D1553792

Classics and Contemporary Thought

Edited by Thomas Habinek

I *Catullan Provocations: Lyric Poetry and the Drama of Position,* by William Fitzgerald

II *Reading Sappho: Contemporary Approaches,* edited by Ellen Greene

III *Re-reading Sappho: Reception and Transmission,* edited by Ellen Greene

IV *Tragedy and Enlightenment: Athenian Political Thought and the Dilemmas of Modernity,* by Christopher Rocco

V *Warriors into Traders: The Power of the Market in Early Greece,* by David W. Tandy

VI *Imperial Ideology and Provincial Loyalty in the Roman Empire,* by Clifford Ando

VII *Horace and the Gift Economy of Patronage,* by Phebe Lowell Bowditch

VIII *The Gift of the Nile: Hellenizing Egypt from Aeschylus to Alexander,* by Phiroze Vasunia

The Gift of the Nile

The Gift of the Nile

Hellenizing Egypt from Aeschylus to Alexander

PHIROZE VASUNIA

University of California Press

BERKELEY   LOS ANGELES   LONDON

The publisher gratefully acknowledges the generous contribution to this book provided by Joan Palevsky.

University of California Press
Berkeley and Los Angeles, California

University of California Press, Ltd.
London, England

Library of Congress Cataloging-in-Publication Data

Vasunia, Phiroze, 1966–.
    The gift of the Nile : hellenizing Egypt from Aeschylus to Alexander /
Phiroze Vasunia.
        p.   cm.—(Classics and contemporary thought; 8)
    Includes bibliographical references and index.
    ISBN 0-520-22820-0 (cloth : alk. paper)
    1. Egypt—Civilization—To 332 B.C.   2. Greece—Civilization—
To 146 B.C.   3. Egypt—In literature.   4. Historiography—Greece.
5. Greek literature–History and criticism   I. Title.   II. Series.

DT61.V36   2001
932'.007'2038—dc21   00–067241

Manufactured in the United States of America
10   09   08   07   06   05   04   03   02   01
10 9 8 7 6 5 4 3 2 1

Contents

Series Editor's Foreword   vii

Acknowledgments   xi

Chronology of Ancient Egypt   xiii

INTRODUCTION   1
   Framing the Issues   1
   Sources—and a Blueprint   10
   Historical Background   20

1. THE TRAGIC EGYPTIAN   33
   Splitting the Danaids   40
   Egypt as Locus for Male Fertility   43
   Blackness and Death   47
   Marrying the Egyptians   53
   Doubles in *Helen*   58
   To Die For   64

2. SPACE AND OTHERNESS   75
   The Pharaoh's Space   77
   Mapping Egypt   87
   Symmetry and Inversion   92
   The Traveler's Eye   100
   Egyptian Space   103

3. IN AN ANTIQUE LAND   110
   Absolute History   112
   The Legacies of the Past   117
   Egypt and the Trojan War   121

Egyptian Time   126
In an Antique Land   131

4. WRITING EGYPTIAN WRITING   136
    Graphomania   138
    The Tyrant's Writ   142
    The Gods of Writing   146
    Plato's Grammatology   155
    Egyptian Writing   159
    Writing and Control   176

5. READING ISOCRATES' *BUSIRIS*   183
    Busiris the Egyptian   185
    Reading Isocrates' Speech   193
    The Paradox of Parody   199
    Isocrates, Plato, Athens   207

6. PLATO'S EGYPTIAN STORY   216
    A Graphic History   218
    From Isocrates to Crantor   226
    Athens and Atlantis   236

7. ALEXANDER'S CONQUEST AND THE FORCE OF TRADITION   248
    Greeks and Macedonians   252
    Homer and Alexander   253
    Herodotus and Alexander   256
    Aristotle and Alexander   261
    The Conquest of Egypt   265
    Epilogue   282

Appendix: *Fragmentary Greek Historians on Egypt,*
to 332 B.C.E.   289

Abbreviations   307

Bibliography   309

Index   337

Illustrations follow page 182.

Series Editor's Foreword

It is a pleasure to welcome Phiroze Vasunia's study to the series *Classics and Contemporary Thought*. The series seeks to establish connections between specialized research on Greco-Roman antiquity and broader inquiry in the humanities, arts, and social sciences. Vasunia's book, *The Gift of the Nile: Hellenizing Egypt from Aeschylus to Alexander*, fits this description admirably. Its topic, Greek views of Egypt in the classical period, is a timely one, relevant to debates over the formation and transmission of European identity, the social function of classical literature and art, and the historical relationship among African, European, and Asiatic peoples and cultures. And its interdisciplinary approach is both novel and welcome, since Vasunia brings to the discussion expertise in the Greek as well as the Egyptian traditions, sensitivity to the role classical accounts of Egypt have played in later imperialist and Orientalist discourse and action, and, in particular, a clear understanding of the social function of images of other peoples and places within Greek, particularly Athenian, culture.

In essence, Vasunia brings to light what we might call the Greek myth of Egypt. His concern is not so much with the verifiable history of relations between Greece and Egypt as it is with the use (and abuse) of that history by Greeks for the purpose of creating an authoritative story of what it means to be an Egyptian and, by implication, what it means to be a Greek. Neither empirically true nor wholly fantastic, Greek discourse on Egypt spoke to the needs of Greeks. It cannot be expected to meet later standards of historical objectivity or to convey accurate details about events and persons, much as some readers might want it to. But it cannot be dismissed as insignificant or inconsequential either, since as myth it shaped the thoughts and actions of real people living a real history; in other words, it exerted authority. What is more, since the Greeks who developed, transmitted, and, in the case of Alexander the Great, lived the myth of Egypt, in turn captured the imagination of later generations and became part of the West's myth of itself, so the classical Greek myth of Egypt has persisted even to this day and exerts its authority over museum-goers, politicians, and filmmakers, not to mention scholars in diverse disciplines and of varying dispositions.

Some aspects of the Greek myth of Egypt explored in this book will be familiar to the general reader. For example, Professor Vasunia calls attention to Greek writers' emphasis on Egypt's great antiquity, although he makes the additional point that in the classical world, as today, Egypt's past too often served as an excuse not to reckon with Egypt's present. Other aspects of the Greek myth of Egypt may be more immediately recognizable only to specialists in literary or cultural theory yet are not for that reason less significant to an understanding of the myth of Egypt and its hold on Greece and its admirers. Hieroglyphs, as Vasunia shows, figure prominently in Plato's influential account of the dependence of writing on speech. Yet this account ignores key differences between Greece and Egypt both in stories about the invention of writing and in the operation of their respective graphic systems. Indeed, hieroglyphs challenge the very relationships between script, speech, and referent that Plato seeks to make stable. Egyptian attitudes toward space, as represented by Greek writers, corroborate, for these same writers, a self-aggrandizing distinction between an Egypt that is inevitably autocratic and an Athens that is inherently progressive. Yet as Vasunia shows, Greek accounts of Egyptian space and its control range from the incomplete to the inaccurate and tell us much more about Greek self-definition than they do about Egyptian practice. Similar misapprehensions or misrepresentations shape Greek accounts of Egyptian religion, politics, and sexuality, all of which are explored in this wide-ranging study.

If there is a single overarching theme to *The Gift of the Nile*, it is that Greek discourse on Egypt is part of a larger process whereby Greeks define themselves in relationship to various non-Greek peoples. Put thus, Vasunia's observations will perhaps not seem unexpected to classicists who have in recent years studied Greek representations of "the barbarian," or Greek notions of ethnicity. Where Vasunia is able to advance such investigations is in showing how concern with identity permeates even such seemingly esoteric or abstract topics as the origin of writing, techniques of measurement and mapping, and the nature of the linguistic sign. Moreover, Greek discourse on Egypt, as analyzed by Vasunia, complicates the simple "us versus them" model of cultural difference that might seem implicit in Greek depictions of non-Greeks as barbarians, since Egypt, even under

Persian rule, is never quite reduced by Greek writers to a polar opposite to Greece. The classical Greek myth of Egypt, while certainly a striking example of self-serving, ethnocentric thought, also opens up the possibility of a more subtle sense of cultural difference and potential cultural exchange than the polarizing dichotomy of Greek and barabarian. In the hope of continuing such exchange into the present Vasunia weaves into his account of Greek views of Egyptian time, space, and politics brief summaries of the same issues as articulated within Egyptian writing and art. Indeed, one of the most attractive features of this book is the continuous juxtaposition of Greek and Egyptian perspectives. This practice makes clear the problematical nature of Greek mythologizing about Egypt. But it also opens the door to further exchange between the scholarly disciplines of Classics and Egyptology, inviting investigation of difference, rather than dichotomy, between their respective fields of study.

Incorporation of Greek as well as Egyptian source material; sensitivity to the role the Greek myth of Egypt has played in later thought and action; and, most important, careful explanation of how representations of Egypt negotiated conflicts and anxieties internal to Greek culture: these are the defining characteristics of a study that will appeal to students of ancient Greece, ancient Egypt, and their respective legacies. If its title, *The Gift of the Nile*, strikes some as a potentially misleading cliche, it is a cliche that—like the texts studied here—assumes new meaning in the context of Vasunia's groundbreaking analysis. As he makes clear, it is not simply Egypt's fecundity, or its generous contribution to (and imagined withdrawal from) later stages of civilization that is conveyed through the imagery of "the gift of the Nile." The term "gift" also implies the possibility of exchange, and through Vasunia's study we gain a clearer sense of Egypt's participation in several overlapping systems of exchange—exchange of ideas, skills, and resources among the peoples of ancient Africa, Europe, and Asia; professional exchange between classicists and Egyptologists and among scholars of literature, anthropology, and cultural studies; exchange between past and present, as recognition of the mythic nature of Greek discourse on Egypt heightens our awareness of the continuing hold of myth in cultural interaction today; and exchange, as the title of this series suggests, between *Classics and Contemporary Thought.*

Thomas Habinek

Acknowledgments

I am happy to acknowledge the many people who have helped me with this book. In the first place, I would like to express my gratitude to Susan Stephens, Marsh McCall, Andrea Wilson Nightingale, and Daniel Selden, for reading and improving an earlier version of the text. I would also like to thank the following for advice and helpful criticism: Clifford Ando, John Baines, Fernanda Bashaw, Martin Bloomer, Joseph Boone, Stanley Burstein, Erin Carlston, Whitney Davis, Carolyn Dewald, Jennifer Eastman, Rhiannon Evans, Vincent Farenga, Ellen Finkelpearl, Reuven Firestone, Hilary Garland, John Gould, Tom Hare, Molly Ierulli, Heather James, Michael Jameson, Stephanie Jed, Philippa Levine, Deborah Levitt, Antonio Loprieno, Stephanie Lysyk, Thomas Martin, Lisa Maurizio, Tara McPherson, Richard Neer, Viet Nguyen, Peter O'Neill, Vijay Prashad, Pietro Pucci, Claudia Rapp, Brendon Reay, Joseph Reed, Margaret Rosenthal, Miguel Schmid, Hilary Schor, Jon Soske, Greg Thalmann, Kate Toll, Susan Treggiari, Mehmet Yavuz, and Katerina Zacharia. I also wish to thank Tom Habinek for his counsel and encouragement; for his comments on a draft of the manuscript; and for the invitation to publish the book in his series at the University of California Press. Lastly, I am extremely grateful to my parents and to my sisters for their love and their support, in general, and especially while I was making the final revisions to the manuscript in Bombay.

Chronology of Ancient Egypt

All dates before 664 B.C.E. are approximate.

3050 B.C.E.	Foundation of Egyptian State
2920–2575	Early Dynastic Period First Dynasty (2920–2770)
2575–2134	Old Kingdom
2134–2040	First Intermediate Period
2040–1640	Middle Kingdom
1640–1532	Second Intermediate Period
1550–1070	New Kingdom
1070–664	Third Intermediate Period Twenty-first Dynasty, Tanite (1070–945) Twenty-second to Twenty-fourth Dynasties, Libyan (945–712) Twenty-fifth Dynasty, Nubian (712–664)
664–332	Late Period
664–525	Twenty-sixth Dynasty, Saïte Psammetichus I Necho II Psammetichus II Apries Amasis Psammetichus III
525–404	Twenty-seventh Dynasty, Persian Cambyses

	Darius I
	Xerxes I
	Artaxerxes I
	Darius II
404–399	Twenty-eighth Dynasty
	Amyrtaios
399–380	Twenty-ninth Dynasty
	Nepherites I
	Psammuthis
	Hakoris
	Nepherites II
380–343	Thirtieth Dynasty
	Nectanebo I
	Teos
	Nectanebo II
343–332	Thirty-first Dynasty, Second Persian Period
	Artaxerxes III Ochus
	Arses
	Darius III
332–30	Greek Period
30 B.C.E.–395 C.E.	Roman Period
395–640	Byzantine Period

Introduction

Egypt haunted Greece for a hundred and fifty years, leading up to and in-cluding the year 332 B.C.E., when it was invaded by Alexander. The litera-ture and art of this period is thick with Greek representations of Egypt and Egyptians. The topic of this book is these representations and the ways in which they facilitated Alexander's invasion. In addressing the literature on Egypt from this period, my central concerns are issues of identity, other-ness, and cultural anxiety. How did the ancient Greeks represent Egypt? What rhetoric of alterity was used or put into place by Greek intellectuals in connection with Egypt? What local anxieties, assumptions, and preju-dices does the Greek discourse on Egypt reveal?

FRAMING THE ISSUES

A number of scholars have discussed the ways in which the self is framed as the other of the other, or, within the field of Greek studies, the ways in which Greeks defined themselves and their polities in opposition to barbar-ians and barbarian institutions. The basic example of this phenomenon of self-definition is said to occur during the aftermath of the Persian Wars, in the early fifth century B.C.E., when the notion of the barbarian begins to harden and take on pejorative connotations, and when Hellenes begin to ar-ticulate conceptual, political, and linguistic differences between themselves and barbaroi.[1] In opposition to the soft and sybaritic subjects of the luxu-rious monarch, many Greeks defined themselves as freedom-loving inhab-

1. Hall 1989 argues for Greek self-definition through tragedy in the wake of the Persian Wars; her work is complicated by Miller 1997, who emphasizes Athenian receptivity to Achaemenid Persian culture.

itants of democratic city-states who were able to triumph over the Persians because of their different way of life. Egypt, too, was subject to an othering process in Greek literature, as the evidence from a range of authors indicates. This book follows earlier studies by examining the representation of Greek identity in the literature: self-representation is an inevitable part of all Greek works that refer to Egypt, even when such self-representation is not explicit. What distinguishes Egyptians from several other barbarians in Greek texts is that whereas Egyptians are not always portrayed in a negative light and do not always serve as a negative foil, they nonetheless occupy a series of different and sometimes contradictory positions in the Greek discourse on Egypt. Accordingly, a whole series of attitudes needs to be examined in connection with the issue of Greek self-definition.

One of my concerns, then, is to discuss these Greek writings against the background of a Greek (which usually denotes Athenian) society engaged in the practice of self-definition. In representing Egypt to domestic audiences, the Greek writers were, in effect, commenting on themselves as much as on Egyptians. To say the word "Egypt" was to invoke a knowledge that played itself out asymmetrically in ethnic terms; it was to invoke a discourse that intersected with Greece's notions of itself and with what it viewed as the barbarian world. Corresponding to the loss or distortion in passing from the Egyptian *Hwt-ka-Ptah* to the Greek Αἴγυπτος was the production of a conceptual realm in which the Greek designation signified possibilities of realization and fulfillment.[2] Nevertheless, negotiating between admiration and appropriation resulted in the creation of a country that was both promoted, on account of Egypt's accomplishment, and tamed, to render a suitable format for Hellenic self-presentation. This study of ideology, therefore, examines how Greek writers went about representing a barbarian nation as a subject for domestic contemplation; at the same time, it attempts to expose the contradictions among and between the anxieties, desires, and practices that informed Greek representations of that barbarian nation, Egypt.

A study that simply creates an opposition between self and other, as my remarks suggest, fails to comment fully and meaningfully on the complex portrayal of Egypt in any period of Greek literature. For one thing, terms such as "self" and "other" are often unstable, giving the idea of two monolithic and homogeneous categories. This book posits a Greek identity

2. See Astour 1965, 81, and Bernal 1987, 95, for the Egyptian root of the Greek name. The name for Egypt appears in Mycenean as the adjective *ai-ku-pi-ti-jo*.

that is less fixed and more variable than such an idea implies, an identity that responds variously to the competing appeals emerging from within and without the culture. Such a view of Greek identity follows from the diversity and variety of the texts and authors concerned with Egypt, each of which was conditioned by different pressures and politics. Moreover, the representations themselves reveal an anxiety over issues of identity and selfhood. Beneath the portrayal of the Egyptian Busiris as a xenophobic and murderous king there lurks the Greeks' fear that human sacrifice had been practised in their own past; beneath the acknowledgment of Egypt's antiquity lies the uncertainty over Greece's own history. In considering these anxieties and complexities, I have tried to avoid working within a framework that relies solely on the distinction between self and other, and have attempted to follow Sara Suleri's lead in breaching "the incipient schizophrenia" of critical analysis.[3]

Having cautioned against relying on a simplistic binarism, let me turn to an example that draws on more than two groups. In his book on Moses, the Egyptologist Jan Assmann speaks of "Europe's having been 'haunted' by Egypt," by which he means that "there was always the image of Egypt as the past both of Israel and of Greece and thus of Europe."[4] But the functions that pharaonic Egypt serves in the discursive traditions associated with Israel and Greece are not the same. In the case of Israel, as the first few books of the Hebrew Bible indicate, pharaonic Egypt stands as the land from which the Exodus takes place. It typifies the past that needs to be rejected because it is the country of slavery and a false, idolatrous religion. The assertion of the true religion, Mosaic monotheism, is predicated on the repudiation of paganistic polytheism. English expressions such as "Egyptian bondage" and "Egyptian darkness" follow from this tradition of the Hebrew Bible and the Exodus story. Against pharaonic Egypt in the He-

3. Suleri 1992, 4.
4. Assmann 1997, 9. See also 208–9: "The meaning of the Biblical image of Egypt and the target of this discourse can easily be defined in retrospect. The Biblical image of Egypt means 'idolatry.' . . . The Egypt of the Bible symbolizes what is rejected, discarded, and abandoned. Egypt is not just a historical context; it is inscribed in the fundamental semantics of monotheism. It appears explicitly in the first commandment and implicitly in the second. Its role in the Exodus story must be sharply distinguished from the roles that Assyria, Babylonia, the Philistines, and other Iron Age powers including Late Period Egypt itself play in the historical and prophetic books of the Bible. Egypt's role in the Exodus story is not historical but mythical: it helps define the very identity of those who tell the story. Egypt is the womb from which the chosen people emerged, but the umbilical cord was cut once and for all by the Mosaic distinction."

brew Bible, one can set other nations such as Persia, or Assyria, or even Egypt of the Late Period. Persia, for instance, is treated with favor in the Hebrew Bible—this treatment may in part be due to the aid given by Cyrus to the reconstruction of the temple at Jerusalem in the period when the Torah was being assembled and consolidated—and even in the New Testament, where the Magi may be taken for Zoroastrian priests. If from the Hebrew Bible we turn to Greek literature, however, it appears at first glance that Egypt and Persia switch roles. In Greek literature, it is Persia that is often reviled, while pharaonic Egypt takes on the role of a historic and accomplished civilization, as the evidence from Herodotus suggests. Thus, ancient Greek literature portrays Egypt and Persia in a manner that seems to reverse the portrayal of these nations in ancient Hebrew literature.

This view, which is deliberately schematic, needs some qualification, starting with the different worldviews of the ancient Greek and Hebrew peoples. The Greeks practised a polytheistic religion that on their own reckoning showed a considerable degree of assimilability or translatability. Herodotus was able to write that a large number of foreign customs and religious practices entered into Greece and became classified and thought of as Greek. The monotheism ascribed to Moses, on the other hand, drew its founding myth from the story of partition and separation from a foreign land; it depended on the rejection of the Egyptian past as pagan and idolatrous. As Assmann writes, "Whereas polytheism, or rather 'cosmotheism,' rendered different cultures mutually transparent and compatible, the new counter-religion blocked intercultural translatability."[5] Far from allowing for translation in this sense, he implies, the religion of Mosaic monotheism functioned through estrangement.

Leaving aside the Hebrew Bible for the moment, I would like to consider the Greeks and Egyptians from this perspective because it allows me to reflect on an issue that recurs throughout the Greek texts, concerning the Greeks' inheritance from Egypt. Readers of Herodotus, Plato, and Aristotle inevitably come across statements about the antiquity of Egypt; the Egyptian invention of writing, geometry, and philosophy; or the contribution of Egyptians to the Greek religious tradition. The Greeks appear to show an esteem for Egyptian knowledge that they never show for Persian or even Babylonian science. Persia is rarely credited by the Greeks as being the homeland of knowledge, but the Greeks frequently credit Egyptians with scientific, philosophical, and religious learning, and admit to intellectual in-

5. Assmann 1997, 3.

fluences from Egypt. "From the historian's point of view," Mary R. Lefkowitz writes, "what is most interesting about these claims of cultural dependency is the respect shown by Greek writers of all periods for the antiquity
of Egyptian religion and civilization, and a desire somehow to be connected
with it. At first, the notion of a Greek debt to Egypt is understood as something natural and respectable, like the obligation of pupil to teacher."[6] As
Lefkowitz suggests, of course, any notion that a culture holds to be self-
evident, natural, or respectable calls out for analysis. It is true that Greeks
borrowed much from Egypt, as they did from ancient cultures in West Asia
and elsewhere; some of the evidence for the transmission from Egypt to
Greece is supplied below. But Assmann's point about the difference between cosmotheism and monotheism indicates that the Greeks also had a
framework through which to see themselves as learning and borrowing
from others. The Greeks were seeing themselves as adapting and borrowing institutions from Egyptians, and in fact the younger civilization was
marking out itself as the trustee of the new culture. One might interpret
this phenomenon as a desire for appropriating and assimilating Egyptian
cultural formations, and think of it variously as the transfer of sacrality, or
the transfer of ethnic accomplishment, or perhaps the transfer of cultural
identity. Greece was creating itself anew in the era after the Dark Ages, and
Egypt had a long and distinguished cultural record that was available to
those who wished to inscribe, codify, and canonize their own, more recent,
endeavors.

Not all Greek texts and writers about Egypt follow this attitude, however, and alongside the desire for the appropriation of culture there exist
Greek fantasies and fears that also need to be investigated. I have referred
to Busiris, who reflects some fears of the Greeks, namely, fears of human
sacrifice and foreigners, and could refer as well to the sons of Aegyptus,
who wish to marry their "Greek" cousins against their wishes, or to the
blustering king Theoclymenus, who wishes to keep Helen in Egypt and
away from her husband, Menelaus. Some of these apprehensions are present in the same texts that refer to Egypt's history and antiquity, so that
Plato's priest comes up with a fantasy story in which Egypt's eight thousand years of civilization are surpassed by Athens' nine thousand years, or
again, Herodotus' history contains examples of Egyptian kings who come
close to behaving like the worst despots from Persia. In these cases, as we
shall see in the chapters that follow, the Greeks found it necessary to pro-

---

6. Lefkowitz 1997, 249.

ject outwards what they were opposed to, in order to preserve the presiding fictions and ideologies of their own societies.

Edith Hall may be correct in saying that only the Greeks among ancient peoples "invented a term which precisely and exclusively embraced all who did not share their ethnicity."[7] If both the Egyptians and Persians were called barbarians by the Greeks, the Egyptians nonetheless occupied a multiplicity of positions in the Greek discourse on the other. To Greek writers, Egyptians are inventors, philosophers, priests, historians, tyrants, rapacious cousins, or murderous hosts. In fact, the flexibility of Egypt in this cultural discourse points to its special place in the logic of otherness, for Egypt serves as the condition for the possibility of a Greek discourse on barbarians as such. What is interesting in Greek pronouncements is that the most accomplished and the most vile Egyptians are equally barbarians, no more and no less than Persians, Babylonians, Scythians, or Indians. The discourse on Egypt is so wide-ranging and is implicated in so many differing intellectual, social, and religious concerns that it gives the student of culture the opportunity to discern the modalities that govern ancient Greek thought on the barbarian. To study Greece's Egypt is, therefore, to understand the limits and parameters within which the barbarian functions and to appreciate the flexible but ultimately circumscribed space that no foreigner can transcend in the Hellenic imagination.

From my remarks so far, it will be evident that I am also making a case for a political reading of these texts, an expression it is as well to leave ambiguous. For, in the first place, the discursive tradition facilitates Alexander's conquest, in which he put an end to Persian control of Egypt and inaugurated a new period of Greek-Macedonian rule. No Greek reference to Egypt in the years before Alexander is innocent of this gross fact, as I hope to show in the last chapter, however sentimental the reference may appear, and however distant it may seem from Alexander's invasion and the subsequent rule by the Ptolemies. Secondly, the texts that I am considering derive from a period in which Egypt was for long stretches under the rule of Persia. This reality should be kept in mind when we look at these texts: some of them may reflect Greek views about Persia triangulated through the situation of Egypt, and some may reflect the feelings, however mediated, of a local population subject to Persian suzerainty. Lastly, these texts need to be considered in the light of Greek military involvement in Egypt before Alexander. The Athenians launched an expedition to assist Inarus

7. See Hall 1989, 4, with the comparative evidence gathered there.

and the Egyptians in their revolt from Persian control during the *pentecontaetia*, an expedition that failed in the face of Persian opposition. In addition, numerous Greek mercenaries were active in Egyptian affairs from as early as the reign of Psammetichus I (or Psamtik), in the seventh century B.C.E. Greek military involvement in Egypt before Alexander, whether through mercenaries or Athenian ships, appears to prefigure the profound change wrought by the king on relations between Greece and Egypt.

What is striking about Greek discourse on Egypt, nevertheless, is the literature's persistent avoidance of the sociopolitical realities of contemporary Egypt. The Greek literature on Egypt invokes, creates, and perpetuates various notions of Egypt that are often at a remove from the contemporary scene. As Christian Froidefond observes in his work on the "Egyptian mirage" in Greece, few writers apprehend the country as it exists at the time of their writing.[8] There appears, instead, a homeostatic view of a country removed from the present, a view that often focuses on the antiquity of Egyptian civilization, the invention of writing, the scribal tradition of chronicling the past, and the contributions of the Egyptian philosophical and religious systems to Greek counterparts. By directing attention to an Egypt devoid of political tensions and contemporary social realities, the surviving literature from Aeschylus to Alexander also obscures the distinctive political, social, and cultural developments of the period in Egypt. The double Persian occupation, the intervening era of independence, and the Greek settlements in Naukratis scarcely influence the bulk of the Greek texts. It is true, of course, that to an extent the contents of these literary works are governed by the choice of genre or mythological theme. One cannot expect Euripides' work to touch upon contemporary events in the same ways as do the writings of historians such as Thucydides. While Thucydides is explicitly composing a work of contemporary history, Euripides is working within a mythical framework set in a distant and heroic past. But we should then ascertain what it is about the Euripidean representation of Egypt that allows the playwright to invoke certain associations with Egypt in the context of his treatment of, for instance, the Helen myth.

Within the general rubric of representing Egypt, it would be simple merely to parrot what the Greek authors say about Egypt, without reading these texts as works of specific authors, writing at specific moments in Greek history. If we were to read the Greeks' exaltation of Egypt as an unmediated gesture of praise, as some critics have done, we would be ignor-

8. Froidefond 1971.

ing the anxieties and fantasies to which I have referred, and we would be replicating the ideology of Hellenism, since the Greek authors themselves pose the issue of Egypt by borrowing from the rhetoric of praise and blame. But the rhetoric a society employs for any given purpose is never natural, just as its method of engaging with foreigners is never natural. To study the rhetoric used by a society in its engagement with foreigners means not just to subject to inquiry the nature of the rhetoric at work, and the engagement with the other that is mediated by the rhetoric; it means also to interrogate the category of the obvious and to inquire into the interests at play, the strategies involved, and the sociopolitical limits imposed on society, for itself and by itself, in its encounter with foreignness. To avoid a deterministic analysis of the texts, we need to investigate the representational dynamic that allows these texts to deem something as Hellenic and something as barbarian. At times, I have chosen to interrogate this dynamic by the introduction of Egyptian evidence, at the risk that the comparative evidence may bring into the discussion its own particular dogmas and constraints. There is the further risk of setting up an all too easy dichotomy between Greek and Egyptian material, and then discovering points of opposition between the two traditions. I hope to have addressed the problem, at least partially, by posing the question of the representing of Egypt, not just at the cultural level, but at the level of representation itself (as explained in chapter 4).

It is worth remarking that Egyptian representations of the foreign, the exotic, and the other, across three millennia of ancient civilization, offer a useful counterpoint to Greek representations of Egypt.[9] By tradition, Egypt and Egyptian society were part of the ordered cosmos, while non-Egyptians such as Nubians, West Asiatics, and Libyans figured as chaos and disorder. Official ideology promoted the view of a homogeneous and uniform society within an Egyptian world empire that was coterminous with the ordered cosmos. Nevertheless, as John Baines remarks, the uniformity maintained by the elite ideology was belied by the immigration of foreigners, such as Nubians, Asiatics, and Libyans, to whom Egypt remained open throughout antiquity.[10] Texts of the New Kingdom, for instance, contain narratives of travel outside Egypt and contact with foreigners in West Asia. The first Greek peoples represented in Egyptian sources may be the island-

9. For Egyptian representations of foreigners, see *LÄ*, s.v. "Fremdvölkerdarstellung"; Loprieno 1988; Valbelle 1990; Baines 1996; Bresciani, in Donadoni 1997, 221–53.

10. Baines 1996.

ers from Crete, who appear as tribute-bearers in depictions from the New Kingdom, a period in which Myceneans (Keftui) also subsequently visited Egypt. Enemies of Egypt were represented, in all periods, as bound foreign captives or by the Nine Bows, which the pharaoh trampled over, as a sign of his, and Egypt's, superiority: trampling the enemy also implied a subjugation or containment of the chaos represented by the hostile other. In this worldview, foreign rulers from Libyans and Ethiopians to Assyrians and Persians were likened to the god of disorder, Seth, returning to Egypt in order to attack the throne of Horus.

By juxtaposing Egyptian material with the Greek sources, I have tried not to reduce all my observations to the charge of ethnocentrism— assuredly, every ancient text that I discuss is guilty of it—but to examine the particular set of assumptions, politics, and biases that are evident in the Greek representations of Egypt. Writing in Arabic about India, in the early eleventh century, al-Biruni points out that Indians differ from "us" (he was from Ghazna) in every possible way: language, religion, customs, antagonism to foreigners, and national character. But he adds: "we must confess, in order to be just, that a similar depreciation of foreigners not only prevails among us and the Hindus, but is common to all nations towards each other." [11] His plea for moving beyond basic prejudices is well taken, being exemplified in the fabulous treatise on India that survives (*Ta'rikh al-Hind*): I have attempted to refer to specific rhetorical devices, ethnographic representations, or historical exclusions in this study of the Greek literature on Egypt. It should be clear that references to a Greek discourse on Egypt in this book do not entail a monolithic or unitary structure, but assume a number of works of varying provenance and focus. The many texts referring to Egypt in the years before Alexander contribute to a heterogeneous body of writing that has differing emphases, rhetorical strategies, ideological motivations, and historical legitimacy. Nevertheless, it is important to understand the elements that are common to these texts, and to appreciate that like the British writings on India from 1600 to 1800 "they constantly refer to, reproduce, counter and build on one another." [12] Several of the following chapters single out for examination meaningful elements and themes within the work of a given author. The arrangement does not imply that, for instance, Herodotus is important to this study only for his elaboration of Egyptian space and time, or Plato only for his opinions on the written word. On the contrary, it will be evident that themes

11. Sachau 1992, vol. 1, 20.
12. Teltscher 1995, 3.

recur and intersect across the works of authors. The weight or prominence vouchsafed to any one subject varies from author to author, but this is un-surprising given the range of texts and the differing levels of authorial openness to others.

SOURCES — AND A BLUEPRINT

"Put simply," says Stanley M. Burstein, "references to Egypt and its cul-ture occur in the works of almost every surviving classical author."[13] It would take someone who has read and understood every surviving classi-cal author to assess the truth of that statement; nonetheless, the general va-lidity of the claim is not in doubt, since references to Egypt occur widely in Greek and Latin works from antiquity. As Burstein also notes, however, only four sustained Greek accounts of Egypt have survived: book 2 of He-rodotus, book 1 of Diodorus, book 17 of Strabo, and Plutarch's *On Isis and Osiris*.[14] To these texts can be added a few written in the tradition of late antique mysticism and Neoplatonism: Iamblichus' *On the Mysteries of the Egyptians*, Horapollo's *Hieroglyphica*, and the *Hermetica* (or *Corpus Her-meticum*) once ascribed to Hermes Trismegistus.[15] The works of many other authors, such as Hecateus of Abdera, Manetho, and Chaeremon, survive in quotation; most of these were assembled by Felix Jacoby in *Die Fragmente der griechischen Historiker*, but Jacoby's selection omits some writers, such as Eudoxus of Cnidus (ca. 400–350 B.C.E.), whose work is available in a sep-arate edition.[16]

This book concentrates on the Greek writers before Alexander's inva-sion, especially writers in the fifth and fourth centuries. I have given some

13. Burstein 1996, 592.

14. For historical commentaries on these texts, see Lloyd 1975, 1976, and 1988a (Herodotus 2); Burton 1972 (Diodorus 1); Yoyotte, Charvet, and Gompertz 1997 (Strabo 17); and Griffiths 1970 (Plutarch, *On Isis and Osiris*). See also Aristides, *Oration* 36.

15. For the text of Iamblichus, see des Places 1996; for the Greek text of Ho-rapollo, see Sbordone 1940 (which differs from the popular Latin translation of the early modern period in important details); and for the *Hermetica*, see Nock and Fes-tugière 1972–73 (with the English translation in Copenhaver 1992).

16. See *FGrHist* vol. III C, which contains entries numbered 608a to 664, plus number 665, a lengthy appendix. For Eudoxus, see Lasserre 1966 and the appendix below. In addition to the writers in *FGrHist*, see also *FHG* and the index to vol. 4. Hecateus of Abdera is *FGrHist* 264, Manetho is *FGrHist* 609 (see also the text and translation in Waddell 1940, and a newer translation in Verbrugghe and Wicker-sham 1996), and Chaeremon is *FGrHist* 618 (see also the text and translation in van der Horst 1984).

consideration to Homer and the pre-Socratics, but I have tried to restrict my argument to the fifth and fourth centuries up to the Greek conquest, on the grounds of historical and societal continuity.[17] In practical terms, the authors and works that refer to Egypt in this period, and that are discussed in this book, are as follows: Aeschylus' *Suppliants;* book 2 of Herodotus; Euripides' *Helen;* Plato's *Phaedrus, Timaeus,* and *Critias;* and Isocrates' *Busiris.* I have also brought in artworks as necessary, for instance, vase paintings in the case of Busiris. The appendix contains a translation of the fragmentary historians of Egypt who were active in the time before Alexander; these and other authors are also treated in this book as appropriate.[18] A few of these texts may strike readers as marginal, but they may be no less important for that, since a great deal of psychological effort may have been expended by the culture to ensure their marginality.

What functions does Egypt have in this Greek discourse? What does it make possible for Greeks to apprehend in the fifth and fourth centuries B.C.E.? What obsessions, desires, and anxieties does it reveal on the part of the Greeks? What stereotypes about it are propagated by Greeks? To answer these questions is to enter into a discussion that draws on a range of sources and materials, varying in age and provenance, on the subject of cross-cultural interaction. In laying out the blueprint for this project, however, it may be possible to suggest the contours of the chapters that follow, and to signal some of the intellectual resources of which I have availed myself in making my argument.

To start at a basic level, it can be said that the teleological scheme proposed in this book reflects contemporary work carried out in colonial and cultural studies. In claiming that the Greek discourse on Egypt provided the ideological background to Alexander's invasion (chapter 7), I am setting up a relationship between knowledge and power, or literature and politics, that has also been explored by scholars in other disciplines: this is evident from the publications of the Subaltern Studies collective, for instance, or such works as Michel Foucault's *Discipline and Punish* and Edward Said's *Orientalism.* These books have shown how "Empire follows Art," to quote

17. The use of Alexander as a turning point in Egyptian history is made in antiquity as well: see *FGrHist* 610 F 2 (last paragraph) and Diodorus 1.23.

18. I have not attempted to discuss every reference to Egypt in the fifth and fourth centuries or earlier. Froidefond 1971 assembles almost every reference to Egypt in the period from Homer to Alexander. For brief introductions to the Greek reception of Egypt, see Zecchini 1989; Kákosy 1995; Burstein 1996; and Hartog 1996, ch. 2.

William Blake, but also how colonialism and modes of domination appropriate knowledge-discourses and cultural production in the service of starkly political ends. They have demonstrated how the European study of non-European cultures has led to colonial hegemony and political control. And they have argued how discourses that seem the most benign can come to have a crucial influence on mechanisms of authority and command. Reliance on such work may appear to some as ahistorical, reductive, and blind to local specificities. I do not wish to obfuscate the genuine differences that divide the classical Greek world of the fifth and fourth centuries from the age of modern European imperialism. Nevertheless, the power-knowledge model, for all its simplicity, has an explanatory value that it is naive to dismiss. For too long Herodotus has been read as a mere ethnographer or historian of the exotic (as if these were unproblematic roles in themselves), and not also as an auxiliary to empire-building in the ancient world. Taken together, Herodotus, Homer, Aristotle, and other Greeks were a defining part of the ideological background that shaped Alexander's conquest of Egypt.

The stereotype of Egypt as the land of the dead is one of the oldest connected with that culture: "one big undertaker's emporium" is what Rudyard Kipling called it.[19] The Greek discourse on Egypt exploits this idea ruthlessly in drama, where issues of erotics, desire, and race are configured in relation to death (chapter 1). Aeschylus and Euripides bring together death, sex, Egypt, black men, and potential rape in *Suppliants* and *Helen* respectively. In both plays, it is Greek men who intervene to save the lives and the chastity of Greek women from the threatening clutches of Egyptian men. The context for their actions is the blackness of Egyptian men in *Suppliants*, the underworld coloring of Egypt in *Helen*, and the pervasive association between blackness and death in the Greek imagination. These plays, therefore, give a peculiar and forceful direction to the hoary, if vague, correlation between the Orient and sex. The plays clearly signal that Greek women detest sexual relations with the deathly and deadly black men of Egypt: Helen and the suppliant women would sooner die than have sexual intercourse with hypervirile Egyptian males. In giving this repudiation as their response to Freud's question ("What does woman want?"), furthermore, *Suppliants* and *Helen* give the Athenian male a space for self-definition and a stage on which to tame the threatening other. The Athe-

19. R. Kipling, *Letters of Travel* (London, 1920), 185, also quoted in Gregory 1999, 185.

nians construct this phantasmatic other to disguise the relations between Greek men and women and between Greeks and foreigners in their own city-state, with its mask of a democratic society. The fantasy substitutes for the real and defers confrontation with it: the real itself is too painful to describe because its revelation would expose the fraudulence of the political fictions the city tells itself.

Herodotus' Egyptian writings both reveal a desire for the mastery of space and time in Egypt and project this desire for mastery onto Egyptian elites (chapters 2 and 3). Pharaohs such as Sesostris are seen dividing up, and indeed redefining, Egyptian space by a host of construction projects; and Egyptian priests are portrayed as capturing all of their history in their annalistic records. This containment of space and time by Egyptians is paralleled by Herodotus' own text in different ways: first, his book captures Egypt's dimensions, its length, width, coastline, the depth of the neighboring seabed; and second, his work presents a history of Egypt in which the past is turned into a monument in which the country of the present finds little, if any, mention. We might say that the mastery over space and time that he ascribes to the pharaohs parallels the mastery of his narrative. The effect of Herodotus' text is to locate this spatiotemporal monolith in Greece's past, so as to make possible in the present the transfer of sacrality (cultural, historical, political) that I have already mentioned. Moreover, Herodotus' text also fosters Greek self-definition by emphasizing the otherness of Egyptian culture. What is remarkable about the work, nevertheless, is that its othering mechanism, which is couched in an idiom of grandeur, ultimately turns on an obsessive domination of the other's space and time. This is the kind of domination that Edward Said, Timothy Mitchell, and Mary Louise Pratt have analyzed in their important studies. This kind of domination puts Egypt on display, but in a manner that is disingenuous because, although it gives the illusion of a "multi-subjective, contingency-oriented account," it insists on the authority of the Greek observer at its core.[20] No less disingenuous, to adopt Mitchell's vocabulary, is the manner in which the work presents Egypt as if were on display at an exhibition, but leaves open where the exhibition ends and where the world begins, or where the idea ends and where the place begins. Concerning this cluster of issues,

20. C. Meier, "Historical Answers to Historical Questions: The Origins of History in Ancient Greece," Arethusa 20 (1987):41–57, 44, also quoted in Greenblatt 1991, 123, who observes further that "the spatial extension Herodotus achieves is comparable to the temporal extension that he elegantly invokes" (186).

one is tempted to draw an analogy with Grauman's Egyptian Theatre in Los Angeles, built in 1922 and renovated in 1998, in which the theatre itself stands for the containment of space and time and for the slippage between the familiar and the foreign.

This theatre was first built at a time when, as Antonia Lant has written, cinema drew on ancient Egypt for themes and inspiration and, indeed, used Egypt as "a means of explaining, legitimating, but above all conceptualizing the new motion picture medium."[21] Of course, the use of Egypt as a means to think through the place of technology and the arts of representation in a culture goes back far beyond cinema to Plato (chapter 4). In a famous story given to Socrates, in *Phaedrus*, Plato describes the invention of writing. Letters, it turns out, were invented by the Egyptian god Theuth, who then presented them to the king Thamus. But Thamus, like Socrates, is skeptical about the benefits of the written word, and is unable to accept them without qualification and restriction. This story reveals more about Plato's metaphysics and grammatology, as Jacques Derrida has pointed out, than Egyptian traditions of writing. If the story betrays a fear of mimesis and the slipperiness of signs, it is nonetheless precisely through the unceasing movement of signs that Egyptian hieroglyphic writing functions. Thus, Plato's use of Egypt and the Egyptian writing system to score a point against written discourse is contrary to the basic principles of the hieroglyphic tradition. He resorts to Egypt in order to further the mischief of his own metaphysics. In addition, the contrast between Greek and Egyptian traditions about writing also emerges in authors such as Aeschylus and Herodotus, in whose work, as Deborah Steiner has argued, writing has sinister connotations that bind it more closely to the barbarian world than to Greek city-states: writing is enigmatic, harder than the spoken word to limit semantically, and subject to a variety of interpretations or misinterpretations in the absence of the author. Thus, these comments and representations of Egyptian language point more to Greek concerns about control and otherness than to any true knowledge of the writing system.

Anxieties and stereotypes of another sort are brought out in the figure of Busiris, the Egyptian king who is said to have routinely sacrificed Greek visitors until Heracles put an end to him and his nefarious activities (chapter 5). The Greek and Roman tradition, with few exceptions, accepts the idea of the xenophobic Egyptian, though the Egyptian tradition has no record of King Busiris and little, if any, proof for human sacrifice in general.

21. Lant 1992, 87.

At first sight, one Greek who does appear to contradict this Greek tradition is Isocrates, who wrote a speech in praise of the Egyptian king. But the speech is a display-piece, a parody of a serious encomium, and as such it only reinforces the worst Greek fears about the king: far from undoing the mainstream tradition, Isocrates' speech confirms and reinvigorates it. Thus, Isocrates conforms to the general pattern of those Greeks and Romans who repeatedly use human sacrifice as a marker of cultural variance. When it is considered that there is a great deal more evidence for human sacrifice among Greeks than Egyptians, the conclusion is inescapable that the story of Busiris is another example the Greeks constructed in order to cover up their own domestic fears. As we shall see later, moreover, Isocrates also uses the speech about Busiris to advance his own philosophical and political position in his rivalry with Plato, just as Plato uses other Egyptian themes for his own purposes.

An Egyptian tale that calls out irresistibly for investigation is Plato's story of Atlantis, narrated by Critias in *Timaeus* and *Critias* (chapter 6). In these dialogues, Plato puts in the mouth of an Egyptian priest the story of Athens' great triumph over Atlantis eight thousand years ago. Long before the Persian Wars, it appears, Athens had come to the rescue of civilization by repulsing a barbarian threat. It is significant that this story, the truth of which is maintained by Socrates and Critias, is attributed to an Egyptian priest in Saïs, as if the narrative of Athens' victory acquires credibility and legitimacy from this source. It is even more significant, however, that the story turns on a notion of history that, like Hegel's, insists on Europe as its sovereign subject, and that refers to Egypt only insofar as it intervenes in this paean to Athenian bravery. But behind this story one finds not so much an Egypt of Plato's day or an Egypt with a recognizable past, but rather a Greek desire to be a part of world history, with Greece at the center and Egypt displaced elsewhere. This portrayal of history, incidentally, has the double effect of making Egypt the place of wisdom and learning that Greeks come to visit, and also a place at the periphery since this transfer of knowledge occurred a long time ago.

It remains to point out, briefly, that the Greek writings on Egypt have acquired a history and left an impression on discourses and traditions which continue into the present day. In the United States, as Daniel L. Selden has remarked, Egypt has served as a site of contestation in two different but not exclusive ways. First, a number of African American writers since the nineteenth century asserted that Egypt was a black African civilization that influenced Greece and, therefore, also the civilizations of modern Europe. Support for this assertion was taken from Herodotus, Strabo, Diodorus,

Pliny, and Josephus, who had said that Egyptians were black or had woolly hair, and who were believed to provide evidence for the cultural impact of Egypt on Greece. So W. E. B. DuBois noted that, according to Aeschylus, the Greeks were descendants of Io's "mulatto son, 'black Epaphus.'" But second, African Americans also invoked the biblical tradition of Exodus, to which I referred above, and depicted Egypt as the land of affliction. This image was then applied by African American figures such as David Walker, Malcolm X, and Martin Luther King, Jr., to the United States itself, which was figured "as Egypt, a place of captivity, ruthlessness, toil, and unremitting pain, from which they perennially longed to escape."[22] For some of these writers, it was Ethiopia, not Egypt, where the seeds of civilization were sown, and it was from Ethiopia that culture spread to Egypt and thence to Greece and Europe. As Selden notes, "Afrocentrism and Ethiopianism, as they developed in nineteenth-century America, were thus two sides of the same coin, complementary parts of a large-scale vision of cultural exile and redemptive return, which defined the place of Africa and Africans in history."[23] In either case, as with Plato's dialogues much earlier, Egypt remained the nation to appropriate in the scripting of one's history.

The first-mentioned of these two traditions evolved, initially through the work of Cheikh Anta Diop, into the Afrocentrist school of history, in which Egypt is described as the source of European civilization. In his multivolume project, *Black Athena*, Martin Bernal has continued the Afrocentrists' arguments by saying that Greek culture and civilization derived from Egypt.[24] Bernal has shown in detail how racist and anti-Semitic scholarship in the eighteenth and nineteenth centuries systematically denied, ignored, or suppressed the influence of Egypt and West Asia on ancient Greece. Bernal's work also indicates how European imperialism influenced classical scholarship in the eighteenth, nineteenth, and early twentieth centuries, and it has reminded contemporary scholars of the need to be wary of colonialist and ethnocentric agendas in the historical study of the ancient world. I have found Bernal's sociological study of European classical schol-

22. Selden 1998a, 196 (also the source of the quotation from DuBois). See also Young 1994.
23. Selden 1998a, 198.
24. Bernal 1987 and 1991. For the response to Bernal's work, see Lefkowitz 1996; Lefkowitz and Rogers 1996 (with large bibliography); and the review articles by Stanley M. Burstein in *Scholia* 5 (1996): 3–16 and Molly M. Levine in *Classical Philology* 93 (1998): 345–63. For a book-length exploration of the sociological issues raised by the debate over *Black Athena*, and for the responsibilities of American intellectuals in the controversy, see Berlinerblau 1999.

arship in the eighteenth and nineteenth centuries quite useful, and I welcome an enterprise that has put the historical study of classical scholarship on an entirely new footing. Moreover, I applaud him for working toward his stated "political purpose" of reducing "European cultural arrogance," and hope that his books will lead to more progressive research methods and a greater degree of methodological awareness in the study of the ancient Mediterranean.[25] Concerning the ancient Greek sources, my remarks should indicate that I am less concerned than Bernal with establishing historical facts, and more interested in representation, rhetoric, and the politics of literature. I take it as axiomatic that there were contacts between Greeks and Egyptians in the period under study and suggest that for this very reason the representations and misrepresentations of Egypt by Greek sources need to be subjected to deep scrutiny. In this book, with some methodological self-consciousness, I hope to examine a particular case of ethnocentrism, localized to the fifth and fourth centuries B.C.E., to inquire into its methods and its grammar, and to investigate the factors that motivated it, the ideologies that sustained it, and the real and sometimes devastating uses to which it could be put by Greeks.

In Europe, Egypt's place in intellectual history can be traced from antiquity to the Renaissance and the Enlightenment.[26] It is a testimony to the power of the Greek discourse that some of the same themes reappear in these later periods, by which time a whole range of Greek and Roman writings on Egypt were available. The obsession with Egypt's antiquity, the fascination with hieroglyphs, and not least the expedition by Napoleon, who styled himself after Alexander, indicate that Europeans were approaching Egypt through the writings of classical Greek and Roman writers. In the Renaissance, scholars such as Marsilio Ficino and Athanasius Kircher, believing that the Hermetic corpus and Horapollo's treatise came from pharaonic Egypt, reconstructed Egyptian philosophy and theology on the basis of these texts and without a knowledge of hieroglyphs.[27] This Egyptian revival, the first phase of Egyptomania, took different if complementary di-

25. Bernal 1987, 73.

26. For introductions to the European reception of Egypt in these periods, see Iversen 1993, chs. 3 and 4, and Whitehouse 1995. For a general survey of Egypt in Western thought, see Donadoni, Curto, and Donadoni Roveri 1990. An extensive bibliography concerning the history of European and U.S. interest in Egypt is available on the World Wide Web at http://www.kv5.com/html/bibliography.html.

27. The "Hermetic" tradition is also attested among medieval Muslim works, for instance, in the *Akhbar al-zaman* of the eleventh century: see Haarmann 1996, 618–21.

rections: Egypt was depicted as the land of wisdom and ancient learning; hieroglyphs were thought of as part of a profound symbolic system; and Egypt was conceptualized as a historical civilization extending back further than the chronological span given in the Bible.[28] Isaac Casaubon's devastating exposé of the Hermetic corpus as a product of late antiquity, not of the pharaonic era, seemed to cause some decline of the Egyptophilia that had swept through Europe, but it nonetheless was unable to prevent the Egyptomania that followed in the end of the eighteenth century.[29] Mozart's *Magic Flute* and then Napoleon's expedition to Egypt occurred at the height of this next phase of Egyptomania, which paved the way for the decipherment of hieroglyphs by Jean-François Champollion in the 1820s. As in antiquity, then, an Egyptian discourse was an important part of Europe's life and politics before and after an act of imperialism brought Egypt under foreign rule; as in antiquity, the discourse was deeply intertwined with the domestic agenda (Hermeticism, Freemasonry, theology) of European intellectuals and writers.[30]

28. The division into three parts is made by Assmann 1997, 18, with further references to each part.

29. For a lavishly illustrated treatment of this Egyptomania and the art it generated from 1730 to 1930, see Humbert, Pantazzi, and Ziegler 1994.

30. The ancient Greek writings about Egypt, which had an impact on American and European intellectual and political life, also appear to have structured the formation and development of Egyptology and to have shaped some of its core assumptions. This influence on Egyptology is, perhaps, not surprising since many professional European Egyptologists come to their discipline via prior training in the classical Greek and/or Roman civilizations. Here is a lengthy and heartfelt lament about their discipline from the authors of a book on Egyptian religion: "... Egyptology has still not succeeded in resolving the contradiction it has trapped itself in: convinced of the high cultural and ethical level of the civilization it studies, it is nevertheless haunted by the feeling that the Egyptians' conceptions of the divine fall short of this level. To be sure, one strongly suspects that this contradiction never existed in reality, but rather stems from the fact that our conceptual tools are poorly adapted to the analysis of a culture they were not designed for. This conceptual inadequacy is in turn constantly exacerbated by the imperious, if unconscious, need to treat everything Egyptian as fundamentally assimilable, in its underlying structures, to one or another feature of the contemporary world. From the beginnings of Egyptology, the specialists have always been inclined to make qualitative judgments—this is a symptom of their often well-disguised concern to show us an Egypt that conforms, on the one hand, to notions of moral and aesthetic decorum palatable to a majority, and, on the other, to our mode of logical thinking. Whether in the domain of beliefs, artistic expression, lifestyle, or writing, Egypt is glorified, in the scholarly works or the proliferating exhibitions devoted to it, only for those aspects of its civilization that command an approving consensus based on the most widely shared contemporary values. Egypt becomes acceptable only when fitted out with the identity we, applying our modes of thinking and being, foist

The fascination with Egypt in Europe and the United States reminds us that the discourse on Egypt had real consequences in concrete situations, whether in the plight of African American slaves, or in colonial invasions by the French and the British. Similarly, it bears mentioning that Egypt itself was not only a discursive construct, but a real place with a distinctive politics and a lived history. As such, it was invaded by Persians, Greeks, Romans, Arabs, Turks, the French, and finally the British. Given the multiplicity of positions that Egypt assumed in separate imperial visions, "Egypt could not be held in place simply as an Other, for it served as the *entry point* . . . it signified a foothold, a staging point."[31] Even earlier than the fifth century B.C.E., there were too many cross-cultural connections and shared histories to allow for such a phenomenon. On the other hand, Egypt's implication in several international discourses allowed it to take on different meanings for different peoples, often simultaneously. It was a place of higher learning, and it was a land of captivity; it participated in Africa and in Asia, or in Africa and in Europe, or in Asia and in Europe; Egyptians were the oldest people in the world and the second oldest people in the world; Egypt was pharaonic, Greek, Roman, Christian, and Islamic. In this book, which is a study of representations and the meanings that representations can assume, there is a risk of setting aside historical experience in favor of textual and artistic analysis. I have attempted to meet

---

upon it—at the cost of seeing what is alien to us in Egyptian culture as no more than a mask behind which a higher reality is concealed. Indeed, this reality is considered the 'higher' the more it can be made to seem like the ultimate source of some aspect of *our* contemporary world. We are less interested in acquiring knowledge *of* Egypt than in recognizing ourselves *in* Egypt" (Meeks and Favard-Meeks 1996, 3). What is striking about this comment is less its focus on the fact that conceptual inadequacies affect Egyptology—every discipline suffers from conceptual inadequacies—than the sense that these inadequacies recapitulate, point for point, the problems that we can identify as endemic to the ancient Greek traditions about Egypt: an acknowledgment of cultural accomplishment that is nonetheless undermined by condescension on the part of the observer; the need to treat everything Egyptian as fundamentally assimilable to features of the contemporary world; and the construction of Egypt as a screen for the projection of domestic concerns. As this quotation itself implies, however, not all Egyptologists now cling to the assumptions outlined here, and increasing numbers of Egyptologists have evaluated and considered their work in the light of the sociopolitical conditions that have shaped the discipline.

31. Lant 1992, 98. Lant is referring to Egypt as an entry point for colonialists on the sea voyage from Britain to India during the days of the Raj. I interpret her comment to mean that Egypt occupied an in-between position (historically, geographically, discursively) which allowed it to participate simultaneously in East and West: see ch. 2.

such a risk by introducing historical material at appropriate junctures in the discussion.

HISTORICAL BACKGROUND

The histories of Hellenes and Egyptians in the Late Period make Greek representations and misrepresentations of Egypt seem especially problematic, since ties between the two cultures are attested at many levels, political, economic, cultural, military, and mercenary.[32] Greek intellectuals often write as if Persia never ruled Egypt after 525, or as if few foreigners exerted political pressure in the Late Period. Indeed, the range of foreigners involved in the Late Period of Egyptian history can be appreciated when it is considered that contemporary sources are in hieroglyphs, demotic, cuneiform, Aramaic, Hebrew, Phoenician, Carian, and Greek. No less significant a practice by several Greek writers is the underplaying of contacts between Greeks and Egyptians in the fifth and fourth centuries. Further, while a vague acknowledgment of cultural debt to Egypt is often made by Greek writers, especially Herodotus, there is no sense of specific Egyptian contributions to Greek art and architecture. In general, the historical details of cross-cultural interaction call into question the motivation behind the Greek representations of Egypt. The critical reader is compelled to confront the deliberate role of Greeks in defining their object, and to insist that the occultation of this object was carried out in favor of the writers' own interests. To paraphrase Raymond Schwab's remark about Orientalism, if Greek writers were trying at all to weaken the wall between Greece and Egypt, the dismantling was done to their own advantage.[33]

While both Egyptians and Persians were always classified as barbarians, the perceived distinctions between Egyptians and Persians ensured that they were received differently by Greeks in lived experience, works of the imagination, and the overlap between these. In describing Persia, contemporary political events are seldom forgotten by Greek writers in the fifth and fourth centuries. Concerning Egypt, Greek writers, with very few exceptions, hardly advert to sociohistorical realities and contacts, and often choose to represent their Egyptians in ahistorical contexts and apart from the attendant condition of Persian rule. But this elision concerning Egypt

32. The following narrative is based on Kienitz 1953; Gyles 1959; Drioton and Vandier 1975; Bresciani 1968 and 1984; Ray 1987 and 1988; James 1991; Lloyd 1994.
33. Schwab 1984, 1.

occurs mainly at a textual level. In the area of historical encounters, relations between Greeks and Egyptians were often triangulated by the Persians, since the Persians played an important part in the histories of both countries in the fifth and fourth centuries. The founder of the Persian empire, Cyrus (Kurush) himself, planned an invasion of Egypt but died before he could undertake it, and his son Cambyses (Kambujiya) led the expedition in 525 to become the new king of Upper and Lower Egypt, at the expense of Psammetichus III, the last king of the Saïte dynasty.

The Persian control of Egypt covered two periods, divided by an intervening stretch of native rule—and these, together, are the years when the Greek texts that form the subject of our study were composed. The first period, inaugurated by Cambyses, lasted from 525 until the successful revolt by Amyrtaios of Saïs in 404; the second was introduced in 343 by Artaxerxes III Ochus, and continued until the arrival of Alexander in 332.[34] Cambyses was the only Persian king to acquire the pharaoh's full titulary; he died in Syria in early 522, after leaving Aryandes behind as satrap (in demotic, *hstrpn*).[35] He was followed as pharaoh by Darius (Darayavaush), son of Hystaspes, and this king visited Egypt three times, once with Cambyses as a member of his retinue, the second time in 519 when he suppressed a native rebellion, and a third time in 497/6 to preside over the opening of the great canal between the Nile and the Red Sea.[36] Darius also restored the House of Life in Saïs, helped construct the temple of Hibis in the oasis at Kharga, made contributions to temples in Elkab, Edfu, Abusir, and Mem-

---

34. Perhaps as a result of these conquests, both Cambyses and Artaxerxes III Ochus were portrayed by Greeks as enemies of Egyptian religion. Although this is a case of Greeks acknowledging Persian activities in Egypt, it should be noted that the Greek accounts are probably fabrications. Cambyses' treatment of the Apis bull is mentioned by Herodotus 3.29; Plutarch, *On Isis and Osiris* 44; Aelian, *Animal Peculiarities* 10.28; and early Christian writers. Ochus' treatment of the bull is in Plutarch, *On Isis and Osiris* 11. The Graeco-Roman writers also attributed other misdeeds to Cambyses: see Herodotus 3.27–38; Diodorus 1.46; Strabo 17.1.27; Pliny, *Natural History* 36.9. The Egyptian evidence does not agree with this view, and two Apis bulls are attested in Cambyses' reign; see Posener 1936, 30–36, 171–75. According to the Demotic Chronicle, Cambyses did reduce the revenues granted to all but three temples in Egypt, and this action may explain some of the hostility; see Griffiths 1970, 290, 468; Bresciani 1984, 359–60; and Ray 1988, 255–61. On Apis in general, see Meeks and Favard-Meeks 1996, 136–40.

35. The titulary is given in the statue inscription of Udjahorresne: see the transcription in Posener 1936, 1–26; translation in Lichtheim 1980, 36–41; and analysis in Lloyd 1982.

36. See texts and discussion of the canal stele in Posener 1936, 48–87, 180–81. The Greek testimonia include Herodotus 2.158, Diodorus 1.33, Strabo 17.1.25.

phis, and in the fourth year of his reign initiated the codification of the laws of Egypt.[37] There is no evidence for a visit to Egypt by any of Darius' successors in the first period of Persian rule, which persisted through the reigns of Xerxes (Khshayarsha) and Artaxerxes I (Artakhshathra), and came to an end in the reign of Darius II, but presumably the satrap managed the satrapy on the king's behalf and exacted the annual tribute.[38]

"The history of fourth-century Egypt has, at least on the surface, a strikingly 'post-colonial' look to it. It is not simply Achaemenid Egypt without the Achaemenids; it is an Egypt in which the idea of the Achaemenids is always present."[39] The expulsion of the Persians by Amyrtaios in 404 was followed by a period of Egyptian rule marked by feuding among noble families from the Delta. The sovereignty of Egypt fell successively and rapidly into the hands of various Egyptians who came from the north. However, these kings had to contend not just with internal rivals, but with Persian rulers who were reluctant to admit their loss of authority over Egypt. Egyptians, Persians, Athenians, and Spartans were all involved in a tangled series of events that eventually culminated in Alexandrian / Ptolemaic rule. For instance, the Persian threat was one reason why Nepherites I (Nefeuret) entered into an alliance with Sparta, in the autumn of 396, at substantial expense.[40] Akhoris (Hakor or Hakoris) extended this policy, since he made an alliance also with Evagoras of Cyprus and recruited the Athenian Chabrias, both of whom must have aided him in his repulse of Persian forces in 385. Nectanebo I (Nakhtnebef) engaged in a massive program of temple-building,[41] but this activity did not prevent him from thwarting a Persian attack in the spring of 373; he was fortunate that another attack, in the 360s, was postponed when the satraps of Asia Minor diverted the Persian king's attention. In 366 and later, he too appears to

37. The restoration of the House of Life is mentioned in the inscription of Udjahorresne. For the Persian kings' building activities, see Bresciani 1958, 177 ff. The codification of the laws of Egypt is attested in the Demotic Chronicle and in Diodorus 1.95; see further Reich 1933.

38. In the fifth century, the satraps were Aryandes (Aryavanda), Pherendates (Farnadata), Achaemenes (Hahamanis), and Arsames (Arsama). The activities of these satraps and other Persian functionaries are most easily apprehended through the Aramaic evidence, accessible in Cowley 1923, Kraeling 1953, Driver 1957, and Grelot 1972.

39. Ray 1987, 80–81.

40. Kraeling 1953, 79. For the Twenty-ninth Dynasty, see in general Traunecker 1979.

41. For the temple-building of Nectanebo I and Nectanebo II, see the lists in Kienitz 1953, app. 10; Ray 1987, 82, 87–88; Lloyd 1994, 353–54; Arnold 1999, ch. 5.

have solicited help from Athens and Sparta.[42] His co-regent and successor, Takhos (Teos or Djeho), attempted to deprive the Persian empire of Palestine and Phoenicia with the assistance of Chabrias and Agesilaus of Sparta, but events took a startling turn when Takhos' nephew rebelled and persuaded Agesilaus to come over to his side as well. With Agesilaus' help, this nephew, Nectanebo II (Nakhthorheb), returned to Egypt and assumed the throne after defeating another claimant from Mendes, while Takhos was forced to seek refuge from no less a personage than the Persian king.[43] Nectanebo II, another contributor to temple-building, ruled for 18 years, but he was finally incapable of preventing Artaxerxes III Ochus from capturing Memphis in the late summer of 343. This was the king whom Alexander replaced during his invasion of 332.

The complicated history of these elites reveals only part of the contacts between Egyptians and Greeks. Greek-Egyptian relations are attested as early as the Minoan era and, to a smaller degree, in the time between the Mycenaean era and Psammetichus I, but the first Greek settlements in Egypt are conventionally dated to the reign of that Egyptian king.[44] An obscure instance of contact occurs in the century before his rule, in 711, when the Egyptian king Shabako returned the Greek "Yamani" in chains to Sargon. Yamani (the name means the "Greek"—cf. Arabic) had attempted to stir up the city of Ashdod against the Assyrian king, and had fled to Egypt after he failed.[45] Passages in the *Iliad* (9.379–86) and *Odyssey* (books 4, 14, 17) also suggest some kind of awareness of Egypt among early Greeks, especially the country's wealth and the Delta's vulnerability to pirates.[46] According to Greek sources, Ionian and Carian pirates helped Psammetichus I

42. Kienitz 1953, 94–95.

43. See Xenophon, *Agesilaus* 2.28 ff.; Theopompus, *FGrHist* 115 F 106, 108; Nepos, *Agesilaus* 8; Plutarch, *Agesilaus* 36–39 and *Moralia* 214D-E; Diodorus 15.92–93; Polyaenus 2.1; Lyceas of Naukratis, *FGrHist* 613 F 2; Pausanias 3.10; Eustathius at *Odyssey* 10.515; *IG* II² 119; also Kienitz 1953, 95–98, 175–78; Ray 1987, 83; and Lloyd 1994, 341–43. An hieroglyphic inscription from the tomb of a physician who participated in the Phoenician expedition is identified in von Kaenel 1980.

44. This is not to minimize the extensive material evidence for contact between Egypt and Greece from the period before Psammetichus I. For Egyptian objects that have been excavated at Greek sites, see Pendlebury 1930 and the incredibly detailed catalogue in Skon-Jedele 1994.

45. See the Assyrian text in Pritchard 1969, 285; with Lloyd 1975, 12–13; Boardman 1980, 45, 112; and Braun 1982, 32.

46. See Froidefond 1971, ch. 1; also Lloyd 1975, 120–23; Burkert 1976 for the *Iliad;* Braun 1982, 33–35; and West's comments in Heubeck, West, and Hainsworth 1988 for the references to Egypt in *Odyssey* 4.

gain control over Egypt, but according to Assyrian sources, Psammetichus started his rule as a vassal of the Assyrians. The truth is probably that Psammetichus began as king of Saïs under Assyrian patronage and then, with the support of Greek and Carian mercenaries, moved to dominate the whole country and freed himself of Assyrian influence.[47]

Greek representations of Egypt are especially surprising given that Greeks began to live in the Delta in large numbers in the seventh century B.C.E. It was probably in Psammetichus' reign that Greeks began to inhabit the site at Naukratis (Kom Ga'if), where the earliest Corinthian pottery is dated to between 630 and 620, thus providing early signs of the trading activity that was to make Naukratis famous.[48] The town itself lay about ten miles from Saïs and fifty from the sea; archaeologists have identified the remains of the Hellenion described by Herodotus as well as a scarab factory and temples of Aphrodite, Apollo, Hera, and the Dioscuri. The stele of Nectanebo I in Naukratis mentions the imposition of duties of ten percent on imports coming through the town and a tax on goods manufactured locally.[49] Exports from Egypt to Greece in the Late Period were corn, papyrus, linen, alum, faience, and works in ivory and bronze, while imports from Greece were wine, olive oil, and silver.[50] The east Greek pottery at Naukratis derives from Rhodes, Chios, Samos, Miletus, Clazomenae, and Lesbos, and there are also large finds of Spartan, Corinthian, and Athenian vases.[51] Names on these finds, presumably those of persons offering them as dedications, run from a Herodotus on an Athenian cup of the fifth century to a Rhodopis and an Archedice on other objects.[52]

But it is not just Naukratis in which Greeks lived in the Late Period, for Greeks resided in and Greek objects made their way to numerous other

47. The Greek sources include Herodotus 2.147–52; Diodorus 1.66; Polyaenus 8.3; cf. Aristagoras of Miletus, *FGrHist* 608 F 9; these are balanced against the Assyrian sources in Braun 1982, 35–37.

48. For a general survey of the archaeological material pertaining to contact between Egypt and Greece in the eighth to sixth centuries, see Guralnick 1997. For accounts of Naukratis, see Austin 1970, 22–33; Lloyd 1975, 24–29; Boardman 1980, 118–33; Braun 1982, 37–43; and the ongoing reports of W. D. E. Coulson and A. Leonard, Jr. The ancient sources are brought together in Bernand 1970, chs. 11–15. I have not seen Astrid Moller, *Naukratis: Trade in Archaic Greece* (Oxford, 2000).

49. See the translation in Lichtheim 1980, 86–89, with the discussions cited in Lloyd 1975, 28.

50. Austin 1970, 35–37; Boardman 1980, 129–31; Braun 1982, 39–40; Skon-Jedele 1994.

51. Austin 1970, 25–27; Boardman 1980, 122–25.

52. Boardman 1980, 132.

places in Egypt. Tell Defenneh, the ancient Daphnae, was a frontier post that in Apries' day gave asylum to Jews, including Jeremiah.[53] Most of its Greek pottery dates to the reign of Amasis (Amhose II, 570 –526)—but it seems to lack Greek objects datable after 525, the year of Cambyses' invasion. Greek pottery from the sixth century has also been found at a site close to Tell Defenneh, identified as Migdol, as well as at Memphis, Abusir, Luxor, Karnak, Edfu, and even Nubia.[54] Greek vases dated to after 500 and found in Egypt are mainly Athenian. One clay vase made by the Athenian potter Sotades in about 460 was found in Memphis; it has the shape of a camel led by a Persian and a black African; another clay vase made by Sotades in 460, found in Nubia, has the shape of an Amazon woman mounted on a horse.[55] Hoards of Greek silver coins have been found in Tell Defenneh, Memphis, Naukratis, and elsewhere. Coins from Thrace and Macedonia predominate among hoards dated to the era before the fifth century, but coins from Athens dominate among hoards dated after about 500; in fact, Athenian coins become increasingly popular after the early fifth century and remain the foreign coinage of choice in the fourth century.[56]

Some of this money went to the Greek mercenaries, military forces and military advisers who were active in several campaigns waged by Egyptian rulers of the Late Period.[57] Psammetichus I's early attempts at consolidation reveal the level of his reliance on Greek and Carian mercenaries, and his son Necho (Nekau) II hired Greek soldiers in the battle of Carchemish, in 605, when Nebuchadnezzar defeated the Egyptian king.[58] Necho also may have had "triremes" built for his naval forces, perhaps by both Greeks and Phoenicians.[59] His successor, Psammetichus II, placed Greeks in his

---

53. See Jeremiah 43.6,–7, where the town is known by its Hebrew name Tahpanhes; other names are Baal-Zaphon, Greek Daphnae (see Herodotus 2.30), and the modern Tell Defenneh. Hebrew sources for the Late Period in general include 2 Kings, 2 Chronicles, Ezekiel, and Josephus (*Jewish Antiquities* 10) as well as Jeremiah.

54. For Migdol, see Herodotus 2.159 (Μαγδώλῳ, Μαγδόλῳ, or Μαγδάλῳ); Exodus 14.1–2; Jeremiah 44.1, 46.14; Ezekiel 29.10; Boardman 1980, 134–35. For the other sites, see Austin 1970, 33–34; Boardman 1980, 133–41.

55. Boardman 1980, 138–40, with illustrations.

56. Austin 1970, 37–40; Lloyd 1975, 30–31; Boardman 1980, 130; Braun 1982, 40.

57. In general, see Parke 1933; Austin 1970, 15–22; Lloyd 1975, 14–23; Boardman 1980, 115–17; Braun 1982, 49–52.

58. Boardman 1980, 51, 115; Braun 1982, 49; James 1991, 715–17.

59. Lloyd 1972 and 1980; Basch 1977 and 1980; see also the references in Lloyd 1988a, 160. On the growth of Egyptian maritime policy in this period, see James 1991, 721–26.

navy and employed Greek soldiers in his Nubian campaign, among the latter being those who left graffiti at Abu Simbel: "When King Psammetichus came to Elephantine, those who sailed with Psamatichos son of Theocles wrote this; and they came above Kerkis as far as the river allowed; and Potasimto had command of those of foreign speech and Amasis of the Egyptians; and Archon the son of Amoibichos wrote us and Peleqos son of Eudamos."[60] A sarcophagus indicates that Potasimto was "commander of the Greeks" in Psammetichus' Nubian expedition, which also included Jewish troops.[61] Greek mercenaries were favored by Apries, but they were unable to save him his throne, and Amasis became pharaoh in 589. A stele at Elephantine records a later attempt by Apries to regain the crown "while Greeks without number are coursing through the Northland," ostensibly on Apries' behalf, but this attempt too was unsuccessful.[62] The Greek sources, including Herodotus, present Amasis as a committed philhellene, nevertheless, and eight Greek writers plus Herodotus mention his dedications at the temple of Athena at Lindus in Rhodes.[63] When Cambyses launched his invasion of Egypt, he benefited from the treachery of Phanes of Halicarnassus, a mercenary under Amasis.

There is poor information about the fate of Greek mercenaries in Egyptian service during the Persian period, but Greek forces continued to influence Egyptian events in the fifth century, notably in the revolt of Inarus.[64] The insurrection of Inarus, which started in 463 in the reign of Artaxerxes I, began in the western Delta and quickly spread. Inarus asked Athens for help in his struggle against the Persians, and he was answered by the helpful diversion of a fleet of two hundred ships under Charitimides, originally intended for use against Cyprus. Inarus' army defeated Persian land forces at Papremis and killed the satrap Achaemenes, while Charitimides dealt severe losses to Persian naval forces on the Nile. The ensuing backlash from Persia came in the 450s, when Megabyzos, satrap of Syria, recaptured Memphis and then besieged Inarus and his Greek allies on the

60. Translation from Braun 1982, 50; see Bernand and Masson 1957; ML no. 7.
61. Austin 1970, 57; Braun 1982, 50–51.
62. Translation and discussion of the stele in Breasted 1906, 509–12.
63. Herodotus 2.182, 3.47. The chronicle from Lindus Temple supplies the names of Herodotus, Poluzalos, Hieron, Agelochus, Aristion, Aristonumos, Onomastos, Xenagoras, and Hierobulos (*FGrHist* 532, paragraph 29).
64. Herodotus 3.12, 15 and 7.7; Thucydides 1.104, 109–10; Isocrates 8.86; Diodorus 11.71, 74–75; Ctesias, *FGrHist* 688 F 14; Posener 1936, 190; Kienitz 1953, 69–73; Driver 1957, 92–96; Salmon 1965; Libourel 1971; Lloyd 1975, 38–49; Ray 1988, 275–76; Robinson 1999.

island of Prosopitis. The Persians captured or killed most of the besieged and sent Inarus to Persia for execution, and in 454 they intercepted and destroyed an Athenian fleet bringing reinforcements. There is a garbled record of Amyrtaios offering resistance in 449 when part of Cimon's fleet was diverted from Cyprus to Egypt, but little else is known of the Egyptian's actions. Later, another Amyrtaios took advantage of Persian weaknesses and restored the country to native Egyptian rule in 404. In the fourth century, more Greeks, notably Chabrias and Agesilaus, intervened in the military affairs of Egypt.

The Egyptian cults in Athens further illustrate cross-cultural interaction between Egyptians and Greeks. The cult of Ammon ('Άμμων) and the cult of Isis ('Ισις, or Είσις) are recorded among the religious associations of Piraeus in the classical period. The former was, of course, the transplanted cult of the Egyptian god Amun, whose name probably means "the hidden one." The oracle of Ammon had already been consulted in the fifth century by such Athenians as Alcibiades and Cimon.[65] By the middle of the fourth century, there was a sanctuary of Ammon in Piraeus, and it became an official state cult by 363/2.[66] This cult was open to citizens as well as to foreigners, and the priest of the cult in about 330 was one Pausiades of Phaleron.[67] Later, even one of the sacred triremes of Athens was called "Ammonias" ('Άμμωνιάς) after the god.[68] Concerning the cult of Isis, whose name may mean "mistress of the house of life," an inscription indicates that the goddess' presence was established in Piraeus before 333/2.[69] Scholars have conjectured variously that the cult was established by Lycur-

65. See Plutarch, *Cimon* 18.6–7 and *Nicias* 13.1. For Zeus Ammon, see chapter 7 below.
66. By about 363/2, a number of dedications were made by the Athenian demos to the cult of Ammon (*SEG* 21.241): ὁ δῆμος ὁ Ἀθηναίων . . . δίδωσι τῶι Ἄμμωνι (see also *SEG* 21.562). In 333/2, a state sacrifice was made to Ammon: see *IG* II² 1496.96–97: this inscription lists sacrifices to Agathe Tyche, Demokratia, Eirene, Hermes Hegemonios, and Zeus Soter as well as to Ammon. The sanctuary of Ammon is also mentioned in *IG* II² 338 in connection with the building activities of Pytheas of Alopeke. Further, Athenian records indicate that a *phiale* was dedicated to Ammon in about 375 (*SEG* 21.549). For the evidence concerning Ammon in Athens, see Woodward 1962. There is no evidence of the cult in Athens after 260 B.C.E.
67. For Pausiades of Phaleron, see *IG* II² 410.19.
68. See Aristotle, fr. 443 (Rose) = scholia to Demosthenes, *Oration* 21.171 (*Against Meidias*), sec. 580 (Dilts), and Photius, *Lexicon*, s.v. Πάραλοι and Πάραλος.
69. See *IG* II² 337. For Isis in classical Athens, see Simms 1989. The evidence for this cult is very slender; it is next attested in the second century B.C.E. For the Egyptian cults in Hellenistic Athens, see Dow 1937 and Mikalson 1998, 30–31, 37–38, 146, 151–54, 275–77; and cf. Brady 1935 and Classen 1959.

gus, who dominated Athenian politics for a decade after 338, or even earlier by his grandfather, the Lycurgus who was lampooned in Attic comedy
for his Egyptian connections.[70] Unlike the cult of Ammon, however, this
was not a state institution, but an exclusively foreign one that admitted
no citizen members. Perhaps the members of this cult were Egyptian and
other metics, or foreign sailors and traders with interests in Athens. To the
material evidence for the Egyptian cults in Athens, we should also add that
Ammon and Isis are mentioned by Greek sources such as Pindar and Herodotus.[71] During the classical period, then, the two Egyptian deities were
known in Greek intellectual and literary circles as well as in their cultic establishments in Piraeus.

Contacts between Greece and Egypt must have been responsible for
Egyptian influence on Greece and Greek culture in the Late Period. Greeks
borrowed from Egypt in religion, myth, geometry, medicine, and literature, but the nature and extent of the impact of Egypt on Greece in these
realms is a matter of controversy and ongoing debate.[72] It is uncontrover-
sial to remark that Greek monumental sculpture and stone architecture reflect Egyptian traditions.[73] Buildings of stone were rare in Greece, which
relied on wood and brick, and in the Near East, where brick was the preferred medium, but they were present in Egypt on a monumental scale long
before the seventh century. By the end of that century, Greeks were constructing buildings out of stone and were eventually led to use the Doric
order in their columns. Greeks also borrowed the palm capital from Egypt,
such as found in the ruins at Luxor, although Greek architects did not put
this style to widespread use. Greek *kouroi* clearly are adaptations of Egyptian stone statues, with the difference that the Egyptian statues are clothed
and the Greek naked. Other sculptured objects in Greece also seem to be
the result of borrowing, for example, the row of marble lions at Delos made
in the sixth century. Scholars have further detected Egyptian traits and mo-

70. Simms 1989. Aristophanes' *Birds* 1296 refers to Lycurgus as Ibis. The scholia remark that people thought Lycurgus was Egyptian "either by race or in character" (ἢ τὸ γένος ἢ τοὺς τρόπους), and indicate that the comic poets Cratinus
(*Maids of Delos*, fr. 32 PCG) and Pherecrates (*Savages*, fr. 11 PCG) also made fun
of Lycurgus for his Egyptian connections (scholia at *Birds* 1294).

71. See Pindar, fr. 36 (Maehler) for a poem to Ammon; and cf. Pausanias 9.16.1.
For Ammon in Herodotus, see 1.46; 2.18, 32, 42 (also gives the name "Amun"), 55.
For Isis in Herodotus, see 2.41–42, 59, 61, 156, 176; 4.186.

72. This is a large and controversial subject: see e.g. James 1985; Morenz 1968;
Boardman 1980, 141–53; Braun 1982, 53–56; Bernal 1987 and 1991; Asante 1990.

73. Iversen 1957; Boardman 1978, ch. 4; Boardman 1980, 143–53; Davis 1981.

tifs in many kinds of Greek art, from bronzes in Sparta to vases and statuettes in Rhodes to specific scenes on vases in Athens and Corinth. As this evidence demonstrates, Egypt made a significant contribution to the evolution of classical Greek art and architecture. Assuredly, the Egyptian influence on Greece makes it impossible to retain the old opinion of scholars such as Ulrich von Wilamowitz-Moellendorf, who wrote about "the peoples and states of the Semites and the Egyptians which had been decaying for centuries and which, in spite of the antiquity of their culture, were unable to contribute anything to the Hellenes other than a few manual skills, costumes, and implements of bad taste, antiquated ornaments, repulsive fetishes for even more repulsive false divinities." [74]

The distance between the historical material just considered and the Greek texts examined below is delicately traversed within a set of distinctions drawn by François Hartog. In his book *Mémoire d'Ulysse*, Hartog distinguishes between a "voyage in Egypt" *(voyage en Égypte)* and an "Egyptian voyage" *(voyage d'Égypte)*. The "voyage in Egypt" refers to the journey made by Greeks such as Chabrias and Agesilaus who traveled across the Mediterranean and engaged in Egyptian politics, or by Greek traders who brought their ships to the Deltaic cities and sold oil for wheat. It has been described at some length in the pages immediately preceding. On the other hand, the "Egyptian voyage" has an imaginary dimension; it is "the voyage as a discursive operator and narrative scheme: the voyage as gaze and as resolution of a problem or response to a question." [75] This is the gaze of literary and philosophical authors and texts, and "the gaze of the Greek tourist, who never ceases to evaluate the other by the measure of the same and knows, at bottom, always from where he returns, or . . . the gaze, finally, which never ceases to revisit the past and to reappropriate it for itself in order to restore it, by 'rediscovering' the signs and traces of an ancient Greek identity in order to recompose and reactivate it." [76] As Hartog im-

74. *Homerische Untersuchungen* (Berlin, 1884), 215, also quoted in Burkert 1992, 2–3.
75. Hartog 1996, 15–16.
76. See Hartog 1996, 16. The sentence reads in full: "This is the gaze of the Greek tourist, who never ceases to evaluate the other by the measure of the same and knows, at bottom, always from where he returns, or, on the contrary, the gaze from afar which, by a detour elsewhere, puts the same at a distance, puts it into question even, this gaze which, through recourse to the elsewhere and the valorization of the other, translates the doubt of the same about what it is, the gaze, finally,

plies, the imaginary "Egyptian voyage" is not interested in Egypt or Egyptians in themselves, in their historical specificity, or in their particular accomplishments. This voyage is a way of reflecting back on Greekness, on Greek selfhood, and on Greek anxieties of identity. It is the idea of the "Egyptian voyage" that reinforces Arnaldo Momigliano's pronouncement on Greek intellectuals' reluctance to learn foreign languages and on their lack of genuine interest in other cultures.[77] This view, in turn, complements Emmanuel Levinas' comment on the founding voyage of Odysseus himself. Odysseus also says he passed through Egypt, but his "adventure in the world," Levinas writes, "is only a return to his native island—a self-satisfaction *[complaisance]* in the Same, a misunderstanding *[méconnaissance]* of the Other."[78] For both Momigliano and Levinas, as for Hartog after them, the Greek gaze on foreigners and foreign cultures is characterized by closure, misrecognition, and a deficiency in intellectual curiosity. This gaze is directed more to the question "Who are we, the Greeks?" than to the question "Who are the Egyptians?" and hence it fails to provide a true and sensitive understanding of non-Greek peoples.

Many of the texts analyzed in this book are self-reflexive and reveal more about the authors than the Egyptians they describe. But self-reflexivity takes several forms. In *Tristes Tropiques,* Claude Lévi-Strauss

---

which never ceases to revisit the past and to reappropriate it for itself in order to restore it, by 'rediscovering' the signs and traces of an ancient Greek identity in order to recompose and reactivate it" (C'est le regard du touriste grec, qui ne cesse d'évaluer l'autre à l'aune du même et sait, au fond, toujours de quoi il retourne, ou, au contraire, le "regard éloigné" de qui, par le détour l'ailleurs, met à distance le même, voire le met en question, ce regard qui, à travers le recours à l'ailleurs et la valorisation de l'autre, traduit le doute du même sur ce qu'il est, le regard, enfin, qui n'a de cesse de reparcourir le passé et de se le réapproprier pour se réassurer, en "retrouvant" les signes et les traces d'une antique identité grecque à recomposer et à réactiver).

77. Momigliano 1978, 7–8, 148–50. Concerning Egyptian, there are some highly dubious exceptions that are mentioned in later sources: Diogenes Laertius (8.3) says that he read in a work by Antiphon *(On Men of Outstanding Merit)* that Pythagoras learned the Egyptian language (φωνή); Clement of Alexandria *(Stromateis* 5.4.20.3–21.3) and Porphyry *(De cultu simulacrorum* fr. 10) claim to understand the language; and Plutarch writes as if he too knows the meanings of certain hieroglyphs *(On Isis and Osiris).* However, Chaeremon (frags. 12, 20D, 25D), Ammianus Marcellinus (17.4.11 and 22.15.30), and Horapollo (in his *Hieroglyphica)* do show a deeper understanding of hieroglyphs than other surviving Greek and Latin writers: see Iversen 1993, 46–50. None of these authors provides evidence of a substantial and wholly correct knowledge of hieroglyphs: see ch. 4.

78. E. Levinas, *L'humanisme de l'autre homme* (Paris, 1972), 43, quoted in Hartog 1996, 16.

writes, "The first thing we see as we travel round the world is our own filth, thrown in the face of mankind."[79] Where a writer like Lévi-Strauss explicitly directs attention to the reflexive aspects of his narrative, Greek texts are self-reflexive in less direct ways: Is the story of the war between ancient Athens and Atlantis also about the war between Athens and Sparta, or is it about the conflict between Athens and Persia? Greek writings about Egypt touch on Greek ideas of tyranny and history, as in Herodotus, on gender politics, as in Aeschylus and Euripides, on anxieties of writing technology, as in Plato, or on human sacrifice, as in Isocrates. Self-reflexivity is entailed also by explorations of otherness, if the self can be acceptably defined as the other of the other. These texts interrogate others and otherness up to the limits imposed on the authors by their cultural context. What are the possible ways of being a barbarian? What does it mean for a barbarian culture to transmit ideas and inventions to Greece? What are the ways of being a barbarian without being a Persian at the same time? Questions of this ilk open outward and provide a space for the barbarian to take shape and color, but, ultimately arrested by closure and containment, they are also pointers to Greek self-fashioning. Thus, the Greek "tourists" who visit Egypt use it to explore issues of self-identity and seek wisdom in Egypt's ancient accomplishments, but seldom forget in the end the location from which they have started out. These travelers are interested not in discovering new ways of life that challenge and transform their own, but in affirming and completing the vision of the world that they set off with on their voyages.

Beyond the claims of pure self-reflexivity and the binarism on which it depends, there is still a terrain to cover and an opportunity for historical detail to be brought to bear on the "Egyptian voyage." For it is true that the line between the voyage in Egypt and the Egyptian voyage is not clearly demarcated, and that each voyage informs the other kind. Herodotus' work on Egypt contains numerous descriptive passages that have since been corroborated by Egyptology, archaeology, or non-Greek sources, though many of the details have been qualified or rejected. Similarly, Thucydides is used by modern historians to establish the size and chronology of the Athenian expedition to Egypt in the middle of the fifth century. Authors like these can give information or interpretation about local history or cross-cultural contact that is substantially different in tenor and content from more imaginary and more self-interested reconstructions of Egyptian life found in Greek texts, sometimes even in other places in their own texts.

79. Lévi-Strauss 1992, 38.

Conversely and importantly, voyages in Egypt were also influenced by Greek discourses that accumulated over the decades. Compelling and powerful representations drawn from Greek traditions about Egypt enhanced the appeal of the country for an imperialist such as Alexander. Scores of mercenaries and traders were attracted, like Alexander, no doubt in part because of what was reported and fantasized about Egypt. These voyages in Egypt were conditioned and prepared for by Egyptian voyages, and it can be affirmed that the two types of voyages continually influenced, inspired, moved, and shaped each other.

Egypt so haunted and fascinated the Greeks that they were bound to represent it in their works. Their preoccupation with Egypt raises a host of interconnected topics: otherness, selfhood, Greekness, imperialism, the power of description, the performative force of linguistic and extralinguistic discourses, and the disconcerting relationship between events and texts. But the Greeks also used Egyptian culture to engage their own problems and to interrogate their own peculiarly Greek fixations. In moving between their attention to Egypt and their attention to themselves, or in moving over the area in common, they generated a body of literature teeming with narratives and counternarratives, interpretations and overinterpretations, deep questions, deeper anxieties, and wildly imaginative fantasies. In their work, they showed how self-satisfying and elusive and how stimulating and troubling it is to study other cultures, and with this demonstration they made possible literary Europe's most persistent and adaptable obsession, namely, the barbarian.

1   The Tragic Egyptian

Why the Orient still seems to suggest not only fecundity but
sexual promise (and threat), untiring sensuality, unlimited
desire, deep generative energies, is something on which one
could speculate: it is not the province of my analysis here, alas,
despite its frequently noted appearance. Nevertheless one must
acknowledge its importance as something eliciting complex
responses, sometimes even a frightful self-discovery. . . .

Edward Said, *Orientalism*

With Athenian tragedy, Greek anxieties about a sexual threat from Egypt
assume a forceful and violent apotheosis.[1] In Aeschylus' *Suppliants* and
Euripides' *Helen*, the Egyptianness of male pursuers is refracted through
issues connected with death and the dissolution of desire.[2] Today, to speak
of Egypt as the land of the dead means to follow one of the oldest stereotypes of Western literature and to disregard the Egyptological evidence
that "Egyptian funerary religion was primarily life-affirming, with build-

1. This chapter is largely concerned with Aeschylus' *Suppliants* (a play in his
Danaid trilogy) and Euripides' *Helen*. Other ancient Greek plays that dealt with
Egyptian themes are now lost or very fragmentary. For instance, Phrynichus composed *Aigyptioi* and *Danaides* (*TrGF* 3 F 1 and 4), titles which parallel the names of
plays in Aeschylus' Danaid trilogy. Timesitheus, too, composed a play called *Danaides* (*TrGF* 214 F [1]). Theodectes composed *Lynceus*, which was based on Aegyptus' son Lynceus, who married Hypermestra, one of the Danaids (see Aristotle, *Poetics* 11 and 18 = *TrGF* 72 F 3a). Even two comedies called *Danaides* are attested,
one by Aristophanes (frs. 256–76 *PCG*), and the other by Diphilus, a poet of New
Comedy (fr. 24 *PCG*). Other lost plays on Egyptian themes include Aeschylus' *Proteus* (the satyr-play of the *Oresteia*) and Euripides' *Busiris*, also a satyr-play. For
comic plays about Busiris, see also Antiphanes frs. 66–68 *PCG* (= Kock, vol. 2, 37–
38); Cratinus fr. 23 *PCG* (= Kock, vol. 2, 289); Ephippus fr. 2 *PCG* (= Kock, vol. 2,
251); Epicharmus, frs. 81.10 and 82, and see fr. 223 *CGFP*; Mnesimachus fr. 2 *PCG*
(= Kock, vol. 2, 436). For Busiris, see further chapter 5 below. For the scattered references to Egypt in comedy, see Froidefond 1971, 224–28; also the entries under
"Egypt" in the index to Long 1986; and Simms 1989 (in connection with Athenian
interest in Isis).
    2. References to *Suppliants* are from FJW, and to *Helen* from J. Diggle's OCT
of Euripides, 3 vols., 1982–94. Translations of *Suppliants* are modified from Friis
Johansen 1970, and of *Helen* from Richmond Lattimore's version in the Chicago
series.

ings, rituals and prayers designed to maintain an individual's life and status beyond the transition of death, which was regarded as an unpleasant
necessity."[3] The stereotype can be found in Aeschylus and Euripides, who
are strikingly efficient in their marshaling of deathly images to describe
Egyptians. The Danaids, in *Suppliants,* prefer marriage with death to marriage with their Egyptian cousins; Helen's rescue, in Euripides' play, unfolds
against the backdrop of an Egypt that is at all times made to resemble the
underworld. Each play configures marriage between Egyptians and Greek
in proximity to death and each play depicts an Egypto-Greek marriage as a
violent disruption in the order of things. Inevitably, the plays do not handle
the issues of ethnicity and gender in the same ways: Aeschylus' play emphasizes the blackness of Egyptians, and Euripides' play stresses their "barbarian" character. Even the word *barbaros* has slightly different connotations in Aeschylus and Euripides.[4] When Egyptians ask to marry Greeks,
however, both *Suppliants* and *Helen* deny Egyptians their desire for marriage with Greek women (with the exception of Hypermestra) by depicting
these suitors as deadly and marriage with them as dangerous.

The conflict between male and female and between Egyptian and Greek
thus becomes most vivid through the portrayal of Egypto-Greek marriage
as death for women. There is crucial stress on gender and ethnicity in these
texts. To take gender, sexually aggressive behavior appears as the chief
characteristic of the Egyptian males. It is the males who insist on their procreative capabilities, while it is the females who fly away from the males'
desire for conjugal union. To take ethnicity, the plays maintain a barrier
between Greeks and Egyptians, for all the slippage discerned in *Suppliants,* and the texts can offer no better response to the question "Why can
an Egyptian man not marry a Greek woman?" than to assert "Because he
is an Egyptian." Athenian tragedy is unable to bring Greeks and Egyptians
together, in contrast to the unions between Greeks and Egyptians that were
occurring in towns such as Naukratis, and in contrast to the military support rendered to the Egyptian resistance against the Persians in the 460s
and later. For tragedy, the social and political cooperation between Egyptian
and Greek is belied by a fantasy of mythical conflict; for tragedy, the Egyptian's desire for the Greek is foreclosed through his very otherness.

In drawing attention to the problematic status of Egyptians in Greek
tragedy, I refer as well to the affinity in ancient Greek culture between
death and blackness, since it is among the cluster of ideas connected with

3. Robert K. Ritner, in Silverman 1997, 132.
4. Bacon 1961, Saïd 1984, Hall 1989.

death and blackness that Egyptians are portrayed by the playwrights, especially by Aeschylus. Greeks and Egyptians construed racial categories in ways that are foreign to modern conceptualizations of the issue, although more recent scholarship has challenged the older judgment that there was no color prejudice among Greeks and Romans.[5] I have tried in my analysis to reorient notions of blackness within the framework of Greek thought and do not claim that the Greeks assumed a racist privileging of any somatic category in their culture. Nevertheless, Greeks certainly acted on the basis of ethnocentrism and cultural prejudice, which at times were informed by somatic judgments. Aeschylus' use of color symbolism and of images of blackness in representing Egyptians is a cultural statement calling for investigation. If blackness was often associated with death in ancient Greek thought, then for a Danaid to want to marry black death was flatly to spurn the hand of her black cousin. Such a gesture takes on added meaning when it is also remembered that the Danaid killed her husband, and was punished with banishment to the underworld. Why must Aeschylus refer repeatedly to this color and to these images in order to portray Egyptians in his play?

This intersection of ethnicity and gender in Greek tragedy will come as no surprise to any one familiar with the history of European literature. Prompted by Gustave Flaubert's writings, Edward Said has remarked on the "almost uniform association between the Orient and sex."[6] As Said notes, Flaubert was merely one of many Western writers from different eras to make this association between the Orient and sex, whether it involved the eroticizing of the natural landscape, the feminizing of the colonized man, or the promise of sexual experience unattainable in the metropolis. Greek tragedians do not necessarily make the same sexual suggestions as one

5. Thompson 1989 has complicated and revised the observations in Snowden 1970 and 1983 concerning the lack of color prejudice in Greek and Roman antiquity. Tuplin 1999 argues that it is not accurate to refer to Greek ethnic prejudice as racist. However, Rosivach 1999 has shown the racist underpinnings of the Athenian ideology of slavery.

6. Said 1978, 188. The encounter with the dancing-girl Kuchuk Hanem, in Esna, brilliantly typifies Said's claim: see the Egyptian travel notes in Flaubert 1972, 112–19. In passages that resonate deeply with issues of race, desire, transnational dislocation, and the politics of representation, Flaubert describes Kuchuk's body ("heavy shoulders, full apple-shaped breasts") and the dance routine ("Kuchuk's dance is brutal. She squeezes her bare breasts together with her jacket") that precedes sex with her. When he adds "I have seen this dance on old Greek vases" (*J'ai vu cette danse sur des vieux vases grecs*), however, he does not say whether he thinks the dancers in the vases are Greek or Egyptian. On Flaubert in Egypt, see also chapters 2 and 3 below.

finds in Flaubert, Gérard Nerval, and Richard Burton. Aeschylus and Euripides open up a space for sexual conflict and intervention in forestalling the cross-cultural intimacy that could have been exemplified in the successful marriages of Egyptians and Greeks. Into this fantasy space will come Greek men ready to ward off Egyptian assailants and eager to give safe passage home to Helen.

It is nonetheless entirely correct, after Said, to insist on the implications for Greek selfhood and subjectivity of the association between Egypt and sex. This question of Greek self-fashioning, which was touched on in the introduction, is raised by a passage of Herodotus in the context of the Danaids. Making a well-known claim, Herodotus discusses the origins of a rite attached to the worship of Demeter:

> And again, about the rites of Demeter that the Greeks call the Thesmophoria, let me hold my peace—save in so far as it is right for me to speak. It was the daughters of Danaus who brought this rite from Egypt and taught it to the Pelasgian women. Afterwards, when the Peloponnesus had its population driven out by the Dorians, the rite perished, and it was the only people in the Peloponnesus who were not driven out but remained—namely, the Arcadians—who preserved it. (2.170–71)

Herodotus notes that the rites of the Thesmophoria were brought to Greece by the Danaids, but some scholarly commentators believe his statement about the Danaids to be "historically worthless."[7]

The search for what is and is not historically sound in Herodotus is unending, quite apart from the problem of how one situates one's beliefs in connection with historical positivism. When Herodotus claims that the Danaids brought the rites of the Thesmophoria from Egypt to Greece, he may be forwarding observations that are "historically worthless," but he is being consistent with his repeated statements of the Egyptian origins of certain Greek practices and ideas, including "the names of nearly all the gods" (2.50), and his statement is valuable for a history of the Greek perception of cultural borrowings from Egypt. As we shall see in chapter 3, Egypt is one of the chief sources for Greek cultural borrowings according to Herodotus' history. In connection with his claim that the Danaids brought the Thesmophoria to Greece, we should recall that he elsewhere identifies Isis with Demeter and that he notes a physical resemblance between the Egyp-

---

7. See the commentary in Lloyd 1988a, 210. Herodotus seems to suggest that these Greek rites were the same as the "mysteries" of Osiris, although the connection is left implicit. The Greek terms μυήσεις and μυστήρια do not have a direct counterpart in the religious thought of Egypt: see Griffiths 1970, 390–92.

tian goddess and Io. For Herodotus, thus, there is both a transplanting of Egyptian rites onto Greek soil and a correlation between Egyptian and Greek divinities.[8]

Aeschylus' *Suppliants* diverges from Herodotus' text to the extent that it reverses the direction of the cultural borrowing. It is likely, as some scholars suggest, that one of the lost plays of the Danaid trilogy enacted the introduction of the Thesmophoria to Greece by the Danaids. But whereas Herodotus ascribes cultural origins to Egypt, Aeschylus describes a movement from Greece to Egypt and then back from Egypt to Greece that serves to affirm the anteriority of Greece over Egypt. The playwright follows the broad outlines of the Greek myth in which Io travels from Greece to Egypt, and begets offspring with names such as Libya, Aegyptus, and Danaus, the eponymous founders of various ethnic peoples. Attributing names such as these to Greek heroes suggests the priority of Greek civilization over the Egyptian, and asks the audience to believe that the lines of Libyans and Egyptians, for example, derive from the Greeks through Libya and Aegyptus. Aeschylus is intervening in a debate on cultural origins that was current in sixth-century and fifth-century Greece, a debate that is reflected, for instance, in the writings of Hecateus of Miletus and Anaximander.[9] Herodotus also was a part of this intellectual debate, but while he often grants priority in civilization to Egyptians and others, Aeschylus appears to locate his tragedy against a genealogical background that grants ethnic anteriority to the Greeks.[10] In his *Inachus*, Sophocles may have adopted a similar tradition as Aeschylus, but in addition he gives Zeus a black complexion in

8. Herodotus *identifies* Isis with Demeter (2.59), but points to the *resemblance* between Isis and Io when he says that "the image of Isis is female in form, but with a cow's horns, as the Greeks represent Io" (2.41). The latter claim about Io appears to have a basis in fact, both in its description of Isis, and in its suggestion that the Egyptian goddess lies behind the representation of the Greek Io in the fifth century. It should be noted that Plato's student Heraclides of Pontus (quoted by Plutarch, *On Isis and Osiris* 27) identifies Isis with Persephassa (Persephone), and Callimachus identifies Isis with Io (*Epigrams* 57.1). See Witt 1966, 59, for Athenian knowledge of Isis in the fifth century. For Isis and Demeter, see West 1984, 297 n. 25; for Isis and Io, see Griffiths 1970, 392–93, 443; Thomson 1973, 136, 285; Seaford 1980, 26–27. For the introduction of Egyptian gods in Greece, see Brady 1935, Dow 1937, and Classen 1959, with the references given in the introduction above.

9. On ethnic identity and cultural genealogy, see Hall 1997. For Hecateus of Miletus, see the appendix below; for Anaximander, see the materials at DK 12.

10. See also the Hesiodic *Ehoiai* for assimilation of foreign peoples to Hellenic stemmata; Bickerman 1952; West 1985, 144–54; cf. Froidefond 1971, 105–10, for *Suppliants* in particular. According to Herodotus, Aeschylus even came up with a mythological innovation through an idea that he stole from Egypt (2.156).

order to explain the difference in pigmentation between Greeks and those who are ostensibly descended from a union between the god and Io. As we would expect, the blackness of Zeus in Sophocles' play is also linked to his role as Zeus Chthonius, the lord of the dead.[11]

Within this climate of speculation in cultural anthropology and of competition in claims to ethnic priority should be placed the depiction of Egyptians in *Suppliants* and *Helen*. When a Greek playwright shows Egyptian men as tyrannical, lascivious, feral, and threatening to Greek chastity, he points not just to characteristics in barbarians, but also invokes the terms of a serious discussion over cultural issues. If a tragedy represents white men saving black women from black men, as in *Suppliants*, or a white man saving a white woman from a black man, as in *Helen*, a whole series of questions is raised concerned with national identity, including those bound up with ethnicity, gender, and self-fashioning.[12] Again, questions about ethnicity, gender, and self-fashioning are raised when, in *Suppliants* and *Helen*, sensual excess is displaced in such a way that Egyptian hypervirility demands the intervention of Hellenic men. Greek tragedies are part of the process of subject formation insofar as they reflect and fashion cultural identities, in particular the identity of the male citizens who produced and consumed these plays. This identity was defined in relation to barbarians, gods, women, and slaves, for instance, although it is not always certain in what ways and with what effects the various vectors converged on individual subjects. No small measure of the importance of *Suppliants* and *Helen* lies in the ways in which these plays engage issues of identity and self-fashioning.

From a slightly different perspective, the tragic theatre also expresses Greek men's desires, camouflaged under such idealized notions as *sophrosyne*, and transposes them onto Egyptian males. Both plays are about the abduction of Greek women by Egyptian men, yet the foreignness of the men should not occlude our recognition of the fantasy that is being enacted on stage: these Egyptian men are vehicles for the exploration and realization of Greek men's covert desires. The "generalized perversion"[13] of the

---

11. Sophocles, *Inachus* fr. 269a *(TrGF)*. See Seaford 1980 and n. 38 below.

12. I am adapting Spivak's statement about white men saving brown women from brown men in her discussion of British legislation concerning *sati:* see Spivak 1988, 296–308.

13. I borrow the phrase from the slightly different context of Alloula's study of the Western male gaze in the modern period: Alloula 1986, 95. See Boone 1995 for modern Western fantasies of Eastern sexual decadence, with particular reference to Egypt in a homoerotic context.

Nilotic or the psychosexual demands of the Egyptian can be read as a projection of the Greek male's fantasies or as a mirror in which he can see the other and recognize the self. Admittedly, the study of these fantasies shows us the complexity of the Greek confrontation with Egypt: to the extent that the staging of these plays focuses the audience's attention on the Greek male's fantasies, the dramatists are also mounting a critique of Greeks and Greek culture through their work. In truth, no reader of the plays can fail to see the engagement with contemporary Greek ideas and practices that occurs in the plays of Aeschylus and Euripides, whether or not the playwrights are addressing male fantasies. It is essential to acknowledge that in different ways Aeschylus and Euripides are subjecting Greek fantasies, sexual anxieties, and societal prejudices to the most provocative criticism by means of their poetry. But precisely because literature here is so polished, complex, and brilliant, and precisely because it shows itself so richly capable of interrogating society from within, we are called upon as critics and readers to understand its inflections and contradictions. Greek ethnocentrism was never a simple phenomenon, and ultimately it was the limit that the Greek playwrights were unable to transgress.

In these two plays, Greek men have to fight on behalf of women to rescue those women, as the Argives wage war against the Egyptians in the later part of Aeschylus' trilogy, and as Menelaus and his men resort to violence against Theoclymenus' subjects. In both cases, however, the women take an active part in inciting this violence against their male oppressors. The Danaids first plead for assistance from the Argives and then murder their husbands on the wedding night, while Helen devises the ruse by which she and her husband deceive Theoclymenus, and she cheers him on during the subsequent massacre. Nevertheless, tragedy ultimately cannot tolerate female empowerment, and so the Danaids are punished by exile to Hades, and Helen's fame is not secured in her marriage to Menelaus in Sparta, but relegated to her cult by the Dioscuri.[14] As well, Euripides' use of a phantom *(eidolon)* itself is predicated on the assumption of a duplicitous Helen who journeyed to Troy with Paris, and thus *Helen*, like Stesichorus' palinode, reinscribes the tradition of the ambiguous female even as it appears to denounce the deceptiveness of the Iliadic Helen.[15] It is naive to suppose from these tragedies that Aeschylus and Euripides are for or against Greek women, or for or against Egyptian men. Greek trag-

14. For this reading of the end of *Helen*, see Foley 1992, 145–48.
15. Stesichorus' palinode is discussed from this perspective in Bassi 1993 and Porter 1993.

edies constantly put into question traditional demarcations of social realities, whether these deal with ethnicity, gender, rites of passage, or the ideologies of the polis. At the same time, tragedies are also liable to locate the exploration of these issues within boundaries circumscribed by the values of a dominant elite. In *Tragic Ways of Killing a Woman*, Nicole Loraux has written that the tragedies "gave the Athenian spectator the controlled pleasure afforded by an enjoyment of the deviant when it is acted out, reflected upon, and tamed."[16] The same could be said about the tragic Egyptian.

AESCHYLUS' *SUPPLIANTS*

Aeschylus' *Suppliants* was first produced, probably in 463, as the initial play in a trilogy.[17] The other two plays in the trilogy were *Egyptians*, of which nothing survives, and *Danaids*, of which there are two fragments. The satyr-play that accompanied the trilogy was *Amymone*, of which three brief fragments remain.[18]

SPLITTING THE DANAIDS

Before asking "What does it mean to be Egyptian in *Suppliants?*" we need to ask also "How many Egyptians are there in the play?" or rather "Who are the Egyptians in the play?" When they arrive with their father in Greece as refugees from Egypt, the Danaids plead as suppliants before the Greek king Pelasgus by appealing to their ties with Greece in order to

---

16. Loraux 1987, 65.

17. For the date, see Lloyd-Jones 1990. The date is not certain, and Sommerstein 1997, following Sicherl 1986 and Rösler 1993, argues for a later date of 461. My views of the trilogy are guided by Garvie 1969, 163–233; Podlecki 1975; FJW, vol. 1, 40–55; Winnington-Ingram 1983, 55–72; Seaford 1987, 110–19; and Conacher 1996, 104–9. Rösler 1993, after Sicherl 1986, suggests that *Egyptians (Aigyptioi)* was the first and *Suppliants* the second play in the trilogy. The ancient sources concerning Danaus and the Danaids contradict one another on many details, and hence also make reconstruction difficult of Aeschylus' trilogy. For the full range of ancient sources, see *LIMC*, s.v. "Danaides" and "Danaos."

18. In its reference to sexual aggression, river waters, and fertility, the account of Amymone contained in Apollodorus (2.1.4) suggests that Aeschylus' satyr-play continued to explore the themes of the trilogy: "But the land of Argos being waterless, since Poseidon had dried up even the springs because of his anger at Inachus for testifying that it belonged to Hera, Danaus sent his daughters to draw water. One of them, Amymone, as she was searching for water, threw a dart at a deer, and hit a sleeping satyr. He, starting up, desired to force her, but Poseidon appearing on the scene, the satyr fled, and Amymone lay with Poseidon, and he revealed to her the springs at Lerna."

strengthen their claim to sanctuary (fig. 1). Danaus and the Danaids are descended from Epaphus, who was conceived in Egypt by Zeus and Io, the daughter of Inachus, king of Argos. The Danaids have ties to both Greece and Egypt, and the Zeus to whom they fervently pray is both their forefather and the god of suppliants—not to mention of other things, since among the numerous titles attested in the play are "Zeus who guards suppliants" (Ζεὺς Ἀφίκτωρ, 1) and "Zeus, god of the suppliant" (Ζεὺς Ἱκέσιος, 347), but also "Zeus the savior" (Ζεὺς Σωτήρ, 26), "Zeus the merciful" (Ζεὺς Αἰδοῖος, 192), "Zeus impartial" (Ζεὺς Ἑτερορρεπής, 403), and "Zeus, god of strangers" (Ζεὺς Ξένιος, 627). In fact, multiple affinities characterize the Danaids, since in addition to the many ways in which they are associated by their *genos* with Greece, Egypt, and Zeus, they also occupy ambiguous positions in society as virgins and suppliants.[19]

If we restrict ourselves for the moment to the issue of ethnicity, we find a splitting occurs in *Suppliants*. The Danaids stress their links to Argos and Greece when they are supplicating (274, 323, 652; cf. 278, 330, 632), yet they also mention their black skin (70–71) and their ties by *genos* to the sons of Aegyptus when they wish to invoke incestuousness as a bar to the proposed marriage (8). Pelasgus remarks on their barbarian (βαρβάροισι, 235) appearance when he first sees them, but soon concedes to the Danaids, "True, you seem to me from ancient times to have part in this land" (325–26). Despite Julia Kristeva's observation "that the first foreigners to emerge at the dawn of our civilization are foreign women—the Danaides," then, it is better to say that the Danaids retain a dual ethnicity and claim, or have imputed to them (933), either one according to situation or need.[20]

No such splitting of ethnic origin seems to be attributed to the sons of Aegyptus, although they also descend from the same union of Io and Zeus that eventually produced their cousins. It is true that opportunities for the male cousins to speak in *Suppliants* are limited, and that they might forward claims to kinship in the lost plays of the trilogy, perhaps in *Egyptians*. In his *Oresteia*, Aeschylus does emphasize different sides of the character of Agamemnon in different plays of the trilogy. In the Danaid trilogy, however, if the sons of Aegyptus had a stronger claim over the Danaids

19. See Zeitlin 1996, 127–36.
20. Kristeva 1991, 42. Kristeva's observation also appears to be based on the view, now no longer held by scholars, that *Suppliants* was produced before *Persians*. On the issue of ethnic splitting, see the discussion in Kurke 1999, 320–22, who also discusses the ways in which the Danaids ultimately persuade Pelasgus that they are "legal tender" in Argos.

in Egyptian law rather than Greek law, as some believe, they would have wished to play down their own and the Danaids' Greekness. To judge from what survives, the sons of Aegyptus are uniformly presented as Egyptian and Nilotic.[21]

It is also true, furthermore, that in this play the word "Aegyptus" (Αἴγυπτος) denotes the Danaids' uncle, and not the country Egypt, to which Aeschylus refers by various circumlocutions that usually incorporate the Nile. Aeschylus appears to have used the word Αἴγυπτος in the sense "Egypt" on only one occasion (fr. 193 Mette, quoted below), thus reversing Homer's practice in which the river is always designated by ὁ Αἴγυπτος ποταμός and not by ὁ Νεῖλος.[22] Nevertheless, the Athenian audience would have little difficulty in identifying Egypt as the land of the Nile, and the men's ethnicity is never explicitly put into doubt in *Suppliants*. The identification of the country with the river assumes added significance when the Nile's reputation for male fertility is considered, while such phrases as "sons of Aegyptus" (Αἰγύπτου παίδων, 9) also heighten the sense of Egypt as the locus for the procreative powers of the male, where the genitive's primary reference (the hero Aegyptus) admits of semantic ambiguity or indeterminacy (hero or country).

A double splitting occurs in *Suppliants*. In the first instance, the sons of Aegyptus and the daughters of Danaus are differentiated from each other in terms of their ethnicity, although both families are the result of the Egyptian intercourse of Zeus and Io. The Danaids' suitors are Egyptians, and they are uniformly presented as foreign, non-Greek, and barbarian. Secondly, Danaus' daughters themselves recognize, or attempt to establish, ties of kinship to the Argives and to their Egyptian pursuers. By a chiastic split, the pivot of which is centered on Egypt, Io's trajectory from Greece to her final destination in Egypt is reversed, but without Io's detours, by the flight of the Danaids from Egypt to Greece, when their Egyptian cousins act as the gadfly. Simultaneously Greek and barbarian, the Danaids find themselves described as ἀστόξενοι by Pelasgus (ἀστοξένων, 356), "foreigners connected with the city,"[23] a term that captures their double status,

---

21. This may be paralleled in the contemporary iconographic evidence. However, the identification of the Danaids and the sons of Aegyptus on some of the vases is not certain: see Eva Keuls' articles in *LIMC*, s.v. "Danaides" and "Danaos."

22. Homer, *Odyssey* 4.477, 581; 14.258. The word Νεῖλος occurs first in Hesiod, *Theogony* 338, and a lost epic poem, *Danais* (fr. 1 Kinkel = fr. 1 Davies). See Froidefond 1971, 22–24, 73–74. This lost epic, *Danais*, must have contained an account of Danaus and the Danaids.

23. See the discussion and translation of this oxymoron in FJW at 356.

though, in truth, their sex would keep them from gaining political franchise in the city. The Danaids can manage this chiastic splitting off into Egyptians and Greeks thanks to the consummation of Zeus' lust on the banks of the Nile. Yet, while Io's travails ended with the begetting of a child whose descendants multiplied as prodigiously as the evidence of fifty sons and fifty daughters shows, the Danaids, with the exception of Hypermestra, are to transform the traditional occasion for a fecund union into a night of murder.[24]

EGYPT AS LOCUS FOR MALE FERTILITY

Let us turn to the Greek idea of Egypt as the focal point for the procreative powers of the male. In her essay on the trilogy, Froma Zeitlin has discussed the politics of Aeschylus' work from a feminist perspective, and claimed that the Danaids are caught between two paradigms of eros: one is defined by the aggressive behavior of the Egyptian cousins, and the other by the softer touch of Zeus, who impregnated their ancestor Io, and for whom (as Father) they have erotic yearnings. The solution to this dilemma is, according to Zeitlin, the eros that draws on both force and persuasion, that is, the eros that Aphrodite describes in the marriage of Heaven and Earth that is mentioned in a fragment of *Danaids*.[25] What emerges from Zeitlin's detailed analysis of the trilogy is the unmistakable notion that Egypt serves as the locus for male fertility and reproductive powers, and that Egypt's status as such is demonstrated not just by the cousins' actions but by Zeus' as well.

The emphasis on male fertility in an Egyptian locale is exploited by Aeschylus in at least two separate plays: he describes Zeus' impregnation of Io beside the Nile in the central episode of *Prometheus Bound* as well as in *Suppliants*. The chained Prometheus places Io's encounter with Zeus in her future travails. Harassed by the gadfly and persecuted by Hera, Io will come

24. See Gantz 1978, and Detienne 1989, 41–57, on "une violence fondatrice de mariage."
25. Aeschylus, fr. 125 (Mette): "Holy Heaven longs to pierce Earth, and the passion of Love seizes Earth to attain that union. Rain falling from Heaven in the act of love impregnates Earth, and for mortals she brings forth food for cattle and the life-giving wheat of Demeter. And from that moist marriage the leafy season of the trees comes to its fulfillment. Of all these things, I am the cause" (ἐρᾷ μὲν ἁγνὸς Οὐρανὸς τρῶσαι Χθόνα, / ἔρως δὲ Γαῖαν λαμβάνει γάμου τυχεῖν, / ὄμβρος δ' ἀπ' εὐνάεντος Οὐρανοῦ πεσὼν / ἔκυσε Γαῖαν, ἡ δὲ τίκτεται βροτοῖς / μήλων τε βοσκὰς καὶ βίον Δημήτριον, / δενδρῶ{ν}τις ὥρα δ' ἐκ νοτίζοντος γάμου / τέλειός ἐστι· τῶν δ' ἐγὼ παραίτιος).

44   *The Tragic Egyptian*

to Canopus, near the place where the Nile flows into the Mediterranean Sea, and where Zeus will, by his touch, both return her to her earlier anthropomorphism and impregnate her with Epaphus. This Epaphus, whose name reflects the tactile circumstances of his conception,[26] will reap the fruit of the land watered by the Nile, and the Danaids will descend from him in the fifth generation and travel from Egypt to Argos (813–15, 846–69). In the Danaid plays, probably composed before *Prometheus*, Aeschylus had followed an outline similar to the Promethean version, with changes in some of the details. In *Suppliants*, for instance, Hera and not Zeus is responsible for Io's metamorphosis into a cow (299), and the reproductive powers imputed to the god's touch are extended to include his breath as well (577). Zeus' success in fathering Epaphus in Egypt remains constant in both plays.

Suppliants is particularly instructive for a consideration of Zeus' procreative and life-giving capacities. After the god causes Io's pregnancy by breath and touch,[27] the whole land cries out, "This is in truth the offspring of life-growing Zeus" (φυσιζόου γένος τόδε / Ζηνός ἐστιν ἀληθῶς, 584–85). The epithet φυσίζοος, which qualifies γῆ or αἶα in early Greek poetry and denotes "wheat-growing,"[28] here emphasizes Zeus' role in the conception of Epaphus. That Zeus is "life-giving" or "life-producing" is also made apparent by the use of Ζηνός to draw attention to the root of ζῆν, a false etymology assuredly, but pervasive among ancient Greek writers nonetheless.[29] Moreover, Zeus the genitor and life-producer also assumes the position of the Danaids' father (139, 592; cf. 811, 885). Apart from any reference to Zeus as the father of the gods, and apart from any Oedipal attachment to Danaus projected onto Zeus,[30] the term "father" must signify his life-giving, procreative, and generative capabilities. And the same verse that makes Zeus "father" also calls him "planter" (592). Zeus the gardener

26. See also *Suppliants* 45, 313–15, 535, 1066; Sophocles, fr. 269a.34; Apollodorus 2.1.3; scholia to Euripides, *Phoenician Women* 678; Nonnus, *Dionysiaca* 3.284–86.
27. The imagery of "touch and seizure" and "breath, wind, and storm" in *Suppliants* is discussed in Murray 1958, 32–41. Later Greek sources record impregnation by a god's touch or breath among Egyptian beliefs: see Norden 1924, 76 ff.; Vürtheim 1928, 47–48; Kranz [1933] 1988, 105; FJW at *Suppliants* 17; Zeitlin 1996, 149–50. For an Egyptian perspective on this mode of creation, see Assmann 1997, 182–84; and for Egyptian attitudes to marriage, fertility, pregnancy, and childbirth, see Robins 1993, 56–91.
28. *Iliad* 3.243, 21.63; *Odyssey* 11.301; cf. Herodotus 1.67.
29. See FJW at 585.
30. See Caldwell 1974, 53–54; FJW at 811; Zeitlin 1996, 144.

plants his seed in the ground, and Zeus himself, by his own hand (592), raises and cultivates the life-form that emerges.[31] In pronouncing their blessings on Argos and its gods, the suppliant Danaids pray that "Zeus bring the fruits of the land to perfection with crops in every season" (688–90). Not quite your garden variety deity, Zeus, the great artificer (594–95), the begetter (206), the planter, and the father of the Danaids, manifests procreative powers and an enabling fecundity in Aeschylus' play.

Zeus' impressive powers of bringing to life are all the more striking, from the perspective of our inquiry, since they are put into effect on the banks of the Nile. Rivers often assume connections with fertility in Greek literature, and the Nile of Aeschylus proves to be no less compelling in this respect.[32] In a fragment from an unidentified play, he writes of the Nile's "refreshing tide," and how "all luxuriant Egypt, filled with the sacred flood, makes Demeter's life-giving grain spring up" (fr. 193 Mette). Even in a play ostensibly dedicated to the conflict between Persians and Greeks, he describes the great river as πολυθρέμμων [many feeding] (*Persians* 33), the root (τρέφειν) of which appears later in *Suppliants* in connection with the Nile, "Νεῖλος . . . τρέφει" [Nile . . . nurtures] (497–98). In *Suppliants*, the Danaids worship "the water of the Nile which touches no one with disease" (561), until they direct their devotion to the rivers of Argos late in the play. Presumably, the Nile's purity made it amenable for service as the place where Zeus ended the madness given to Io by Hera (586–87). The Danaids further elaborate the Nile's qualities toward the end of *Suppliants* when they call it "the cattle-nourishing water which makes life-giving blood grow forth and be in bloom for mortals" (855–57).

The Nile's waters were renowned for their fertility among the ancient Greeks, as the Danaids' statement indicates.[33] Aristotle thought of the Nile as "highly fecund and nourishing because of the moderate heat of the sun's rays" (in Strabo 15.1.22), while Theophrastos in his treatise on waters went further and used the superlative (πολυγονώτατον, in Athenaeus 41f). An intriguing comment is provided by a scholiast to Aeschylus' play when he writes that "the Nile's water is conducive to male birth: Zeus drank from it and fathered Ares" (at 857). We find again an example of the male god's

---

31. The imagery of *Iliad* 14. 346–51 is especially suggestive in this respect. When Hera seduced Zeus and they made love, "beneath them the bright earth made fresh-sprung grass to grow, and dewy lotus, and crocus, and hyacinth thick and soft that kept them from the ground. On this they lay, and were clothed about with a cloud, fair and golden, from which fell drops of glistening dew."

32. See Borthwick 1963, 231–41.

33. See Bonneau 1964, 107, 130; Froidefond 1971, 72–83; FJW at 561, 855.

procreative talent displayed in the context of Nilotic waters, despite the ambiguity surrounding the term "male birth" (ἀρρενογόνον). And the notion of the fertility of the Nile and Zeus is confirmed further by the scholarly view of the identification between the two in *Suppliants*.[34]

The issues of fertility and procreation raised by the story of Io find a parallel in the episode with the Egyptian slave-girl Hagar from a slightly earlier narrative, the book of Genesis.[35] When Abram is unable to father children out of Sarai, he follows her advice, takes the slave Hagar as wife, and makes her pregnant. However, Sarai later feels contempt for Hagar and drives her into the wilderness, where an angel speaks to her by a spring of water.

> The angel of the Lord found her by a spring of water in the wilderness, the spring on the way to Shur. And he said, "Hagar, slave-girl of Sarai, where have you come from and where are you going?" She said, "I am running away from my mistress Sarai." The angel of the Lord said to her, "Return to your mistress, and submit to her." The angel of the Lord also said to her, "I will so greatly multiply your offspring that they cannot be counted for multitude." And the angel of the Lord said to her, "Now you have conceived and shall bear a son; you shall call him Ishmael, for the Lord has given heed to your affliction. He shall be a wild ass of a man, with his hand against everyone, and everyone's hand against him; and he shall live at odds with all his kin." (Genesis 16.7–12)

Genesis later names Ishmael's twelve sons, who occupy territories up to Shur, which is across from Egypt in the direction of Assyria (25.12–16).

Let us restrict comparative commentary on the myth of Io and this rich narrative to our immediate purposes.[36] It is striking that in Greek and Hebrew traditions the question of fertility is raised, and that in both the male's procreative powers retain their fecundity and are emphasized. The Greek myth combines contact with the god and impregnation by him in the mo-

34. See Froidefond 1971, 81, for Zeus and the Nile. It may be that Zeus' epithet φυσίζοος reflects an identification between him and Amun-Re: see Kranz 1933, 106. Zeitlin 1996, 149–53, also discusses the theme of reproduction in *Suppliants*.

35. See also Jeremiah (46.20): "A beautiful heifer is Egypt—a gadfly from the north lights upon her." Astour 1965, 92 n. 1, situates the gadfly "as a tool of divine wrath for chasing and persecuting somebody" within West Semitic beliefs. For the gadfly in the Greek tradition, see Davies and Kathirithamby 1986, 159–64. For Io and the *oistros*, see Padel 1992, 120–21.

36. The Greek myth of Io may well derive from a Semitic or Near Eastern source: see Astour 1965, 80–92, esp. 86–87; Bernal 1987, 88–98; and West 1997, 442–46.

ment when Zeus touches Io, while the biblical text separates Hagar's impregnation by Abram from her contact with the divine, which occurs by the spring. Yet, Hagar is promised numerous offspring by a god as she rests by a body of water, just as Io conceives the first member of a vast family by the Nile. Io's descendants include Libya, Egypt, and Danaus, who establish communities of people in their name; Hagar's descendants, while not the twelve tribes of Israel, are twelve princes who also establish communities according to their tribes. The analysis could be extended further, but let us observe for the moment the conjunction between fertility and water in the Hebrew text, and the conjunction between male procreative powers and the Nile in the Greek. When we turn to Greek drama, we find that the Nilotic man suffers from the lack of a female partner for his powers of reproduction; indeed, it is the sexual aggressiveness of Egyptian men that repulses women in tragedy.[37]

BLACKNESS AND DEATH

I see a warship. . . . I see its curtains and its billowing sail. Now
the ship's prow looks toward us, threatening, across the watery
stretches, and heeds too well the guiding rudder at its stern. Now
the black limbs of the sailors show clear against their white and
flowing robes. Now the whole panoply of ships has come into view,
the leading ship has furled its sails, and now the steady beat of oars
sounds its approach to shore. (713–23)

Black Aegyptiads are hunting for a marriage with black Danaids. The "sunburned" blackness of Egyptians in *Suppliants* (154–55) is consonant with the blackness of Egyptians in contemporary Greek sources. Herodotus called the Egyptians "black-skinned and woolly-haired" (μελάγχροές

---

37. A story attested in Pindar (as quoted in Strabo) and Herodotus grants sexual aggressiveness even to Egyptian he-goats. There is also a suggestion here, perhaps, of the sexual depravity of Egyptian women and of the depravity of the land in general, but neither source elaborates on the attitude or willingness of the female participants in this form of bestiality. See Strabo 17.1.19: "Here, also, are an Hermupolis and a Lycupolis, and Mendes, where they worship Pan and, among other animals, the he-goat. And as Pindar says, the goats there have intercourse with women: "Egyptian Mendes, by the bank of the sea, the end of the Nile's branch, where goat-mounting he-goats have intercourse with women" (Αἰγυπτίαν Μένδητα, πὰρ κρημνὸν θαλάσσας / ἔσχατον Νείλου κέρας, αἰγιβάται / ὅθι τράγοι γυναιξὶ μίσγοντα, Pindar fr. 201 Maehler)." Herodotus says this kind of intercourse took the form of a public exhibition (2.46). On Strabo's passage, see further Yoyotte, Charvet, and Gompertz 1997, 112.

τε . . . καὶ οὐλότριχες, 2.104; cf. 2.57), and an unidentified dramatist wrote that "the sun, shining with its light, will turn your skin Egyptian" (χρόαν δὲ τὴν σὴν ἥλιος λάμπων φλογὶ/αἰγυπτιώσει, TrGF Adespota F 161). Epaphus in *Prometheus Bound* is also said to be black or dark (κελαινὸς ῎Επαφος, 851), while lines 53–54 in Sophocles' *Inachus* are probably a reference to his "dark" father, Zeus, ὁ πολυφάρμ[ακος . . ./κάρβανος αἰθός (fr. 269a TrGF).[38] Further, it is suggested, on the basis of the popularity of blacks on vases from the sixth century onward, that black masks made it possible for playwrights such as Aeschylus, Phrynichus (in his *Danaids*), and Epicharmus (in his *Busiris*) to exploit the contrast between the black skins of Egyptians and the white skins of Greeks.[39] While tragedy puts forward environmental explanations for difference in appearance or physiology of the various peoples of the world—for example, the heat is responsible for the blackness of Egyptian skin—it does not anywhere attribute ethnic character to environment or climate; in this respect, tragedy differs from such other works as Herodotus' history and the Hippocratic treatise *Airs Waters Places*.[40]

Death in Greek thought is also famously black: "black Hades," for instance, is the expression used by Sophocles in *Oedipus Tyrannus* (29).[41] The references to blackness in *Suppliants* do not just foreshadow the moment when the Danaids will murder their husbands on that wedding night of horror, but also imply that the impending marriage of the Danaids is a marriage with death. Such an implication coheres with the conflation of wedding and funeral rituals that is well attested in Greek tragedy. The Danaids allude to the blackness and sunlessness of Hades and the under-

---

38. Seaford 1980 argues that the black stranger is Zeus Chthonius and alludes to the Egyptian Osiris; West 1984 finds in this black Zeus a Greek aetiology for the black appearance of Egyptians and for their allegedly generic cunning; but Hall 1989, 140 n. 113, suggests that the dark stranger may be Hermes.

39. See Hall 1989, 139–40, with Pickard-Cambridge 1968, 162; Snowden 1970, 158–59; 1976; and 1983, 63–64; and Irwin 1974, 130–31. See also FJW at 154. And see the "black noses" mentioned by Sophocles in his fragmentary play, *Ethiopians*, fr. 29 TrGF.

40. See Herodotus 2.35–36 and *Airs Waters Places* 12–24; Backhaus 1976; Jouanna 1981; Hall 1989, 173; Tuplin 1999, 62–69; Thomas 2000, ch. 4; and cf. FJW at 155. See also chapter 2, below.

41. See the references assembled in Winkler 1992, 12–18; and Padel 1992, 78: "Death is a dark covering. Those who die enter the covered underworld, a darkness. . . . The underworld's dark is overdetermined. Earth is 'dark.' To bury someone is to 'cover' them in earth; to kill them is to 'cover them in night.' . . . 'Black earth' drinks the blood of the dying." References to these and other quotations concerning the blackness or darkness of death can also be found in Padel 1992, 78–79.

world by invoking their own sunburned blackness, and state that they will hang themselves if they are unable to flee their cousins' lust:[42]

> May the seed of a mother, mightily solemn, escape men's beds, ah me, unmarried, unvanquished. If not, we, the black sun-smitten race, will come with our boughs to the earth-dweller, Zeus of the dead (gracious to strangers): we will die by the noose, if we are not heard by the Olympian gods. (151–61)

Since Hades is traditionally identified as the "Zeus of the underworld,"[43] the Danaids seem to be expressing a preference for seeking out his realm over entering into marriage with the Aegytiads in this world. In fact, the Danaids explicitly voice the desire to be married to death rather than to their Egyptian cousins:

> I am undone with fear. Sooner may I meet my fate by hanging than suffer the man I abominate to touch my skin. May I die before that, and Hades be my lord and master. How can I find a seat high up in the air, near which the watery clouds become snow? Or a crag, slippery, steep, lonely, overhanging, distant, visited only by vultures, to bear witness to my deep plunge, before I ever celebrate a wedding with a tearer against my heart's will? . . . Let death come, let it reach me before the marriage-bed. (786–805)

"Escape odes," familiar enough to readers of tragedy, are sung by females and often make reference to birds in flight. The Danaids' emphasis on vertical movement in this ode recalls the Greek idea that relates the position of the hanged woman *above* the ground to the motion of the woman who throws herself *down* to her death. As Loraux observes, "The same word, *aeirô*, which means elevation and suspension, applies to these two flights in opposite directions, upward and downward, as though height had its own depth: as though the place below—whether it be the ground, or the world under that—could be reached only by first rising up."[44] The Danaids' "deep plunge" (796–97) is thus associated with their desire to kill themselves by hanging. This death by hanging or hurling oneself from a steep rock is preferred to sexual contact with the Egyptian men. Further, the words used to signify "touch" (χριμφθῆναι, 790) and "tearer" (δαίκτορος, 798) have definite sexual connotations and in this context can refer only to rape.[45] On the other hand, ἀνάσσοι [be my lord and master] (791), which

42. See FJW at 154–55.
43. See FJW at 158.
44. Loraux 1987, 18.
45. See FJW at 790 and Loraux 1987, 11.

the Danaïds apply to their potential relationship with Hades, can be used to describe the relationship of a husband to a wife. Therefore, the Danaïds are saying that they would rather escape into marriage with Hades than suffer the sons of Aegyptus to touch them, tear them, and rape them.

Links between blackness, death, and the sexual desire of the Aegyptiads are explored by the Danaïds in other sections of the play, both before and after the passage just quoted. After mentioning that Zeus' desire "flares everywhere, even in darkness, with black mishap for mortals" (88–90), they call on Zeus to witness the hubris and lust of the Aegyptiads (104–11). They go on to sing words that elaborate this kind of blackness and frenzied desire by inviting comparison with a funeral lamentation: "Of such piteous calamities do I speak in my complaint, shrill, heavy, weeping — woe, woe, conspicuous by funeral woes. Though alive, I sing my own dirge" (112–16). The sexually aggressive Aegyptiads are so far from marrying the Danaïds that they move the latter, not to a wedding song, but a funeral lamentation for themselves. Toward the end of the play, however, when the Egyptian herald arrives to abduct the Danaïds forcibly, the funeral turns into a black dream, and the daughters cry out to Danaus for help, "Oh father, . . . he carries me to the sea, like a spider, step by step, a nightmare, a black nightmare" (885–88). And, as the Egyptian herald comes closer to his object, he is metamorphosed in the Danaïds' vocabulary from a spider in a black nightmare to a beast (897), a snake (896), and a two-legged serpent that rages with lust close to them (895).[46]

Death is a *telos* in the Greek imagination, as scholars have reconstructed it, just as marriage is a *telos* for the young woman in fifth-century Athens. Since the Danaïds wish for a marriage with black death rather than with black Egyptians, death itself must be compared to a *marital telos,* and this idea is found at the conclusion of the drama. In the play's final song, the Danaïds sing that they will pay homage no longer to the waters of the Nile but instead to the rivers of Argos. After describing their transfer of allegiance from one locus of riverine fertility to another, they sing: "And may pure Artemis look with pity upon our band, and may the *telos* of Cytherea not come forcibly upon us.[47] May this prize [ἆθλον] involve death" (1030–

---

46. Given that the Danaïds probably invoke incest as an objection to the proposed marriage, it should be noted that incest is habitually associated with darkness in Greek literature: see Seaford 1990a, 83–84, for blackness and incest.

47. In line 1032, τέλος is an emendation for γάμος of the manuscripts. See the discussion in FJW, who prefer this emendation against such editors as Page, who prints γάμος in his OCT.

33). The word ἆθλον is sometimes used to denote a woman's hand in marriage.[48] For their part, the Danaids refuse the *telos* of the conjugal union over which Aphrodite serves as one of the presiding deities, and choose rather the *telos* of marriage with death. Moreover, the Danaids are not just asking for their own marriage to death to take place by the sterile waters of the Styx, the river of the underworld, but are also alluding again to the forthcoming murder of the Egyptian bridegrooms on the wedding night.

Against this background of death, blackness, and marriage should be read a familiar and lugubrious story, that is, the story of the rapist Tereus, his wife Procne, and her sister Philomela, which ends with their metamorphoses into hawk, nightingale, and swallow, respectively. It is easy to see why the Danaids refer to Procne's plight in the opening song of *Suppliants:*

> If someone who knows bird cries happens to be near, a dweller of the country who hears my lament, he will think that he hears Tereus' wife, the sad, hawk-chased nightingale, who, barred from the green-leaved rivers, voices a novel kind of lament for her old haunts: she composes the song of her child's doom, how he was killed by his own kin, by her hand, a victim of the wrath of an unnatural mother. Even so, I indulge my wailing with Ionian songs, and tear my soft cheek colored by the Nile summer and my heart which is unused to tears. I gather the flowers of lament, anxious if there is someone here to give protection during this, my friendless flight, from the land of Aeria. (58–76)

The Danaids, like the nightingale, are driven away from their haunts beside a river and are chased by hawks, a word used against the Egyptian men elsewhere (224); in both stories, evidently, the body of water serves as a site for the exaggeration of male lust. The Danaids again are black, in this case because of the heat of the Nilotic summer, and again they are in lamentation. The connection between lamentation and death is furthered by the very mention of the nightingale, which has associations with death in Greek literature and especially in tragedy.[49] The same song elicits comparison with a marriage to death when it moves toward its conclusion in which the "black sun-burned race" (154–55) of the Danaids prays to the god of the underworld and threatens to commit suicide by hanging (154–61).

---

48. See the discussion in FJW. In the translation of line 1033, I follow the suggestions made in FJW.

49. For a close parallel, see Aeschylus, *Agamemnon* 1140–49. For the nightingale, see also Aeschylus, fr. 749 (Mette); Sophocles, *Women of Trachis* 962–64 and *Electra* 107–18; Euripides, *Helen* 1107–12 (with Kannicht 1969); Loraux 1998, 57–65; Nagy 1996; and the references in Rehm 1994, 174 n. 122.

Of course, when the Danaids sing about the slaughtered son Itys, whom Procne killed with her own hands, they are alluding as well to the future annihilation of their Egyptian husbands. They "do not know yet—but a tragedian, playing with myths to transform one into the past of the other, knows—that they themselves will soon commit another one of the great feminine crimes."[50]

The well-known punishment of the Danaids should be situated in this thematic context as well, although its place in Aeschylus' trilogy is uncertain.[51] The Danaids are chastised for the murder of their Egyptian husbands, and sentenced to fill a bottomless jar by carrying water in leaking pitchers in the underworld. The irony of their exile is evident, given their statements about Hades in *Suppliants*, but it can be elaborated a little further. Giulia Sissa recalls the story of the vestal Tuccia who proves her virginity by carrying water in a sieve, and suggests on the basis of this and comparable evidence that the leakiness of the jars indicates that the Danaids are no longer virgins when they carry out their penalty in the underworld.[52] In her account, the Danaids kill their new husbands after having sexual intercourse with them. In *The Savage Mind*, Claude Lévi-Strauss comments that the male as eater and the female as eaten is among the most familiar of cultural equations; he also inadvertently reminds us of how the Danaids treat their cousins on the wedding night when he goes on to point to the inversion of this equation in the metonymic notion of the *vagina dentata*.[53] I would add that since the act committed by the Danaids can be seen as a form of castration, the murder is the appropriate revenge by the Danaids for having to marry and gratify sexually men they detest. However, just as the Danaids turn violent on their husbands in a gesture that inverts rape, the punishment the women receive is also suited to their crime. The Danaids are compelled to an endless residence in a black Hades for which they expressed an erotic preference in Aeschylus' play by being forced to convey water in the underworld in jars that proclaim the loss of their virginity.

This thematization of sex and death in *Suppliants* circles us back to a

50. Loraux 1998, 59.
51. The basic study of the motif in classical literature is Keuls 1974. Garvie 1969, 234–35, supplies the bibliography on the subject; see also FJW vol. 1, 50.
52. The anecdote about Tuccia is from Valerius Maximus 8.1.5; see Sissa 1990, 127–72.
53. See *La pensée sauvage* (Paris, 1962), 148, with the discussion in Sissa 1990, 58–59.

passage in Herodotus (2.85–89).[54] Herodotus writes that Egypt, whose inhabitants he knows are black (2.57, 104), has men who are professionals in the art of embalming, and who have made mummification a special craft. The embalmers offer three kinds of preparation, varying in price and quality, for corpses. All three require the dead body to be subjected to various types of treatment, which Herodotus describes in detail, at the hands of embalmers. However, the Egyptians entrust neither beautiful women nor the wives of distinguished men to embalmers immediately after death, but they wait for three or four days to elapse before handing over the bodies to the specialists. They do this, Herodotus claims, to keep embalmers from having sexual intercourse with these women, since an embalmer was once seen committing such an act.

Both Herodotus and Aeschylus make the sexual desires of the Egyptian male into a concern and they seem to locate these sexual desires in proximity to a contact with death. In Herodotus' account, black Egyptian men are no less lustful than the sons of Egypt in *Suppliants*. But while Aeschylus' play insists on women's marriage with death or the male Hades and also makes the women kill the men, Herodotus' text reverses sex roles, and portrays living black men copulating with dead black women, even as it retains the element of sexual aggressiveness that characterizes the Egyptian males of *Suppliants*. In both texts, Egyptian men need to be debarred from Egyptian, or quasi-Egyptian, women on account of the men's exaggerated lust. In the one instance the Egyptian men's lust provokes a desire for an intermingling with death, and in the other the men's lust actualizes and then defers sexual contact with the dead.

MARRYING THE EGYPTIANS

The presentation of Egyptian men in Aeschylus' *Suppliants* needs to be examined in the wider context of marital aspirations and erotic desires in the play. In *Suppliants*, the sons of Aegyptus wish to wed the Danaids, but weddings are deeply problematic in Greek tragedy, even when the two parties

---

54. The passage is discussed in Montserrat 1998; the Greek and Latin passages on mummification are discussed in Dawson 1928. See Sophocles, *Phineus* fr. 712 *TrGF* (= Athenaeus 3.119c): ". . . looking like an Egyptian mummy . . ." (νεκρὸς τάριχος εἰσορᾶν Αἰγύπτιος). Herodotus also recounts the story that the Greek tyrant Periander killed his wife Melissa and then made love to her corpse (3.50, 5.92). If Periander's necrophilia belongs to the topos of tyrants' sexual voracity, the portrayal of tyrants is homologous to the construction of Egyptian men.

consent to the union.[55] One can see why the dramatists were able to exploit or enhance some of the more unsettling elements of a wedding. The bride's passage from virginity to womanhood was subject to ambiguity, tension, and uncertainty, distinct from the tributes and blessings she received during the ceremony. In the language of the day, the bride was likened to a yoked animal, a tamed animal, a ploughed field, or a plucked flower, and in some sources she is described as resentful or on the threshold of death.[56] These comparisons and descriptions might not have disturbed all Greeks, but imaginative dramatists could, and did, explore various negative features of the wedding, regardless of which features were actually associated with a real wedding in fifth-century Athens.

It is self-evident that Greek tragedy emphasizes the problematic and ambiguous aspects of the wedding and of marriage. Again and again, the tragedies draw attention to the taboo regarding certain kinship ties within a marriage, as in Sophocles' *Oedipus Tyrannus,* or the tensions and strains that divide a marriage, as in Euripides' *Alcestis,* or the complete fragmentation of a marriage, as in Aeschylus' *Agamemnon,* or—what in some ways reverses a main theme of *Suppliants*—the male's disdain for marriage, as in Euripides' *Hippolytus.* Parallels between wedding and funeral ceremonies, especially, allowed playwrights to conflate the two and dramatize the failure of a wedding or marriage.[57] The association between marriage and funeral rites, or between the wedding and death, was dramatized in numerous ways and by a variety of tragedies, including Aeschylus' *Agamemnon,* Sophocles' *Antigone* and *Women of Trachis,* and Euripides' *Alcestis, Medea, Suppliants, Women of Troy,* and *Iphigenia in Aulis.*

The Danaid trilogy differs from some of these insofar as it dramatizes in detail the events that lead to a wedding and the married life rather than the experiences of individuals who are already married. Yet, no part of a woman's life in ancient Greece was more fraught with anxiety than the period of virginity that ideally culminated with the *telos* of marriage. In the an-

---

55. Seaford 1987 is an excellent analysis of weddings in tragedy. See also Ormand 1999 for Sophocles, Seaford 1990b for Euripides, and Rehm 1994 for various plays.

56. The sources are collected in Seaford 1987, 106–7.

57. This is emphasized by Loraux 1987, Seaford 1987, and Rehm 1994; cf. Redfield 1982, 188–90, and Jenkins 1983. For useful discussions of the Greek wedding and marriage, see Erdmann 1934; Craik 1984; Oakley and Sinos 1993; Rehm 1994, 11–21, 30–42. For helpful discussions of the funeral, see Kurtz and Boardman 1971, 68–161; Vermeule 1979, 11–21; Garland 1985, 21–37; Rehm 1994, 21–29, 30–42. For further references to both, see Rehm 1994, 154 n. 1.

drocentric view of the dominant elite, virginity and the ability to procreate were what the woman brought to a marriage. It is hardly surprising that these two issues, the loss of virginity and fecundity, are raised in a play that explores the girl's passage to marriage. Given the representation of marriage in tragedy, it is also not unexpected that *Suppliants* would make that passage problematic, as the Danaids' repeatedly expressed fears suggest. If *Suppliants* is concerned with a girl's nervous transition to a wedding and marriage that are to render her a woman, it also places a heightened emphasis on the fearful side of the transition by locating marriage within the constellation of ideas that associates it with abduction, enslavement, rape, and death.

The Danaids evince a deep loathing to marriage with their Egyptian cousins (39, 332, 394, 788–805, 1031–32, 1063–64), and characterize the men's suit as contrary to divine law *(themis)*, impure, hubristic, and incestuous.[58] They also appear to show an aversion to marriage in general, as a number of scholars have noted, as well as a dislike for contact with males (141–53, 392, 426, 528–37, 643, 790, 798–99, 804–7, 818, 1017).[59] It may seem that the Danaids detest not just their cousins, but all men, and therefore it may seem misleading to extract general statements about Egyptian men from this tragedy. Instead of putting the issue in such a way, however, we might rather state that the Danaids' detestation of their cousins is framed by their aversion to the idea of marriage and to the violence of men. The representation of the Egyptian men is part of this representation of a conflict between the sexes and is colored by the representation of that conflict. Far from dismissing the Danaids' dislike of their Egyptian pursuers as a generic loathing, we need to determine the position of Egyptians from the standpoint of the drama's questioning of gender relations, and of "the disquieting potential for sexual violence that lies behind the taking of wives."[60]

It is obvious that Danaus and the Danaids reject the suit of the cousins — and the intensity of their rejection is telling. In his treatment of the tragic wedding, Richard Seaford has argued that the Danaids' attitude "resembles

58. These themes are treated systematically in Lévy 1985. The play's treatment of incest has been the subject of debate: in addition to Lévy, see Garvie 1969, 216–19; Thomson 1973, 289–93; MacKinnon 1978; and FJW vol. 1, 33–40.

59. Many scholars also hold the opposite view. The main references to this unrewarding debate are gathered in Garvie 1969, 211–23. See also FJW vol. 1, 30–33; Lévy 1985; Sicherl 1986; and Seaford 1987, 110–19.

60. Zeitlin 1996, 124. For "the imagery of contrast of male and female," see also Murray 1958, 27–31.

in several respects the attitude associated with the Greek bride or her female companions."[61] In his view, Aeschylus' description tends to the bride's
nervousness about separation, loss of virginity, and possession by the husband. Thus, the Danaids' references to their ancestor Io as "mother" (141,
539) recall both her afflictions and the bride's fear about the violation of the
emotional bond between mother and daughter. Further, the notion of the
man's "taming" (ζεύγνυμι) of the woman occurs regularly in tragedy, and
is used to describe the action of the man in marrying the woman. Words
cognate with "tame" (δαμάζω) also appear to assume significant resonances
in the play. The Danaids have no desire to be the "slave" (δμωίς) of the
Egyptians (335); they imagine themselves as δάμαλις (351), which usually designates an untamed animal, and call on "untamed" Artemis to assist them "untamed" (ἀδμῆτος ἀδμήτα, 149) and then wish "that the
mighty race of our honerable mother may escape men's embrace (ah me),
unwedded, unvanquished (ἄγαμον ἀδάματον)" (151–53). The use of this
vocabulary emphasizes that the Danaids view their marriage with the
Egyptian men as a taming of their natural spirit and as a seizure against
their will.

We might consider, following Seaford, that plant imagery in *Suppliants*
evokes the potential taking of the Danaids' virginity and the corresponding
brutality of the Egyptian men. Danaus warns his daughters that "tender
summer fruit is in no way easy to protect; animals spoil it, and men too of
course" (998–99). Earlier, the Danaids sing a prayer for Argos that reflects
their own private hope: "But let the blossom of its youth be unculled, and
may Aphrodite's bed-fellow, man-slaying Ares, not shear off its tenderest
bloom" (663–66). Similarly, the Danaids' recollection of Io's eating of
flowers in a rich meadow refers to her deflowering, but also to the possibility of their own (538–40). Passages such as this remind us of the Sigmund
Freud who found that a young woman's dreams about flowers indicated
a "fear of being deflowered" and "an over-valuation of her virginity."[62]
Moreover, the Danaids also complicate the literary practice of comparing
the bride or groom to a plant[63] when they use the comparison to express

61. Seaford 1987, 110; for the references to δαμάζω below see his discussion
on 111.

62. Sigmund Freud, *The Interpretation of Dreams*, 377 (Standard Edition),
quoted in Caldwell 1974, 59.

63. See e.g. Sappho fr. 115; cf. Euripides, *Hippolytus* 630, *Medea* 231; Theoc-
ritus 18.30. Plant images can also express the loss of a girl's virginity: Sappho fr.
105 a, b.

their view of their Egyptian pursuers: "Let him [Zeus] look now on mortal insolence, how it starts afresh, the stem which, through desire to marry us, has sprung into bloom with evil and wanton thoughts, being irresistibly goaded by its raving intent, its mind turned to folly by delusion" (104–11). In these passages, the Danaids state their fears about abduction by the Egyptian men and their sexual aggressiveness.

Moreover, Aeschylus also draws on hunting metaphors to make the cousins' suit look unacceptable. As one scholar has observed, the Egyptians are hunting for a marriage with the Danaids, yet marriage is not something to be hunted.[64] Nevertheless, the Egyptian men resemble hunters and the Danaids the hunted, or, in an extension of the same idea, the men are likened to predators and the women to prey. We noted the reference to Procne as a "hawk-chased nightingale" (62). Elsewhere, the men are hawks and the women are doves, liable to be devoured by their feathered fellows (222 ff.), while death lurks in the next few lines (228). To Pelasgus, the Danaids say that they have come as a "fugitive, running around like a wolf-chased heifer on the steep rocks where, trusting in her place of defense, she lows, telling the herdsman of her distress" (350–53). Some verses later, the Greek king promises not to deliver the Danaids "as prey to winged creatures" (510), which prompts the suppliants to remark, in effect, that the Egyptians may not be winged creatures, but are still "more hateful than evil-minded serpents" (511). Yet, the men also revert to being birds, "ravens that have no care for altars" (751–52). Another reference to death is followed by mention of goats (794), vultures (796), being a prey to dogs, and a meal to the birds of the country (800–1); and there is also the Egyptian herald's bestiality as spider (887), beast (897), snake (896), and two-legged serpent (895). One might further adduce a passage in *Prometheus* where the Aegyptiads are hawks, the Danaids doves, and the marriage hunted by the men is said to be "unhuntable" (857–59). Similarly, Zeus' desire in *Suppliants* is, like marriage with the Danaids, not easily huntable (86–87), nor is it something to be tracked down in a hunt. That the men approach marriage as a chase or a hunt illustrates the extent to which they transgress in the prosecution of their violent courtship.

Lastly, a general strategy used by Aeschylus to make the cousins appear hostile is to have Danaus, the Danaids, and also Pelasgus mobilize a whole array of charges and insinuations against these Egyptian males. The sons of Aegyptus are portrayed as hubristic, willing to disregard *themis* and jus-

64. MacKinnon 1978, 81.

tice *(dike)*, and more reliant on brute force (βία) than persuasion (πειθώ). As stated above, they are likened to beasts, and their touch is more loathsome than death itself. They are as willing to disregard the sacred rights of suppliants and become impious (751) as they are ready to stain the holy altars with the blood of virgins. Their herald speaks in mocking tones to the king of Argos, and thereby refuses to adhere to the traditional obligations of the guest. Through this battery of name-calling and seemingly scandalous behavior, however, runs the pervasive theme of the men's lust, which drove the Danaids from Egypt to Greece as suppliants. Where can Egyptian men, hungry for marriage, teeming with lust, and ready to inflict violence, stand in such a conceptualization of the conjugal tie?

EURIPIDES' *HELEN*

> The lover, all as frantic,
> Sees Helen's beauty in a brow of Egypt. . . .
> *A Midsummer-Night's Dream*

DOUBLES IN *HELEN*

"Every Athenian tragedy," Pierre Vidal-Naquet writes, "is a reflection on the foreigner, on the Other, on the double."[65] Euripides' *Helen* has lent itself to interpretation in terms of antitheses, extending far beyond the contrast between Theonoe and Theoclymenus, the two principal Egyptians in the play. The play has given rise to a series of analyses that oppose feminine values to masculine values, Helen to Menelaus, the *Odyssey* to the *Iliad*, peace to war, the private realm to the public realm, inward life to outward action, shame over Troy to glory in Troy, unselfishness to possessiveness, persuasion to force, tragedy to comedy, and so on.[66] The phantom in *Helen* is largely responsible for the driving opposition between reality

---

65. Vidal-Naquet 1997, 119. See Herodotus 2.112–20, discussed in chapter 3 below, for the story of Helen in Egypt. Before Herodotus and Euripides, Stesichorus had denied that Helen went to Troy. See also Anticleides of Athens, *FGrHist* 140 F 18 (= scholia at *Odyssey* 4.355): "Anticleides tells the story that Helen wished for Menelaus and secretly went out of the city. She found a Carian ship and asked the captain, whose name was Pharos, to take her and land her safe in Lacedaemon. They were caught in a storm and went to Egypt, where they landed from the ship. Pharos was killed by a snake. Helen buried him and called the island by his name." On the naming of Pharos, see Hecateus of Miletus, *FGrHist* 1 F 307.

66. See e.g. Solmsen 1934, Zuntz 1960, Segal 1971, Zeitlin 1981, and Sansone 1985.

and illusion that so many critics have found relevant to their discussions of the play. Pietro Pucci writes, in connection with *Helen*, that "the structure of replacement, supplanting, and vicariousness that the supplement [in Derrida's sense] describes in its complex economy is however well presented in our text. The structure of substitution seems to dominate the whole of the play and even its details."[67] The oppositions and substitutions of which Pucci speaks also structure Euripides' presentation of Egypt and the Egyptians in the play. This phantasmatic economy can be traced in the portrayal of Theoclymenus and Theonoe, and in Egypt's status vis-à-vis Troy and Sparta; it leads directly to the idea of Egypt as a double of the underworld.

We ought to distinguish between the main kinds of Egyptians in Euripides' *Helen*, as with Aeschylus' *Suppliants*, before we consider the play's treatment of marriage and death against a Nilotic horizon.[68] The principal Egyptians in the play are Theonoe and Theoclymenus, and accordingly the royal twosome offer "opposed images of virginal purity and lustful (if vulnerable) desire."[69] Among the oppositions and contradictions that constitute Euripides' text is the characterization of the female Theonoe and the male Theoclymenus. As in *Suppliants*, the figure of the male is marked by sexual aggression, and the female by a desire to remain chaste; as with Aeschylus' play, it is the Egyptian male who poses a sexual threat to the eponymous Greek female. In Euripides' drama, moreover, the Greek woman and the Egyptian woman share an aspiration for chastity, although Helen's desire for chastity lasts only until she regains her lost husband, while Theonoe's is presumed to be one of her defining characteristics.

Theonoe and Theoclymenus differ in significant ways, despite the fact that they both are Egyptian and the offspring of Proteus. Whereas the text emphasizes Theonoe's virginity (10, 894, 939, 977, 1032), it depicts Theoclymenus as a lustful male seeking to marry Helen. Theonoe knows the truth of all things (13–15, 317; cf. 530), while Theoclymenus fails to know that the sailor in rags is Menelaus, or that Helen is deceiving him. Theonoe

---

67. Pucci 1997, 47.

68. Euripides' *Helen* is the only surviving fifth-century tragedy set in Egypt; however, satyr-plays such as Aeschylus' *Proteus*, Euripides' *Busiris*, and the other satyr-plays on Busiris probably were set in Egypt (see note 1 above). See also *P. Oxy.* 1176 for a possible fragment by Euripides. Note that Aristophanes' *Women of the Thesmophoria* contains a comic parody of Euripides' *Helen*, among other plays. The Aristophanic scholia contain the following interesting comment: ἐπανουργεῖτε, . . . ὡς δὴ τῶν Αἰγυπτίων πανούργων ὄντων (scholia to *Women of the Thesmophoria* 922).

69. Segal 1971, 559.

aids and abets the Greek couple, but Theoclymenus has a reputation for killing every Greek stranger he can lay his hands on (155); and in fact his ambitions are frustrated by Greeks and by the services rendered to them by his sister. Theonoe acknowledges Greek gods, including Zeus, Hera, and Aphrodite (879–91), but she does not omit to follow the details of Egyptian religious custom.[70] Theoclymenus swears by Apollo (1204), but complains also that Greek customs escape him (1246; cf. 1270), and he has to ask about the manner of a Greek burial (1240ff.).

It is, of course, the male's behavior that holds particular interest for the analysis made in this chapter, and as in Aeschylus' *Suppliants*, it is the male pursuer's conduct that is characterized by violence. Like Aeschylus, Euripides crosses hunting images with the idea of sexual aggressiveness, and shows Theoclymenus hunting for a marriage with a Greek woman. Replete with hunting images, the play depicts the Egyptian's hunt for marriage with Helen in terms no less violent than those applied to the sons of Aegyptus.[71] And, just as the sons of Aegyptus provoke vehement responses from Danaus and the Danaids, so the Egyptian Theoclymenus is described as "barbarian." Throughout *Helen*, the word "barbarian" itself recurs with the pejorative meaning that it had acquired by the time the play was produced in 412; when the term does not refer to Theoclymenus and Egyptians, it refers to Paris and Trojans.[72]

While the revising of the traditional narrative has the apparent effect of improving Helen's reputation in Euripides' play, the suitors Paris and Theoclymenus are both portrayed as reprehensible barbarians.[73] Considered as a narrative, nevertheless, the play reads not so much as another encapsulation of the potential abduction of the illustrious Helen as the *inversion* of that famous scene when Paris sailed off with his prize to Troy. In the traditional version, the barbarian Paris violates his guest-privileges at Menelaus' home in Sparta by abducting or seducing—the ambiguity is part of

---

70. Compare the fumigation in *Helen* 865–67 with Plutarch, *On Isis and Osiris* 79, Pippin 1960, 161, and Griffiths 1970, 565–71. Hall 1989, 150–51, offers good reasons to doubt the further parallels adduced in Goossens 1935 and Gilbert 1949.

71. See *Helen* 62–63, 153–55, 981, 1169–76, cf. 544–45. For Theoclymenus' associations with hunting, see also Segal 1971, 583.

72. See 224, 274, 295, 666, 863–64, 1100, 1507. For the connotations of the word in Euripides' plays, see in general Saïd 1984 and Hall 1989.

73. The shepherd Paris and the hunter Theoclymenus are also both associated with nature. Wolff 1973, 65, mentions the parallels between Paris and Theoclymenus.

the tradition—Menelaus' wife. In Euripides' play, Menelaus is returning from Troy when he is shipwrecked in Egypt. Here, he, the husband, retrieves his wife, Helen, whose fidelity is emphatically impeccable, out of the grasp of the barbarian Theoclymenus, whose courtesies to Helen and the disguised Menelaus are mocked by the Greek husband's violation of guest-privileges. Whereas in the traditional story the barbarian prince abducts or seduces Helen, and transports her from Greece to Troy, in Euripides' drama the husband rescues, or re-seduces, his chaste wife on his way back from Troy to Greece in the territory of a barbarian prince, who also wishes to seduce her.

Helen's trajectory from Sparta to Egypt (to Sparta) is doubled by the displacement of her *eidolon* from Sparta to Troy (to Egypt), so that Helen's seventeen years in Egypt are matched by the phantom's seventeen years in Troy and on the seas.[74] But in inverting the story of Paris' taking of Helen, the play leaves implicit a comparison of Egypt's position with that of barbarian Troy and Greek Sparta. The "lovely-virgin streams of the Nile" (1) that have made the country rich with herds (1260) contrast with the "streams of the Scamander" (52–53; cf. 367–69) beside which, Helen mourns, many souls died in Troy because of her. The Nile's life-giving values are alluded to, as with Aeschylus' *Suppliants*, but now in opposition to the Scamander's waters, where many Greek warriors gave their lives. Further, the "Egyptian" deities connected with water, Proteus, Psamathe, and Nereus (4–15), are portrayed by Helen as beneficent and helpful to her cause, as are Proteus' daughter, Theonoe, and Pontus' daughter, Galaneia (1457–64). The life-sustaining, purificatory, and rejuvenating qualities of the Nile and these marine gods in an Egyptian setting offer an alternative to the bloody world of Troy, tarnished by death and war. A play that makes into a phantom the object of the Greek expedition to Troy calls into question the value-system defined by Troy and indeed the heroic identity developed by military prowess at Troy. Hence, despite the successes in Troy of which he often speaks in the play, Menelaus has to wage another battle on his way out of Egypt, as if to revitalize the glory *(kleos)* won at Troy and nullified by the *eidolon*. To the extent that a Trojan War has to be fought in microcosm by the Greeks in Egypt, however, the contrast between Egypt and Troy becomes less clear since both locales serve as sites for the repossession of Helen through the defeat of her barbarian captors by Menelaus

---

74. Vernant 1983 discusses the *eidolon* within the context of the double in archaic Greek thought. For Helen as the phantom of sexuality, see Loraux 1995, ch. 11.

and the Greeks; to that extent, moreover, the narrative reaffirms the heroic reliance on martial capacities that the *eidolon* makes problematic.[75]

If Egypt is to be compared to Troy, it nevertheless appears also to have connections with Sparta. Both Egypt and Sparta are places where Helen's marital obligations are threatened by the aggression of the barbarian male. Both regions have celebrated rivers that flow through them, the Nile in Egypt and the Eurotas in Sparta, and both regions have similarities in their natural landscapes.[76] In fact, Egypt and the Egyptians confuse Menelaus when he first lands in the strange country, and hears of another Helen. Menelaus asks whether there is some other man called Zeus who lives besides the Nile, and wonders whether he might have stumbled onto another Sparta or Troy (490–96). Yet, while he has arrived at a place that is and is not Sparta, is and is not Troy, the place seems to allow his wife to reverse the infamy attached to her name. Hermes, not Paris, brought the chaste Helen to Egypt, at Zeus' bidding (44–48), and Paris seized only her simulacrum: "I never went to Troy, but it was my phantom" (582). At some level, then, Egypt returns her reputation intact to Helen, and gives Menelaus the opportunity to regain his wife, who is also that earlier Helen of Sparta before Paris, and never was the tainted woman who lived within the walls of barbarian Troy.

Euripides' play raises many doubles, but the most intriguing double involves an Indo-European comparison, namely, the comparison between the phantom Helen and the shadow Sita. In the Sanskrit epic *Ramayana*, Rama fights a war against the demon Ravana, who has seized his wife Sita and taken her to Lanka. After many years, Rama kills Ravana, and brings Sita back home. The parallels between this story and the saga of Helen, Menelaus, and Paris in Greek mythology are numerous, and have been noted by a wide range of scholars. Less well studied are the correspondences between the so-called variant traditions of Sita and Helen from ancient India and Greece. In the *Adhyatma-ramayana*, a work of the fifteenth century, it is not Sita who is abducted by Ravana, but her *chaya* or shadow; the real Sita lives inside a fire while Rama fights against Ravana. In this version, Rama, feigning sorrow for Sita, wages war against Ravana, kills him, and brings back home the shadow Sita, who then enters the fire and vanishes, while

---

75. This is noted by many critics, including e.g. Segal 1971, Foley 1992, Austin 1994, Rehm 1994.
76. The comparison is remarked on in Segal 1971, 572–73.

the authentic Sita comes out of the fire and is reunited with Rama. This tradition of the shadow Sita is also told with various elaborations in other Indian works such as Tulsi Das' *Ramacaritamanasa* and several Tamil texts.[77]

It is interesting to see that the Indian and the Greek "variant" traditions are both concerned with the attempted rape of a woman by a foreigner. While the *Adhyatma-ramayana* retains the focus on Ravana as the rapist, however, the Euripidean Greek version portrays an Egyptian king as the would-be rapist and unwanted suitor of Helen. This Greek tradition is not content merely to split Helen into her real and phantom selves, but chooses further to invent an Egyptian threat to Helen that she and Menelaus must repel, just as the Greeks repelled the Trojans earlier. In her study of the shadow Sita and the phantom Helen, Wendy Doniger writes, "Women may see in these stories the fantasy of splitting in flight from rape, the woman's reaction to sexual violence; the woman's revulsion against the rapist is also expressed in the fantasy of a violent punishment of the man by another man. Many of these stories turn out to be about rape, from which the shadow serves to exonerate the woman, distancing her from any possible defilement at the hands of the demonic rapist or unwanted husband."[78] With a deliberate thoroughness, the Euripidean exoneration of Helen designates not just the Trojan Paris but also the Egyptian Theoclymenus as aggressor, and it devises a scenario in which the fantasy of violent punishment is carried out with expert irony by Menelaus and his aggrieved wife against an array of Egyptians. For all the clumsiness he displays in his attempts at Helen, then, Theoclymenus belongs in this constellation of ideas where the sexual threat comes from a demonic and lustful foreigner.

A possible model for the Indian and Greek traditions also locates the cross-cultural comparison within the horizons of our analysis of Egyptians in tragedy. Doniger makes the appealing case that the Vedic goddess Saranyu influenced the similar but different stories of the shadow Sita and the phantom Helen.[79] Saranyu was married to the Sun, but one day abandoned him and left behind a shadow in her place. Like Saranyu, Sita and Helen have solar connections, the connections being much stronger and clearer in the case of Helen than of Sita.[80] But in both mythological traditions, the sun has two aspects, light and darkness, and both mythological

77. The most systematic comparison of the shadow Sita and the phantom Helen is Doniger 1999, ch. 1. For the *Adhyatma-ramayana*, see also Siddhantaratna 1935, Kapadia 1964–65, and Whaling 1980; for Sita and the *eidolon*, see also Franci 1980.

78. Doniger 1999, 79.

79. Doniger 1999, 43–79.

80. Skutsch 1987.

traditions explore the light / dark duality contained in the figures of Saranyu, Sita, and Helen: ". . . all three of them," Doniger writes, "spend not half their time but half of their essence 'in the dark'—in their shadow forms."[81] Indeed, one of Saranyu's sons is none other than Yama, the god of death. And Helen, too, is associated with Persephone, who must divide her life between the upper world of light and life and the lower world of darkness and death.[82] What Euripides does in his play is take elements of darkness and death that are historically connected to the story of the phantom Helen, and assimilate them to Egypt and Egyptians. In his *Helen*, Egypt is uniformly the land of the underworld and contact with the Egyptians is likened to death.

TO DIE FOR

Egypt's associations with death pervade Euripides' play, where "everywhere there are echoes of death."[83] These associations pile up with frightful regularity, as even a cursory glance at the play reveals. The tomb of Proteus is the focus of the opening scene of the drama, and the characters refer to it and even address it in the course of the play.[84] The chorus of captured Greek women makes death a part of its concerns in various moments, including the first stasimon (1107–64), which is directed to a nightingale (1110), a bird that has associations with death in Aeschylus' *Suppliants*, among other texts. The chorus laments for the distress of Helen and Trojan women as well as of the Greek wives mourning those Achaeans whom Hades took (1111–25). Most vividly, Helen's scheme to deceive Theoclymenus involves a mock funeral at sea for her husband that prompts her to cut her hair, change her white clothing for black, lacerate her face, and carry out other parts of the funeral rite (1087–89, 1186–88), a mode of mourning that repeats what Helen ascribes to the mothers and wives of the warriors who fought at Troy (367–74). This pseudo-funeral, far from being the occasion for Menelaus' last rites, serves rather as the funeral for the Egyptians who are slaughtered by Menelaus and the Greeks on board the

81. Doniger 1999, 62.
82. Clader 1976.
83. Wolff 1973, 64. Egypt's associations with death are also noted by Goossens 1935; Bacon 1961, 137–38; Guépin 1968, 128–33; Pippin 1960, 156; Jesi 1965; Robinson 1979; Foley 1992, 136; Rehm 1994, 121–27. It is sometimes suggested that Homer presents Odysseus' trip to Egypt in the *Odyssey* so as to connect the country to Hades. For a description of Hades in Greek thought, see Garland 1985, 48–76.
84. See 64, 466, 547, 1165–66; and cf. 799–800 and *Women of the Thesmophoria* 887–88

ship that conveys Helen back to Greece. The many underworld associations of Egypt are not in doubt, therefore, and can be found in considerable detail throughout *Helen*.

In an Egypt conceived of as the land of the dead, the interpenetration of marriage and death also occurs in a manner similar, but not equivalent, to that in *Suppliants*. The plays are similar to the extent that Greek women expressly state a preference for marriage with someone other than the sexually forward Egyptian; but the difference between the plays lies in the choice of marital partners. The Danaids state that they would rather marry Hades than the Egyptian men. On the other hand, Helen already has a husband, and she desires to die with Menelaus in order to be with him. As Loraux suggests, Helen's choice "to die with" is the counterpart of the expression "to live with" (συνοικεῖν), which is a common way to express the state of marriage in Greek.[85] Helen's wish "to die with" her husband is a means of reaffirming her marriage, in and by her death, not unlike the Indian woman who committed *sati* by leaping on to the burning pyre of her dead husband.[86] To put the matter another way, Helen would wish to die a death in Egypt in order to emerge in a renewed union with Menelaus.

Helen's wish to die with Menelaus is apparent in an early scene when she swears by the Eurotas that if the rumors of her husband's death are correct, she will commit suicide by hanging or by driving a sword through her body (348–59). To be sure, Theoclymenus' lust plays a part in Helen's wish to be dead as well, although it remains in the background in this scene. In Aeschylus' play, the Danaids repeat that they would rather die by hanging than allow hateful men to "touch" their skin (790), and they would rather plunge to their deaths from a steep rock before marriage with a "tearer" (798). If we may explain Euripides by Aeschylus, Helen is also saying that she would die rather than have the Egyptian Theoclymenus touch her, tear her, and rape her. Moreover, Helen's attitude in this scene is consistent with the moment when she must reintroduce the subject of death in order to convince Menelaus that she has remained true to their marriage bed. To Menelaus' question, "What will make me sure of this [marital fidelity]?" (796), she indicates Proteus' tomb and adds: "I took a suppliant's place here to escape his bed" (799), thereby showing that once again a Greek woman must resort to supplication in order to escape an Egyptian's bed. Menelaus cannot understand why Helen has to supplicate at a tomb, and asks if she does so for lack of an altar or because of barbarian custom (800). Helen's

85. Loraux 1987, 23.
86. Loomba 1993 surveys the scholarship on sati.

noncommittal reply (801) indicates not just that Menelaus' options are off the mark, but also that in this play, too, the libidinous Egyptian has compelled the Greek suppliant to enter into a relationship with death.

Helen's wish to kill herself in Egypt is a reflection of her desire to die with Menelaus, and thus in some way is a reaffirmation of her marriage. Euripides' drama confirms this formulation of women's deaths, "to die with," by supplementing the promise of the woman's solitary death (348–59) with the depiction of both husband and wife in one scene where they swear to die together. In fact, this scene of the joint declaration of death occurs twice, first when Menelaus and Helen recognize each other, and then just after Menelaus appeals to Proteus' tomb, in the presence of his wife and Theonoe. On the second occasion Menelaus asserts that he will kill both Helen and himself, after which the two of them will go the land of the dead and presumably live together there (980–90). The anxiety over the sex drive of the male Egyptian appears to cause an oscillation between marriage with death or a marriage in death whenever an Egyptian man pursues a Greek woman, but whether with death or in death, the place of Egypt in this constellation of ideas is rather gloomy.

The corollary to Helen's desire to die with her husband occurs when Helen persuades Theoclymenus, with Menelaus' help, to allow her to hold a burial ceremony for her dead husband. This burial is depicted by Helen and the disguised Menelaus as the wife's dutiful service to her deceased husband, and thus as an affirmation of the sundered marriage. When Helen's sense of duty makes Theoclymenus anxious, he confesses to her that he is fearful that she might want to die with her husband: "I am afraid longing for him will seize you, make you fling your body down into the tossing sea stunned with delights remembered from him before" (1395–97). Erotic overtones apart,[87] Theoclymenus' statement implies that Helen will want to kill herself for her husband, so that she might rekindle the lost pleasures of their past marriage and rejoin him. What happens, of course, is that the funeral turns into an escape mechanism for Menelaus and Helen, while Theoclymenus' anticipated wedding with her comes to nothing.

Helen and Menelaus save themselves in Euripides' play and manage to steal away from Theoclymenus and Egypt, thus removing the need for them to adhere to their oaths of death. When this "rebirth" of Helen and Menelaus

87. The erotic associations are stated by Kannicht 1969 at 1397.

is considered in conjunction with their "death" in the underworld that is Egypt, we find that the *Helen* relates to similar story patterns in Greek literature and mythology. Parallels with Euripides' particular development of the story of the seizure and return of Helen can be found in other plays by him, including *Alcestis* and *Iphigenia among the Taurians*, which share the basic pattern of descent and ascent in the myths of Persephone and of Orpheus. This pattern also appears with qualifications in old comedy and satyr-plays. It is further true that *Helen* duplicates the *Odyssey* insofar as it repeats the themes of the shipwrecked sailor and "rewooing, recognition, and symbolic remarriage."[88] These similarities between *Helen* and other narratives have occupied many critics, who point especially to the Demeter/Persephone myth and, secondarily, to the *Odyssey* for correspondences with our play.[89]

The story of Persephone and Demeter, in particular, can be used to further the conception of the wedding as a transition for the woman to another household or hearth, or the conception of marriage as rape and death from the perspective of the bride or wife. This myth has obvious correspondences with the narrative of Euripides' *Helen*, given that both stories plot the abduction of a woman into a world of death, her subsequent rescue and return to the upper world, and the establishment of a cult in her honor. A significant difference between the two lies in the marital status of the woman at the moment of abduction, since Kore is unmarried and virginal, and Helen married and a mother; yet scholars have also analyzed the "remarriage" of Helen and Menelaus in terms of the valuation of sex roles in marriage in fifth-century Athens.[90]

Euripides' text itself invokes the myth at two places, first when Helen laments and mourns in a *kommos* to the Sirens (164–78), and then in a stasimon to the Great Mother (1301–68). Given Helen's whereabouts and situation in the early parts of the play, her words to the Sirens about Persephone confirm Egypt as the place of loss, privation, and death for the Greek woman: "sorrow for sorrow, song for song, melody matching my dirges—if only Persephone might send . . . so that in addition to tears from me she might take a hymn to the perished dead down into her halls of

88. Foley 1992, 136.
89. Critics who point to similarities with one or both include Pippin 1960; Wolff 1973, 63–64; Segal 1971, 569–73, 578, 582, 598, 600; Eisner 1980; Hartigan 1981; Foley 1992; Rehm 1994, 121–22.
90. Foley 1992.

night" (174–78). Helen sings of Persephone as an inhabitant of, or sojourner in, the halls of night, but she is also identifying herself with Persephone as a coresident in those dusky chambers inhabited by the dead. Secondly, the long choral ode to the Great Mother, who appears to be Demeter,[91] also describes a woman's search for her lost daughter. The ode's syncretism and the obscurity of the text make it difficult to interpret, but the Kore / Demeter theme is unmistakable, particularly in the loss of the daughter and the deprivation caused by the mother's rage, and this theme too strengthens the correlation between the abduction of Persephone and the abduction of Helen into the land of death. In this respect, one might mention Anne Pippin's view of Theonoe as "a demythologized Demeter, offering, in her religion of justice and the immortal *gnome*, the philosophical counterpart of the Eleusinian compromise, but adding the threat of punishment."[92]

The Persephone story also relates significantly to Aeschylus' Danaid trilogy. Indeed, the central theme of the story, the fear of the male's abduction of the female, is common both to *Helen* and *Suppliants*. All three narratives—the narratives of Persephone, the Danaids, and the phantom Helen—refer to the brutal seizure by the male of the female, and all associate the male abductor with the underworld. As noted above, moreover, Herodotus says that the ritual of the Thesmophoria was brought to Greece from Egypt by the Danaids, and it has been plausibly suggested that Aeschylus' trilogy ended with the establishment of the ritual in Argos. The contradictory message of the myth of the Thesmophoria can appropriately be applied to the Danaids: on the one hand, the story highlights the separation and grief caused by marriage, and certainly forty-nine of the Danaids continue to object to marriage with their cousins. On the other hand, the myth does allow for marriage between Persephone and Hades, and thus assents to "the essential role of marriage in maintaining the body politic" in Greek society.[93] So Hypermestra marries Lynceus, while her forty-nine sisters are punished for murdering their husbands. Hades gets to keep and have his wife, but in a partial and limited way; Lynceus gets Hypermestra as his wife, but in the knowledge that his forty-nine brothers were slain

91. Scholars have challenged the identification, and some, e.g. Dale 1967, find the whole ode irrelevant; but see the persuasive discussions in Kannicht 1969 and Austin 1994, 177–83.
92. Pippin 1960, 159.
93. Zeitlin 1996, 123.

on Greek soil.[94] By this one marriage and at so bloody a price, the Egyptian husband, with his half-Argive wife, is allowed to enter the Greek world (fig. 2).[95]

The tragic Egyptian occupies a consequential and precise place within the larger and more general context of fifth-century Athenian tragedy. This genre's exposition of foreignness and otherness is too well known to require lengthy elaboration here. Suffice it to say that merely four of the thirty-two surviving tragedies and one surviving satyr-play are set, even partly, in the city of Athens. Vidal-Naquet notes that in Euripides' plays alone there are more than a hundred instances of the word *barbaros*, and he hardly exaggerates when he states that all the surviving plays explore the oppositions between insider and outsider, Greek and barbarian, and citizen and non-citizen.[96] The two plays of Aeschylus and Euripides paint the writers' concerns with Egypt onto this wider canvas of barbarians in Greek tragedy, but within the broader picture, Egypt and the Egyptians seldom fare better in their hands than do the other barbarians of tragedy. Most obviously, these barbarians pose a sexual threat to women and they threaten to disrupt the bonds of kinship and supplication. In depicting the Egyptians as black, deadly, rapacious, and dangerous, Aeschylus and Euripides thus graft a particular idiom of otherness onto the protracted and expansive dramatization of the foreign that characterizes Athenian tragedy over the course of the fifth century.

Like most of these fifth-century tragedies, and like the ritual ceremonies

94. It may be that Aeschylus, fr. 125 (Mette), quoted above, refers to the conjugal union between Lynceus and Hypermestra. If Aphrodite is naturalizing heterosexual marriage in the last play, as Aeschylus' fragment implies, the marriage between Lynceus and Hypermestra may be part of a resolution to the conflict between the Danaids and the sons of Aegyptus in the trilogy. However, it should be stressed that this reading of the trilogy depends on a tendentious interpretation of a fragmentary text.

95. Hypermestra disobeyed her father's instructions and spared the life of her husband, Lynceus. Subsequently, "this Lynceus made war on King Danaus, slew him, and took the kingship and his daughter, according to the account of the wise Archilochus" (Malalas, *Chronographia* 4, 68 [Didnorf] = Archilochus fr. 305 [West, dubia]). It is not known whether the slaying of Danaus occurred in Aeschylus' Danaid trilogy: the notion of the violent Egyptian male is consistent with the themes of *Suppliants*. The fourth-century poet Theodectes may well have dramatized Lynceus' killing of Danaus in his play, *Lynceus*.

96. Vidal-Naquet 1997, 112; for *barbaros* in Euripides, see Saïd 1984.

that preceded the staging of tragedies, Aeschylus' *Suppliants* and Euripides' *Helen* ultimately reinforce civic ideology, that is, they reaffirm the set of values prized by the enfranchised, male elite in Athens. Such a relationship between the dramas and civic ideology is patent at many levels, including ethnicity, gender roles, kinship, and supplication, and has been discussed by critics. For the particular purpose of this study, we might note, in the case of *Helen*, that the affirmation of civic values is discernible at a basic level in the defeat of non-Greeks such as Theoclymenus by Menelaus and Helen. Further, the play upholds the institution of Greek-Greek marriage since Menelaus manages to recover his wife and restore her to their conjugal bed in Greece, while it forecloses the possibility of Egypto-Greek marriage. By disavowing marriage between Greek and foreigner, Euripides' play also reaffirms, if indirectly, the Periclean citizenship law, according to which only the offspring of an Athenian father and Athenian mother could be considered an Athenian citizen.

In the case of Aeschylus' *Suppliants,* the expectations of the Danaids and their Egyptian cousins contrast with the behavior of Pelasgus, who instigates a vote to decide whether Argos should give refuge to the women. Thus the democratic behavior of the Greek stands in vigorous opposition to the autocratic decisions that the daughters of Danaus and the sons of Aegyptus call on him to take. It may be that the Danaid trilogy as a whole involved questions of law, political institutions, and the relationship between the two. Jean-Pierre Vernant observes that the play is about *kratos,* "authority," about the range of possibilities covered by that term, about what it is, and on what it depends. "What is authority, the authority of the man over the woman, of husband over wife, of the head of the State over all his fellow citizens, of the city over the foreigner and the metic, of the gods over mortal men?"[97] If it is true, as scholars generally believe, that the trilogy ended with the defeat of Pelasgus and the Argives and with the establishment of Aegyptus as *tyrannos,* then the playwright appears to have been offering a cautionary tale to Athenians against the concentration of authority in one man and a warning to them to maintain democracy over and against rule by a tyrant. In contrast to the negative model of the rule of Aegyptus, however, the play also offers a model on how to incorporate otherness into the very heart of the Greek polis. This follows from the possibility that in Aeschylus' trilogy the Danaids, refugees from the fertile land of the Nile, introduce water to dry Argos; and it follows from the possibility that in the end of the trilogy they are shown to establish the ritual of the

97. Vernant and Vidal-Naquet 1990, 39.

Thesmophoria in the Greek land. The fact that this ritual, in the real world of fifth-century Athens, was limited to women gives the trilogy "a poetic resolution consistent with the fact that ritual is the typical mode of public action allowed to the feminine in the city." [98] Thus, the trilogy ends with the controlled integration of the other and the proper delimitation of women's roles, at the same time that it counsels the Athenians against the negative model of the tyrannical Aegyptus. From this standpoint, Aeschylus' trilogy dramatizes the mythological narrative of the Danaids so as to serve the ideological needs that pervade and sustain the polis.

It needs to be said that the plays are concerned directly with Athenian issues such as citizenship, law and power, gender relations, kinship, and supplication, in addition to the role of the Egyptian barbarian in life and art. As so often happens in Greek texts of the fifth and fourth centuries, Egypt is caught up in contemporary debates, many of which have nothing to do with Greek-Egyptian matters or with Egypt by itself. Some scholars have detected contemporary political statements, linked to the different historical circumstances of the two plays, in *Suppliants* and *Helen*. In the case of Euripides' *Helen*, several readers have noted that the play is commenting on the Peloponnesian War by pointing to the inanity of a Trojan War that was fought over a phantom woman. Concerning Aeschylus' play, Alan H. Sommerstein argues that the playwright is advising Athenians to vote for the ostracism of Cimon. Cimon had probably made a case to the city to favor the supplication of the Spartan Perikleidas, and he in fact was ostracized in 461. Sommerstein writes, ". . . Aeschylus was using tragedy as a political weapon, and using it in the cause of that *demokratia* which may have been coined as a political catchword about this very time, a catchword whose echo is heard in the text of *Suppliant Maidens*." [99] Both Aeschylus and Euripides appear to be intervening in local political debates far removed from Egypt, although their vehicles for doing so are plays that involve Egypt, or Egyptians, or both.

If tragedy's "detour through the other" [100] is essential to its function as a mainstay of civic ideology, the nature of Egypt's otherness is thematized through the use of details that are sometimes legitimately Egyptian, but more often are not attested by any Egyptian source. In addition to details pointed out throughout this chapter, details of dubious authenticity include those features within the tragedies that the drama classifies as Egyptian,

98. Zeitlin 1996, 169.
99. Sommerstein 1997, 79. On this subject, see also chapter 4 below.
100. Goldhill, in Silk 1996, 253.

but which are virtually impossible to attest on the basis of our knowledge of Egyptian history and culture. These Egyptian elements are difficult to accept on historical grounds because, of course, they are chiefly the products of the playwrights' dramatic imagination. Even when it is considered that the plays use mythological themes and therefore require some license, the dramas nevertheless misrepresent geographical and topographical details. So in his study of the geography of Greek tragedy, André Bernand, the author as well of several books about Egypt in the Late Period, notes plainly that Aeschylus' Egypt is a fabulous and fictitious country, and that Euripides' Egypt has more purchase within the dreams of the playwright than in actual observation.[101] Even when some items in the plays rework legitimately attested Egyptian material, those that do this with any degree of sensitivity are very few indeed. The emphasis in *Suppliants* of conception by breath and hand may derive from Egyptian ideas of reproduction; the Danaids' song to the Nile may echo a Middle Egyptian hymn to Hapy, the personification of the inundation; and "the bird of Zeus" (212) mentioned in the play may be an oblique reference to Amun-Re.[102] Similarly, Euripides' *Helen* contains some maritime, zoological, and geographical details that find correspondences in contemporary Egypt.[103] By and large, however, Aeschylus and Euripides exoticize and reshape Egypt to fit the dramatic ends of their plays.

The intersection of these plays and Athenian politics should not, moreover, obscure the important elements of fantasy at work in them.[104] Whatever else these plays are about, they are also about sexual desire, physical possession, and potential rape. By transferring violent sexual impulses to

101. Bernand 1985, 68, 285.

102. For Egyptian themes in *Suppliants,* see Kranz 1988, 98–107; Hall 1989, 144–45; Zeitlin 1996, 149–50.

103. Bernand 1985, 287–89.

104. My remarks on the Greek fantasies reflected by these plays are indebted, in part, to the Lacanian analysis carried out by Slavoj Zizek on Alfred Hitchcock's film, *Rear Window:* see Zizek 1991, 91–93. For a general Lacanian treatment of modern European fantasies of the East, see also Grosrichard 1998: "Thus, while the despotic Orient is indeed the *Other* held up for us to see, it is also the one that *regards* us, in every sense of that word. . . . And this vast literary output . . . is not just the mere result of fashion (or at least, it demands explanation). . . . [H]ow many spying eyes have been imagined in order to strip us of our own secrets! Have we inquired deeply enough into the strange and complex relation that is at the root of this literature's success? An entire century took pleasure in making itself seen through what it burned to go and see; in revealing to itself the truth about its princes, its obeisances, its way of making love—in short, all its madness—through the artifice of a gaze which, it tells itself, is foreign. This gaze, which to me is other,

Egyptian males, Greek men can imagine themselves as rescuers and warriors, or as men who can beat off foreign pursuers and save Greek women from their barbarous clutches. But if we twist Freud's famous question *What does woman want?* and ask instead *What does the Greek man want?*, the plays give the answer that the Greek man wants to do precisely what the Egyptian men are attempting to do in these plays. In other words, Egyptian men are realizing the desires of the Greek male spectators who are watching the dramas. The Greek males are seeing on stage fantasy figurations of the things that could happen to them, or things that they wish would happen to them. They could abduct women; or they could deflower these half-exotic virgins; or they could have Helen of Troy. Considered from this perspective, the reunion of Menelaus and Helen in *Helen,* and the marriage of Hypermestra and Lynceus, if this occurs in the Danaid trilogy, offer "safe" climaxes to these fantasies, climaxes in which the conjugal bond is presented as an escape and release from the preceding violence. In this respect, it is fitting for the remaining Danaids to be punished, in the trilogy, since they carry out frightening and castrating actions on their fateful wedding night. The chastisement of the castrators leaves intact the phallic pride and alleviates the anxiety of the men who regard them. In many ways, therefore, the plays enact the deepest fantasies and fears of the male elites who performed and watched the productions.

There is an Egypt of history, there is an Egypt of myth, and there is an Egypt which is neither wholly historical nor wholly mythical, but is purely tragic. Yet, to claim that the Egypt of Greek tragedy is an Athenian construct is to say that Athens itself is an effect of Egypt. In tragedy, Egypt is an other place, and its alterity gives form, content, and validity to Athens' view of itself. Through the playwrights' dramatic techniques, the city in its self-image remains a place that is not the land of the dead, nor the tyrannical kingdom of a rapacious host, just as it is not Troy, not Sparta, and even not Argos. The meaning and value of this Egypt are decided and fixed by, among other things, the relationship that Athens imagines it has with itself. In this discursive economy, tragic Egypt makes the real possible and allows it to flourish; absent its own history and myth, tragic Egypt makes

knows more about me than I do myself. And when I attempt to go and look behind what I believe to be the point from which, over there in that world, it looks at me, it is myself and our world that I find in the end" (24–25). In the ways that Grosrichard imputes to the seventeenth and early eighteenth centuries, Athenian tragedy repeatedly portrayed encounters between Greeks and barbarians in which the desires, fantasies, and apprehensions of the citizen male were played out in front of the audience.

possible the democratic polis of the fifth century. But the polis has a politics, and the politics imposes limits, and so no measure of dramatic ingenuity can allow Egyptians and Greeks to coexist on an equal footing. In Aeschylus' *Suppliants*, as Ralph Hexter and Daniel Selden remark, marriage between the two groups "is represented as both miscegenetic and semi-incestuous, and hence an agency of ritual pollution (*miasma*): given the overdetermined network of relationships in the family of Aegyptus and Danaos, eponymous founders of the Egyptian and Greek lines and, as such, institutors of the social polity in general, some sort of ethnic or gentilitial contamination would seem to be inevitable."[105] The way to preserve the social polity and to prevent ethnic contamination is to make abhorrent the union between these men and women, just as Euripides' *Helen* also makes abhorrent the union between an Egyptian king and a Greek woman. Against a tragic Egypt, contrived out of this poetics of abhorrence, Athens emerges as the exemplary city-state of the Greeks.

105. Hexter and Selden 1992, 200.

2 Space and Otherness

The writing of Herodotus' history constitutes a privileged moment in the Western discourse on Egypt. Book 2, which contains the bulk of the Egyptian sections, quickly became the most famous and the most influential description of the country and set the pattern for several centuries of Egyptian ethnography. Even in the reign of the Ptolemies, after Greeks settled in Egypt in large numbers and came to know the region more intimately, Herodotus' history remained a text for writers to emulate, to rival, to improve upon, and vigorously to attack. Ethnographers of places other than Egypt also drew on book 2 for its style, rhetoric, and method: such was the case with Alexander's admiral, Nearchus, whose account of India shows clear verbal and stylistic parallels with Herodotus' text.[1] Much later, Lorenzo Valla's Latin translation of 1474 brought Herodotus to a wide readership among humanists, geographers, and explorers. Scores of authors, during and after the Renaissance, were influenced by Herodotus in their descriptions of Egypt and of places distant, strange, or hitherto unknown. Book 2 provided a model to Cortés' associate Gómara, for example, when he recorded the conquest of New Spain. And, although he had his critics, it was not really until Jean-François Champollion's decipherment of hieroglyphs in 1822 that Herodotus began to lose the status he acquired in the Renaissance as an authority on Egypt. With the decipherment, Egyptian sources could be understood and studied for the first time since late antiquity, when knowledge of the ancient Egyptian language was lost. Still, Herodotus' text managed to retain its appeal for scholars and travelers, with

1. See chapter 7 below.

the result that even today his description of Egypt invites comment, scrutiny, and analysis.

The influence of Herodotus' account is due to a powerful rhetoric of otherness as much as it is to richness of detail, narrative sophistication, and the perceived usefulness of the text as a historical source.[2] It is through such a rhetoric that Herodotus theorizes cultural difference, separates Egyptians from Greeks, and describes *them* in relation to *us*. This rhetoric runs through various parts of Herodotus' Egyptian account, including the geographical, ethnographic, and historical sections, and it is what makes the popular features of the text contribute to an inventory of the other. What is the nature of this rhetoric, what are its effects, and what are its implications within the framework of ancient thought? One way to answer these questions is to consider the basic categories through which Herodotus' rhetorical strategy is put into play, in other words, to consider his representation of Egyptian space and time. It was, after all, Herodotus' record of the country's space and time that served for centuries as a crucial paradigm for the description of Egypt and other lands by Europeans. Recurrent stereotypes about Egypt—as the land of the Oriental despot, say, or as an ancient country in which nothing changes—can also be traced back to the author.

I would like to begin this study of Herodotus' words, then, by discussing representations of Egyptian space and time in his text.[3] For convenience, the study is spread over two chapters, chapter 2 being the discussion of space, and chapter 3 the discussion of time. What emerges from the analysis is the recognition that the historian uses space and time in ways that differentiate Egypt from Greece politically and socially and hence that a distinctive significance attaches to Egypt. In his representation of space, Herodotus focuses attention on the despotism of Egyptian history, on the despot's arbitrary rule over Egypt, and on the imbalance of power through which the system of despotism operates. The text implicitly contrasts the freedom and democracy of Greek cities such as Athens with the oppression and autocracy of nations such as Egypt. This chapter locates this particular impression of Egypt within the broader context of Herodotus' representation of Egyptian space. Such a context includes the rhetoric of mapping, the

2. For empirical assessments of Herodotus' historical work on Egypt, see e.g. Morenz 1968; Armayor 1978 and 1985; Lloyd 1988b; Fehling 1989; Pritchett 1993.
3. References to Herodotus are to C. Hude's OCT, 3d ed., 1927; translations are adapted from Grene 1987.

structure of inversion and reciprocity, and the general strategies of geo-graphical description practiced by the narrator.

THE PHARAOH'S SPACE

Yet Egyptian nature is, like human nature everywhere, contradictory. . . . This people admire an iron-handed and lion-hearted despotism; they hate a timid and grinding tyranny.

> Richard F. Burton, *Personal Narrative of a*
> *Pilgrimage to al-Madinah and Meccah*

Herodotus' representations of Egyptian space connect the country with tyranny, monarchy, and autocracy. These are not political systems about which the author has favorable comments to make. Donald Lateiner notes that Herodotus refers to "more than fifty traditional kingdoms and tyran-nies with usurped power" in his history, and never describes them so as to "present tyranny as an attractive or progressive form of government."[4] The actions of autocrats are often scandalous and excessive, and are char-acterized by flamboyant expenditure, humiliation and oppression of oth-ers, and a brash arrogance that leads to downfall. Herodotus' portrayal of autocracies contrasts with his depiction of nontyrannical Greek city-states, as any number of comments from his text show. Lateiner assembles the rel-evant material and summarizes the position thus: "Herodotus considers Greek governments other than tyrannies superior to oriental autocracies because of their relative moderation and humanity: they recognize human dignity and respect persons and ancestral institutions, they require ac-countability to law and custom, and they are able to profit from criticism and select policies wisely."[5]

The actions of Herodotus' Egyptian rulers and his treatment of Egyp-tian space should be read against this larger ethnographic differentiation where the despotism and tyranny of barbarian lands stands in contrast to the freedom and openness of many Greek city-states. This contrast, in turn, was an important issue for many fifth-century Greeks, and especially Athenians, given the centrality of democracy and freedom to the official ideology of the city-state.

Let us turn to Sesostris, the archetypal autocrat, to whom Herodotus de-

---

4. Lateiner 1989, 170.
5. Lateiner 1989, 182.

votes many passages.[6] As the example of this king shows, space in Egypt is constantly invested with royal potential. The pharaohs of Herodotus are often rebuilding Egypt, changing its landscape, erecting monuments of brick and stone, redirecting the flow of the great river, or creating artificial lakes, and Sesostris is one of many royal figures in Herodotus' Egyptian account who transgress the natural order of space by altering, modifying, or transforming the space of Egypt. In Sesostris' case, the alteration to the landscape of Egypt is complete and lasting because of the numerous canals he constructs, but in other cases kings of Egypt build or attempt to build proto-Suez Canals, labyrinths, lakes, temples, and shrines, and thus the alterations to the Egyptian landscape vary in degree and scale. What is interesting about all these modifications of Egypt is that they are sites for the intersection of power and space.

Sesostris redefines the space in which he finds himself, reassigns spatial limits to his own advantage, and transforms the topography. He attempts to "extend the existing" boundaries of Egypt, to use the Egyptian euphemism for imperialism, carries out extensive conquests outside Egypt, and even crosses from Asia into Europe when he invades Scythia (2.103). When he conquers lands whose men put up strong resistance, he sets up pillars inscribed with his name and country and a message indicating that he has conquered them with his power. If he invades lands without encountering significant opposition, he sets up pillars depicting female genitalia (2.102). The king is also unfazed by zones of separation other than a country's boundaries. On his return journey from his conquests, when he finds himself trapped in his brother's house in Daphnae by an enveloping ring of fire, his wife advises him to place two of his sons as a bridge over the fire. He takes this advice and walks to safety over the flaming bodies of his dying children, thus traversing the blazing demarcation of domestic space inside the house and natural order outside by deflecting against kin the arson-murder intended for himself (2.107). In this respect, Sesostris' behavior exemplifies that of the Herodotean tyrant whose actions lead to a "*redefini-*

6. Several ancient Greek authors recount the story of Sesostris; Herodotus (2.102–111, 137) and Diodorus (1.53–58) give the most extensive narratives. He seems to be based on traditions connected with several different Egyptian pharaohs: Senusret I (1965–1920 B.C.E.), Senusret III (1874–1855 B.C.E.), Rameses II (1279–1213 B.C.E.), and also Sheshonq I (945–924 B.C.E.), the Shishak of the Hebrew Bible who raided Jerusalem in about 925 B.C.E. See Lloyd 1988a on Herodotus and Sesostris. A "novelized version" of Sesostris' life also found an audience in antiquity: see the introduction, text, translation, and commentary for the *Sesonchosis* fragments of the early fourth century C.E. in Stephens and Winkler 1995, 246–66.

tion of the boundaries of self and other," that is, between *oikeion* and *allotrion*, and so the Egyptian's maneuvers typify "the tyrannic problem par excellence in Greek thought."[7]

The paradigmatic relationship for the subordination of Egypt to king is that which encompasses the positions of master and slave.[8] "King-subject, master-slave: from the point of view of power, the two pairs overlap," François Hartog observes. "The king is like a master of slaves, and the master is like a king."[9] Sesostris furrows numerous canals in the countryside and allocates a square of equal size to each Egyptian (2.108–9), so that the king marks the space of Egypt in the way that a master brands a slave with stigmata. The master registers a claim of ownership for a slave by stigmatizing the slave's body, while the king asserts his claim to Egypt by marking it with canals and uniform squares. Egypt will bear the signs of this branding for all time, so that what was previously a land of carts and horses is converted into a region lacking both, and every Egyptian now lives on a piece of land no smaller or larger than his neighbor's. The ruler-owner's prerogative is to mark the body of national space, and those marks identify that space as subordinate and as the proper domain of the ruler. Moreover, the intermediaries who carry out Sesostris' injunctions are themselves slaves: he uses hordes of foreign captives to perform the digging of canals and, given the context of its mention in the text, the allocation of square portions of land (2.108–9). Hence, Herodotus' text locates Egyptian space within a dynamic that imports the foreign, subjugated, servile prisoner as the necessary intermediary for the invention of the native realm that becomes in turn subordinate to the ruler's will.

In connection with stigmata and slavery, it should be mentioned that Herodotus' imaginative marking associates Egyptian kings and their practices with the barbarism and servitude that tattoos and brands signified in the Greek and Roman world. Of Greek and Roman attitudes, Dominic Montserrat writes: "Tattoos were inflicted on slaves or malefactors as a punishment, a permanent signifier to their subordinate bodies. As the tattooing needles bit into the skin, they announced that the body being tattooed was penetrable and passive, the ultimate mark of subservience in the ancient world. Thus, even cultic tattooing, which marked the devotion of an initiate to a god, was regarded with some suspicion, because of the symbolic

7. Kurke 1999, 117, in connection with Polycrates.
8. See Hartog 1988, 332–35, and Steiner 1994, 77–78 and her ch. 4, for general analyses of this question.
9. Hartog 1988, 335.

penetration implicit in the tattoo."[10] It will occasion no surprise, therefore, to find in Herodotus a reference also to cultic tattooing in book 2. Mentioning a temple of Heracles near the Canopic mouth of the Nile, he says, "If a runaway slave takes refuge in that, no matter whose slave he may be, and has put upon himself certain sacred tattoos (στίγματα ἱρά), thereby surrendering himself to the god, no one may lay a hand on him. This is the law, which is the same from the beginning right up to this time of mine" (2.113). Herodotus' remark links together slave status and stigmata in the context of the Egyptian temple, with the additional stipulation that this is how things have always been in the country—but, in a Herodotean twist, the slave is also said to gain divine protection if the tattoos are inflicted in this temple. Let us note in passing that in ancient Egypt tattoos assumed a range of different social meanings, depending on the tattooed individual, the appearance of the tattoo, and the place on the body where the tattoo was made. Tattoos could signify the foreign or servile status of the individual, as in Herodotus, but they could also take on aesthetic or religious values; and women were more commonly tattooed than men.

The idea of the servility of the Egyptian state in relation to its royal master emerges also from the reign of Amasis, the last of the Egyptian kings mentioned by Herodotus in book 2. Amasis, too, marks the space of Egypt when he builds a marvelous propylaia to the temple of Athena in Saïs, great sphinxes of stone obtained from the quarries of Memphis and Elephantine, a gigantic monolithic chamber conveyed from Elephantine to Saïs by 2,000 men, and a prostrate statue which is 75 feet long (2.175–6). The country accommodates 20,000 cities in his time (2.177), and, what is important to a Greek writer, he makes a grant of the city of Naukratis to the Greeks in Egypt (2.178). But Amasis also knows that he has enslaved the people of Egypt. When the Egyptians show reverence to an image made out of his golden footbath, he indicates to them that they worship now what used to be a receptacle for vomit and urine. He resembles the footbath, he says, since he was formerly an ordinary citizen, but is now the king and the rightful object of their honor. "That was how," Herodotus notes, "Amasis conciliated the Egyptians to the justice of their slavery (δουλεύειν) to himself" (2.172).

If Egypt has to remain servile, however, then Egypt must always have a king or master to whom it belongs, and this is precisely what Herodotus

---

10. Montserrat 1996, 76. On Greek and Roman tattooing, see in general Montserrat, 1996, 75–78; and Jones 1987. For Egyptian tattooing, see Keimer 1948 and Bianchi 1988. See also Sextus Empiricus, *Outlines of Pyrrhonism* 3.202

makes clear in his Egyptian logos. Writing about the successors to Sethos, the priest of Hephaestus and ruler of Egypt, Herodotus states that the Egyptians were unable to live without a king, so they divided up the country into twelve parts, each under the rule of one king (2.147). The Egyptians are capable of seeking liberty, as Hartog says, but not of living with it.[11] In other words, Egypt needs a king to retain its identity as Egypt, and the Egyptians must have a ruler to administer their country, so they themselves set up a higher authority.

Yet in this case the Egyptians establish not one but twelve kings, each with a province of his own. Like Sesostris apportioning squares of equal size to his subjects, or, rather, like the reverse of that earlier geometrization of Egypt, these Egyptians divide up their country into twelve parts for twelve rulers on equal terms. The kings rule the country and agree not to destroy each other and not to seek to have more than one of the others (2.147). The twelve are to rule their twelve provinces as equals in all respects and they strengthen their alliance by marriages between their families. In this manner, once again after Sesostris, the space of Egypt is geometrized and saturated with the power of the king.

The twelve kings also leave behind a labyrinth with twelve courts as a memorial of their reign (2.148). The twelve courts of the labyrinth provide an obvious fit to the twelve kings and twelve provinces of Egypt; thus the particular geometrization of space in the description of the labyrinth corresponds to the general geometrization of Egypt. Herodotus furthers the identification between Egypt and the labyrinth by the use of verbal echoes in his writing. Earlier in book 2 he states that Egypt has "more wonders in it than any other country and more works that are beyond description (λόγου μέζω) than anywhere else" (2.35). When he comes to discuss the labyrinth, he writes, "I saw it myself and it is beyond description (λόγου μέζω). . . . The pyramids, too, were beyond description (λόγου μέζονες), and each of them is worth just as much as many of the great works of the Greeks, but the labyrinth surpasses even the pyramids" (2.148). We find that both Egypt and the labyrinth are impossible to represent in language, though the narrator attempts the exercise in any case. What emerges from both representations is a space that is framed to a geometrical design and invested with the power of kings.

In the manner of Sesostris' geometrization and the twelve kings' monument, the pyramids are sites for the intersection of despotic power and space. The pyramids are ways for kings to mark the Egyptian landscape

11. Hartog 1988, 324.

and, as with the labyrinth, the pyramids are "beyond description." The description of the pyramid of Cheops, for example, raises issues of power, despotism, servility, and geometrization. Cheops is said to drive his people into extreme misery before he builds his pyramid, closes the temples, prevents the people from sacrificing in them, and orders all the Egyptians to work in pursuance of his own ends (2.124). Gangs of one hundred thousand people haul the stones from quarries in the Arabian mountains to the Nile, and then after the load crosses the river, another team hauls the stones to the Libyan mountains. The workers have to build a road on which to drag the stones, and the road itself is, in Herodotus' opinion, the equal of the pyramids. Ten years in the building, the road runs more than fifty stades and has a breadth of ten *orguiai*. Each side of the square base of the pyramid (which takes twenty years to build) is eight plethra, which is also its height. Perhaps with Herodotus in mind, Aristotle mentions the pyramids of Egypt as measures that allow the tyrant to keep his subjects perpetually at work and in poverty.[12] It is the historian's narrative that presents this distinctive equation as intrinsic to Egypt.

Egyptian Whore, Greek Courtesan

With the separate accounts of Cheops' daughter and Rhodopis, Herodotus reveals his bias as he briefly develops these stories of pyramids and power. In the case of Cheops' daughter, Herodotus has her move between prostitution and despotism; but in Rhodopis' case, the author offers a more appealing view, one marked by the charm of a Greek courtesan. The text not only makes the association between sex and the Orient, but also reflects the author's ethnocentrism in matters of gender and space.

Herodotus records that Cheops prostitutes his own daughter to pay for the pyramid when his finances fall short (2.126). As Deborah Tarn Steiner remarks on the position of women in the cluster of ideas surrounding Herodotus' Egyptian king, "Rapacity, self-aggrandizement through compet-

12. Aristotle, *Politics* 1313b: "And it is a device of tyranny to make the subjects poor, so that a guard may not be kept, and also that the people being busy with their daily affairs may not have leisure to plot against their ruler. Instances of this are the pyramids in Egypt and the votive offerings of the Cypselids, and the building of the temple of Olympian Zeus by the Pisistratidae and of the temples at Samos, works of Polycrates (for all these undertakings produce the same effect, constant occupation and poverty among the subject people); and the levying of taxes, as at Syracuse (for in the reign of Dionysius the result of taxation used to be that in five years men had contributed the whole of their substance)." Aristotle mentions the pyramids along with the projects of Greek tyrants; it is as if he cannot resist bringing up the pharaohs' behavior in the context of oppressive tyranny.

itive building, the degrading treatment of women, and indentured labor are the burdens of the gravestones' literal and symbolic messages."[13] The daughter obliges her father by selling herself for money, but she also asks the men that visit her to make her a gift of one stone each. These stones are used to build another pyramid, each side of which is one and a half plethra. Thus, alongside Cheops' edifice of oppression and exploitation stands a similar marvel, an expression of man's exploitation of woman, but also of female ingenuity and woman's sexuality. However, the counterexample to the anecdote of Cheops' daughter is the story of the famous Rhodopis (2.134–35). In his account of a pyramid made by the king Mycerinus, Herodotus points out that Rhodopis cannot have paid for Mycerinus' pyramid, contrary to the beliefs of some Greeks. The courtesan should be dated to the reign of Amasis and not Mycerinus, writes Herodotus, and she was freed by Charaxus, the brother of the poet Sappho.[14] "In sexuality her gifts became so great that she gained a fortune—great indeed for a Rhodopis, but not reaching to the construction of such a pyramid" (2.135).

The pyramid serves as the site of transgression for the Oriental princess as well as the Oriental despot. What is interesting about the story of Cheops' daughter is that the Egyptian woman exploits men's sexual desires to further her own love of power. She exploits men's sexual desires by selling her body in return for money and she manifests love of power by having a pyramid built for herself. Rather than succumbing to the degradation of prostitution, the Egyptian princess turns that feature of her life to her own advantage by a gesture of self-aggrandizement. A number of scholars have observed that in Herodotus only tyrants and kings feel eros as a transgressive force: "the *despotes* is prey to desire *(eros)*, both sexual desire and desire for power, illegitimate love and love of power."[15] For example, Pausanias has the desire (ἔρως) to become tyrant (τύραννος) of all of Greece (5.32), and conversely, Cambyses desires his sister (3.31). But Cheops' daughter is not prey to eros; instead, she uses illegitimate love to ensure that she will have a monument to herself. She usurps the role of the despot, but she also alters the notion of despotic eros as transgressive force, since she delinks the desire for power from desire for sex, by putting the latter at the service of the former.

13. Steiner 1994, 138.
14. "Charaxus, when he had freed Rhodopis, returned home to Mytilene," Herodotus writes, "and in one of her poems Sappho made bitter mockery of him" (2.135). It is believed by some scholars that Sappho, frs. 5, 15 (West), contain reproaches to her brother in connection with a courtesan named Dorikha.
15. Hartog 1988, 330. See also Benardete 1969, 137–38; Hall 1989, 208–9.

Rhodopis' reputation contrasts with that of Cheops' daughter, and it is instructive to compare the Greek woman's story with the Egyptian's, although both individuals furnish the association between prostitution and the pharaonic aspiration for monumentality. Rhodopis, a Thracian slave, belongs to a Samian man, who is also the master of Aesop, the writer of fables. She becomes a courtesan in the Greek community at Naukratis, a city whose courtesans are said to be especially talented. Rhodopis possesses a marvelous sexual expertise, though Herodotus finds it difficult to believe that even she could have amassed enough to pay for a pyramid. Cheops' daughter belongs to the opposite end of the social scale. Whereas the foreign woman turns to prostitution after receiving her freedom in Egypt, where she was a slave and an outsider, the Egyptian princess makes a similar turn despite her position at the top of society. She turns to prostitution in order to finance her father's pyramid, though in the process she manages to have erected a testament to her own prowess. For the non-Egyptian Rhodopis, the practice of selling herself enables her to acquire a minor fortune that is sufficient to make a dedication of roasting-spits at Delphi, though not to fund a pyramid. Her sexual skills allow her to increase her social standing through garnering of money and service to the gods, and by these means she seeks to move away from the periphery and toward the center of acceptability. The Egyptian uses her sexuality to fund part of her father's pyramid, according to Herodotus, and her prostitution points rather to a father's wickedness. But her next action is to emulate her royal father and have a pyramid built for herself, so that her behavior encompasses playing the whore and playing the princess simultaneously. Such conduct is possible, perhaps, only for a barbarian woman in Herodotus' text.[16]

Gustave Flaubert, a self-declared lover of prostitutes, read these sections of Herodotus and was captivated by the story of Rhodopis. The notes that he took during his travels to Egypt in 1849 and 1850 refer to the story of

---

16. For Herodotus' treatment of women in general, see Rossellini and Saïd 1978, and Dewald 1981; cf. the story of Pausanias and the woman of Cos (9.76). For a different reading of these particular episodes, see Kurke 1999, 176–77, 220–27, who believes that "Herodotus's narrative of Rhodopis systematically exposes the disembedded economics involved in the circulation of *hetairai* and thereby demystifies the aristocratic system of which the *hetaira* is a part" (220). Unlike Kurke, I do not read Herodotus' account of Rhodopis in terms of irony and parody, but I agree with this scholar that "the daughter's pyramid stands as a monumental accounting-sheet, commemorating and quantifying her forced prostitution. In the process the king is exposed as a tyrant, and his monumental ambitions as the extreme of depravity (notice how Herodotus introduces the story: ἐς τοῦτο δὲ ἐλθεῖν Χέοπα κακότητος . . .)" (222).

Rhodopis' pyramid. In the preliminary version of *Education Sentimentale*, he wrote that Jules

> adored the courtesan of antiquity as she came into the world on a day of bright sun, the beautiful and terrible woman who built pyramids with presents from her lovers; before her the rugs of Carthage were unrolled and Syrian tunics displayed; to her were sent amber from the land of the Sarmatians, feather-beds from the Caucasus, gold powder from the Senaar, coral from the Red Sea, diamonds from Golconda, gladiators from Thrace, ivory from the Indies, poets from Athens. The pale creature with eye of fire, the embracing, strangling viper of the Nile.[17]

Partly through the astonishing glitter of its prose, and partly through the crossing of eroticism and a largely Eastern geography, the passage embodies the kind of response that an Egyptian setting generated among Europeans of the nineteenth century. Rhodopis, after all, was Greek, not Egyptian, and in historical terms the thought of a Greek courtesan receiving these gifts in Greece would have been too absurd for us to contemplate. Yet, it is precisely in Egypt that this picture of ornament and sensuality becomes plausible for Flaubert: "The pale creature with eye of fire, the embracing, strangling viper of the Nile." This is another way of saying that the embroidered preference for the Greek courtesan over the Egyptian whore is glamorized here and complete.

Persian Egypt

The kings of Persia rival the earlier Egyptian rulers in their transgressive behavior, their excess, luxury, cruelty, and danger. Charges of physical violence occur frequently in Herodotus' depictions of Persians. The Persian kings in Herodotus impale their enemies, or hack off their noses, ears, arms, and legs.[18] To quote one example from the many cases of spatial transgression, Cyrus punishes the Gyndes river by dividing it into 360 channels (1.189). Egypt was under Persian rule in Herodotus' day, and when his Persian kings go to Egypt, they attempt to surpass even the pharaohs in transgressing the natural order of things in Egypt. As Cambyses promises his

---

17. Flaubert 1972, 54. See also Flaubert 1972, 126: "I have tried in vain to do something with my oriental tale, and for a day or two I played with the story of Mykerinos in Herodotus (the king who slept with his daughter). But it all came to nothing. By way of work, every day I read the *Odyssey* in Greek. Since we have been on the Nile I have done four books; we are coming home by way of Greece, so it may be of use to me" (letter dated March 13, 1850). For a sympathetic reading of Flaubert's writings on Egypt, see Finlay 1983.

18. See 3.69, 79; 7.35, 238; 8.90; 9.172.

mother, "Mother, when I am a man, I shall turn Egypt upside down" (3.3). Cambyses remembers these words, Herodotus adds, when he becomes a man and plans his expedition against Egypt. After he invades Egypt, Cambyses indeed violates the established customs of the country. He outrages the body of the deceased Amasis by having it whipped, stabbed, and then set on fire (3.16). When he sees Egyptians celebrating the appearance of the god Apis, he forms the suspicion that the people are rejoicing at his plight and puts them to death; later he attempts to stab the Apis calf in the belly, strikes the thigh instead, but kills the holy animal nonetheless (3.27–29).[19] Cambyses' successor, Darius, attempts to continue pharaonic policies when he works on a project initiated by the Egyptian Nekos, a canal that would lead to the Erythraean Sea (the Indian Ocean). An oracle had stopped Nekos, the son and successor of Psammetichus, from prolonging the agony of his workers by telling him that he was doing the work of the barbarian, an apparent allusion to Darius. Nekos, incidentally, suffered the death of 120,000 Egyptians in his attempt to reconfigure space and build this canal from the Nile to the Erythraean Sea (2.158).[20]

Just as the Egyptian kings brand the space of Egypt as servile, the Persian rulers too maintain the servility of the country. The Egyptians, who were enslaved (δουλωθέντες, 7.1) by Cambyses, revolt from the Persian empire in the last years of Darius' reign when the king is still reeling from the shock of his defeat at the battle of Marathon. He resolves to wage war against both them and the Athenians, but he dies before he can execute his plan, and Xerxes accedes to the throne. Xerxes subdues the Egyptian rebels and makes the slavery (δουλοτέρην, 7.7) of Egypt harsher than it was under Darius, which is no surprise, since he is an expert at marking the slave body. It is he who attempts to build a bridge across the Hellespont. Like a master treating a slave, he lays three hundred lashes on the Hellespont and

19. On Cambyses' treatment of the Apis bull, see the introduction and chapter 7.

20. Using words that resonate with the themes of chapters 2 and 3, Aristotle relates the attempt to make the canal (*Meteorology* 352 b 20 ff.): "The whole land of the Egyptians, whom we take to be the most ancient of men, has evidently come into existence and been produced by the river. This is clear from an observation of the country itself, and the facts about the Red Sea suffice to prove it too. One of their kings tried to make a canal to it (for it would have been of no little advantage to them for the whole region to have become navigable; Sesostris is said to have been the first of the ancient kings to try), but he found that the sea was higher than the land. So he first, and Darius afterwards, stopped making the canal, lest the sea should mix with the river water and spoil it. So it is clear that all this part was once unbroken sea" (trans. E. W. Webster). Among other things, this passage thematizes the obsession with royal power, the reconfiguring of space, and the ancientness of Egyptians as programmatic for Greek representations of Egypt.

lowers a yoke of fetters into the sea when his bridge collapses (7.35). Egyptian papyrus helped hold together the bridge (7.25, 34).

At the start of this chapter, I said that I was interested in the general issue of space and time as a means to understanding the rhetoric of otherness in Herodotus' Egyptian history. Thus far I have been considering autocratic behavior and Egyptian space, and now I would like to turn more closely to the rhetoric used by Herodotus to represent Egyptian space. The following sections examine this question through the rhetoric of mapping, the structure of inversion and reciprocity, and the general strategies of geographical description employed by the narrator. Lastly, I also present Egyptian material and consider Egyptian conceptualizations of space against the background of Herodotus' work.

MAPPING EGYPT

Herodotus' account of Egypt focalizes a representational technique that thrives on enumeration, surveying, measuring, and mapping. The writer's representation of the country involves a specific rhetoric of setting and framing, a rhetoric that borrows vocabulary from surveying, classifying, listing, and ordering. This is explicable in terms of the intellectual developments—the development of maps, for example, or Pythagoras' spherical model of the earth, or the invention of the *periplous* (the narrative of a sea voyage)—that informed Herodotus' interest in spatial, topographical, and geographic phenomena. These revolutionary developments were disseminated widely, even to the mainland Greek city-states such as Athens, where they exerted an influence on the political self-image of the isonomic, democratic city. By the end of the sixth century, there was "a certain coincidence between the geometric vision of the world, such as it was being formulated by Anaximander, and the political vision of a rational and homogeneous city, such as it was achieved by Cleisthenes."[21] These developments contributed to the production of knowledge about the world and were attempts to fashion totalizing but reductive structures; they were ways of ordering up the world before the gaze of the human subject.[22]

The development of maps in particular seems to have affected the Greek

21. Lévêque and Vidal-Naquet 1996, 81.
22. For a treatment of this general problem, see Foucault 1970, 125–65. Herodotus' debt to the pre-Socratics is discussed by Immerwahr 1966 and Lloyd 1975, 126–39, 156–70.

experience of space, unlike the case in Egypt,[23] and cartographic practices provide the background to Herodotus' spatializing techniques. The Greeks had known cartography since the time when Anaximander (ca. 610–546 B.C.E.) invented the map, if we believe later authorities.[24] Anaximander was a pupil of Thales at Miletus, where in the early 500s Hecateus "improved" on the first map. Herodotus may have learned of these cartographic developments in his early years in Asia Minor, or later in Athens and elsewhere. At any rate, his work reflects knowledge of the early maps and he refers to maps on at least two well-known occasions in his history. In one case, he registers amusement at the number of people drawing maps with the earth as a circle and Okeanos running around it (4.36). In the second case, the map presents a new order of space, and its viewers have difficulty in reconciling their images of the real objects with what they see on a map (5.49–50).[25] Herodotus' history is in many ways the successor to the first maps. Scholars have argued that Herodotus used maps in the writing of his history, and they have attempted to recreate these maps on the basis of the written work, even if it is hard to supply definitive proof of his reliance on them.[26] Naturally, the map by itself does not suffice as an explanatory or hermeneutic tool with which one may better apprehend Herodotus' narrative structure. Cartographic consciousness as we know it, if it exists at all, came about after several advances to and standardization of the technology had occurred in Renaissance Europe, while planetary consciousness is a still more recent phenomenon in human existence. Nevertheless, the novel modes of thinking about, representing, and ordering the human environment developed by sixth-century Ionians certainly informed

23. There are no secular maps of the country as a recognizable whole on any drawing from ancient Egypt, and the Egyptians seem not to have used their technical expertise at measuring, surveying, and recording small areas of land to produce cadastral maps. The so-called Turin Maps, which date to about 1150 B.C.E., may refer to gold mines at Umm Fawakhir, in Wadi Hammamat. There are also traces of map-like designs on funerary monuments from the beginning of the dynastic period. Further, tombs of the New Kingdom contain drawings of gardens (Wilkinson 1990), and temples of the nineteenth and twentieth dynasties depict landscapes in a map-like manner. The Book of the Two Ways also offers examples of topographical drawings, but these have been likened to a passport to a mythical land of the afterlife rather than a map, and they are "more pictorial than planimetric" (Shore 1987, 120). See, in general, Ball 1942, 7–8; Dilke 1985, 15–16; Shore 1987; Harrell and Brown 1992; *LÄ*, s.v. "Landkarte."

24. Strabo 1.1.11; Diogenes Laertius 2.1–2; and Agathermus (author of a geographical treatise in the third century C.E.) in *GGM* 2.471–87, esp. 471.

25. See also the incident with Strepsiades in Aristophanes, *Clouds* 200–17.

26. See e.g. Myres 1896 and Heidel 1937.

Herodotus' depiction of space, and the map influenced his work in important ways.[27]

Herodotus' mapping of Egypt involves the measuring, surveying, assessing, and calculating that were prerequisites for an accurate map. For
example, Herodotus' preoccupation with the calculating of distances makes
him list the dimensions of Egypt. The length of the Egyptian coastline is
60 *skhoinoi* ("ropes") or 3,000 stades, he tells us, and the road to Heliopolis is 1,500 stades (2.6–7). The latter distance is roughly the same as from
the altar of the twelve gods in Athens to the temple of Olympian Zeus in
Pisa, "roughly" because there is a difference of about 15 stades between the
two lengths. From Heliopolis to Thebes is a journey of nine days by boat,
and the distance is 4,860 stades or 81 *skhoinoi;* and the total from the sea
to Thebes is 6,120. Again, up from Thebes to Elephantine is 1,800 stades.
As Herodotus says, "these are all the stades in Egypt put together" (οὗτοι
συντιθέμενοι οἱ στάδιοι Αἰγύπτου, 2.9). Thus, as if he were describing
a geometrical figure, he offers the reader the measure of Egypt's width,
which is its coastline, and of its length, which is the distance from the sea
to Elephantine.

"These are all the stades in Egypt put together," but the country has
more stades to offer. The road to Meroë, the location of the pharaoh Min's
dam, the canal to the so-called Red Sea, land allotments to the warrior class,
Amasis' building projects, the pyramids, and the labyrinth are some of the
opportunities for Herodotus to mention length, breadth, and depth in his
narrative. He even discusses the depth of the sea at a day's sailing distance
from the coast and Psammetichus' attempt to fathom the depth of one
of the springs of the Nile (2.5, 28). It is only when one travels south and
southwest *outside* of Egypt that one's capacity to quantify space begins to
fail, and one reaches the limits of the world. The Ethiopian city of Meroë is
several days from Elephantine, and beyond Meroë is Asmach, a city settled
by Egyptian deserters (2.30). The journey from Elephantine to the deserters takes four months by river and land (2.31). Beyond these Egyptian deserters, Herodotus writes, no one can tell about the river or the land; the
space is unknown, hence unmeasurable and unmeasured. But within the
inhabited world, and particularly within Egypt, space is surveyed, ordered,
and framed.

According to our text, Egypt occupies a special place in the realm of the
spatializing discourse since it is the home of geometry. As we have seen,

27. Jacob 1992, 273–96, discusses the points raised here in connection with
maps.

Sesostris invented the space of Egypt by turning it into a land of canals and by giving each Egyptian a square of equal size, in return for which he exacted an annual sum. If an Egyptian could prove that the river had carried off a part of his allotment, the king would reduce the yearly tax for that person by a proportionate amount. It was from this that geometry (γεωμετρίη) was discovered, which eventually came to Greece (2.108–9). Egyptians invented the technique of measuring lands, and Egyptians in Herodotus' history at times have geometrical assessments undertaken, as the examples of Sesostris and Psammetichus show. Since Greeks learned the art from them, according to Herodotus, the Greeks' structuring of the world into units and measures is the result of Egyptian ingenuity, so that by measuring Egypt, Herodotus is actually applying a local system of reckoning to the land. In his world, the Egyptians use the rope (σχοῖνος) as their basic measure, just as the Greeks use the stade, and the Persians the parasang. The length of the outstretched arms, or fathom (ὀργυιή), is the measure used by men who are poor in land (γεωπείναι), the stade by those who are less so, the parasang by those who have much land, and the rope by those who have plenty (2.6). Thus, the Egyptians have plenty of land, which they assess by the rope in their geometry.

Where, or what, is the land of Egypt? The Egyptians would agree with Herodotus that natural boundaries contain Egypt and thus provide a suitable frame to its territory. To the north is the Mediterranean, which gives Herodotus' Egypt a coastline that runs from the Plinthine gulf to Lake Serbonis, which lies along the base of the Casian mountain (2.6). Herodotus writes that the land from the sea to Heliopolis is broad, flat, swampy, and muddy (2.7). South of Heliopolis the country is a narrow, confined on either side of the Nile by mountains. The mountain ranges run north to south, one on the Libyan and the other on the Arabian side. A level plain lies between the mountain ranges which is not more than two hundred stades wide at its narrowest part, and south of this the country is wide again, presumably all the way to the first cataract at Elephantine (2.8). But the river heeds no coastline, suggests Herodotus, and even carries off Egypt outside its boundary. If you are still a day's sail off-shore and drop a line into the sea, you will measure eleven fathoms and find mud, which shows how far from the land the silt from the river extends (2.5).

The Egyptian land sits between the two mountain ranges, but the country as a whole is itself an "in-between" country. Herodotus insists that all of Egypt, that is, all the country along the Nile from Elephantine to the Mediterranean, should properly take the names of the two continents Libya and Asia since it lies between them (2.15–7). The Nile, too, is an in-between stream. The river runs through the exact middle of the country, dividing it into two as far as the city of Cercasorus. Here the river separates into three ways, but the direct channel, which issues into the greatest and most famous part of the Delta, the Sebennytic mouth, flows directly through the middle of the Delta and cleaves it into two (2.17). Even the annual inundation is orderly: when the Nile floods, it spreads over the Delta and covers parts of Libya and Arabia for a distance of a two-day journey in either direction (2.19). Thus, Egypt is situated between Libya and Asia, and the Nile flows precisely through the center of Egypt. The corollary to the in-betweenness of Egypt and the Nile is supplied by the Ionians who claim that only the Delta is Egypt.[28] If the Ionians are correct, Herodotus asserts in an opaque section (2.15–16), then they should add the Delta to their list of continents—Europe, Asia, Libya—since the Delta is neither Asia nor Libya, but between Asia and Libya. However, Herodotus claims that the Delta is alluvial silt—the gift of the Nile[29]—a natural formation which has come into existence after Egyptians began living elsewhere in Egypt. Therefore, the Ionians must be wrong. Egypt is not just the Delta, the Nile must be at the center of the country, and the answer to the question "What is Egypt?" is "All of Egypt is that land which is lived in by the Egyptians" (Αἴγυπτον μὲν πᾶσαν εἶναι ταύτην τὴν ὑπ' Αἰγυπτίων οἰκεομένην, 2.17).[30]

28. The view that Egypt consists of the Delta is also alluded to in Aeschylus, *Prometheus Bound* 813–14, where Prometheus refers to "the triangular land of the Nile" (τὴν τρίγωνον ἐς χθόνα / Νειλῶτιν). Herodotus says that this was the view of the Ionians—which may be a reference to Hecateus of Miletus.

29. Herodotus uses the expression to refer not just to the Delta, but to a larger part of Egypt: "For it would be clear to anyone of sense who used his eyes, even if there were no such information, that the Egypt to which the Greeks sail is land that has been given to the Egyptians as an addition and as a gift of the river; and this is true also of the land for three days' journey above this lake [Moeris] of which we have spoken; for it is of the very same kind as the other part of the country. . . ." (2.5). Arrian offers the interesting remark that Hecateus of Miletus as well as Herodotus called Egypt "the gift of the river" (δῶρον τοῦ ποταμοῦ, *Anabasis* 5.6 = *FGrHist* 1 F 301).

30. Aristotle refers to the whole country as a deposit of the Nile; he claims that Egypt was originally not the Delta, but instead the southern region of Thebes (*Meteorology* 351 b 28ff.): "Here [in Egypt] it is obvious that the land is continually getting drier and that the whole country is a deposit of the river Nile. But because the neighbouring peoples settled in the land gradually as the marshes dried, the lapse of time has hidden the beginning of the process. Thus, all the mouths of the Nile, with the single exception of Canopus, are obviously artificial and not natural. And Egypt was originally what is called Thebes, as Homer, too, shows, modern though he is in relation to such changes. For Thebes is the place that he mentions; which implies that Memphis did not yet exist, or at any rate was not as important

Symmetry and inversion characterize Herodotus' description of Egypt, especially the first half of book 2. Whether he is observing Egyptian customs and manners or commenting on the behavior of Egyptian fish, the determining pattern is one of symmetry, inversion, and reciprocity. Moreover, it needs to be said that Herodotus writes from an Hellenocentric perspective, regardless of the identity of the ethnic group he is describing and that he uses symmetry and inversion to point to cultural difference. The ethnocentric perspective is evident also when Greeks are not directly mentioned, as in the comparison between Egyptians and Scythians. Each of these peoples is worthy of description because each offers a contrast to the Greeks in behaviors and customs: the Egyptians provide a contrast from the world of the civilized, and the Scythians from the world of the uncivilized.

Herodotus' use of symmetry and inversion is nowhere more evident than in the first half of book 2; it determines his report of Egypt's geography, its customs, and even its natural life. A striking demonstration of the technique occurs in Herodotus' description of Egyptian fish. The oppositions and rhythms of this passage need to be appreciated at length:

> Fish that go in shoals are mostly not born in the rivers; they are born and reared in the lakes. When the heat is on the fish to conceive, they go in shoals to the sea, the males leading and shedding their seed and the females following and gulping it down and, from this, conceiving. When the fish become pregnant in the ocean, they head back again to their native haunts, both males and females; but now they have not the same leaders, for the leadership has passed to the females. As these lead the shoal, they do as the males did before. They shed their eggs, like millet-seeds, several at a time, and the males, which are following, eat them up. These seeds are fish. From the surviving seeds, the ones which are not devoured, come the fish that are reared. Those of the fish that are caught as they swim toward the sea show bruises on the left of their heads; those on the return journey, on the right. This is because they swim to the sea keeping the land on their left, and, swimming back, on their right, grazing the bank and touching it, as often as they may, so that they do not lose the way through the stream. When the Nile begins to rise, hollow and marshy places near the river begin to fill first, as the water passes through to them from the river, and the moment these are full, all of them are full of small fish. How these come into being I think I understand. The year before, when the Nile receded,

as it is now" (trans. E. W. Webster). See also *Meteorology* 352 b 20 ff., quoted above, and cf. Diodorus 3.3.2.

the fish laid their eggs in the mud, and then, with the last of the water, away went the fish. Then, as the season came around and the water came upon the mud again, these fish hatched at once from the eggs that were there. (2.93)

A whole series of oppositions is made apparent in this piscatory account, including oppositions that involve gender (male and female), ecology (shore and river, river and sea), orientation (left and right), movement (to and from the sea), and potentiality (egg and fish), and these oppositions unfold along two axes, horizontal and vertical. Equally striking is the fact that this is a description not just of fish, but of Egyptian fish. It follows a claim that some Egyptians survive on fish only, and it purports to give an explanation of phenomena that occur in the Nile. Simultaneously an elaboration of a point made in the ethnographic narrative and a scientific explanation of things as they are in Egypt, the passage exemplifies the way in which Herodotus incorporates symmetry, inversion, and reciprocity into his rhetoric of alterity.

But the consequences of so systematic an application of symmetry and inversion as we find in Herodotus' text need to be appreciated. The particular signification actualized in the text does not merely present Egypt to the historian's audience in an unproblematic manner; on the contrary, defining Egypt within systematically arranged coordinates allows Herodotus to frame the country in his writing and in the minds of his readers. The position of a major geographical description at the beginning of the Egyptian account emphasizes the author's technique of spatialization. The reader or listener has to encounter this Egypt before moving on to the ethnographic or supposedly historical narratives; the region has to be oriented, marked off, blocked, measured, and surveyed; it has to be contained within its boundaries, conveniently provided by nature: a sea to the north, mountain ranges to east and west; and it has to be afixed to a material as well as a conceptual map. Egypt has to cohere with the shape, structure, and order of the cartographic imperative, and it has to answer to the demands of a world made up of three women-continents, Europe, Asia, and Libya, where Europe's length matches that of the other two combined (4.42). The position of the Nile is carefully arranged in the center of the country and as the mirror image of the Ister. The behavior of the inhabitants must also fit the pattern, so that Egyptian customs are opposite to those of all other people. Even the sex lives of the fish follow a balanced rhythm: swimming out to the sea, swimming back to their homes, they spawn a damaged brood.

For all the flexibility and relativity built into Herodotus' system of reciprocity, polarity, and inversion, the point of reference inevitably remains

Greek. In one of his inversions, Egyptian women stand while they are uri-
nating, and men sit while they do so. This example seems to undermine at
least two Greek convictions, since by assimilating the Greek man to the position of the Egyptian woman, Herodotus at the same time confounds distinctions between male and female and between Greek and barbarian.[31] But
the normative standard for Herodotus is rooted in Greek custom. When he
tells us, in the same passage, that "the most of what the Egyptians have
made of their habits and their customs are the opposite of those of other
peoples," the exaggerated claim reminds us that he is referring to the
Greeks. He is struck by the habits and customs of the Egyptians because
they are opposed to his own, and he is judging and evaluating the foreigners' behavior in relation to the behaviour of his own people. "All Herodotean
logoi are ethnocentric, with the Greeks at the centre, from 1.1.1 (ἐπὶ τήνδε
τὴν θάλασσαν)."[32] In describing and assessing different customs and habits, Herodotus moves between sameness and difference, and the point of
fixity he chooses for these cultural comparisons is undeniably Greek.

Consider his description of Egyptian customs. Herodotus applies symmetry, inversion, polarity (ἔμπαλιν, 2.35), and analogy (ὡς ἐγὼ συμβάλ-
λομαι τοῖσι ἐμφανέσι τὰ μὴ γιγνωσκόμενα τεκμαιρόμενος, 2.33) to
the case of Egypt, and he does so within the constraints of a system based
on environmental determinism. The locus classicus for the belief that environmental factors affect national character is the Hippocratic treatise *Airs
Waters Places* (12–24), though traces of the view are also discernible in the
works of Sophocles and other writers.[33] The belief is even stated explicitly
in the first sentence of Edward William Lane's popular account, *Manners
and Customs of the Modern Egyptians*, first published in 1836.[34] Herodotus combines inversions and oppositions with environmental determinism;
for him, just as the Egyptians have a peculiar climate and a unique river,
so they have made their habits and customs opposite to those of other peoples (2.35).

> Among them, the women run the market and shops, the men weave
> at home; and whereas in weaving all others push the woof upwards,

31. See Cartledge 1993, 58–59.
32. Lateiner 1989, 147.
33. Lloyd 1976, 146–47; Thomas 2000, ch. 4.
34. Lane's introduction begins with the following words: "It is generally observed that many of the most remarkable peculiarities in the manners, customs,
and character of a nation are attributable to the physical peculiarities of the country. Such causes, in an especial manner, affect the moral and social state of the modern Egyptians. . . ."

the Egyptians push it downwards. Men carry burdens on their heads, women on their shoulders. Women urinate standing, men sitting. They relieve nature indoors and eat outdoors in the streets, giving the reason that things unseemly but necessary should be done in secret, things not unseemly should be done openly. No woman is dedicated to any god, male or female; men are dedicated to all deities, male or female. Sons are not compelled against their will to support their parents, but daughters must do so though they be unwilling.

Everywhere else, priests of the gods wear their hair long; in Egypt they are shaven. Among all other men, it is the custom, in mourning, for those who are especially afflicted to have their heads shaven; Egyptians are shaven at other times, but after a death they let their hair and beard grow. Other people keep the daily life of animals separate from their own, but the Egyptians live with their animals in the house. Whereas all others live on wheat and barley, it is the greatest disgrace for an Egyptian so to live; they make food from a coarse grain which some call spelt. They knead dough with their feet, and gather mud and dung with their hands. Other men leave the genitals as they were at birth, except for those who learned from the Egyptians, but the Egyptians circumcise. Every man has two garments, every woman only one. The rings and sheets of sail are made fast elsewhere outside the boat, but inside it in Egypt. The Greeks write and calculate by moving the hand from left to right, but the Egyptians from right to left. That is what they *do*, but they *say* they are moving to the right and the Greeks to the left. They use two different kinds of writing, one of which is called sacred and the other common. (2.35–36)

As with Herodotus' observations of Egyptian fish, the range of oppositions is breathtaking, and again the oppositions are an integral part of an ethnographic narrative of difference. The presumption to speak for "everywhere else" and for "all others," as we saw, points to Herodotus' Hellenocentrism, since the field of reference is Greek rather than universal: the contrast is between Egyptians and Greeks, no matter what universality is imputed to Hellenic custom by the writer. The claim to universality is also inconsistent, since Herodotus acknowledges the limits of his inquiries at other points in his history and admits that his ethnography is partial and incomplete. In this regard, it should be stated that some ancient Greeks were unable to accept the validity of all of Herodotus' reports concerning non-Greek peoples. Aristotle, for example, referred to his account of Egyptian fish as "a very simple-minded and popular story," and called him a *mythologos*.[35]

---

35. Aristotle, *Generation of Animals* 3.5 (755b6); Aristotle's knowledge of Herodotus is also apparent elsewhere in his works, e.g. *History of Animals* 8.28.3 (606), 3.22 (523); and *Poetics* 9.2 (1451); and see chapter 7, below.

The complexity and Hellenocentrism of Herodotus' system, which perceives the world through a grid of symmetry and inversion, are brought out with force in the intercultural comparison between Scythia and Egypt. As Hartog and James Redfied have shown, the narrative offers a number of comparisons between Scythia and Egypt, with Greece occupying the implicit and excluded position of the third term.[36] Although Herodotus does not himself always oppose the two cultures, the contrast is stark and unavoidable. Each culture poses a countermodel for Greeks, one by the elaboration of its civilization, the other by its lack of civilized life. Greece remains the absent third term, from which the polarities flow outward in search of comparison and contrast, and to which they ultimately return bringing clarity and illumination. The examples and oppositions are copious and they bear repeating in detail. I present them as follows:

> Egypt has more wonders than any other country (2.35). Scythia's rivers
> are its wonder; apart from its rivers, Scythia has only one wonder, the
> footprint of Heracles (4.82). The Scythians claim they are the youngest
> of all people (4.5). The Egyptians used to claim they were the oldest
> until the experiment of Psammetichus proved otherwise (2.2). The
> Egyptians keep records and annals (2.77, 145), the Scythians have no
> continuous recorded history. Egyptian inventions are the most numer-
> ous in the world. The one thing that the Scythians have invented better
> than any other people is their ability to flee the conqueror: if the Scyth-
> ians wish to avoid their enemy, that enemy cannot engage them (4.46).
> The Egyptians worship different deities in different ways and in various
> places. The Scythians all revere the same few gods, although the Royal
> Scythians also offer sacrifice to Poseidon (4.59). The Egyptians seem to
> have invented the rites of Dionysus (2.49); the Scythians find it shame-
> ful to indulge in Dionysiac orgies (4.79). Egyptians do not practice hu-
> man sacrifice (2.45). Scythians revel in human sacrifice, drink the blood
> of their enemies, and use human blood during their oath-taking cere-
> monies (4.64, 70).
>   Turning to spatial and geographical phenomena, Scythia and Egypt
> are closed systems, neither borrowing customs from other people (2.79,
> 91; 4.76). The furthest the Egyptians have traveled is to Scythia (2.103).
> The furthest travel of the Scythians brings them into contact with the
> Egyptian Psammetichus, who persuaded them to go no further south
> than Palestine (1.105). Both are "in-between" countries, since Scythia
> sits between Europe and Asia, and Egypt between Libya and Asia. He-
> rodotus attributes a major river to both regions, and the rivers are im-

36. See Hartog 1988, 15–19, and his article in *Annales ESC* 34 (1979), 1137–54, which is the basis for Redfield 1985. I have relied especially on Redfield's article for the comparison between Egypt and Scythia.

portant points of comparison: in one instance, he notes that the Nile is "equal" to the Ister (2.34), in another, that they are "equal in measure" (2.33). He describes the upper course of the Nile by analogy with the known lower section of the Ister, and he uses the known lower section of the Nile to give the correct orientation of the equivalent part of the Ister (2.33). The Nile divides Egypt into two, and the Ister divides Europe into two. The Nile rises among the desolate and marginal Libyans, the Ister among the desolate and marginal Celts (2.33, 4.49). The one river rises in the west, and then flows east before turning *north* into Egypt, the other rises in the west, and then flows east before turning *south* into Scythia. The Nile issues into Egypt, which lies opposite the mountainous part of Cilicia on the northeast coast of the Mediterranean; from there to Sinope on the Black Sea is a straight journey for about five days; Sinope is opposite to the Ister where it issues into the sea (2.34). Hence, the Nile is equal and opposite to the Ister. The rivers are mirror images of each other at a horizontal plane running across the length of the Mediterranean.

Scythia has many rivers whereas Egypt has only one (4.47–53, 82); but the Egyptian river was divided by Sesostris into numerous canals, the number of which is only slightly greater than the Scythian rivers (4.47). Egyptian canals are artificial and built by humans, Scythian rivers are natural. Before Sesostris, Min, the first ruler of Egypt, also sought to influence the course of the river. In Min's time, the northern part of Egypt was marsh land (2.4); but afterward the Egyptians controlled the river, and made the Delta fit for inhabitation (2.15). On the other hand, the Scythian territory existed before the Scythians and was empty (4.5–11). While the Egyptians live in fixed settlements and towns, the Scythians are nomadic. The division of the Nile into canals prevents the Egyptians from using carts and horses (2.108), but the nomadic Scythians live in wagons and ride horses. There is no rain in Egypt (2.14), but the country gets its water from the Nile, which contrary to all other rivers rises in the summer and sinks low during the winter (2.19). In Scythia, the winter is different from winter in all the other parts of the world since hardly any rain falls in that season; however, the rain hardly ever stops during the summer (4.28).

There is no end to the search for order and pattern in Herodotus' work,[37] but, in fact, he is not the first or the only Greek writer to fashion his work in accordance with a system of symmetry or inversion.[38] The sophistic polarity between *physis* and *nomos,* the Aristotelian table of opposites attributed to a Pythagorean source (*Metaphysics* 586a), the culture-bound

37. See e.g. Immerwahr 1966, 49 ff.; Froidefond 1971, 115–207; Lachenaud 1980; Longo 1986; Gianotti 1988; Gould 1989, 86–109.
38. Lloyd 1966.

antitheses of man and woman or free and slave, and the pervasive use in Greek of *men-de* clauses are instances of dual symbolic classification in Greek thought.[39] While the approach has some explanatory power, it is not enough to say that Herodotus' spatializing discourse works to principles of symmetry and inversion. Interpreting Herodotus' text in this way is useful to the degree that it lets us see some of his structuring techniques, but such an interpretation would inevitably lead us to a totalizing reading that would subsume all of the text within a dyad and would contravene an analysis the purpose of which is to examine the constitutive elements of a spatializing discourse. Without entering into the intentional fallacy, we can also state that in attributing this system to Herodotus' text, we are coming close to repeating a rhetorical and thematic signification constructed by the author himself, and hence that we are subject to the manipulation of the text. Our notion that Herodotus uses a system of symmetry and inversion may be itself the mechanical elaboration of a controlling Herodotean trope. If the text does not begin to deconstruct at this point, at least the complications associated with these statements can easily be multiplied, and impel us into deep aporia.

Instead of following the lead of this global binarism, I would rather draw attention to the ethnographic effects of Herodotus' reliance on polarity and inversion. In the classical period itself, Sophocles and the fourth-century comic poet Anaxandrides, among others, used inversions to mark out differences between Greeks and Egyptians.[40] In the fifteenth century, Roberto

---

39. Vidal-Naquet 1986, 61–82; Cartledge 1993, 13–16, 58–59.

40. See Sophocles, *Oedipus at Colonus* 337–45, which is probably responding to Herodotus (the play was first produced in 401). The fragment from Anaxandrides' play *Cities* is worth considering in detail: "Anaxandrides in *Cities* says, referring to the Egyptians:

[Demos to Egypt:]
I couldn't have allied myself with you,
Our ways and customs differing as they do.
I sacrifice to the gods, to bulls you kneel,
Your greatest god's our greatest treat, the eel;
You don't eat pork; it's quite my favorite meat;
Your worship your dog, mine I always beat
When he's caught stealing; priests stay whole with us,
With you they're gelded eunuchs; if poor puss
Appears in pain you weep, I kill and skin her;
To me the mouse is nought, you see 'power' in her."
    (*Athenaeus* 7.299f = fr. 40 PCG, trans. J. M. Edmonds)
The reference to priests is also noticed by Eustathius, with interesting commentary. See the notes to fr. 40 in *PCG*.

da Sanseverino, an Italian condottiere, wrote a Herodotean description in the account of his travels to Egypt and the Middle East.[41] In his version, slaves are masters, the mad are considered saints, women wear trousers, and donkeys have their hair cut. Such inversions were not uncommon in travel accounts from the period, Jeannine Guérin Dalle Mese has shown, and they occur in the writings of Pietra Martire d'Anghiera, Jean Palerne, and Francesco Suriano, all of whom wrote works about their journeys to Egypt.[42] But the impact of Herodotus' inversions is hardly restricted just to Western observers of Egypt, and no less an observer than al-Biruni, whose travels to India occurred in the eleventh century, came up with this intensely oppositional description:

> We shall now speak of certain strange manners and customs of the Hindus. The strangeness of a thing evidently rests on the fact that it occurs but rarely, and that we seldom have the opportunity of witnessing it. If such strangeness reaches a high degree, the thing becomes a curiosity, or even something like a miracle, which is no longer in accordance with the ordinary laws of nature, and which seems chimerical as long as it has not been witnessed. Many Hindu customs differ from those of our country and of our times to such a degree as to appear to us simply monstrous. One might almost think that they had intentionally changed them into the opposite, for *our* customs do not resemble theirs, but are the very reverse; and if ever a custom of *theirs* resembles one of *ours*, it has certainly just the opposite meaning.
> They do not cut any of the hair of the body. Originally they went naked in consequence of the heat, and by not cutting the hair of the head they intended to prevent sunstroke.
> They divide the moustache into single plaits. . . .
> They let the nails grow long. . . .
> The Hindus eat singly, one by one, ...
> They have red teeth in consequence of eating areca-nuts with betel-leaves and chalk.

41. Roberto da Sanseverino, in G. Maruffi, ed., *Viaggio in Terra Santa per Roberto da Sanseverino* (Bologna, 1888), 150–51, quoted in Guérin Dalle Mese 1991, 191: "E per dire una piacevolezza, per recreazione de li animi de quelli che legano questo itenerario, quattro cosse tra l'altre sono in tute quelle parte de' Mori molto differente e contrarie a le nostre de ponente e ad ogno altro politico vivere: la prima è perchè, come è dicto, niuno può esser soldano che non sia schiavo venduto, cioè cristiano renegato, ch'è tanto a dire questo che li schiavi sono signori; la seconda, li mati sono reputati e tenuti per sancti, perchè dicono che non possano più pecare, e da tuti sono ben veduti, ben tractati e ben onorati; la terza, le femine portano brage, e li omini comunemente non le portano; la quarta, li asini loro sono rasi, e li omini non portano le barbe."
42. See Guérin Dalle Mese 1991, 190–202.

They drink wine before having eaten anything. . . .
They beat the cymbals with a stick.
They use turbans for trousers. . . .[43]

One does not know what is more remarkable, the details that al-Biruni offers, or the transference of the system from Egypt to India. But in the use of inversions that simultaneously betray their own prejudices and serve as markers of cultural difference, these voyagers are the heirs of Herodotus.

THE TRAVELER'S EYE

How are the implications of Herodotus' presentation of Egyptian space played out at the level of the narrative? The narrator maintains his authority over space by a gesture that depicts the Egyptian landscape in terms that suggest his own ability to possess and judge the scene. One of the strategies at work in Herodotus' text is the mastery predicated between the narrator and space, and there are obvious ways in which the text conveys this mastery to the reader. First, the narrator speaks out of a position of authority. He arranges his material, places his words here or there, and in this or that manner, dispenses emphasis to a point, or passes lightly over a detail. He represents, signifies, and configures space in his attempt to abbreviate the distance between what is language and what is not. He sees, hears, inquires, measures, and records the results of his labors: "Herodotus of Halicarnassus sets forth here the results of his inquiry" (Ἡροδότου Ἁλικαρνησσέος ἱστορίης ἀπόδεξις ἥδε).

Second, the narrator uses the authoritative vantage point to instill belief in his account of space.[44] He quotes the archives of Egyptian priests, reports things that he has himself seen or heard, and invokes sources in a variety of ways. In addition, he sometimes mentions variant accounts without appearing to vouch for the belief of any one in particular. The quoting of sources, even when the narrator eschews entering into the question of their veracity, is a means of winning over the reader's sympathies and a subtle way of eliciting the reader's support on the many occasions when he presents evidence without calling attention to truth or falsity. As Michel de Certeau writes of quoted language, "With its referential function, it introduces into the text an effect of reality; . . . it discretely functions like a machinery that extracts from the citation a verisimilitude of narrative and a validation of knowledge. It produces a sense of reliability."[45] Third, the text

43. Sachau 1992, vol. 1, 179–80.
44. For the second and third points discussed here, see Hartog 1988.
45. de Certeau 1988, 94.

mediates the unknown by the familiar, and it presents space in Greek terms and as a Greek construct. The names of Greek winds designate the points of the compass, for example, and the stade functions as the basic unit of length to which all other linear quantities may be assimilated. Of course, Herodotus was a Greek writing in Greek, and therefore it would have been impossible for him not to fashion a text that was to some extent Helleno-centric. However, Herodotus the "translator" assumes authority in the eyes of his readers because before he translates, he has to have the capacity to convert alien discourses and knowledge into a Greek idiom.

In her study of the rhetoric used by Victorian explorers of the Nile and Africa, Mary Louise Pratt writes about the "monarch-of-all-I-survey" passages that occur repeatedly in travel accounts of the period. The "relation of *mastery* predicated between the seer and the seen" that Pratt finds in the literature is evident also in the panoptic technique that appears in Herodotus' landscape descriptions.[46] The narrator's gaze is all-encompassing and it reveals knowledge of the entire Egyptian landscape, from the north to the south, from the east to the west. The reader finds the measurements of extraordinary distances supplied by the text down to the last stade, for instance, Heliopolis is 81 *skhoinoi* or 4,680 stades from Thebes (2.9). Even apart from the access to feats of calculation and surveying that such figures imply, the panoptic gaze determines the shape of various geographical sections:

> But for one going (ἰόντι) further and above Heliopolis, Egypt is a narrow country. On the one side the mountains of Arabia stretch along it, bearing from north to south and even stretching toward what is called the Erythraean Sea. In it are the quarries that were cut out for the pyramids that are in Memphis. This way the mountains turn and end in those places of which I speak. Their greatest length from east to west is, I learn, a two months' journey, and the parts toward the east yield frankincense. That is this range of mountains. But, towards Libya, Egypt is bounded by another range of rocky mountains, wherein are the pyramids. These mountains are all covered in sand, and they run in the same direction as the Arabian hills, which run southward. Above Heliopolis there is not much land—not, that is, of land that is Egypt;

46. Pratt 1992, 204. For a discussion of the monarch-of-all-I-survey trope in travel writing, see Pratt 1992, esp. 201–8. The expression occurs first in William Cowper's poetry *(Verses Supposed to be Written by Alexander Selkirk)*, and then explicitly in travel writings about Egypt as well. See W. H. Bartlett, *The Nile Boat, or Glimpses of the Land of Egypt* (London, 1849), 109: "I was a monarch of all I surveyed, and amused myself with arranging everything in the nicest order." On this subject, see also Gregory 1999, 120–31.

for here Egypt is narrow for the distance of a fourteen days' journey upstream the river. Between these aforementioned mountain ranges the land is flat, and it seems to me that, at its narrowest, it is not more than two hundred stades from the Arabian mountains to those that are called Libyan. Beyond this Egypt is again a wide country. Such is the nature of this land. (2.8–9)

The passage provides a vast range of information about a region that is a significant distance beyond Heliopolis. We read that the mountains on the Arabian side of the Nile extend all the way to the Erythraean Sea. But before the narrator moves further, he informs the reader that the stones used in the pyramids of Memphis were quarried from these mountains and that the eastern parts yield frankincense. Then the narrative shifts to the mountains on the Libyan side, and we find out the salient features of these geological formations. After the account of the mountains on the Libyan side comes a description of the land up to Thebes. Thus, the vision of the reader traverses the landscape from Heliopolis to Thebes, and the text obliges with details about distance and appearance. As he continues his report beyond the passage cited, the narrator's field of information comes to include all of Egypt from the Mediterranean Sea to the land south of Elephantine, to the west to Libya and to the east to the Erythraean Sea. Of course, Herodotus does not later shy from giving an account of the inhabited world in his narrative. As far as Egypt is concerned, it is striking that the narrative does not present the country from a centrally fixed point of view. The narrator's gaze moves over and along with the space that he is describing. Since the space under consideration is enormous, however, the narrator filters it to the reader in a highly reductive and totalizing manner.

The discourse that uses the principle of panopticism serves to naturalize the space of Egypt by flattening and denuding it. The excerpt contains no reference to human beings other than the narrator, and it presents to the reader a landscape void of people. At the beginning, an impersonal dative participle with no clear antecedent, "for one going" (ἰόντι), directs the reader's attention to the absence of a distinctive human element in the account. The landscape appears as it would to an unnamed person traveling above Heliopolis. In fact, the person's journey (2.5–9, 29–31) from the Mediterranean coast to Elephantine and further guides the orientation and sequence of the geographical sections in general. But no human being could command the breathtaking sweep of the narrative, and the perspective offered by the description contrasts with the suggestion of an anonymous traveler moving south along the Nile. The text detaches the space of Egypt from its residents and describes the region's geographical features.

Only after it has established the coordinates of this discursive spatialization does it enter into a discussion of the Egyptians. Absent, too, are aesthetic judgments of any sort. The narrative does not qualify the beauty, appeal, attractiveness, or even the color of the mountains or the countryside. This is Egypt, measured, packaged, quantified, stripped of its inhabitants, and lacking any aesthetic flavor. Nature itself has produced this Egypt, and the narrative presents it to the reader in a quasi-direct fashion.

When the narrator does turn to a sustained discussion of the people, he presents them within the system of symmetries and oppositions outlined above. These Egyptians live in no town or village in particular, they have no distinctive names, their customs are common to all Egyptians, and they exist only in so far as they fit the system. It is only after this oppositional discourse of Egyptian behavior that the text moves on to name specific practices in the context of particular locales, although it is still restrained in naming individual Egyptians until the account of the kings gets underway (2.99). Textual reticence about the names of Egyptians, apart from a few kings, occurs in the early passages despite the fact that Herodotus maintains that he compiled the relevant sections on the basis of his sight (ὄψις), his judgment (γνώμη), and his inquiries (ἱστορίη, 2.99). He adds that he bases his later account of the kings (i.e., 2.99–182) on Egyptian logoi as he heard them, with his eyes again acting as supplementary tools, but these sources, too, permit him to name only royal Egyptians and not commoners. If Egypt is unable to survive without kings, and its space is constantly and pervasively charged with autocratic power, then the tyranny of the kings over the space of Egypt finds a parallel in the mastery of the narrator over the landscape.

EGYPTIAN SPACE

Among the lines of inquiry opened up by Herodotus' work is the use of space as part of a meditation on different ethnic groups and on different political institutions. Space in Herodotus' text is integral to the distinctions explored by the historian between the world of the polis and the world of the barbarian, between democracy and autocracy, and between Greeks and non-Greeks. The historian asks his readers to contemplate what it means to live in a space or place and what the space says about its inhabitants, and to consider the relationship that a people has with the space which it inhabits. Concerning the description of Egypt, a double impetus drives the spatial elaboration in Herodotus' work, where the first realizes a space organized on principles of geometry and the second presents transgressions of the same space as evidence of the autocrat's political mastery. Accordingly Herodotus first offers a carefully geometrized and symmetrized model in the manner recounted above, as he conceptualizes the country and the landscape. But secondly, the relationship that he institutes between the Egyptian king and the country revolves around issues of absolute power and transgression. The king treats Egypt as his own personal possession, subjects it to whatever changes suit his whims and desires, and exults in marking it with vain monuments such as pyramids, palaces, and temples. Thus, Herodotus' exposition of Egyptian space is central to his rhetoric of otherness and drives his presentation of political differences between Greeks and Egyptians.

Since by commenting on autocracy and power Herodotus' Egyptian descriptions have a political dimension, it will be worthwhile here to state first the Greek and then the Egyptian contexts to his spatial politics. As with the case of maps discussed earlier in the chapter, the Greek polis lies in the background to Herodotus' inquiries about foreign communities, and its shape and scheme provided him with a paradigmatic example against which he represented other settlements. Athens can be mentioned here not only because Athens is the best known of the Greek city-states, but also because it was the city where Herodotus gave readings of his work and in which he lived for part of his adult life. As Jean-Pierre Vernant has indicated, Athens appropriated the model of the house with the hearth at its center by producing a communal hearth with the agora, acropolis, and political institutions at its center. Following Vernant, Pierre Lévêque and Pierre Vidal-Naquet have also pointed to the isonomic self-image of the democratic city, and to the geometrical reciprocity and symmetry that informed civic space. Thus, the post-Cleisthenic community was based on a clearly demarcated civic and political center, the agora and the acropolis, in relation to which "all the various points occupied by the citizens appear symmetrical and reversible."[47] Further, sanctuaries, monumental buildings, and sacred cult-sites also determined the space of the Greek city-state during its formative development in the archaic and classical periods. François de Polignac has demonstrated how the sanctuary at the margin of the urban community stood for the city's proprietorship over the sanctuary and how the sanctuary's monumental buildings denoted the collective na-

47. See Lévêque and Vidal-Naquet 1996 and Vernant 1983, 214, with 176–89; cf. Vernant 1982, 125–26. Vernant's emphasis on a fixed, circular, and central hearth should be read against the archaeological evidence described in Jameson 1990, 105–6, and the sociological analysis in Lefebvre 1991, 246–50, 330–35.

ture of the city's decision-making apparatus.[48] At several levels, therefore, the democratic ideology of the polis in its own self-image was transferred onto spatial conceptualizations as well.

It hardly needs to be said that the fraudulence of this model of the democratic city is evident to modern observers from the mechanisms of exclusion and inclusion that also characterized Athens in the fifth century. For one thing, principles of *isonomia*, reversibility, and symmetry collapsed when it came to Athens' aggressive behavior and imperialism over other city-states. Concerning the specific issue of space and gender, moreover, the texts associate Athenian women more with the domestic interior of the household than with the public life outside the home.[49] This is a telling indication of the situation of women in the androcentric worldview, since the exclusion of women from the political center of power was replicated on the intellectual plane in terms of a spatial discourse. In this sense, Athenian women, even those freeborn and of citizen families, were localized to a space inhabited by barbarians, metics, and slaves. For all the delusions and fictions of Athenian spatial ideology, however, the notions of equality, symmetry, and reversibility were central to the ancient city's image of itself as a democracy. In this image, power was placed in the center and subject to open discussion and debate, while decisions were made by the law courts and the Assembly, made up of Athenian citizens, and not by tyrants or autocrats. Despite the partial and illegitimate status of the democracy, then, the mainstream Athenian conceptualization of sociopolitical space was closely connected to the practice of open citizenship and the exercise of citizens' rights.

This conceptualization of space, as Lévêque and Vidal-Naquet suggested, was linked by Herodotus as well to the isonomic democracy of Athens.[50] If

48. See de Polignac 1995.

49. If the archaeological evidence belies the seclusion of women that the texts call for, however, then the displacement of women was ideological rather than physical. The archaeological material is presented thus in Jameson 1990, against Walker 1983. For the theoretical problems involved in writing about Greek concepts of space, see Algra 1995, 7–30.

50. Lévêque and Vidal-Naquet 1996, chs. 4–5. Herodotus himself offers no lengthy and explicit commentary on democracy in his own voice (he uses *demokratia* or a variant three times in his work), and I do not wish to simplify his attitude to this political system and to *isonomia*, nor do I wish to suggest that he was an unabashed admirer of Athenian democracy. For Herodotus' political theory, see Raaflaub 1987; Saxonhouse 1996, ch. 2; and Kurke 1999, ch. 3. Saxonhouse notes the historian's emphasis on equality (*isonomia* and *isegoria*) rather than on democracy per se; Kurke finds stories that valorize as well as condemn *isonomia*, but ultimately sees traces of allegiances to *isonomia* in the histories.

Herodotus' interest in linking the spatial and the sociopolitical comes from his Greek background and informs his geographies, it is remarkable to see the varied uses he makes of his spatializing discourse: where in the Greek case he uses symmetry and geometry to develop his presentation of equality under the law, in the Egyptian case he uses symmetry and geometry to describe the autocratic, hubristic, and transgressive rule of kings. His presentation of Egyptian space as symmetrical and geometrical is not entirely inconsistent with Egyptians' representations of their own country. Nevertheless, whereas Egyptians also conceived of their country in terms of symmetries, axes, and limits, they conceptualized the relationship between the king and space in ways quite different from Herodotus' in his work.[51] Both the overlaps and the discrepancies are important to our understanding of Herodotus' ethnographic and political observations, and can be spelled out in slightly greater detail.

For an example of the Egyptian concern with symmetry, the position of the Nile within Egyptian thought is an excellent reference point. Just as Greek texts often assume the center of the earth to be at Delphi, Egyptian writers take the centrality of the Nile for granted.[52] The Nile rises in the south, flows over five cataracts, contributes to a Deltaic formation, and empties into the Mediterranean Sea. It would be apparent to a person standing on the banks of the river at Thebes, say, that the stream flows from the south to the north. Accordingly, the sense of orientation expressed in Egyptian texts is toward the south; the Egyptians australized themselves toward the source of the Nile. When one travels north in Egyptian texts, one travels downstream, and to go south, one moves upstream. Evidence from the later period contains descriptions of property in which the points of the compass are supplied in the series south, north, east, west, which implies that the primary orientation of the writers was directed toward the south.[53] Since one oriented oneself toward the source of the river, one could refer to the south by saying "face," while the normal expression for "north" can be linked to "back of the head." The word for "east" is the same as that for "left" and, correspondingly, the same word denotes "west" and "right."[54] Since the Euphrates flows south rather than north, the Egyptian texts describe it as "that circling water which goes downstream in going up-

51. Wilson, in Frankfort et al. 1949, 39–70, and Lesko 1991, 116–22, are helpful for their discussions of Egyptian views of space.

52. For this discussion of the Nile, see e.g. Wilson in Frankfort et al. 1949, 39–70; Morenz 1973, 46–47; Lesko 1991, 117.

53. Shore 1987, 127–28.

54. Sethe 1922. See Plutarch, *On Isis and Osiris* 32.

stream," or "that inverted water which goes downstream by going south."
Since it rains very seldom in Egypt, lands where it does rain often are said
to have a "Nile in the sky." The hieroglyphic word for non-Egyptian lands
(khasut) is the same as that which means "hill country" or "desert," thus
contrasting, at least at the level of signs, domestic fertility with what is foreign, barren, sterile, and non-Nilotic.[55] In stressing the centrality of the
river to the civilization, Herodotus is thus articulating a position that is attested thoroughly in local traditions.

But this picture of an Egypt axially oriented along the Nile, a picture
that is reinforced by Herodotus, needs to be qualified in ways that far ex-
ceed the Greek writer's grasp of the country. In addition to the south-north
axis of the river, there was the east-west axis of the moving sun.[56] According to the Pyramid Texts, the day-barque ferried the solar sphere across
from the east to the west during the day, and then the night-barque from
west to east below the earth at night. Thus, in Akhenaten's new capital city
of Akhetaten, "[t]he main thoroughfares of the capital . . . ran parallel to
the course of the Nile, cut at right angles by the path of the sun, so that cir-
culatory patterns in the city replicated the form and movement of the cosmos."[57] Egyptian texts privilege the eastern end of the east-west axis since
the orient is the land of the sun's appearance, its rising and birth, while the
occident is connected with the sun's disappearance, its setting and death;
hence, the east was also "god's land." And just as the Nilotic axis divided
the country into east and west, or left and right, the plane of the sun's displacement separated the two regions of Upper Egypt and Lower Egypt.

The symmetry behind such notions as an east-west axis or the division
between Upper Egypt and Lower Egypt informed other areas of Egyptian
belief and perhaps even led to the conceptualization of a vertical axis, for
the sky had its counterheaven and the earth an underworld. The concept
of symmetry itself, which admits of certain complications, has important
ramifications for Egyptian thought and practice. The symmetry also appears in Egyptian art and architecture, so that temples were aligned along
a definite axis. However, the symmetry in temples also accepted minor
variations from the scheme, and the ideal was "lively yet careful deviation
from a set pattern."[58] Moreover, while symmetrical principles may have

55. The ancient name for Egypt is *Kmt*, or "Black Land," the land of black alluvial silt, which Egyptians distinguished from *Dsrt*, or "Red Land," the desert.
56. *LÄ*, s.v. "Weltbild."
57. Selden 1998b, 398.
58. Hornung 1992, 82.

contributed to the organizing of earth and sky, Egypt's boundaries, though the work of nature itself, were almost, but not quite, symmetrically arranged: the first Nile cataract at Aswan, the Red Sea, Sinai, the Mediterranean Sea, and the Libyan desert. As Herodotus perhaps implies, nature had given these borders to Egypt, and the pharaohs would protect the flat lands within; boundary stones in Nubia threatened trespassers with death. From another standpoint, however, the boundaries of Egypt were infinite, since the pharaohs officially presented themselves as rulers of the whole world.[59]

Although Herodotus presents the kings as transgressing space and as doing violence to the natural symmetry of things, the Egyptian representations of the pharaohs' building activities point not to transgression and violation, but rather to extension and replication. The king's building projects involved not just numerous workers and administrators, but also nearby settlements to hold the staff and allow for planning of the building activities. In his discussion of the Egyptian background to Callimachus' poetry, Daniel L. Selden remarks that these affiliated settlements show "that the Egyptian city differed in fundamental ways from the Greek *polis:* never an originary or self-determining corporation, Egyptian towns always followed from and remained dependent on a conceptually prior religious or royal building."[60] Far from being just monuments to the king's vanity, as Herodotus implies, these building projects brought together a diverse group of interconnected interests and workers. Selden correctly observes how "such architectural projects were fundamental to the maintenance and growth of the Egyptian state, which coalesced politically, economically, and culturally around monumental building projects of this type, particularly temples, palaces, and tombs."[61]

It was the Egyptian temple, furthermore, that served as the model for all kinds of monumental building projects, whether they were temples, palaces, or tombs. The temple ("god's house") itself was modeled both on the cosmos and the creation. The floor of the temple gradually rose as it progressed toward the sanctuary, which itself was a symbol of the primeval

---

59. See e.g. an inscription erected by Queen Hatshepsut: "Lo, the god knows me well, Amun, Lord of Thrones-of-the-Two-Lands; he made me rule Black Land and Red Land as reward; no one rebels against me in all lands. All foreign lands are my subjects; he placed my border at the limits of heaven" (Lichtheim 1976, 28–29, translation modified). On ancient Egyptian limits and symmetries, see Hornung 1992, 73–92.

60. Selden 1998b, 395.

61. Selden 1998b, 394

mound that had emerged from the primordial waters of Nun. In addition, the hieroglyphic texts and illustrations of deities on the walls were such that it would be true to echo Erik Hornung's assessment that "the temple mirrors the entire cosmos."[62] This basic cosmological scheme was replicated in Egyptian tombs, pyramids, palaces, and urban settlements. It is not unusual to find Egyptian texts of different historical periods referring to pyramids or cities as primeval mounds. Even Alexandria, for all its Greek background, was founded on a site "clearly reminiscent of creation's primeval mound," and the city's "site and layout . . . were classically Egyptian in character."[63] In short, despite the suggestions made by Herodotus, the monumental building project in Egypt was not presented or conceived as a topographical violation or spatial transgression, but rather in terms of continuation, consolidation, and repetition.

Ultimately, Herodotus' reflection on Egyptian space is a political declaration. Like the domestic spaces of the Greek city-states, Egyptian geography can be described in the language of geometry and symmetry, but unlike the Greek city-states, Egyptian spatial symmetries do not for Herodotus betoken an open democracy or the popular exercise of power, but rather are constructed in such a way as to invite their repeated and constant violation by kings. This relationship between the Egyptian kings and space is not surprising coming from the historian who felt the country was so soaked in despotic power that he once remarked it was impossible for Egyptians to exist without a king. On the other hand, seeing the building activities of Egyptian kings as transgressive and as monuments to personal vanity runs counter to Egyptian views of pharaonic building projects. Even as it ignores Egyptian attitudes to monumental building projects, such a gesture relies on the distinction between the world of the pseudodemocratic polis and the world of the monarch, between freedom and despotic rule, and between the Greek and the barbarian. Beneath Herodotus' spatial descriptions lies a conviction that connects the polis to autonomy and equality under the law, and the supposition that Egyptian barbarians are incapable of living in democratic freedom.

62. Hornung 1992, 116.
63. Selden 1998b, 398–99. For Alexandria, see also chapter 7.

3   In an Antique Land

In *A Thousand Miles up the Nile* of 1877, Amelia Edwards, a founder of the Egypt Exploration Fund and of a chair of Egyptology in University College London, wrote of the native Egyptian "as wearing the same loincloth, plying the same shaduf, ploughing with the same plough, preparing the same food in the same way and eating it with his fingers from the same bowl as did his forefathers of six thousand years ago."[1] In one form or another, the idea of Egypt as a country rooted in the distant past has featured in Western descriptions since antiquity. On more or less the same scaffolding as Edwards, Gustave Flaubert had earlier put together his own elaboration of the idea of Egyptian antiquity. In a letter written in Cairo and dated January 15, 1850, he writes of his impressions of Egypt. The letter forms part of an unimpeachable pattern of appreciating Egypt in an antique vein from Herodotus' words to the tourist guidebooks of today.

> Anyone who is a little attentive *re*discovers here much more than he discovers. The seeds of a thousand notions that one carried within oneself grow and become more definite, like so many refreshed memories. Thus, as soon as I landed at Alexandria I saw before me, alive, the anatomy of the Egyptian sculptures: the high shoulders, long torso, thin legs,

---

1. Edwards 1877, ix. In 1863, Lucie Duff Gordon wrote even more evocatively, "Nothing is more striking to me than the way in which one is constantly reminded of Herodotus. The Christianity and the Islam of this country are full of the ancient worship, and the sacred animals have all taken service with Muslim saints. . . . This country is a palimpsest in which the Bible is written over Herodotus, and the Koran over that. In towns the Koran is most visible, in the country Herodotus" (Gordon 1969, 65). On Gordon's letters from Egypt, see Gendron 1986. The work of authors such as Edwards and Gordon raises questions about Orientalism and European travel writing about Egypt in the nineteenth century: on this subject, see the sources and analysis in Gregory 1999.

etc. The dances that we have had performed for us are of too hieratic a character not to have come from the dances of the old Orient, which is always young because nothing changes. Here the Bible is a picture of life today. Do you know that until a few years ago the murderer of an ox was still punished by death, exactly as in the time of Apis?[2]

Flaubert's reference to the Bible may be consistent with the traditional use of that text as a guide to the customs and geography of the Middle East,[3] but the language of rediscovery and refreshed memories is extraordinary. Implicitly or explicitly, he is making at least three claims about Egyptian culture: first, it goes back an inordinately long distance into the past, perhaps even by thousands of years; second, Egyptian customs have changed little or not at all over this span of time; and third, Egypt is both other than the Europe in which Flaubert lives and the home to ideas, beliefs, and manners that flourish in Europe—hence, the emphasis on rediscovery and refreshed memory and on the Bible. In fact, these claims do little more than distill, across two thousand years, the remarks made by Herodotus, who advances one of the most compelling and influential ancient treatments of Egyptian temporality.[4]

Even a casual reader of Herodotus will be struck by the number of references to the age of Egyptian civilization. Examples include the description of Psammetichus' experiment, the records of the priests, the borrowings of Greek religion, and Hecateus' famous genealogical investigation. I do not propose to verify the bulk of such examples, or to assess Herodotus' dates and relative chronologies for their historical legitimacy. Many schol-

---

2. Flaubert 1972, 81.

3. For the influence of the Bible and Christianity in travel literature about Egypt from 1320 to 1601, see Guérin Dalle Mese 1991, 120–261.

4. The power of the ancient model is noticeable to disconcerting effect in popularizing twentieth-century accounts of the ancient world. See, for example, Edith Hamilton's *The Greek Way*, 2d ed.(New York, 1930): "In Egypt, in Crete, in Mesopotamia, wherever we can read bits of the story, we find the same conditions: a despot enthroned, whose whims and passions are the determining factor in the state; a wretched, subjugated populace; a great priestly organization to which is handed over the domain of the intellect. This is what we know of the Oriental state to-day. It has persisted down from the ancient world through thousands of years, never changing in any essential. Only in the last hundred years—less than that—it has shown a semblance of change, made a gesture of outward conformity with the demands of the modern world. But the spirit that informs it is the spirit of the East that never changes. It has remained the same through all the ages down from the antique world, forever aloof from all that is modern. This state and this spirit were alien to the Greeks" (also quoted in Hare 1999, 216). In a sense, this entire chapter is an attempt to explain why it was possible for Hamilton, an avowed admirer of Greek texts, to propagate so "extreme and naïve" (Hare's words) an interpretation.

ars have made inquiries along these lines,[5] and the fact that Egypt is an ancient and accomplished civilization is not a subject of debate. I would like, rather, to reflect upon the effects of Herodotus' narrative and see what sort of Egypt his text produces. Herodotus' account consistently projects the beginnings of Egyptian history further back in time than Greek history, so that Egyptians are seen as precursors of Greeks, even though both continue to exist in the time of Herodotus. The text relegates Egypt to an allochronic past, while it appropriates for the Greeks an historical narrative in which Egypt once played a foundational part. This momentum is also discernible as Herodotus, in effect, reshapes Greece's founding myths to make them concur with the temporal position he assigns to Egypt in his inquiries.

Herodotus' temporal organization should be studied in the light of the temporalizing within the democratic polis of Athens, where in the fifth century a particular kind of time was integral to the construction of democratic ideology and imperial hegemony. This temporality, the privileged though not the only mode of time associated with Athens, is referred to by some scholars as "political time" and linked to the collective decision-making apparatus of the city: "[i]t is the temporality of the chief organs of the democracy, the courts and the assembly, where decision depended upon the authority of the citizen body, but where this authority was expressed as the consensus of an instant, a consensus that was sovereign like the demos itself, was unconstrained (though perhaps swayed) by earlier decisions, and was not binding on future decisions."[6] The focus on the past in the Egyptian history, therefore, poses a contrast with the present-oriented temporality of the Athenian democracy, and in depicting Egyptian society as fixedly ancient, Herodotus is also implicitly drawing a contrast between two political systems, namely, between the tyrannical, despotic, fundamentally autocratic civilization of Egypt and the isonomic, democratic city-state of Athens. As we shall see in detail below, the temporal shape given to Egyptian history by Herodotus is part of a set of sociopolitical distinctions applied to the world of the Greek city-states and the world of the barbarian.

ABSOLUTE HISTORY

Herodotus prepares for the history of the conflict between Persians and Greeks, which takes up the second half of his histories, by describing the nations defeated by the Persians before they encountered the Greeks. The

5. See e.g. Mitchell 1956; Strasburger 1956; Miller 1966; Lloyd 1975, 171–94.
6. Csapo and Miller 1998, 102.

unexpectedness of the Greek victory is foreshadowed through an account of Persia's rise to military and imperial greatness in the first half of the histories, which relate in detail the conquests of Lydia, Babylon, and especially Egypt. As Herodotus characterizes them, these were civilizations in a sense that the Greece of his own day was not, with monumental "histories" far in excess of the past that was attached to the Greeks. Almost as incredible as the triumph of Greece over Persia, he implies, was the subjugation of the ancient civilization of Egypt by Persia; if even Egypt could fall to Persia, there was little hope for smaller nations that came in the way of this relentless power. According to the Herodotean worldview, Greece's eventual defeat of Persia was all the more remarkable given Persia's vanquishing of the Eastern civilizations.

What was the consequence of this scheme for the history of Egypt? In his study, *Time and the Other,* Johannes Fabian uses the expression "denial of coevalness" to refer to the temporal distancing that he finds in modern anthropological writing. Fabian refers to Herodotus only in passing, but his comment seems to apply so readily that I would like to develop this argument in connection with it. For, by consistently projecting Egyptian beginnings at a remote point in history, Herodotus' narrative circumscribes, arrests, and closes off time in Egypt. To be sure, his history of Egypt contains numerous details, anecdotes, and the military conquests of kings. Nonetheless, Herodotus' Egyptian history, for itself and in itself, unlike his Persian and Greek histories, lacks explicit themes and does not form part of a historical continuum. It is a "monumental history" that succeeds in turning its subject into Shelley's monument: "I met a traveller from an antique land/ Who said: Two vast and trunkless legs of stone/Stand in the desert. . . ."

It is instructive to consider the structure of Herodotus' Egyptian account when approaching the temporality it presents. Scholars often divide his Egyptian book into two parts, the first consisting of chapters 1 to 98, and the second of chapters 99 to 182; the first few chapters of book 3, which also contain details about Egypt are set aside by commentators because they give an account of Cambyses' activities, and hence do not seem to cohere with the more "Egyptian" material in book 2. In this scheme, the first part of book 2, chapters 1 to 98, is primarily concerned with ethnography and geography, while the second part, chapters 99 to 182, is concerned with the activities of Egypt's kings.

This schematization of Herodotus' work has its advantages and disadvantages, but it also foregrounds the questions of temporality that we are considering here. Like many anthropological works, the Egyptian ethnography of the first part is scripted in the "ethnographic present," to use a phrase for a phenomenon that Fabian describes at some length, the effect of which is often to posit a categorical and ahistorical view of a society.[7] Since Herodotus wrote his ethnographies of Greeks, such as the Spartans, in the present tense as well, it cannot be inferred that this practice is unique to his Egyptian ethnography. Nevertheless, the use of the ethnographic present in the first part of book 2, combined with such devices as the repeated use of the word "always" (αἰεί) with regard to Egyptian practices, is programmatic for the temporality of book 2 as a whole, as is evident from a consideration of the second part.

It is customary to divide the second part into two smaller sections, the first consisting of chapters 99 to 142, the discussion of the early pharaohs, and the second of chapters 147 to 182, which addresses the relatively recent period of Saïte rule. The value of the first of these sections is famously unclear to modern historians of Egypt because of its broad sweep. Several rulers are named in chronological order by Herodotus in this section (Min, the queen Nitocris, Moeris, Sesostris, Pheros, Proteus, Rhampsinitus, Cheops, Chephren, Mycerinus, Asykhis, Amysis, and Sethos), but with the proviso that in the years between Min and Sesostris there are 330 rulers who are not named, besides the two (Nitocris and Moeris) mentioned in the text. Moreover, the Egyptological record shows that the order of the pyramid builders (Cheops, Chephren, and Mycerinus) is incorrect; they belong before Moeris. On the other hand, the second section, chapters 147 to 182, provides dates and regnal years that largely correspond to external evidence for Egyptian history, to the extent that Herodotus' account of Saïte rulers (Psammetichus, Nekos, Psammis, Apries, Amasis, and his son, Psammenitus, mentioned in book 3) still informs modern political histories of this period in Egyptian history.

Nevertheless, the narrative that unfolds across the two sections that constitute the second half of book 2 is perfectly consistent and intelligible within the logic of Herodotus' text itself, for the unifying themes in the second half of book 2 are the wonderful and the monumental.[8] This interest is signaled by the writer himself, who justifies the length of his treatment of Egypt with the claim that "it has more wonders in it than any country in the world and more works that are beyond description than any-

7. An example: "They drink (πίνουσι) out of bronze cups, rinsing these every day—not one man doing so and another not, but all of them. They wear (φορέουσι) linen clothes that are always newly washed—being especially careful about this. They circumcise (περιτάμνονται), out of cleanliness, preferring to be clean than to seem fair in appearance" (2.37).
8. This is sometimes noted: see e.g. Drews 1973, 57.

where else" (2.35). The effect is to give the reader a host of details, anecdotes, and marvelous achievements such as the construction of the labyrinth. Thus, King Moeris digs Lake Moeris, builds two pyramids inside it, and the propylaia to a temple of Hephaestus (2.101, 149); Mycerinus attempts to disprove the oracle that promises him only six more years of life, by turning night into day through keeping lanterns lit at night, and so getting twelve years instead of six (2.133); and Psammetichus contrives to gain the throne by pouring libations to the gods out of his bronze helmet (2.151). A great number of similar anecdotes and details are offered by Herodotus, especially in connection with the Saïte period, but ultimately they appear because they are part of the record of wonders and monuments, not of a historical continuum: the Pyramids, Min and the building of Memphis, Nitocris' revenge, Apries' palace, Amasis' propylaia, and Sesostris' foreign conquests. As Robert Drews remarks in connection with Sesostris, "Sesostris' empire, in the *Histories*, is unrelated either to its temporal context or to subsequent history and is meaningless for both."[9] From the perspective of wonder and the monument, even the scholarly debate over the position of the pyramid builders appears misguided, since Herodotus was less interested in establishing the chronological order of these pharaohs than in describing their achievements.

What is noticeable about Herodotus' Egyptian history is how it both delivers more and less than what one expects of a fifth-century Greek: more, because the writer, in relating the account of Egypt's past, begins his history an impossibly long time ago and thereby turns Egypt into an absolutely historical civilization; and less, because his account of Egypt's history, by ending with the arrival of the Persian king, Cambyses, omits the details and a thematic discussion of Egyptian history from 525 B.C.E. to his own era. Herodotus' concern with the rise and humiliation of the Persian empire, thus, leads to a kind of annalistic history which allows for the wonderful and the monumental, but not an Egyptian history that contextualizes the Egyptians who live in the present. No less a philosopher of history than Hegel believed that Herodotus presented Egyptian history as a series of stories from the *Arabian Nights*, while the scholar Stanley M. Burstein characterizes the work "as a chronicle of deeds of great kings, with little effort made to organize the account in terms of major historical themes."[10]

9. Drews 1973, 60.
10. Burstein 1996, 593. See G. W. F. Hegel, *The Philosophy of History*, trans. J. Sibree (1857; reprint, Buffalo, N.Y., 1991), 219; Hegel does not appear to take exception to this view.

When this treatment of Egyptian events is considered along with the "ethnographic present" so widely used in the first half of book 2, the conclusion is inescapable that the Egyptians' biographies, actions, gestures, and plans are elements of a narrative that consistently archaizes Egypt and denies it coevality. The narrative explicitly works according to various categories—autopsy (ὄψις), hearsay (ἀκοή), opinion (γνώμη), and inversion (ἔμπαλιν), for instance—which have been subject to detailed criticism by a variety of scholars. Such a narrative allows the encapsulation of personalities, events, and circumstances, but the narrative dynamic yields to the static imparted to Egypt in Herodotus' semiotization of the country, and the overall frame of Herodotus' Egyptian account is a stable, fixed, and immobilized time. Within the constraints of the discourse, therefore, the text generates the notion of an eternal and unchanging Egypt at the heart of Herodotus' inquiries.

While Herodotus' account was the most influential of the fifth- and fourth-century histories of Egypt, he was writing in a context in which the antiquity of Egypt was already established as a field of inquiry.[11] Hecateus of Miletus (ca. 500 B.C.E.) made Greek myth and legend the basis for the Egyptian account that appeared in his *Periegesis:* this is the implication of a passage in Herodotus (2.143–45, F 300), and of some quotations, which refer to place-names such as Pharos (F 307) and Canopus (F 308) that Hecateus derived from the crew of Menelaus' ship. It appears that Herodotus reversed this emphasis, since he said Egypt was much older than did Hecateus, and he claimed that Egypt was the home of several Greek gods. In effect, both writers were Hellenocentric: Hecateus insisted on the antiquity of Greece and the priority of Greek myth; Herodotus created a framework for Egypt' antiquity and influence that was dependent on Greece as its point of reference. To judge from the references in ancient authors, Herodotus' account, by the force of its authority, squashed the impact that Hecateus' might have had on the Greek understanding of Egyptian history, though it was also charged by some that Herodotus had plagiarized large sections of Hecateus' work.[12]

Herodotus also had a greater impact than two of his successors, namely, Hellanicus of Lesbos, writing at the end of the fifth century, and Aristagoras of Miletus, in the middle of the fourth, who were the authors of *Aegyp-*

11. For the fragments of Hecateus, Hellanicus, Aristagoras, and Eudoxus, see the appendix below.

12. For Hecateus and Herodotus on Egypt, see Pearson 1939, 81–90; West 1991; Burstein 1996; with Jacoby's commentary to *FGrHist* 1 F 300–324.

tiaca that, on the available evidence, offered only slight contrasts with Herodotus' account. Hellanicus appears to have supplied details not mentioned in Herodotus concerning Amasis' reign (608a F 2), while he turned to myth as an instrument to understand Egyptian phenomena such as the inundation of the Nile (F 4). Aristagoras is said to have written about the Apis bull (F 4) and about relatively recent events in Egypt concerning Gynaikospolis, the city of women (F 8). It is possible that Hellanicus and Aristagoras offered different conceptions of Egyptian temporality from Herodotus, given these references to relatively recent events, but the absence of a narrative context makes it impossible to arrive at a firm conclusion about the nature of their histories.

The chief reconfiguration of Herodotus' historical schema, as Burstein has argued, probably came from Eudoxus of Cnidus, but even he was not able to overturn the powerful impact of the Herodotean model. Eudoxus (ca. 400–350 B.C.E.) is said to have traveled to Egypt and to have been the source for the Egyptian information in Plato, under whom he studied. Eudoxus' claim that the Egyptians used the word "year" to refer to what the Greeks called "month" indicates that he substantially revised the absurdly huge span of years assigned to Egyptian history by Herodotus, Plato, and others. Moreover, "Eudoxus foregrounded the role of the Egyptian priests in his interpretation of Egyptian life, ascribing to them an extensive knowledge of science and philosophy and assigning to them a central role in Egyptian culture instead of treating them primarily as sources of information as Hecateus and Herodotus had done."[13] In this view, Eudoxus refashioned the Herodotean schema on two counts, the priority of Egypt over Greece and the Hellenocentrism of his Egyptian history. However, it is not until the Hellenistic period that substantial and certainly attested restatements of Herodotus' vision of Egypt's past appear, and it was not until late antiquity when Christian chronographers used Eudoxus' work to justify an historical continuum that they perceived in the Bible. In the fifth and fourth centuries B.C.E., however, Herodotus' picture of a static Egypt in the distant past largely set the pattern for the reception of Egyptian history in Greece.

THE LEGACIES OF THE PAST

Herodotus' text is the founding work, whether acknowledged as such or not, for the assumption in Flaubert, Edwards, and others that Egypt is rooted in the remote past, and his archaizing practices are widespread

13. Burstein 1996, 597.

enough in book 2 to be considered definitive for his treatment of Egyptians. According to Herodotus, Egyptian temporal moments have the same quality, and Egyptian history takes place in one time, which is closed, static, and unchanging.[14] It is this quality of Egyptian time that allows writers such as Flaubert to claim that nothing changes in the Orient, or that the murderer of an ox is still punished in the ancient manner. The consequence of Herodotus' treatment is to define the relationship between Egypt and Greece so as to contain Egypt in a static past and to designate Greece as the country of the present.

I begin this topic with some observations on the question of cultural transmission. Herodotus' allochronic discourse allows him to present Egypt as the school of Hellas partly since Egyptian history extends further back in time than Greek history. The Egyptians are capable of inventing a number of practices and concepts, according to Herodotus, since they have made an early start in the race of time, and since they are barbarians rather than savages.[15] Later, the Greeks adopt these inventions from them. The roster of Egyptian inventions and practices, most of which the Greeks acquire, includes geometry, astrology, holy assemblies, processions and services of the gods, the names of nearly all the gods, a Dionysiac ritual, contempt for craftsmen, and perhaps circumcision, though the Ethiopians may have invented the last.[16] Of course, the Egyptians are not the only people who are inventors and teachers, nor the Greeks the only beneficiaries of alien wisdom. Herodotus writes that the Greeks learned from peoples other than the Egyptians: from the Babylonians such things as the sun-clock, sundial, and the twelve divisions of the day (2.109); from the Libyans, the robe and aegis of the statues of Athena, the crying out of ὀλολυγή, and the practice of harnessing four horses together (4.189); and from the Phoenicians, the alphabet (5.58). And barbarians pass on their customs not only to Greeks but also to other barbarian peoples, just as the Ethiopians learned good manners from the Egyptians (2.30), the Phoenicians and Palestinian Syrians learned circumcision from the Egyptians (2.104), and the Persians learned worship of Aphrodite Ourania from the Arabians and Assyrians (1.131).

14. It may be helpful here to point out that the time of Herodotus' Egyptians does not adhere to a linear model, where the ordering relation is irreflexive, antisymmetric, and transitive, nor does it help to think of Egyptian time in cyclical terms; rather, he closes off Egyptian time from the present. See Serres 1979 for some of these terms.

15. See Hartog 1988 on this distinction.

16. Respectively, 2.109, 82, 58, 50, 49, 167, 104.

The Egyptians occupy a special place in this traffic of custom and learn-ing, since they are clearly the most prolific inventors and teachers, and the Greeks borrow more from them than from any other people. They have learned men with excellent memories, Herodotus observes, and they are unlike the people around the Black Sea, who, apart from the Scythians, rank among the stupidest nations of the world and have produced no learned men (4.46). The Greeks, in turn, also have a special place in Herodotus' cir-culation of inventions, since the Greeks themselves do not, in general, in-struct any other nation in Hellenic practices, but they remain beneficiaries of barbarian wisdom. There is one exception—the Persians learned peder-asty from the Greeks (1.135). Excepting pederasty, Greek customs and in-ventions appear to be restricted to the boundaries of Greece, while those of non-Greeks circulate in an open system of various non-Greek peoples.

Catherine Darbo-Peschanski has shown that it is the *temporality* of He-rodotus' narrative that explains the remarkable asymmetry by which Greeks have so few customs that other nations such as the Egyptians adopt, while they are themselves characterized repeatedly as recipients of foreign cultural influence.[17] The Greeks occupy progressive points in Herodotean time, but Egyptians and other non-Greek nations are always burdened by their situation in the past. In brief and scattered comments, Herodotus takes his inquiry back to the original moments when Hellas assumes its identity. He refers to the Dorians becoming Lacedaemonians and to Pelas-gians becoming Athenians (1.56). His position on the Pelasgians is confus-ing, since he identifies the Athenians with Pelasgians, but also maintains a distinction between the two groups (1.56–58).[18] At any rate, he does state that the Pelasgians were barbarians, and that Hellas grew "from something small to be a multitude of peoples by the accretion chiefly of the Pelasgians but of many other barbarian peoples as well" (1.58). For Herodotus, bar-barians contribute to the formation of Hellas and its constituent peoples such as Lacedaemonians and Athenians.

17. See Darbo-Peschanski 1989, 233–43.

18. The literature on the Pelasgians is vast and often contradictory. See McNeal 1985 for this passage in Herodotus. The ancient literary evidence is collected in Lochner-Hüttenbach 1960. Tuplin notes, "What both the Pelasgian myth and the story of Cadmus show is that barbarian origin is acceptable, so long as one escaped the barbarian tendency to stagnate in primitive conditions, both socio-political and linguistic. For the tonguelessness of barbarians is a piece of primitivism, not just a metaphor for incomprehensibility. Greek emerges in some fashion out of a barbar-ian linguistic background, and, as Plato claimed to recognise in the etymological playroom of his dialogue *Cratylus*, still retains barbarian words" (Tuplin 1999, 62).

According to the logic of the narrative, barbarians can learn the inventions of other barbarians, or teach inventions to others, just as Pelasgians and other non-Hellenes can learn from other peoples or instruct them. Yet, Herodotus' text allows Hellenes only to acquire knowledge and virtually prohibits Hellenes from handing over knowledge to non-Hellenes, so that Hellenes cannot transmit their learning to barbarians after the former have made the transformation from barbarian (or Pelasgian) to Hellene. Barbarians, in turn, acquire nothing from the Hellenes as Hellenes, although barbarians once played a role in the formation of Hellenes. If barbarians cannot learn Hellenic practices or discoveries, however, they may never become Hellenes; they remain barbarians. Whereas barbarians live in a time that is bracketed off and closed, Hellenes have evolved from barbarians, and have taken on such names as Athenians and Lacedaemonians. But in Herodotus' text, Hellenes never become barbarians since they develop and progress over barbarians by the assimilation of barbarians.[19]

Non-Greeks live in a separate temporal frame where they do not acquire Greekness, hence Herodotus' statement that the Egyptians refuse to follow the customs of other nations, especially those of the Greeks, makes sense (2.49, 91). He remarks elsewhere that the Scythians, too, do not use foreign, particularly Greek, customs (4.76). If Herodotus would grant the transmission of Greek *nomoi* (customs), the Greekness of these *nomoi* would be diluted, and not to allow the dispersal of Greek *nomoi* among barbarian nations is a way of preserving the essence of Greece. But he seems to make a point of Egyptian insularity. The Egyptians, he writes, follow their ancestral customs and take no others to themselves at all (2.79); they follow the same customs at all times, handing them down from one generation to the next without alteration. The Linus song, for instance, is sung in Greece, Phoenicia, Cyprus, and other nations. "There are so many matters," Herodotus observes, "at which I marvel among the Egyptians, but certainly one is from where they got the name of the Linus song. It is clear that they have sung it forever (αἰεί)" (2.79). He adds that the Egyptians have sung this song of lamentation at least since the time of Egypt's first king, who ruled more than eleven thousand years before his inquiries (2.142). This impression of Egyptian stability is reinforced by Herodotus' priestly informers, who claim on the basis of their records that in ten or more millennia the sun's movements deviated from the norm four times: twice the sun rose from where it usually sets, and twice it set in the place

19. See Hall 1989, 149, 171, and Tuplin 1999, 61, for the overlap between "the past" and "the elsewhere" in Greek thought.

from where it usually rises. Nevertheless, although even the sun suffered change, Egypt and the Egyptians remained constant, for in all these millennia "nothing became different among the Egyptians . . . neither products of the earth nor products of the river, nor yet in respect of diseases or death" (2.142). Thus, Herodotus' articulation of Egyptian history unfolds within a peculiar temporal organization, one whose closure proves impossibly final for the Egyptians and whose inertia is difficult for them to overcome. Within the confines of this overarching vision, Herodotus expounds powerfully the inability of Egyptians to rise out of their historical condition and to engage the social and political realities of the present day.

EGYPT AND THE TROJAN WAR

In Herodotus, as in numerous Greek writers, Egypt is inextricably tangled up in questions concerned with myths and origins, and the writer naturally finds a place for the myth of Helen and the Trojan War in the Egyptian sections of his histories. His text uses the story of Helen and the Trojan War in a special way in his narrative of the war against Persia. Egypt is semiotized and appropriated by Herodotus so that it occupies pivotal and identical positions in the two great narratives of East-West conflict, the Trojan War and the Persian War. Of course, Herodotus was not the first to say that Helen never sailed to Troy, as Stesichorus wrote poems on the subject, and he was also not the only writer to say that she stayed instead in Egypt, as Euripides' tragedy makes clear. I discussed Euripides' *Helen* in chapter 1, and here I would like to evaluate Herodotus' treatment of the story of Helen in Egypt against the background of myth and time in his history.

Let us reflect on Herodotus' statement that the priests' annals refer exclusively to human rulers, and that divinities lived in Egypt before mortals commenced their reign. The last king to rule Egypt before the twelve who ruled jointly, Herodotus writes, was Sethos, a priest of Hephaestus. The Egyptian priests counted 341 generations from their first king to this priest of Hephaestus, and Herodotus supplies the figure of 11,340 years as the calendrical equivalent of these 341 generations.[20] He writes: "In 11,340 years, said the priests, there had never been a god in man-shape; nor, moreover, neither before nor thereafter, among the rest of those who became kings of Egypt, had any such thing happened. During this time, they said . . . nothing became different among the Egyptians, for all these disturbances,

20. See Henige 1974 and Ricoeur 1985, 160–71, for generational succession and historiography.

neither products of the earth nor products of the river, nor yet in respect of diseases or death" (2.142). Recorded history in Egypt covers an immense period and encompasses more than 341 generations from the first human king to Sethos. Herodotus does not tell us how many years or generations separate his enunciative situation from Sethos, although he suggests that Hecateus' visit occurred in the 345th generation from the beginning of human rule. In any case, more than 11,340 years separate his fifth-century Greek audiences from the start of recorded history in Egypt. In all these years, moreover, human beings lived in Egypt, but not one god or anthropomorphic deity. There were gods who ruled Egypt, but their sovereignty preceded that of human rulers: Horus was the last of the divine rulers of Egypt, Herodotus notes elsewhere (2.144).

Herodotus' remark seems to posit a historical continuum in which divine beings precede human beings, but it does not conflict with the intellectual currents that shaped his and others' historiography in archaic and classical Greece. Many Greeks of the period did not maintain a clear distinction between myth and history, but incorporated narratives that we would describe as mythic into their historical texts.[21] Greeks recognized myth as a part of ancient history, they believed that mythic events actually happened, and until Thucydides and Plato, *logos* and *mythos* were interchangeable for "story."[22] This is not to say that Greeks accepted traditional accounts of gods and heroes uncritically, since the critique of myth is almost as old as the Homeric poems in Greece. But the criterion for criticism was credibility, that is, the degree to which the tradition seemed true, reliable, and plausible. Further, Greeks were able to distinguish between narratives about humans and narratives about the divine, heroic, supernatural, or bestial. Given these criteria, Greeks believed that heroes and other semi-divine entities once inhabited the Earth, and that these lived within roughly the same geographic limits as humans inhabiting the Earth in the fifth century B.C.E. Even the temporal dimension of heroes was not different from humans, since they merely lived in the distant past and belonged to an older and stronger race than the present one.

Herodotus' history illustrates these qualities of the mythic. When the Athenians and Tegeans quarrel over who has the best claim to the left flank in the battle line, the two sides refer to stories from the mythic past and to the actions of the Heracleidae and of Polynices against Thebes (9.26–7). Both sides appear to be using traditional narratives with mythic elements

21. See e.g. Brillante 1990 and Graf 1993, 121–41.
22. See Brisson 1982; and cf. Pindar, *Olympian* 1.28–29.

as descriptions of events from the past. In another passage, Herodotus mentions Polycrates of Samos and Minos, the son of Zeus and Europa: "Polycrates is the first of the Greeks we know to lay plans for the mastery of the sea, except for Minos of Cnossus and any of those that before him were lords of the sea. But Polycrates is the first of the human race to do so . . ." (3.122). The author is maintaining a distinction between human and nonhuman, and also implying that the actions of the nonhuman occur in an earlier time than those of the human. While Herodotus maintains that the rule of mortals on Earth follows that of the gods, he does not often venture into descriptions of activities in that divine time and he uses the heroic ancestor or divine figure rather as a limit or point of departure. In the case of Polycrates, for instance, he cites Minos as another figure who has had sovereignty over the sea, but then refrains from discussing his sea power. When he writes about the Lacedaemonians, he gives the Greek view about "the kings of the Dorians back to Perseus—leaving out the god" (6.53). He leaves out the name of Zeus, because he is not taking his account back further than the heroic Perseus to his divine father. His genealogies of the Spartan kings Leonidas and Leotykhides go back in both cases to Heracles, but not beyond (7.204, 8.131), and there are numerous other examples of this kind of genealogical accounting. He accepts divine and human periods in his chronological frame, but shies away from probing the nature of the former. He does not implicate gods in his inquiry and, indeed, does not choose to consider how gods produced humans. For Herodotus, as Darbo-Peschanski observes, humans are already there as a homogeneous race.[23]

Yet, if there is a place in his history where the narrator makes an attempt to consider the Greek gods and even their origins, it occurs in his Egyptian sections. The Greeks, he claims, received their gods and religious practices from Egypt. The names of all the gods always existed in Egypt, except for Poseidon, the Dioscuri, Hera, Hestia, Themis, the Graces, and the Nereids (2.50). The Egyptians were also the first people to organize holy assemblies, processions, and services of the gods (2.58), and the Greeks acquired their religious customs from the Egyptians. Herodotus also writes that the similarities in the methods of divination at Thebes in Egypt and at Dodona in Greece suggest an Egyptian origin for the oracle at Dodona (2.53–7). As for Heracles, both his mortal parents, Amphitryon and Alcmene, have distant Egyptian connections. The Greeks got Heracles' name from the Egyptians and foisted it on Amphitryon's son. Herodotus writes that Heracles certainly is an ancient Egyptian god, and he variously attests his stay in

23. Darbo-Peschanski 1989.

Egypt at 15,000 (2.145) or 17,000 years (2.43) before Amasis, when, as we saw above, gods ruled the country. These gods lived and reigned in Egypt and one of them acted as supreme ruler (2.144). Horus, whom the Greeks call Apollo, was the last of the divine beings to rule Egypt after he deposed Typhon, while Dionysus, Herodotus adds, is the Greek name for Horus' father, Osiris (2.144).

Egypt is not just the home of the Egyptian counterparts of the Greek gods, but also the locale for the mythic action of Greek heroes. Already in the proem, Herodotus indicates an Egyptian destination for the hapless Io. In book 2, he dwells at length on the story of Helen and the Trojan War, and according to him, Egyptian priests have their own version of what happened to Helen. By this account, when Paris carried off Helen from Sparta, he was blown off course to the Canopic mouth of the Nile. Paris' servants deserted their master and accused him to Thonis, the warden of this Nilotic mouth, of stealing Helen and injuring Menelaus. Thonis, in turn, arrested Paris and haled him off to Memphis, where the king Proteus judged that he would keep Helen for himself until such time as Menelaus should come to claim her in Egypt, and he gave Paris three days to leave the country (2.113–15). When Menelaus and the Greeks besieged Troy and demanded back Helen and the property that Paris stole with her, the Trojans replied that the Egyptian Proteus had Helen and the goods in question. The Greeks realized that the Trojans were speaking the truth after they captured the citadel, and dispatched Menelaus to Proteus. Menelaus arrived in Memphis, declared what had happened, received good hospitality, and retrieved Helen and all his possessions (2.118–19). In offering this version of Helen's abduction and return, Herodotus demonstrably accepts the reality of Paris' theft of Helen and of the war between the Greeks and Trojans, and also the notion that Helen never went to Troy, but was left by Paris in Egypt. He notes that he concurs with the priests' view that the Trojans did not have Helen and that the Greeks did not believe them when they stated this: "And the reason of this, if I may declare my opinion, was that the divinity (τοῦ δαιμονίου) was laying his plans that, as the Trojans perished in utter destruction, they might make this thing manifest to all the world: that for great wrongdoings, great also are the punishments from the gods. That is what I think, and that is what I am saying here" (2.120).

The inclination to ascribe the destruction of Troy to a divinity suits the mythical time imparted by Herodotus to Egypt. The Helen episode involves figures from Greek myth and, moreover, Herodotus recognizes the mythical nature of his narrative. In the first place, he writes that Homer knew of Helen's Egyptian sojourn and consciously left it out of his epic poetry

(2.116). In Herodotus' view, Homer, along with Hesiod, clarified the existence of the gods, gave the gods their names, and created a theogony for the Greeks (2.53). Secondly, Herodotus refers explicitly to the cult of Helen when he refers to a shrine of the "foreign Aphrodite" (ἱρὸν τὸ καλέεται ξείνης Ἀφροδίτης, 2.112) in the precinct of the Egyptian king Proteus, and then guesses that this is Helen's shrine; and later he alludes to her temple at Therapne in Laconia (6.61) and to her abduction by Theseus (9.73).

Herodotus' text both Hellenizes and mythologizes Egypt, but the time of Helen and the Trojan War lies in Greek—not Egyptian—myth. Egypt's gods lived in an extremely remote past and therefore they cannot appear in events as recent as the Trojan War. And although the priests claim their annals contain accounts of human beings only, they must have in mind Egyptian humans, since from the Greek perspective these are incidents from the heroic past. So Egypt serves as the setting for incidents in Greek myth in which Greek gods and heroes engage each other, and Herodotus Hellenizes the name of the Egyptian king, whom he refers to only as Proteus. Further, the narrative does not simply use Egypt as the location for Helen's stay away from Troy; it appropriates Egypt and the Egyptians. Herodotus specifically invokes the Egyptian priests as the source for much of his narration about Helen and he uses the authority of the priests to support his own account of the events: "Part of these matters, the priests told me, they learned from their researches; but they said that what happened in their own country they knew for absolute fact" (2.119). As Helen's stay in Egypt finds confirmation in ancient and respected priestly memories, Egyptian kings mingle with Greek heroes in this variation on one of the central narratives in the Hellenic religious and literary traditions.

Egypt occupies an interesting intermediate position between European Greece and barbarian Asia in Herodotus' narrative. The war between the Greeks and Trojans was, for Herodotus, a war between European Greeks and Asiatic barbarians, as his proem makes clear. When he evaluates the Persian and Phoenician *logoi*, for instance, he considers the events of the Trojan War as possible causes for the Persian Wars, the example par excellence of the conflict between European Greeks and Asiatic barbarians. He appears in the proem to disavow these *logoi*, but in terms that suggest that he sees the Trojan War fundamentally as a struggle between Greeks and Asiatics. Yet, the chief villain of this war, Paris, finds himself constrained to stop over in Egypt, and he has to negotiate Egypt and overcome its obstacles before he can return to Asia. The Egyptian king strips Paris of his prize, but Paris manages to sail home alive. For the Asiatic Paris, therefore, Egypt is the land that interrupts his return home and deprives him of his prize. Indeed, Troy comes crashing down in flames for the sake of a woman he never managed to bring home because of Egypt and its king. Egypt functions as a necessary hurdle for the Asiatics in Greek myth, in a role that prefigures its position in the narrative of the Persian Wars. When the Asians return, now as Persians, to wage war against Greeks, they too must pass through a troublesome Egypt. Cambyses conquers Egypt, and his successors Darius and Xerxes must deal with uprisings in the country. Thus, Herodotus' choice of narrative strategy presents Egypt as the necessary point through which the Asian threat to Greece must pass and encounter difficulties.

Further, Herodotus' construction of the Trojan War as the precursor of the war between Greeks and Persians entails his projecting the two in a particular temporal sequence. The Trojan War precedes the Persian Wars in such a way that its relation to the future event is not flexible or undetermined, while the Persian Wars unfold in terms that are already encoded in the earlier, mythical, and heroic struggle of Greeks and non-Greeks. Egypt occupies the same space in both narratives and is appropriated for the stories of both wars as the site of delay, danger, threat, hindrance, and annoyance to Greece's enemies. The text even incorporates Egyptian sources into its stories of fulfillment. The priests verify for Herodotus that Paris had to leave behind Helen in Egypt, or that Cambyses lost his senses in the country, so that Greece's enemies appear as a distant, barbarian, and Asiatic people who are ready to despoil Hellas of its inhabitants or possessions. But Egypt is intermediary, it straddles two continents, and though the Greeks call the Egyptians "barbarians," the Egyptians themselves refer to foreigners by the term "barbarians" (2.158). In a word, Egypt is neither Asian nor Greek. Therefore, and not disregarding Egypt's service as the homeland of Greek learning and wisdom, the narrative can align this foreign country with Greece and against its foes.

EGYPTIAN TIME

I have been suggesting that Herodotus depicts Egyptian history as captive to the past and as flat and static, in contrast to the forward-driven nature of Greek history. It would be instructive, now, to check Herodotus' discursive momentum, and consider briefly what ancient Egyptians themselves thought about Egyptian history and Egyptian time.[24] I do not say that He-

---

24. See Sauneron and Yoyotte 1959; Assmann 1975; Hornung 1966 and 1992, ch. 8; Redford 1986; and Baines 1989. I have found Baines' treatment of time very useful and follow him closely here; cf. *LÄ*, s.v. "Zeit," and Bochi 1994.

rodotus is necessarily misleading in his attitude to Egyptian history, but that the Egyptians' sense of their history and the concept of time is more complicated and interesting than the Greek text allows. The Egyptians, far from conceiving of themselves as inhabitants in a time that is static, closed, and bracketed off, had a sense of their rich past and found numerous ways to mobilize it in their present-day activities. This conception of history and time compares strikingly with the attitude displayed by Herodotus in his account of Egypt. Where Herodotus depicts Egyptian history as closed and static, the evidence suggests a readiness among Egyptians to mobilize the past in many areas of life; where Herodotus points to the sameness of time in Egypt, the evidence shows the Egyptian historical record as celebratory, ritualized, and stylized, but nonetheless amenable to change; where Herodotus invokes the divine as a limit or point of departure, the evidence indicates that the separation between religious and secular is harder to make for the ancient Egyptians, who conceived of history as a religious festival. These statements should not be taken to imply that the ancient Egyptians believed in, or lived through, an insufficient model of history; on the contrary, for the Egyptians, to borrow a turn of phrase from Clifford Geertz, this was how their history was.[25]

The comparison of these approaches to time and history can be made concrete through a discussion of two features of Egyptian time. The first point concerning the Egyptian material is that Egyptian history needs to be looked at as a celebration, and that its basic tone is ceremonial. The Egyptian historical records posit a historical scheme that is based on a stylized and ritualized view of history, so that history is in many ways regarded as a great festival or celebration. Secondly, Herodotus' statements about the sameness of time in Egypt should not obscure the fact that Egyptians of various periods also valued and, to use John Baines' expression, "mobilized the past"—in fact, the evidence for the Egyptians' "mobilization of the past" is very extensive.[26]

To turn to the first point, Egyptologists such as Erik Hornung have for some years now recognized the ceremonial and ritualized character of the Egyptian historical tradition.[27] In its ritualized and stylized aspects, Egyptian history thus resembles that of other cultures studied by anthropologists, an example being the theatre-state of Negara, which has been discussed by Geertz, among others. In the Egyptian case, however, it is fair

25. Geertz 1980, 136.
26. Baines 1989.
27. Hornung 1966 and 1992, ch. 8.

to say with Egyptologists that "history is stylized but not falsified." On the one hand, "the overall historical picture yielded by official inscriptions and pictures is heavily determined by recurring, typical events;" and on the other, "Egyptian historical records [such as the Palette of Narmer] attest to a keen awareness that individual people and events are unique."[28] In the Egyptian view, history is a religious drama or religious festival or religious celebration in which all of humankind takes part, with the pharaoh in the central role. Thus, the tone of history is dictated by the official annals, which were maintained by Egyptian priests and scribes from the time of the earliest dynasties; history is stylized and follows the pattern of the annalistic tradition. The annals are prescriptive as well as descriptive, and they record what has happened in the past, but also set the tone for what is happening in the present and will happen in the future. The annals typically begin afresh with each new king, so that time as well begins anew with the ascension of the new monarch. This ritualized scenario should not be taken to reflect historical determinism, since new events do occur and are recorded as such in the annals, sometimes "to the astonishment of the entire land."

The chief agent of this celebration is the king, who rules on earth as the protector of *maat*, for the present and the future. His role in what we would call the historical record—Egyptian does not have a word for "history"—is oriented to the future.[29] The creator places him on earth "for ever and ever, judging mankind and propitiating the gods, and setting order *(maat)* in place of disorder. He gives offerings to the gods and mortuary offerings to the spirits."[30] The royal inscriptions habitually refer the king's achievements and behavior to the gods and to the future. In the ongoing struggle between Horus and Seth, the king rules as the incarnation of Horus and as the restorer of *maat*. The accession to the throne represents the triumph of Horus and hope for the resurrection of Horus' father Osiris: "the coronation was always held on the 1st Day of the 1st Month of the Season of *Prt*, the Day of the New Year Feast of Horus the Behdetite immediately after the Festival of Khoiak which celebrated the resurrection of Osiris."[31] A new government provides the opportunity for a new beginning, but the aim of the new pharaoh is to restore *maat* as it was at the time of creation; therefore, moving toward the future is also moving toward the remote past.[32]

28. Hornung 1992, 152.
29. See Baines 1989, 132–33.
30. A Middle Kingdom text quoted by Assmann 1970, 22.
31. Lloyd 1975, 97.
32. Hornung 1992, 164.

Secondly, Herodotus' text should not conceal the fact that Egyptians of various periods also valued and mobilized the past. The earliest annals date from about 500 years after the founding of the first dynasty in about 3000 B.C.E.[33] These annals do not posit divine predecessors to the first kings. Later, between about 2500 and 1500, the texts begin to incorporate a golden mythic age as immediately anterior to the first human kings.[34] In the Middle Kingdom, the texts may portray the Old Kingdom as part of the glorious past or as part of a mythical antiquity; or they may mention it for a particular event or situation. As an example of the last type, the texts often refer to Snofru's reign in the fourth dynasty.[35] Builders of the Middle Kingdom also imitated Old Kingdom capital styles and reused stone from Old Kingdom pyramids.[36] But the Middle Kingdom itself was the classical period for Egyptians of a later era. The Egyptians of the New Kingdom, especially the Ramessid era, made more use of the past than their forebears, and their art shows awareness of specific periods and earlier building projects.[37] Such records as the Turin Canon impose divisions on the annalistic testimony and single out prominent figures.[38] The many mortuary texts are future-oriented, but still use the past in their narratives; however, some evidence from the New Kingdom reveals a shortening of the range of historical perspective in terms of dynastic founders and periods.[39]

The Egyptians of the fifth century B.C.E., when Herodotus composed his work, had the greatest historical perspective in ancient Egypt. The Late Period in general also favored archaism in various media—perhaps this was a response to the pressures of foreign domination or the desire of foreign rulers to appropriate native traditions.[40] All the monumental inscriptions are in Middle Egyptian, which remained the classical language. The Bentresh Stela claims to be a decree of Rameses II, but is more likely from the Persian or perhaps the Ptolemaic period.[41] Archaism in the Memphite

33. Redford 1986.
34. Kákosy 1964a and 1964b; Otto 1969.
35. Instruction for Kagemini, Prophecy of Neferti, P. Westcar, all translated in Lichtheim 1973, 60, 140, 216–17. See Baines 1989, 136.
36. Fischer 1959; Goedicke 1971.
37. Baines 1989, 141–44.
38. Gardiner 1959.
39. Baines 1989, 144: "One text presents Haremhab as the founder of a period within a century of his death."
40. For Late Period archaism, see Bothmer 1960; Brunner 1970; Nagy 1973; Assmann 1985, 484–86; *LÄ*, s.v. "Archaismus." For the response to foreign pressure, see West 1991, 154.
41. Translation, commentary, and bibliography in Lichtheim 1980, 90–94.

Theology tricked many modern experts into thinking it was from the Old Kingdom, but now scholarly consensus dates it to the Twenty-fifth dynasty.[42] Rulers of the Late Period, including the Persian kings, continued to project themselves as followers of traditional pharaonic dogma in many matters of cult, defense, and administration.[43] The deification of personages from the past flourished more in the Late Period than in earlier times: Imhotep and Amenhotep acquired their own cults in this era.[44] Moreover, the priests, who served also as guardians of memory, retained much of their influence in the Late Period. The inscription of Udjahorresnet mentions the care given to the temple of Neith at Saïs by Cambyses and Darius.[45] Psammetichus I and Psammetichus II both appointed their daughters as High Priestess in the temple of Amen at Thebes.[46] The great wealth of the temples, attested in such earlier documents as the Harris Papyrus of Rameses III and the Wilbour Papyrus of Rameses V, persists in the temple of Ptah at Memphis and religious estates in Buto. But when the priests suffered maltreatment from rulers, they could strike back by obliterating the latter from history and memory, and this is the punishment recorded by the Demotic Chronicle for Xerxes, who seized the temple estates in Buto.

In all these ways, then, the Egyptians adopted modes of recording, assimilating, and scrutinizing their past. They had canonical and powerful means of describing past events, endowing them with particular significance, and sifting through what was worthy of notice and what was not. There are Egyptian texts that conform even to the relatively narrow definition given by Donald Redford in which history counts as "the telling of events involving or affecting human beings (not necessarily, though usually, in narrative form), which took place prior to the time of composition, the chief aim of which is to explain those events for the benefit, predilection and satisfaction of contemporaries, and not for the enhancement of the writer's personal reputation."[47] In making these claims for an Egyptian historical sense, however, it is a mistake to impose Greek concepts or categories on the ancient Egyptian material, or to insist that Egyptian methods of

42. Junge 1973.

43. Lloyd in Trigger et al. 1983, 293–99.

44. Wildung 1977.

45. Lloyd 1982 supplies an analysis of the main problems and a comprehensive bibliography.

46. Lloyd in Trigger et al. 1983, 302–4.

47. Redford 1986, xiv. For examples of these texts, which come from different periods, see the Annals of Thutmose III, from the New Kingdom (translation in Lichtheim 1976, 29–35), and the Victory Stele of Piye, from the Late Period (translation in Lichtheim 1980, 66–84).

relating to the past correlate to particular modern historiographical notions. The reader needs to approach ancient Egyptian texts with methodological self-awareness and with rigorous attention to local cultural assumptions and specificities. "The Egyptian vision of the world," Christopher Eyre cautions us, "moves seamlessly between the physical and the biological, the tangible and the metaphysical, the measurable and the mythological."[48] So also the Egyptians' relationship to past times and events weaves in and out of historical categories that may or may not be familiar from modern historiography. But it is true to assert, in a manner that Herodotus only begins to imply, that ancient Egyptians had a rich sense of their past, and of commemorating, celebrating, and absorbing it.

IN AN ANTIQUE LAND

Instead of speaking further about the Egyptian historical sense and how it compares with what Herodotus writes, I would like to conclude by moving in a slightly different direction. The title of this chapter derives from the first line of Shelley's poem "Ozymandias," but it is also the title of a book by Amitav Ghosh. In order to carry out the research for his book, Ghosh himself traveled to Egypt and lived there for a number of months, and so he also devotes some of the book to an account of his own experiences in modern Egypt. His book deals in part with the problem of historical time, and his formulation of the problem is worth considering at length.

> Within moments a dozen or so people had crowded around me, and I was busy affirming that yes, in my country there were indeed crops like rice and wheat, and yes, in India too, there were peasants like the fellaheen of Egypt, who lived in adobe villages and turned the earth with cattle-drawn ploughs. The questions came ever faster, even as I was speaking: 'Are most of your houses still built of mud-brick as they are here?' and 'Do your people cook on gas stoves or do they still burn straw and wood as we do?'
>
> I grew ever puzzled as I tried to deal with this barrage of inquiries, first, by the part the word 'still' played in their questions, and secondly by the masks of incredulity that seemed to fall on their faces as I affirmed, over and over again, that yes, in India too people used cattle-drawn ploughs and not tractors; water-wheels and not pumps; donkey-carts, not trucks, and yes, in India there were many, many people who were very poor, indeed there were millions whose poverty they would scarcely have been able to imagine. But to my utter bewilderment, the

48. In Silverman 1997, 92.

more I insisted, the more sceptical they seemed to become, until at last I realized, with an overwhelming sense of shock, that the simple truth was that they did not believe what I was saying.

I later came to understand that their disbelief had little or nothing to do with what I had said; rather, they had constructed a certain ladder of 'Development' in their minds, and because all their images of material life were of those who stood in the rungs above, the circumstances of those below had become more or less unimaginable. I had an inkling then of the real and desperate seriousness of their engagement with modernism, because I realized that the fellaheen saw the material circumstances of their lives in exactly the same way that a university economist would: as a situation that was shamefully anachronistic, a warp upon time; I understood that their relationship with the objects of their everyday lives was never innocent of the knowledge that there were other places, other countries which did not have mud-walled houses and cattle-drawn ploughs, so that those objects, those houses and ploughs, were insubstantial things, ghosts displaced in time, waiting to be exorcized and laid to rest. It was thus that I had my suspicion of what it might mean to belong to an 'historical civilization', and it left me bewildered because, for my own part, it was precisely the absoluteness of time and the discreteness of epochs that I always had trouble in imagining.[49]

Herodotus' Egyptian history is written out of a double movement of appropriation and displacement, so that, on the one hand, the narrative appropriates Egyptian history by making Egypt the site for events from Greek myth and by making it the precursor to Greek history and, on the other hand, the narrative also signals a displacement away from Egypt by rendering Egyptian time as static and closed, in contrast to forward-driven Greek time. When we consider Egyptian conceptions of the past, we find by comparison that history and time are configured and lived through categories not easily assimilated to Herodotus' text. In Ghosh's account, nevertheless, Egyptian villagers in our own day have come into contact with modernity and yearn for a developmental economics that will remove them away from the temporal ghosts about them into a mechanized, industrialized future. And in this account, it is striking that as a consequence of their engagement with capitalist modernity, Egyptian villagers show a type of historical sense that is closer to Herodotus' Greeks than to their ancestors, the ancient Egyptians.

In fact, the overlap between the modern developmental model and the

49. Ghosh 1992, 199–201.

ancient Greek model has been noticed and discussed by scholars of the ancient world. Eric Csapo and Margaret Miller have explained the correspondence between the two kinds of temporalities by the emergence of democracy and empire both in ancient Athens and in Europe of the seventeenth and eighteenth centuries, when modern constructions of time took hold.[50] These scholars are wary of overexact analogies, however, and they caution that a plurality of temporalities can exist in a given society, that early modern Europe and ancient Athens do not offer precise parallels, and that temporality in the postmodern twentieth century is not analogous to the ancient temporality either. These words of caution should not be brushed aside, nor should the realization that "democracy" was realized in a very limited sense in the Europe of the seventeenth and eighteenth centuries as well as in ancient Athens. For our purposes, nevertheless, and without disregarding the genuine differences between ancient Athens and other periods, it is worth reflecting on limited democracy and empire as mediating factors for one kind of temporality, and in particular on how these forces shaped the dominant temporality of fifth-century Athens.

In ancient Athens, as noted at the start of the chapter, this temporality was connected to the ideology of the democratic city-state and the establishment of a political calendar. As with the spatial organization mentioned in the previous chapter, the Cleisthenic reforms of 507/6 were a turning point in this regard too, since they imposed an arbitrary structure on Athens' civic life even as the lunisolar calendar continued to order the rhythms of the religious life. Cleisthenes appears to have divided the year into 10 periods, each of 35 or 36 days, in order to match his division of Attica into 10 tribes; he also increased the membership of the Council *(Boule)* from 400 to 500 citizens, all of whom were elected by lot, 50 from each tribe. Hence, each tribe's members functioned as the working committee *(prytanis)* of the Council in turn over the course of the 10 periods, and so the fiction of an egalitarian society was manifest in the regulation of the civic calendar. As Pierre Lévêque and Pierre Vidal-Naquet write, "Temporal organization was copied upon *[se calque sur]* spatial organization: to have the prytany was, for a tribe, both to occupy such a position in the course of the political year and to delegate fifty of its own members to the public hearth at the heart of the *polis*."[51] Moreover, it was according to the prytanies that the government dated its decisions and actions, including armistices, reval-

---

50. Csapo and Miller 1998. This essay offers a useful orientation to important questions connected with the study of time in classical Athens.

51. Lévêque and Vidal-Naquet 1996, 15.

idation of extant laws, and the drawing up of financial records.[52] The prytany calendar promulgated the democratic ideal of equality for all and established a temporal frame of reference for the city's body politic; it was
also a way for the city to acquire control over time.

But the fifth century was also a period when Athens was flexing its political weight overseas and attempting to establish an empire. "The Athenian Empire," Csapo and Miller write, "is the first Greek foreign enterprise
that can be characterized as a programmatic pursuit of power for its own
sake through unlimited territorial expansion and the subjection of other
states."[53] While the city was establishing its democracy, it was also exer-
cising power outside its boundaries in attempts to practise its hegemony
over other city-states. Accordingly, Athenian "temporality expressed itself
best in the treatment of foreign wars, imperial victories, social class and
slavery because the conception of time was inseparable from the conception
of power, and power was something one gained necessarily at another's expense."[54] The temporality of Athens' pseudodemocracy was thus the same
as the temporality of imperialism. Wide-ranging in scope and effective in
its interpellation of subjects, the temporality of the city-state was the basis
for the promulgation of particular regimes of power inside and outside the
city. On the one hand, it was a means for the state to maintain its modes
of production, to run its political life, to regulate its social calendar, and to
preserve the values and hierarchies of the dominant ideology, and, on the
other, it guided the city in harnessing its resources for the acquisition and
control of overseas territories.

Ghosh, in the passage quoted above, and Fabian, in his study on coevalness, both remind us that the important thing about narratives of temporality is their ending. The villagers in modern Egypt know about the post-
industrial world outside their village, and believe their lives to be incomplete
until they can lay their hands on the latest mechanized products of the capitalist world economy. This is the ladder of evolution that they have constructed for themselves, and until they arrive at that materialist finale, they
see their lives as unfinished and stuck in the past. For the Athenians in the
fifth century, the emphasis of the dominant temporality was on the present and the near future, and not the distant future. The Athenians did not
believe in progress in itself, as scholars have often remarked, and the democracy never turned into a full, participatory democracy, with rights for

52. Bickerman 1980, 34–35.
53. Csapo and Miller 1998, 88.
54. Csapo and Miller 1998, 124.

women, metics, and slaves. Christian Meier notes that the present was a "special level of achievement" and "a limit that was hardly ever transcended."[55] What this means in political terms is the valorization of fifth-century Athenians and the democracy as a particular *telos,* and this is also the point where temporality enters into Herodotus' history of otherness. By situating his temporalities in the context of fifth-century Athens, we see that the historian was also privileging the Greek present and the political system of imperial democracy over and above the static temporality of Egypt and its despotic past.[56] For Herodotus, geographic and ethnic distance are translated into temporal distance, and temporality becomes another means of depicting the otherness of the foreign culture: his work takes societies that are coeval and represents them along a temporal continuum. By using temporality as a marker, Herodotus was posing a contrast between different practices of power, institutions of government, and codes of social life; and by giving Egyptians and Greeks different temporalities, he was drawing attention, obliquely but profoundly, to what he saw as the fundamental distinctions between the two cultures in terms of their histories, their politics, and their internal relations of power.

55. Quoted in Csapo and Miller 1998, 123.
56. As I noted in chapter 2, Herodotus' attitude to Athenian democracy and to Athens' empire is not one of unrestricted approval, and I do not wish to suggest that he wholeheartedly or necessarily endorsed Athenian imperialism. The basis for his comparison does seem to be the temporality of fifth-century Athens, however. See chapter 2, n. 50 above.

4 Writing Egyptian Writing

Like much of the early literature generated by Greeks about Egyptians, the historian's text records an impression of cross-cultural collision and at the same time glimpses in vexation at it. "They use two different kinds of writing (γράμμασι)," Herodotus observes, "one of which is called sacred (ἱρά) and the other common (δημοτικά)." The remark seems accurate enough as it stands, although it leaves out the hieratic script.[1] More interesting than this omission is the use of writing as an indication of cultural variance, an indication hinted at in the dual nature of Egyptian writing, but made explicit in the words that precede—for Herodotus finds in the Egyp-

---

1. Herodotus 2.36. Within the Graeco-Roman tradition, only Porphyry and Clement of Alexandria distinguish between three different kinds of Egyptian writing: today, Egyptologists refer to the three as demotic, hieratic, and hieroglyphic. See Porphyry, *Life of Pythagoras* 12, and especially Clement of Alexandria, *Stromateis* 5.4.20: "Those instructed among the Egyptians learn first of all the genre of Egyptian letters which is called 'epistolographic' (τὴν ἐπιστολογραφικὴν); secondly, the 'hieratic' genre (τὴν ἱερατικήν) which is used by the sacred scribes; finally and in the last place, the 'hieroglyphic' genre (τὴν ἱερογλυφικήν), which partly expresses things literally by means of primary letters and which is partly symbolic. In the symbolic method, one kind speaks 'literally' by imitation, a second kind writes as it were metaphorically, and a third one is outright allegorical by means of certain enigmas" (αὐτίκα οἱ παρ' Αἰγυπτίοις παιδευόμενοι πρῶτον μὲν πάντων τὴν Αἰγυπτίων γραμμάτων μέθοδον ἐκμανθάνουσι, τὴν ἐπιστολογραφικὴν καλουμένην· δευτέραν δὲ τὴν ἱερατικὴν, ᾗ χρῶνται οἱ ἱερογραμματεῖς· ὑστάτην δὲ καὶ τελευταίαν τὴν ἱερογλυφικήν, ἧς ἣ μέν ἐστι διὰ τῶν πρώτων στοιχείων κυριολογική, ἣ δὲ συμβολική. τῆς δὲ συμβολικῆς ἣ μὲν κυριολογεῖται κατὰ μίμησιν, ἣ δ' ὥσπερ τροπικῶς γράφεται, ἣ δὲ ἄντικρυς ἀλληγορεῖται κατά τινας αἰνιγμούς). On this passage in Clement, the commentary of Alain le Boulluec (Paris, 1981: Sources Chrétiennes no. 279) is essential. See also the discussion in Marestaing 1913, 105–8; Vergote 1939; and Iversen 1993, 41.

tian writing system a reflection of the inverted world inhabited by the Egyptian people: "The Greeks write and calculate moving the hand from left to right, but the Egyptians from right to left." Given the location of these remarks within a discourse on the general alterity of Egypt and Egyptians, one is tempted to formulate a universal theory of topsy-turviness according to which Greek words and things find their polar opposite in Egypt. Herodotus goes on: "That is what they *do*, but they *say* they are moving to the right and the Greeks to the left" (2.36).[2] The Egyptians, thus, agree with Herodotus when he claims that they orient their writing in a direction opposite to that of the Greeks, but the names they give to the two orientations reverse the Greek's description by changing left for right and right for left. To follow the impracticable logic of this assertion to its consequences is arduous, however, because of the bewildering disjunction between terms for left and right across the two cultures, and no amount of mental exercise can resolve the obscurity.[3] Let it, therefore, serve as a cautionary reminder to us not to repress the encounter of Greeks and Egyptians through the reductive idiom of binarism, and rather to read that encounter within a more productive language of difference.

Notwithstanding the confusion he causes his readers, Herodotus occupies a strategic place in the history of Greek views concerning Egypt and writing, whether it is a question of a description of Egyptian writing per se, or of the uses to which writing is put by the Egyptians. He is strategic by reason of his primacy, since his is the earliest surviving text to engage the subject of writing in the context of a sustained narrative about the Egyptian people. It is true that Hecateus may have discussed the topic earlier, but

2. The use of writing as a marker of cultural difference is exemplified in a passage by al-Biruni that stands in a direct line of descent from Herodotus: "The Hindus write from the left to the right like the Greeks. They do not write on the basis of a line, above which the heads of the letters rise whilst their tails go down below, as in Arabic writing. On the contrary, their ground line is above, a straight line above every single character, and from this line the letter hangs down and is written under it. Any sign *above* the line is nothing but a grammatical mark to denote the pronounciation of the character above which it stands" (Sachau 1992, vol. 1, 172–73).

3. Herodotus may also be making a joke here since when he says that the Egyptians write to the right, he uses the word *epidexia*, which can mean "auspicious, lucky" or "proper, correct." In his account, it is as if Egyptians had pointed to their leftward writing and said that they were writing their words "right," which in Greek is also "to the right." See Lloyd 1976, 162. However, Herodotus is also undeniably playing with absolute notions of right and left in this passage and with notions of intercultural translatability.

his comments are known to us partly because of Herodotus, and Hecateus' work survives only through quotations in other authors.[4] Herodotus' place is strategic also because the questions formulated by the historian seem to recur with a disconcerting persistence in subsequent literature. What social and political status does this type of technology have within the culture? To what extent does it constitute a specific mode of ethnologic thought, with its own particular order? Why do Greek sources across the ages persist in referring to Egyptian writing? In the context of this line of thought should be understood the demarcation—evident in Aeschylus and Plato as well as Herodotus—of Egypt as the graphic space par excellence, of Egyptian writing as the inscribed marker of despotic power, of the Egyptian god as the inventor of writing, or of Egyptian temples as the repository of archival memories. Across these Greek views of Egyptians and writing, moreover, runs an apprehension about the written word, especially at the levels of orality and signification, as is exemplified most vividly in Socrates' discourse to Phaedrus. The strangeness of this apprehension is made clearer when the assumptions underlying the Platonic story are set off against the attitudes of the Egyptians themselves to writing.

GRAPHOMANIA

In no persons is the mastery of graphic space manifest more visibly than in the priests of Egypt. To describe what the priests reveal to Herodotus from their written records means to relate much of what he recounts in book 2 of his history. I offered some remarks in chapters 2 and 3 about the figuration of space and time in Herodotus, and it will be useful now to consider what his text indicates about the priests in connection with their writing activities. It is not just that the priests continually make entries in their papyrus records; the effect of Herodotus' presentation is to shape Egypt

---

4. Scholia to Dionysius Thrax, 183 Hilgard (= *FGrHist* 1 F 20): Πυθόδωρος δὲ ἐν τῷ περὶ στοιχείων καὶ Φίλλις ὁ Δήλιος ἐν τῷ περὶ χρόνων πρὸ Κάδμου Δάναον μετακομίσαι αὐτά φασιν· ἐπιμαρτυροῦσι τούτοις καὶ οἱ Μιλησιακοὶ συγγραφεῖς Ἀναξίμανδρος καὶ Διονύσιος καὶ Ἑκαταῖος, οὓς καὶ Ἀπολλόδωρος ἐν Νεῶν Καταλόγῳ παρατίθεται. See Jeffery 1967, 152–53. These same scholia also say that Anticleides of Athens, the author of a book on Alexander of Macedon, attributed the invention of the alphabet to Egyptians: Ἀντικλείδης δὲ ὁ Ἀθηναῖος Αἰγυπτίοις τὴν εὕρεσιν [τῶν στοιχείων] ἀνατίθησι (scholia to Dionysius Thrax, 183 Hilgard = *FGrHist* 140 F 11b). Cf. Pliny, *Natural History* 4.67 (= Anticleides of Athens, *FGrHist* 140 F 11a): "Anticleides says that a certain person of the name of Menos, in Egypt, invented letters fifteen years before the reign of Phoroneas, the most ancient of all the kings of Greece, and this he attempts to prove by the monuments there."

and Egyptian history as dependent on the written word. The country serves for Herodotus as the locus of graphic activity and as the place where history and time are inextricably bound with the written word. By presenting Egypt to his readers with the express aid of the priests' written annals, Herodotus channels Egyptian history to his audience in a manner that regulates this chronicle in terms of its relationship to writing. The text fashions a portrait of a country in which writing serves as a defining factor, and in which the passage of time (chronology) or the succession of generations (genealogy) is understood by the device of writing. Egypt exists as the site of a graphic energy of such intensity in the historian's work that it becomes natural for Greeks henceforth to think of Egypt in conjunction with its deep antiquity, its vast archival resources, and its writing system.

Herodotus encounters the priests who write down episodes of Egypt's vast history in their annals at Memphis, Thebes, and Heliopolis, and he is told that the Heliopolitans are the greatest record-keepers (λογιώτατοι) among the Egyptians (2.3). Perhaps, the Heliopolitans are the same as "those who live around the sown parts of Egypt" because, according to a later part of Herodotus' text, these people "are great in cultivating the memory of mankind and are far the greatest record-keepers (λογιώτατοι) of any people with whom I have been in contact" (2.77). Leaving aside the particular graphic capacities of the Heliopolitans, we learn that some priests disclose to Herodotus matters connected with divinity from their annals, since, he says, even these matters were divulged to him in conversation with the priests, although he is reluctant to set forth accounts that deal with the divine in his narrative (2.3). It is the priests who unfurl the full glory of Egyptian history for their Greek visitor, beginning with Min, the first king of Egypt, and continuing down through the names of an additional 330 kings—a roster that is eventually expanded to encompass 341 names (2.142). These names occur in the lists of papyrus (βύβλου) that also divulge the information that eighteen of Egypt's kings were Ethiopian, and one was not really a king, but, being female, a queen (2.99–100).

The priests' written records contribute to the construction of recorded time in Egypt, in addition to making the country the eternal site of graphic activity. Since I have already discussed this material in chapter 3, however, I will repeat only a few of the salient details from Herodotus. By the historian's reckoning, the priests' written records signify an immense period of 341 generations or 11,340 years. Hecateus was in Thebes, as we recall from chapter 3, and he traced his genealogy and connected himself to a god in the sixteenth generation, but the priests answered the Greek wordsmith by constructing a genealogy of their own reckoning, and refused to accept that a man had been born from a god (2.143). For the last 345 generations none of the high priests had any connection to a god or hero, the priests said to Hecateus, although they also noted that there were gods who were rulers of Egypt before these men (2.143–4). Herodotus supplies further the information he receives from the priests concerning these divine beings who ruled Egypt in the distant past. Pan is thought to be the youngest of the gods in Greece but he is the oldest for the Egyptians and belongs to a group of gods known as the Eight; Heracles is of another group, the Twelve; and Dionysus is of a third group, which was born out of the Twelve. The number of years between Dionysus and Amasis is reckoned as being 15,000 and between Heracles and Amasis 17,000 (see 2.43). "The Egyptians claim that they know these matters absolutely because they are continually making their calculations and continually writing down the number of the years" (2.145). Thus, for Herodotus, writing constitutes the quintessential Egyptian activity, at once central to its priestly class, integral to the priests' conception of their own past, and a sign of the country's immense history.

Not long after Herodotus, Plato offers his own mélange of written texts, Egyptian priests, and the incredible antiquity of Egyptian civilization. As with my discussion of Herodotus, I refer to another part of this book for a fuller treatment, and I shall not dwell in this chapter on the remarks Plato makes in *Timaeus* and *Critias:* I consider these works in chapter 6, in connection with the story of Atlantis. I note here the affiliation, in these dialogues, of the Egyptians to writing and of the Greeks to a culture that relies primarily on the transmission of ideas by oral means. Ambiguities in *Timaeus* and *Critias* make it difficult to assess the precise role of writing among the Greek recollections in the narrative, but it is nonetheless clear that, by contrast with Greece, the broad association of Egypt with the written word is prevalent as much in Plato as in Herodotus. We shall come to see that Plato's use of writing, like Herodotus' work, raises troubling questions about the Greeks' ethnocentrism in matters of history, temporality, and politics. About these very subjects, Michel de Certeau observed, "History is homogenous to the documents of Western activity. It credits them with a 'consciousness' that it can easily recognize. History is developed in the continuity of signs left by scriptural activities: it is satisfied with arranging them, composing a single text from the thousands of written fragments in which already expressed is that labor which constructs time. . . ."[5] What is interesting in the Platonic case, nevertheless, is that graphic consciousness is imputed to Egyptians and then, in turn, put in service of a

5. See de Certeau 1988, 210.

larger "historical" narrative that is ultimately more revealing about Greek notions of time and history.

The assertion of this graphomania is not to deny the Egyptians the ability to exploit oral language in the traditions handed down to us by Herodotus and Plato. In *Timaeus* itself, the recollection of the history of the originary Athens is not purely derived from written records, since the sacred texts of the Egyptian priest are based on hearsay (ἀκοῇ, 23a), and the priest himself appears to be speaking from memory because he invites Solon to consult the actual writings (τὰ γράμματα, 24a) at a later time. Herodotus also reminds us, at the beginning of book 2, of Psammetichus' experiment to determine the oldest people in the world, and this experiment, related to the historian by the priests, places a strong significance on oral discourse. The Egyptians concede priority in age to the Phrygians, according to Herodotus, since the first word *spoken* by two children raised in isolation, "bekos," was the same as the Phrygian word for bread. For once, therefore, it appears that an issue concerned with the antiquity of Egyptians is posed in terms of an oral rather than a written framework. A passage from Plato's *Philebus* also bears consideration in the light of our discussion:

> We might take our letters again to illustrate what I mean now. . . .
> The unlimited variety of sound was once discerned by some god, or
> perhaps some godlike man; you know the story that there was some
> such person in Egypt called Theuth. He it was who originally discerned
> the existence, in that unlimited variety, of the vowels—not "vowel"
> in the singular but "vowels" in the plural—and then of other things
> which, though they could not be called articulate sounds, yet were
> noises of a kind. There was a number of them, too, not just one, and
> as a third class he discriminated what we now call the mutes. Having
> done that, he divided up the noiseless ones or mutes until he got each
> one by itself, and did the same thing with the vowels and the inter-
> mediate sounds; in the end he found a number of the things, and af-
> fixed to the whole collection, as to each single member of it, the name
> "letter." It was because he realized that none of us could get to know
> one of the collection all by itself, in isolation from the rest, that he
> conceived of "letter" as a kind of bond of unity uniting as it were
> all these sounds into one, and so he gave utterance to the expression
> "art of letters," implying that there was one art that dealt with the
> sounds. (18b-d)

Socrates, too, gives overt emphasis to oral discourse, sound, and utterance by describing Theuth's activities in Egypt. Whether the effect is intended or not, however, it should be added that Socrates' description of phonic intervals and linguistic differences in connection with Theuth also draws on an analogy that is made possible by writing and by knowledge of letters (see 17a-b).[6]

THE TYRANT'S WRIT

François Hartog, Stephanie West, and others have argued that Herodotus' work usually associates writing more closely with barbarians than with Greeks.[7] In her study of the myths and images of writing in ancient Greece, *The Tyrant's Writ*, Deborah T. Steiner follows these scholars by opposing writing and tyranny to democracy and oral discourse in Herodotus' histories, and she finds that writing "gathers both sinister and pejorative associations, and appears within a complex of activities designed to illustrate the despotism of the Oriental monarchs."[8] For Herodotus, Steiner observes, "to write . . . is to enter the world of the tyrant, to set oneself on the side of the autocrat, the oppressor, the enslaver."[9] Eastern kings set up more inscriptions than did any other type of individual in Herodotus' history.[10] Examples of written objects created by Eastern tyrants are commemorative pillars, boundary stones, graves, statues, catalogues, inventories, dispatches, coins, and seals. On the other hand, Herodotus' Greeks indulge more in oral discourse, debate, and discussion than in written communication, although he never explicitly privileges speech over writing. Herodotus' use of writing, then, has obvious implications for the stereotype of oriental despotism and for the civic ideology of the democratic polis.

Among the numerous instances of barbarian writing, the more flamboyant examples of the despot's exploitation of the written word occur in the Egyptian sections of Herodotus' history. Herodotus does not specify whether Sesostris actually inscribed hieroglyphs on his monuments, as was usual for such displays in ancient Egypt, but the king's ostentation

---

6. The point is stressed in Derrida 1981: "As in Saussure's *Course in General Linguistics,* the scriptural reference becomes absolutely indispensable at the point at which the principle of difference and diacriticity in general must be accounted for as the very condition of signification. . . . The scriptural 'metaphor' thus crops up every time difference and relation are irreducible, every time otherness introduces determination and puts a system in circulation. The play of the other within being must needs be designated 'writing' by Plato in a discourse which would like to think of itself as spoken in essence, in truth, and which nevertheless is written" (162–63).

7. Hartog 1988, 277–81; West 1985; Thomas 1992, 130.

8. Steiner 1994, 127.

9. Steiner 1994, 128.

10. See West 1985 and Steiner 1994, 132.

could have taken advantage of the pictorial character of the script: "Now, wherever he encountered men of bravery, who strove for freedom, among such folk he set up pillars in their lands that declared his own name and country and how he had conquered them by his own power. But when he had taken over cities without a fight and easily, for them he also made records on the pillars in just such terms as he used for the men who were brave, but, you see, he also had female genitalia drawn thereon because he would make clear that they were cowards" (2.102).[11] The historian asserts that most of the pillars that Sesostris had erected inside Egypt are no longer standing in his time, but that he saw some in Palestinian Syria with the inscriptions and the genitalia (2.106). He also saw two statues of Sesostris in Ionia; each was almost seven feet, with a spear in the right hand, a bow in the left and from one shoulder to the other, across the breast, an hieroglyphic inscription saying: "I won this land with my shoulders." Rulers of Egypt other than Sesostris are also recorded as commemorating their achievements by the written word. Cheops' pyramid, another monument to pharaonic extravagance, also bears Egyptian writing on it that discloses the amounts spent on radishes, onions, and garlic for the men who built it (2.125). An interpreter translates the writing for Herodotus, and puts the sum of money at sixteen hundred talents of silver. And the kings Asuchis and Sethos are also responsible for inscribed messages (2.136, 141).

With Aeschylus, who completed his *Suppliants* before Herodotus published his histories, Egyptian writing is also used to foreground the distinction between Greeks and Egyptians by linking writing with autocracy and anti-democratic values. It is true that *Suppliants* tends to complicate dichotomous relationships by giving the Danaids familial links to Greece and Egypt, as we saw in chapter 1, or by making a monarch into a mouthpiece for democratic sentiments. However, many of the attacks made in the play cluster around the space of Egypt, and in at least one passage the drama seems to cast aspersions against Egypt and its mode of written discourse, while Egyptian behavior and Egyptian writing invite broadly similar terms of denigration. The brute force of βία, the reluctance to rely on persuasive language, the disregard for Greek custom and the proclivity for writing on papyrus drift into the general locus of the sign "Egypt."

11. Herodotus' report about Sesostris and female genitalia may have some basis in fact. See Hare 1999, 110–11, who observes that Senusret III (1874–1855 B.C.E.) had the phallus determinative on the Semna stela mutilated as a derogation of the Nubian enemy. On Sesostris, see also chapter 2 above.

Whereas Herodotus does not explicitly pose the general opposition of oral and written discourse, Aeschylus' play appears both to pose the dichotomy forcefully and to raise questions of propriety about writing. Pelasgus convenes an assembly of the people of Argos to decide whether to give refuge to the fifty Danaids and their father Danaus. Pelasgus rules over Argos as its king, but, like an orator in democratic Athens, he uses πειθώ (523), persuasion, to sway the assembly into giving sanctuary to the refugees. The Argive people announce their decision in favor of the Danaids through voting pebbles after they have heard Pelasgus, whom Danaus calls δημη-γόρος (623), a word used of public speakers in fifth-century Athens. When the Egyptian herald blusters on stage, he threatens and orders the Danaids to follow him, and his stratagem depends on force (βία), rather than persuasion (πειθώ). The herald allies himself against the rule of law and with the lawless behavior typical of barbarians and tyrants in Greek tragedy.[12] Earlier in the play, even the Danaids revealed traces of their barbarian colors by telling Pelasgus that as sole ruler he need not wait for and defer to the people's verdict (370–75), thus contrasting Athenian democracy with barbarian highhandedness. But in his words to the herald, Pelasgus respects the popular assembly and stands by its decision (940–49):

ταύτας δ' ἑκούσας μὲν κατ' εὔνοιαν φρενῶν
ἄγοις ἄν, εἴπερ εὐσεβὴς πίθοι λόγος·
τοιάδε δημόπρακτος ἐκ πόλεως μία
ψῆφος κέκρανται, μήποτ' ἐκδοῦναι βίᾳ
στόλον γυναικῶν· τῶνδ' ἐφήλωται τορῶς
γόμφος διαμπάξ, ὡς μένειν ἀραρότως.
ταῦτ' οὐ πίναξίν ἐστιν ἐγγεγραμμένα
οὐδ' ἐν πτυχαῖς βύβλων κατεσφραγισμένα,
σαφῆ δ' ἀκούεις ἐξ ἐλευθεροστόμου
γλώσσης. κομίζου δ' ὡς τάχιστ' ἐξ ὀμμάτων.

You could lead them away voluntarily, with good will, if pious logos should persuade them; a city's unanimous vote has decreed thus: never to surrender the host of women to force; the nail of this resolve has been driven in piercingly so as to remain fixed. This message is not inscribed in tablets nor sealed in the folds of papyrus; you hear it clearly from the tongue of a free man. Now get out of my sight.

Apart from bringing together several key shibboleths (πείθω, λόγος, βία), the passage contrasts the oral discourse of the Greek king with the written

12. See Hall 1989, 190–200.

discourse of the Egyptians. The way for the herald to carry off the Danaids lies through persuasive language; only if the herald's persuasiveness is effective will the Greeks allow him to lead away the women. Greeks will never submit to brute force. This decree, resolved by the Argive people in a pseudodemocratic assembly, is said to have a nail "driven in piercingly so as to remain fixed"—surely an allusion to the notices "nailed up" in the Athenian agora for all residents to see. Not all writing is suspect, therefore. Written texts that are publicly discussed and displayed, visible to all citizens in the democracy, and unanimously sanctioned before publication are preferred to the private, hidden writings on wax tablets or sheets of papyrus. The former can be read out by the lips of free men, while the latter are characteristic of barbarian violence and deception. By saying to the herald "you hear it clearly from the tongue of a free man," Pelasgus points out that he is reiterating the Argives' decree orally, and also that he is not just speaking out but reading out a public notice of that decree, which contrasts with the antidemocratic papyrus imputed to the Egyptians.[13]

What is also noteworthy about these passages from Aeschylus and Herodotus is the inconsistency in the attitudes of Greeks to inscriptions, so that the publicly displayed written text in Athens evokes the notional openness of Athenian democracy, and the monumental inscription put up by barbarians such as the Egyptians signifies the tyrant's power. Whereas the Athenian text solicits oral discussion and disputation, by this logic, the barbarian monument in contrast epitomizes the autocracy and despotism of its ruler. By setting forth the written text in the public arena, the Athenians believed that they were allowing the text to be consulted and freely discussed and that they were not encouraging the clandestine transfer of information. Jean-Pierre Vernant states the Greek attitude thus:

> To put a text in writing is to set down one's message *es meson*, at the center of the community—that is, to place it openly at the disposal of the group as a whole. By being written down, the *logos* is brought into the public square; like magistrates who have just discharged their duties, it must now give an account of itself before all and sundry and justify itself in the face of the objections and challenges that anyone has the right to bring against it.[14]

---

13. The passage from *Suppliants* is also discussed in Petre 1986; Steiner 1994, 166–68; Detienne 1996, 105. See also *Suppliants* 991–92 and *Prometheus Bound* 811.

14. Vernant 1990, 207; similar statements in Vernant 1982, 52–54, and Detienne 1996, 91–102. For speech ἐς μέσον in Herodotus, see 1.207; 3.80, 83, 142; 4.118, 161; 7.8, 164; 8.21, 73.

Yet the Greek attitude conveys only some of the consequences of public writing, since the monumental inscription can also serve the ideology of the democracies that cause it to be erected.

Herodotus is following what he saw or heard about foreign practices when he associates writing, especially writing on monuments, with Egyptians and other barbarians, and he is faithful to the evidence to the extent that monumental writing did promote elite ideologies in Egyptian and other non-Greek cultures. However, to state the matter thus is misleading since the setting up and display of written texts on stone in Greek public places points to one way in which writing promoted the ideology of Greek states. In Greece, the stone inscriptions had a value that was often more symbolic than "documentary," which in fact paralleled their use in Egypt. The tribute lists on the Athenian acropolis listed the names of those states that paid tribute to Athena and so to Athens and its imperial hegemony. Public erection and public display were conditions in certain decrees or treaties; it was not enough for the city to place a copy of the text in its "archives," which in any case were never as bureaucratized as those in ancient Mesopotamia or Egypt. The archives were not formalized or systematically organized, and we may doubt whether Greeks used writing for strictly administrative purposes. No evidence exists for an "archive mentality" in places such as Sparta, which had no archives at all, or Athens, where the Metroön was established in the late fifth century.[15] Even when the city placed a copy of a treaty in its archive, it referred to the monumental rather than the archival version as the treaty itself. Hence, many public inscriptions contained written threats to warn readers not to destroy them. In cases where curses intensified the inscription's directives, as they did in Teos, for example, the monumental display obviously enhanced the weight of the curse.[16] As Rosalind Thomas observes, "public, exemplary, and monumental inscriptions were probably the most characteristic public use of written record in the service of the classical city-state."[17]

THE GODS OF WRITING

Well then, what I heard was that there was at Naukratis in
Egypt one of the ancient gods of that country, the one to whom
the sacred bird they call the ibis belongs; the divinity's own name

15. For Sparta, see Cartledge 1978 and Boring 1979. For a view different from mine concerning Athens, see Sickinger 1999, who argues that "documents on stone formed only a small part of the much larger picture of Athenian public records" (5).

16. For Teos, see ML no. 30.

17. Thomas 1992, 140; cf. Sickinger 1999.

was Theuth. The story was that he was the first to discover number
and calculation, and geometry and astronomy, and also games of
draughts and dice; and to cap it all, letters. King of all Egypt at that
time was Thamus—all of it, that is, that surrounds the great city
of the upper region which the Greeks call Egyptian Thebes; and
the god [Thamus] they call Ammon. Theuth came to him and
displayed his technical inventions, saying that they should be
passed on to the rest of the Egyptians; and Thamus asked what
benefit each brought. As Theuth went through them, Thamus
criticized or praised whatever he seemed to be getting right or
wrong. The story goes that Thamus expressed many views to
Theuth about each science, both for and against; it would take
a long time to go through them in detail, but when it came to
the subject of letters, Theuth said, "But this study, my king, will
make the Egyptians wiser and improve their memory; what I have
discovered is a *pharmakon* of memory and wisdom." The other
replied, "Most scientific Theuth, one man has the ability to beget
the elements of a science, but it belongs to a different person to
be able to judge what measure of harm and benefit it contains for
those who are going to make use of it; so now you, as the father of
letters, have been led by your affection for them to describe them
as having the opposite of their real effect. For your invention will
produce forgetfulness in the souls of those who have learned it,
through lack of practice at using their memory, as through reliance
on writing they are reminded from outside by alien marks, not
from inside, themselves by themselves: you have discovered a
pharmakon not of memory but of reminding. To your students
you give an appearance of wisdom, not the reality of it; having
heard much, in the absence of teaching, they will appear to know
much when for the most part they know nothing, and they will be
difficult to get along with because they have acquired the
appearance of wisdom instead of wisdom itself."

Phaedrus 274c–275b[18]

The problem of spoken and written discourse arises quite notoriously in
Plato's *Phaedrus,* a dialogue which also raises the question with reference
to Egypt. Analysis of Socrates' story of Theuth and Thamus needs to di-
verge in at least two directions, however, one to account for the graft of
the Egyptian tradition concerning Thoth onto a Greek text, and the other
to evaluate the story's claims about writing and speech from an Egyptian as
well as a Greek perspective. To move in the first direction will require un-

18. Translations of Plato's *Phaedrus* are modified from Rowe 1986.

derstanding of the differing traditions associated with Greek and Egyptian inventors of writings, with Prometheus, Palamedes, and Orpheus on one side and with Thoth on the other. To move in the second direction will entail a discussion of the critical assumptions that lie behind the Greek and Egyptian writing systems.

Greek Inventors

The contrast between Greek and Egyptian attitudes to writing is reflected, in part, in the difference between the reputed inventors of the technology in each culture. *Greek* inventors of writing such as Palamedes, Orpheus, and even the Platonic Theuth figure in narratives that refer to the deleterious, harmful, or destructive consequences of writing, whereas the *Egyptian* Thoth represents the sacrosanct and performative nature of the hieroglyphic script. Numerous Greek texts demarcate writing as an area of anxiety, in contrast to the Egyptian traditions surrounding the god Thoth that reflect the vital and cosmic power of writing within the culture. This cross-cultural difference about inventors is important and can be developed with a few particulars.

The qualities surrounding Greek inventors of writing such as Prometheus, Palamedes, and Orpheus should be compared to Thoth's creative and performative powers.[19] The originary myths about writing in Greece contrast vividly with the Egyptian ideas concerned with Thoth—as Marcel Detienne and David Frankfurter submit—since the Greek myths either locate the written word in proximity to anxiety and deceit, or render it subordinate to the musical, the aural, and the oral.[20] Prometheus' deception of Zeus and his subsequent chastisement are the background to the lines in *Prometheus Bound* where the Titan includes writing among the gifts he gave to humankind (459–61).[21] Similarly, Palamedes' inventions other than writing—dice, measures, the art of posting sentinels—convey the

---

19. I do not treat here all the purported inventors of the alphabet. A full list of inventors would have to include Palamedes, Orpheus, Theuth, Prometheus, Hermes, Danaus, and Cadmus. See Jeffery 1967; Harrison 1998, n. 96; and n. 4 above.

20. See Detienne's essay "L'écriture inventive (entre la voix d'Orphée et l'intelligence de Palamède)" in *Critique* 475 (1986): 1225–34, reprinted as "Une écriture inventive, la voix d'Orphée, les jeux de Palamède," in Detienne 1989, 101–15; and Frankfurter 1994.

21. Parallels between the story of Prometheus and Theuth-Thamus are often suggested: see e.g. Hackforth 1952, 157 n. 2; Rowe 1986, 208–9; and cf. de Vries 1969, 248; Burger 1980, 93.

slippery nature of the written word,[22] and his fate suggests how writing is conceived as an "instrument of deceit"[23] at its founding moment, since Odysseus destroys him by means of a letter, forged so as to be from Priam to Palamedes.[24] In the case of Orpheus and the Orphic tradition, writing is not so much denigrated as given a smaller significance than orality, voice, and sound.[25] The word *stoicheion,* in the sense of both letter and element, reflects "the tendency of Greek culture to transcend the writing itself, to reach an 'oral' state of pure planetary sound, to abstract ideas from the immediate forms of reality."[26] The Orphic tradition, thus, conceived of writing as the *instrument* for vocalized sound and for the voice of its hero Orpheus, and this remains true even though Walter Burkert is probably correct in claiming that "with the Orphica literacy takes hold in a field that had previously been dominated by the immediacy of ritual and the spoken word of myth."[27]

Socrates adheres to Egyptian beliefs concerning the god's inventive capacities by presenting Theuth as the inventor of writing, it is true, but he

22. Palamedes' inventions are dice, lighthouses, scales, measures, the discus, the art of posting sentinels, and the alphabet: see e.g. Gorgias, *Defense of Palamedes* (DK 82 B 11a) 30; Pausanias 2.20.3 and 10.31.1; Philostratus, *Heroica* 10; scholia on Euripides' *Orestes* 432; Servius on Virgil's *Aeneid* 2.81; Tzetzes, *On Lycophron* 384. The idea that Palamedes invented writing dates back at least to Stesichorus' *Oresteia:* Στησίχορος ἐν δευτέρῳ τῆς 'Ορεστείας . . . τὸν Παλαμήδην φησὶν εὑρεκέναι [τὰ στοιχεῖα]: Page, *PMG* 213 (= scholia to Dionysius Thrax, p. 183 Hilgard). Wüst 1942 assembles the bulk of the ancient evidence concerning Palamedes; Woodford 1994 discusses the evidence, with special emphasis on the iconographic material; cf. Woodford, *LIMC,* s.v. "Palamedes." Nightingale 1995, 149–54, suggests that the story of Palamedes, especially as recounted in tragedy, provides the subtext to Plato's tale of Theuth and Thamus. Parallels between Euripides' *Palamedes* and Plato's tale are also noted in Ferrari 1987, 280–81 n. 2.

23. Frankfurter 1994, 190. For a different reading of the inventions credited to Palamedes and Theuth, see Kurke 1999, 249–53, who argues that the inventions in each case "have a positive moral value in their service to the community" (251).

24. Apollodorus, *Epitome* 3.8; Hyginus, *Fabula* 105; scholia on Euripides' *Orestes* 432.

25. The tradition is ambiguous about Orpheus' status as inventor of writing. Pseudo-Alcidamas, *Odysseus* 24, credits Orpheus with the invention of writing; Plato, *Laws* 677d, has Clinias mention Orpheus along with other cultural heroes such as Daedalus, Palamedes, Marsyas, and Olympus, but does not specify writing; and inversely, Androtion, the fourth-century Atthidographer and student of Isocrates, is recorded in Aelian, *Historical Miscellany* 8.6, as having cast doubt on Orpheus' ability to read and write. See Detienne 1989, 110–11, and Steiner 1994, 195.

26. Frankfurter 1994, 191, following Franz Dornseiff, *Das Alphabet in Mystik und Magie,* Stoixeia 7 (Leipzig, 1925), 14–17.

27. Burkert 1985, 293, also quoted in Frankfurter 1994.

also invokes the framework of the various Greek cultural figures connected with writing: for one thing, Theuth's inventions include games of draughts and dice, number, calculation, geometry, and astronomy; for another, writing figures within the context of a parable that ends with the king's warnings about writing. In short, the anxieties about writing expressed by Socrates in *Phaedrus* fall within the Greek rather than the Egyptian tradition, as is evident from the specific remarks given in the Theuth-Thamus episode and the remarks following the episode. Thamus attacks writing on the grounds that it "will produce forgetfulness in the souls of those who have learned it, through lack of practice of using their memory, as through reliance on writing they are reminded from outside by alien marks, not from inside, themselves by themselves" and on the grounds that it will give "the appearance of wisdom (σοφίας . . . δόξαν), not the reality (ἀλήθειαν) of it" (275a). Socrates adds to Thamus' criticism and claims that writing, like painting, is unable to respond when asked questions and repeats the same thing again and again (275d). The written text also circulates outside the control of its author, Socrates notes, so that "when it is ill-treated and unjustly abused, it always needs its father to help it; for it is incapable of defending or helping itself" (275e). He appears to compare the person who relies on writing to a farmer who plants his seeds in a garden of Adonis, and he calls writing an amusement (παιδιά, 276b).

It would be inconsistent to infer from these remarks that Plato is strenuously opposed to all writing, nor does the Platonic Socrates offer reasons to make such an inference. The effect of Plato's presentation, rather, is to position writing within a zone of apprehension, to caution against its dangers, and to seek a way in which to practice it fruitfully. Socrates says that writing per se (αὐτό γε τὸ γράφειν λόγους) is not shameful (αἰσχρόν) but what is shameful is speaking and writing in an unacceptable way (τὸ μὴ καλῶς λέγειν τε καὶ γράφειν), that is, shamefully and badly (αἰσχρῶς τε καὶ κακῶς, 258d). Later in the dialogue, Socrates introduces the Theuth-Thamus story by observing, "What we have left is the subject of propriety and impropriety in writing: in what way, when it is done, it will be done acceptably and in what way improperly" (274b). Moreover, the *Phaedrus* is replete with various ironies that tend to undermine a straightforward criticism of writing. Not least among these ironies is the fact that the dialogue itself survives in written form, that Phaedrus displays one of the weaknesses of reliance on the written word by asking to be reminded of an earlier part of the discussion (277b), and that Socrates defines a legitimate way of *speaking* as "one that is *written* together with knowledge in the soul of the learner" (276a). Rather than condemning the written word altogether, then, Socrates appears to be advocating a limited use for writing in which it remains subordinate to oral discourse and is placed in the service of philosophical dialectic.

In affirming that Socrates does not reject writing completely in *Phaedrus*, I am giving only a partial reading of Plato's comments about writing, since he treats the question of writing elsewhere in his dialogues, for example in *Laws* (discussed in chapter 5 below), and he also expresses misgivings about writing in two of his *Letters* (the second, 314b-c, and seventh, 341b-345a), though the authenticity of these works is open to question. Further, Aristotle famously distinguishes in *Physics* between what Plato says in "so-called unwritten opinions" and what he says about place in *Timaeus*, although it is hard to determine the precise valuation imputed to Plato's unwritten opinions in this passage in Aristotle (209b14–15). To complicate the study of Plato's treatment of writing, moreover, it should be mentioned that modern scholars themselves are unable to arrive at a consensus on the subject, whether they are considering *Phaedrus* in particular or the Platonic corpus in general. G. R. F. Ferrari, for instance, distinguishes between three different interpretations of Plato's remarks about writing in *Phaedrus* and then proceeds to modify one of these in pursuit of a fourth.[28] What is certain from a consideration of these studies, nevertheless, is that writing is an area of high anxiety for Plato, whether or not one agrees on the depth of Socrates' criticisms, on the ironies in the text, and on the level of Plato's commitment to the written word.

The Egyptian Thoth

As the functions of Thoth indicate, the Egyptian god poses a strong contrast to the Greek heroes and founders of writing. In Greece, the invention of writing occurs in situations that involve deceit or evasiveness, and the inventors themselves engage in actions that are questionable or merit punishment. But the Egyptian god "was charged with important responsibilities in the administration of the world," and he appears in contexts that point to the sacrosanct and creative nature of writing.[29] The written word was deemed sacred in ancient Egypt, as the Greek term "hieroglyph" correctly implies, and Thoth's role in Egyptian traditions draws out precisely the sacred and the powerful nature of hieroglyphic writing. He appears in the Egyptian narratives as an aide to the creator god, and he is the first to find written language, the god of scribes, the preserver of the cosmic order

28. Ferrari 1987, 206–22.
29. Meeks and Favard-Meeks 1996, 100.

that is *maat*, the apportioner of time, and the overseer of the journey from this world to the next.[30] In some contexts he is the "lord of time" and "the king of eternity," the god "who guides heaven, earth, and the nether world, and makes life for men."[31] Unsurprisingly for the god of writing, his actions tend to the enhancement of societal memory and the conservation of knowledge, both for the society of gods and the society of human beings, that is, for all creation. "To draw up a catalogue of written signs was to draw up a catalogue of all that had been created. It is possible that Thoth kept an inventory of these 'imprints' and could make a tally of them."[32] The evidence, thus, indicates vital discontinuities at several levels between the Greek and Egyptian founders of writing.

Thoth's chief renown comes from his role as the deity who presides over writing, and his activities in this capacity should be emphasized accordingly. Thoth first gives languages to human beings, and hieroglyphic writing is referred to as "a letter written in the writing of Thoth." The god himself often appears in the act of writing, so that books are said to have been written by him as the patron god of scribes, while writers in the House of Life labor under his jurisdiction. A cultic hymn praises Thoth as "he who has given words and script, who makes the temples to prosper, who founds shrines and makes the gods to know what is needful."[33] His connections to writing activities are in many respects more immediate than the Greek gods' ties to writing, and in contrast to the Greek gods who *inspire* their poets to the heights of literary creativity, Thoth actually *writes* texts and functions as an "author," and does not stimulate people to write. In Egyptian texts, divine authorship occasionally replaces scribal authorship—the gods rarely inspire a linguistic composition—and the divine author is usually Thoth: "[Thoth] has written for you with his own fingers the Book of Breathings."[34] In his capacity as the god of writing and hieroglyphs, more-

30. As the escort of the dead, and also as god of writing and as the messenger of the gods, Thoth resembles Hermes, with whom the Greeks identified him. During the Late Period, which witnessed an increase in contact between Egyptians and Greeks, Thoth ascends from being "twice great" to "thrice great," *trismegistos*. However, the explicit equation between Thoth and Hermes Trismegistus first appears in about 165 B.C.E., in Greek and demotic evidence from Saqqara: see Hornung 1982, 186 and n. 156. For this Graeco-Egyptian Hermes, see Fowden 1993, and for the Hermetic writings, see Copenhaver 1992.

31. Boylan 1922, 86.

32. Meeks and Favard-Meeks 1996, 105.

33. Boylan 1922, 95.

34. Divine authorship is discussed in Morenz 1973, 219–21; the citation is from 219.

over, Thoth presides over the choice of the pharaoh's five official titles and with the help of Seshat, the goddess of writing, he registers the years of the pharaoh's reign, "I write for you years without number and hundreds of thousands of *heb sed* feasts."[35] Thus his jurisdiction over the written language helps make him central both to pharaonic power and kingship and to the official commemoration of the royal record.

The opposition between Greek and Egyptian inventors of writing is brought out clearly in Thoth's importance to the maintenance of cosmic order and balance, or *maat.* Like the scribes on earth who may serve as secretaries to the pharaoh, Thoth acts as Re's secretary and helps him with his pen, "Daily Thoth writes *maat* for you."[36] At other times, Thoth serves as the "vizier" at the head of Re's court, or as his "representative" *(stj),*[37] or as his son.[38] As the quotation above implies, Thoth preserves the fragile cosmic order by protecting *maat,* often in the context of his control over language: "I, Thoth, am the eminent writer, pure of hands . . . the writer of *maat,* whose horror is the lie . . . the lord of the laws . . . I am the lord of *maat,* I teach *maat* to the gods, I test (each) word for its veracity. . . ."[39] As Erik Hornung observes, "The sacred eye [of Horus] is often shown in the hands of a baboon—an allusion to Thoth, who healed the eye, brought about reconciliation, and in turn reestablished *maat.* . . . When in the form of a baboon Thoth crouches in the sun god's barge and extends the eye to Re, he indicates the cosmic order of the stars, which unwaveringly follow their course. This too is *maat.*"[40] Against the anxiety and slipperiness that surrounds Greek inventors of writing, then, Thoth appears in Egyptian materials that reaffirm his pivotal influence on the harmony of things and that insist on his continued involvement in human and divine order.

Power over language, it is true, does not fall exclusively to the province of Thoth alone, since such power is manifest widely in Egyptian religion. Nevertheless, the creative powers of language are made explicit for the Egyptian tradition even by the narratives that exclude Thoth. Ptah, too, creates with the help of language: "having first devised the world in his

---

35. Boylan 1922, 85, 87.
36. Bleeker 1973, 119. On the subject of pens: the Egyptian pen was typically a rush, and the Greek pen a reed. In the Ptolemaic period, some Egyptian scribes appear to have used a rush rather than a reed to write Greek. See Tait 1988.
37. Erman 1937, 81; Hornung 1982, 232.
38. Hornung 1982, 236.
39. Bleeker 1973, 119.
40. Hornung 1992, 142.

heart, he then calls it into existence with his tongue."[41] The creator in human form, Atum, uses not his tongue, but generates the first sperm either by masturbation or by spitting and coughing, the latter processes being intimately linked to the organ of spoken discourse. The creator in bird form let loose a shriek that "pierced the original stillness before the sun emerged from the bird's egg."[42] This primordial egg, relics of which were later situated at Thoth's cult center in Hermopolis, is described as "the egg of the great cackler," and even Amun is known as the great cackler.[43] According to the Pyramid Texts, the sun god exploits "insightful planning (Sia), creative statement (Hu), and powerful magic (Heka)."[44] In other texts, the goddess Neith summons "the world into being through seven statements, which in a later magic text become the sevenfold laugh of the creator god."[45] Thus, both Thoth and other deities remind us of the prominence given to the sacred and performative aspects of the written word in the Egyptian tradition.

In emphasizing the negative effects of Thoth's invention in *Phaedrus*, Plato tellingly ignores the mediating and balancing role assumed by the god in his habitual preservation of the cosmic order. Thoth "was at once the Perceptive One *(sia)* and the one who knew everything *(rekh)*. The two kinds of knowledge were harmoniously combined in his person. His peculiarity was to receive the first one *(sia)* and to transmit the second one *(rekh)*."[46] But according to Plato's Ammon, who may be standing in for the Egyptian god Atum, writing has deleterious consequences; it brings about forgetfulness. As Dimitri Meeks and Christine Favard-Meeks observe, "This amounts to saying that the assiduous pursuit of rekh must necessarily lead to the progressive loss of sia, and, ultimately, to the abandonment of creative thought." From an Egyptian perspective, Plato's overvaluation of the creative power of sia and the repetitive power of rekh ignores the equilibrium that Thoth brings to his activities and duties. Thus, contrary to the implications of Plato's story, "Thoth's capacity to handle rekh and sia with equal skill gave him a balanced, even-handed role that led others to compare him to the plummet of a scale and invested his intermediary function with its full significance."[47] Whatever the sources for Plato's story

41. Hornung 1992, 43.
42. Hornung 1992, 42.
43. Morenz 1973, 178.
44. Hornung 1992, 44.
45. Ibid.
46. Meeks and Favard-Meeks 1996, 101.
47. Meeks and Favard-Meeks 1996, 101.

about Theuth and Thamus in *Phaedrus,* the philosopher seems to have been distorting for his own purposes the basic thrust of the Egyptian tradition concerning Thoth.

Thoth and the rest of the Egyptian gods, then, present a clear departure from the archaic and classical Greek figures connected with writing. Unlike the scenario in Greece, as outlined above, the evidence from Egypt celebrates and reconfirms the powerful creative and performative nature of the written word within the tradition. Further, this valuation of writing and the position of Thoth in relation to it are not simply flourishes of a certain moment or phase of scribal importance, but on the contrary are thoroughly attested in all periods of ancient Egyptian history. By the time Plato was composing his story about Theuth, Thamus, and the written word, these traditions surrounding both writing and the gods of writing were firmly established as canonical in Egypt. In imputing his story to an Egyptian source, therefore, Plato is being quite disingenuous and he cannot be taken to represent with any reasonable accuracy the native Egyptian views of Thoth and writing, beyond the claim that connects Thoth with the introduction of the technology. Some of the disconnect that occurs between Socrates' story and the Egyptian traditions about writing we have already explored; a large part of it can be better understood and evaluated in the light of a closer study of Plato's assumptions about writing and of the Egyptian writing system itself.

PLATO'S GRAMMATOLOGY

Both the Socratic attitude to writing in *Phaedrus* and the general tradition this anxiety represents deviate considerably from Egyptian attitudes, as we just saw, even if the Greek philosopher does not repudiate all instances of writing. The divergence between these two cultural traditions can be explicated further by comparing the assumptions that in each case inform the relationship to writing. For this reason, it will be instructive, first, to appeal to one critic's engagement with *Phaedrus,* in order to describe Plato's assumptions, and then to relate by contrast an ancient Egyptian formulation of the same problem.

In his essays on grammatology, Jacques Derrida follows Friedrich Nietzsche, Martin Heidegger, and others by continuing to challenge the foundational polarities of Western metaphysics, through a problematization of conceptions of language: "All the metaphysical determinations of truth, and even the one beyond metaphysical onto-theology that Heidegger reminds us of, are more or less immediately inseparable from the instance of the logos, or of a reason of thought within the lineage of the logos, in whatever sense it is understood. . . ."[48] The Platonic opposition of speech and writing is, for Derrida, the key to a series of polarities that characterize the European philosophical tradition such as presence and absence, man and woman, good and evil, mind and matter, and so on. However, each side of the polarity does not carry equal value; rather, he claims that the philosophical tradition has consistently prioritized the first term in each of the polarities cited above. Thus, the series of polarities are not merely equations of two equal and opposite entities; they are also hierarchical so that speech, presence, man, good, and mind have persistently been valued more highly than writing, absence, woman, evil, and matter. The second term in each polarity is defined negatively in relation to the first, whether as a fall, lack, deviation, error, or distortion.

Concentrating on the relation between speech and writing in *Phaedrus*, Derrida argues not only that Plato "thinks of writing . . . on the basis of *opposition* as such,"[49] but also that the *possibility* of placing writing in opposition to speech is an illusion. For Derrida, speech is already constituted by writing. To demarcate speech as separate from writing, therefore, is to project outside what is already inside. One basis for this conclusion is the number of scriptural metaphors present in the text: when Socrates states his preference for *speech*, he adds that it should be *"written* together with knowledge in the soul of the learner" (276a5–6). The scriptural metaphor, thus, borrows a term "from the order of the very thing one is trying to exclude from it," and also thereby complicates the boundary between the literal and figurative.[50] Another basis for Derrida's view is the description of writing as *pharmakon*, which means both "remedy" and "poison": but neither antonym is an adequate translation and this indeterminacy of the "proper meaning," and indeed the difficulty of "reconstituting the entire chain of significations of the *pharmakon*," make it possible to deny the clear opposition between writing and speech.[51]

48. Derrida 1976, 10. There are few sympathetic readings of Derrida's analyses of Plato's *Phaedrus:* however, see Neel 1988, esp. chs. 5–7, and Zuckert 1996, chs. 7–8.

49. Derrida 1981, 103.

50. Derrida 1981, 149.

51. Derrida 1981, 95–117 (quotation from 96). In regard to the drug, he observes: "The *pharmakon* would be a substance . . . if we didn't have eventually to come to recognize it as antisubstance itself: that which resists any philosopheme, indefinitely exceeding its bounds as nonidentity, nonessence, nonsubstance; granting philosophy by that very fact the inexhaustible adversity of what funds it and the infinite absence of what founds it" (70). See also ch. 5, n. 55 below.

Derrida suggests that the Platonic attitude to writing evades certain questions which make that attitude highly problematic. According to this reading, the Platonic view readily privileges presence, identity, immediacy, and ideality in the linguistic signs that constitute language. Yet Derrida and others dispute that kind of systematization of language, and in particular, they would question the fixed grounding of the sign in another referent. Thus, meaning is produced not because the sign is deeply committed to some referent outside of language, but through its interaction with other signs. Meaning is not immediately present in a sign, but is disseminated along what Jacques Lacan called a "signifying chain"; meaning results from the play of signs that make up this signifying chain. No extralinguistic referent, or no group of such referents, is responsible for the meaning-producing function of language; instead, the movement of the signs generates an effect of the signified which results in meaning. It is this theological effect that Nietzsche identifies in *Twilight of the Idols:* "I fear we are not getting rid of God because we still believe in grammar."

One might argue, following Socrates in *Phaedrus*, that the challenge to the classical view is true of written but not of spoken language.[52] In spoken language, it appears that the speaker's meaning and intentions are immediately present and accessible in the uttered words, and presence and meaning seem to coincide more closely with the spoken word than with the written. The spoken word also usually exists in a given context and situation in which authorial intent and meaning take on more clarity than they would without such context. Conversely, the written text often circulates freely and in the absence of the author; it seems to be at another level of representation from speech and also, therefore, from the speaker's being and consciousness. When the text escapes the control of the author, it can be abused and put in service of ends which the author did not foresee. When questions are asked of it, as Socrates says in *Phaedrus*, the text cannot answer back but remains mute; at the most, it repeats the same words over and over. The written text lacks a "father" who can come to its aid and defend it. Oral discourse seems to obviate these problems of being, deferral, meaning, consciousness, and dialectic by working through presence, intimacy, and limited context.

From the standpoint of a grammatological critique, however, this view of language depends on a naive understanding of speech and, further, is typical of the logocentrism that has pervaded the Western metaphysical

52. See Eagleton 1983, 130, for the formulations in this paragraph.

tradition since Plato. "[S]ince spoken signs, like written ones, work only by a process of difference and division, speaking could be just as much said to be a form of writing as writing is said to be a second-hand form of speaking."[53] Speech is also material, but it happens to be the privileged object of the logocentric system and to be one of those overvalued points in which the ideologies of the sociophilosophical heritage of Europe converge. "In an original and non-'relativist' sense," Derrida observes, "logocentrism is an ethnocentric metaphysics. It is related to the history of the West."[54] For the functioning of these European ideologies, it is necessary to promote speech along with presence, being, truth, and reality. Yet these categories of privilege are themselves the result of a play of signs; they are part of a history that has been supported by the belief in, or search for, transcendental signifieds, whether one calls them God, freedom, truth, or being. Social and political ideologies are responsible for promoting speech over writing, just as they are responsible for privileging man over woman, presence over absence, or self over other. It may be that civilized life is unable to move forward without such hierarchies, but there is a critical responsibility to expose their underpinnings, and to appreciate why writing has been constructed as "the anathema that the Western world has obstinately mulled over, the exclusion by which it has constituted and recognized itself, from the *Phaedrus* to the *Course in General Linguistics*."[55]

Plato displays attitudes to language that appear to be problematic, at least from Derrida's perspectives. But the attitudes ascribed to him above are fairly consistent with his own philosophical system to the extent that this might be ascertained; nor do these assumptions about language seem to be at cross-purposes with each other, and traces of them can be found even in the philosophical work of his student Aristotle.[56] Plato believes in

---

53. Ibid.
54. Derrida 1976, 79.
55. Derrida 1976, 103.
56. See Aristotle, *On Interpretation,* with the critique in Derrida 1976: "If, for Aristotle, for example, "spoken words (ta en tê phonê) are the symbols of mental experience (pathêmata tes psychês) and written words are the symbols of spoken words" (*De interpretatione*, 1, 16a 3) it is because the voice, producer of *the first symbols,* has a relationship of essential and immediate proximity with the mind. . . . In every case, the voice is closest to the signified, whether it is determined strictly as sense (thought or lived) or more loosely as thing. All signifiers, and first and foremost the written signifier, are derivative with regard to what would wed the voice indissolubly to the mind or to the thought of the signified sense, indeed to the thing itself (whether it is done in the Aristotelian manner that we have just indicated or in the manner of medieval theology, determining the *res* as a thing created from its *eidos,* from its sense thought in the logos or in the infinite understanding

absolute truths or meanings that subsist in an area distinct from language and privileges the kind of linguistic sign that comes close to expressing these extralinguistic truths. This is not to suggest that Plato was not himself troubled by language as such, and he and poststructuralism are in complete agreement as far as a general anxiety about language is concerned. Plato's anxiety about language is manifest in many places, including substantial parts of *Cratylus* and book 10 of the *Republic*. In *Cratylus*, Socrates advances his belief that names have a natural correctness and that they are imitations of certain realities. But the dialogue ends with some concession granted to the influence of convention and custom in the formation of names. Consistencies in Socrates' position are not always easy to unravel, and it is possible that the central portion of the dialogue in which Hermogenes and Socrates discuss correctness offers a prescriptive rather than a descriptive linguistics.[57] The *Republic* presents Socrates' celebrated attack on poetry, a part of which sets out the view that language conveys its message at several mimetic removes from an ideal Form. Linguistic mediation imposes distance and difference from a supposed transcendental Form; thus, language is at best an incomplete and at worst a distortionary medium that leaves Socrates yearning for an alternative path to the truth. This comes close to Socrates' view in *Cratylus* that learning the truth about things through words, even if words are rightly conceived, is inferior to learning the truth itself by itself (439a-b). However, both *Cratylus*, with its palinode to undecidability, and the *Republic*, with its insistence on ideal Forms, posit the meaning-filled realm of a transcendental signified on the other side of a linguistic sign.[58]

EGYPTIAN WRITING

The Egyptians, too, appear not to have taken a complacent attitude to language. Far from complacency, in fact, the hieroglyphic texts reveal that the Egyptians explored the problems of language at precisely those points where Plato seems vulnerable to poststructuralist attack. One problem

---

of God). The written signifier is always technical and representative. It has no constitutive meaning" (11). The implied overlap between Plato and Aristotle suggests that the former's assumptions concerning language had a certain currency in Greek thought. If so, the hieroglyphic system poses challenges not just to Platonic, but to broadly held Greek conceptions of writing and language.

57. Baxter 1992.

58. For a semiotic interpretation of Plato's theory of language, see Manetti 1993, 53–69.

arises in the Socratic preference for speech over writing, an approach predicated on the hierarchical dichotomy between speech and writing. But the very idea of a clean split between speech and writing appears in need of serious reexamination in the light of arguments that speech itself is both contaminated by writing and mediated through signification and differentiation. Second, we noted above that the Socratic argument depends on a yearning for a linguistic sign with access to an extralinguistic truth, while it ignores the primary source for the generation of meaning, which is the ceaseless interaction of signs. On both these points—the play of signs and the division between oral and written—the hieroglyphic texts frame the problem in ways importantly different from Plato's Greek.

Characters of the hieroglyphic script are of three main types, each with a typical function.[59] These are logograms, phonograms, and determinatives. A *logogram*, sometimes referred to as "ideogram," is a word that is represented by a picture of the object to which it refers. Thus, a picture of the sun denotes "sun," or in a more developed version, "day." A *phonogram* supplies information about phonetic features of the writing system, that is, about sounds or phonemes. Phonograms denote single consonants, pairs of successive consonants, and groups of three successive consonants. These are usually referred to as uniconsonantal, biconsonantal, and triconsonantal signs. Signs of the latter two types often appear alongside uniconsonantal signs that may "duplicate" part or whole of their phonemic value. Thus, *wr* may be written as a combination of the signs *wr* and *r*. Lastly, a *determinative* occurs at the end of a word and reduces uncertainty about the meaning of a word, often by indicating the general class of words to which the particular word belongs. In this way, words indicating something bad would terminate with the "bad bird" sign, or abstract nouns could terminate with a "book roll." Apart from determinatives, phonograms, and logograms, the hieroglyphic script uses orthograms and calligrams, which have orthographic or aesthetic value, but indicate neither meaning nor sound. A line from any hieroglyphic inscription taken at random will illustrate the ways in which the three major sign categories work and sometimes also orthograms and calligrams. The readability of the script decreases if a balance between the major sign classes is not kept.

The Play of Signs

In his essay on the sign in ancient Egypt, Jan Assmann has usefully distinguished the two aspects of every *inscribed* linguistic sign, its function and

59. See esp. Gardiner 1957; Schenkel 1971 and 1976.

materiality.[60] "Function" may refer to a semantic or phonetic value or a combination of semantic and phonetic values. Here "materiality" refers not to the medium in which the sign is inscribed, but to the physical form of the sign—the two vertical lines and one horizontal line which, when arranged in a certain manner, constitute the capital letter *H*, or the circle with an oblique line that constitutes the letter *Q*. The letter *H* can be displayed on a computer screen, written on paper, papyrus, bark, canvas, and in different fonts, without having its referential, that is, semantic or phonetic, value altered. But the sign must retain its distinctive shape and form if it is to be read as *H*, that is, if it is to retain the functions of that letter.

However, the semantic weight attached to the physical shape or materiality of a sign needs to be minimal if the semantic value of the sign itself is to come across to the reader. The reader who focuses on the shape or form or material aspects of a sign, the reader who chooses to concentrate on the vertical and horizontal bars of the letter *H* or the gentle curvature of letter *Q*, risks losing the meaning of the letter—of the phonemes [h] or [q]—and turning into a mere gazer. Reading becomes more difficult if the material aspect of a sign also itself assumes signification: actualized co-meaning decreases the readability of a sign. It is true that the materiality of the sign cannot be fully effaced, but the materiality needs to be latent rather than pronounced. As Assmann argues, "Generally, the possibilities of a gradual actualization of a latent material cosignification lie within the normal writing system of a culture and are not differentiated as a special script."[61] Nevertheless, such differentiation occurred in the history of the Egyptian writing system where the elaboration of the materiality of hieroglyphs reached almost fantastic proportions. Yet soon after the creation of the hieroglyphic script, another script, the cursive, emerged out of hieroglyphic in which the materiality of the sign was kept relatively low, and which existed side by side, in many cases literally so, with the hieroglyphic. There is a one-to-one correspondence between cursive and hieroglyphic signs so that the basic linguistic structure of the two scripts is the same. Material cosignification in cursive is nonetheless minimal, and the material features of the cursive sign do not interfere with that sign's semanticity. But Egyptians did not shy from tending to the materiality of the hieroglyphic sign. The hieroglyphic script worked through a high degree of actualized cosignification. Of course, deliberate cultivation of the phenomenon should

---

60. Assmann 1994, 17–18. For a semiotic introduction to the ancient Egyptian conception of signs, see Loprieno 1998.

61. Assmann 1994, 24–25.

be linked to the script's prevalence on monumental inscriptions, in contexts of political and religious importance.

By referring to a sign's materiality, we refer to what Ferdinand de Saussure would call its sound-image or graphic signifier,[62] and in ancient Egypt, as any book on hieroglyphs proves, a high degree of attention was given to the graphic signifier. This is true at the level of physical appearance since the inscribed hieroglyph is usually colored and can be three-dimensional, though its depth, if not color, is rarely discernible in scholarly reproductions. This is also true at so basic a level as the frequent reduplication that takes place among the phonetic and logographic components of a word. The word for "anoint" in the Middle Kingdom is transcribed as *wrh* where the standard transcription elides the reduplication of the *r* that appears in the hieroglyphic.[63] Thus, the system generates a complete word with the help of a signifier which appears redundant from a foreign perspective, but nevertheless contributes relevantly to the production of meaning. A similar phenomenon occurs in the case of determinatives: these characters have no phonetic value, and are usually not transcribed into roman letters, but still help in determining the meaning of a word.[64]

Care lavished on the graphic signifier is manifest also in the organization and orientation of hieroglyphs. The conventional spelling of the name of the god Ptah requires three characters. The sky hieroglyph (roughly, a horizontal plank) denotes *P,* the earth hieroglyph (also a horizontal plank) denotes *t,* and the figure of the god Heh denotes *h.* Since Heh usually appears in his hieroglyph with his arms raised, the scribe can visually evoke Ptah's mythological separation of heaven from earth by placing Heh between the characters for sky and earth; and this is exactly how Ptah is drawn in the Memphite theology.[65] Moreover, hieroglyphs were usually laid out in square spaces, and characters were often arranged or rearranged so as to fit into the quadrant. Calligraphic considerations also determined the position of characters. One consideration was to avoid isolating small or short characters, and deliberately to place them between tall or large characters, thus producing a visually harmonious scheme. The term "he who carries the festival text," *hr(j)-hb(t),* may be expressed by three characters, but the character that would be read initially is shorter than the other two, and is placed between them.[66] In some texts from the Old Kingdom, on the

62. See especially Saussure 1959, 65–67.
63. *LÄ,* vol. 2, col. 1190.
64. See Te Velde 1985–86, 64.
65. See Sauneron 1960, 132–33.
66. *LÄ,* vol. 2, col. 1191.

other hand, sizes were varied according to emphasis, and characters even overlapped other characters.

The orientation of hieroglyphs holds particular interest for the study of graphic signification. The inscriptions were usually written so as to be read from the right to the left of the spectator, as is the case in many Semitic languages. The hieroglyphic figures are themselves also shown oriented to the right; that is, they face the beginning of the line. But the rightward orientation was not strictly observed. The orientation was reversed in the case of a doorway, for example, where the inscription might start at the bottom of each foot, and meet up at the top so as to furnish a symmetrical arrangement. The orientation was also altered in other ways familiar to Egyptologists, and Henry G. Fischer has described the phenomenon well.

> The rightward orientation of hieroglyphs is reversed, in most cases, for one of two reasons: either to provide a symmetrical arrangement in inscriptions associated with a doorway or niche, such as a pair of obelisks, or to agree with the direction of a figure facing leftward. In the course of the OK the second type of reversal was applied to the proper left side of seated statues, and then to the back and head end of coffins. Occasionally hieroglyphs were redirected in an inscription for no other reason than to emphasize a shift in the point of view, as when, in some OK tomb biographies, the words "he says" are reversed between the name of the speaker and his statement. Retrograde inscriptions, in which the expected sequence of signs is reversed, are known from the OK but become more frequent in the MK and later; in some of the rarer cases involving horizontal lines the retrograde sequence alternated with the normal one, producing a boustrophedon pattern of reading. More commonly the retrograde sequence is applied to columns of inscriptions written vertically, and only affects the order in which the columns are read, while the arrangement of signs within each column remains normal. The vertical sequence of hieroglyphs is much less variable; it almost always proceeds from top to bottom. A vertical inscription of the First Intermediate Period reverses this procedure, however, and some late MK stelae occasionally show a retrograde sequence of horizontal lines, reading from bottom to top.[67]

The passage is impeccable as a recapitulation of the evidence, but its style heightens the frequency with which the orientation of hieroglyphs was changed from its rightward slant. Fischer more than once makes a claim about the orientation of the script and then qualifies the claim to broaden the scope of alterations substantially. We read initially that the rightward

67. See *LÄ*, vol. 2, cols. 1192–93; see also Fischer 1977 and 1986.

orientation of hieroglyphs is reversed for two reasons, but then it turns out that the orientation was also reversed "for no other reason than to emphasize a shift in the point of view." Further, inscriptions on columns are "almost always . . . top to bottom"—but "a vertical inscription from the First Intermediate Period" and "some late MK stelae" are read in the reverse order, from bottom to top. Thus, as Fischer's remarks indicate, the visual syntax of hieroglyphs remained fluid and often unpredictable, and the hieroglyphs could be oriented in what seems to the modern reader to be a bewildering variety of directions.

The quantity and quality of the characters in the hieroglyphic repertory allowed their exploitation for purposes of graphic dissimilation, orientation, and reorientation. The pictorial aspect of the signs made them especially amenable to use alongside representational art, and the practice is widely attested since the Egyptians exploited the juxtaposition and even integration of hieroglyphic writing and representational art for deliberate semiotic effects. One typology of the relationships between text and representation groups them according to the following heads: primacy of the text; primacy of representation; parallel recourse to text and representation; convergence between text and representation; representation as an aid to the text; text in support of the representation; text and representation in a complementary relationship; texts and representations in "osmosis."[68] A glance at the sign list in the standard Egyptian grammar demonstrates why such a close relationship between writing and art might be possible:[69]

A	55 images of man and his occupations
B	7 images of woman and her occupations
C	20 images of anthropomorphic deities
D	63 images of parts of the human body
E	34 images of mammals
F	52 images of parts of mammals
G	54 images of birds
H	8 images of parts of birds
I	15 images of amphibious animals, reptiles, etc.
K	6 images of fish and parts of fish
L	7 images of invertebrates and lesser animals
M	44 images of trees and plants
N	42 images of sky, earth, and water

68. Vernus 1985.
69. This is Te Velde's count of the list in Gardiner 1957; see Te Velde 1988.

O   51 images of buildings and parts of buildings
P   11 images of ships and parts of ships
Q   7 images of domestic and funerary furniture
R   25 images of temple furniture and sacred emblems
S   45 images of crowns, dress, and staves, etc.
T   35 images of warfare, hunting, and butchery
U   41 images of agriculture, crafts, and professions
V   38 images of rope, fiber, baskets, bags, etc.
W   25 images of vessels of stone and earthenware
X   8 images of loaves and cakes
Y   8 images of writing, games, and music

Middle Egyptian used about 700 such characters, but the number of the characters expanded to more than 5000 in the Ptolemaic period. The press of the Institut Français in Cairo has a font of more than 5000 hieroglyphic characters, but Serge Sauneron was led to lament a while ago that "nevertheless on the publication of each new text of the low epoch, some characters must be delineated which were not known before." [70] The explosion in characters was perhaps due to the cryptographic tradition and the symbolic interpretation of hieroglyphs that became more common with the advent of the Greeks and Romans. [71]

Although the forms of the hieroglyphs remained stable in the centuries before the Graeco-Roman presence, minor innovations and changes did take place, so that clothing and fashion on human figures in the hieroglyphs adjusted to contemporary usage, and the introduction of the chariot into Egypt in the Eighteenth Dynasty gave birth to a new hieroglyph. [72] The truncation and mutilation of hieroglyphic humans and animals also occurs, especially in texts written on coffins and in burial chambers. [73] Living characters were killed off in this way simply to foster their identity with the dead; or they were abbreviated so as to prevent them from harming the dead; or the feet of the human and animal characters were amputated so as to prevent them from walking off to regroup into new and threatening combinations. In addition, some dangerous animals, for example, crocodiles and snakes, had daggers drawn through them. [74] This is also

---

70. Sauneron 1960, 132.
71. See in general Iversen 1993 for this phenomenon.
72. *LÄ*, vol. 2, col. 1193.
73. See Lacau 1913; Te Velde 1985–86, 66–67; and *LÄ*, vol. 2, col. 1195.
74. *LÄ*, vol. 2, col. 1195.

the case with the Seth-animal, which in the last millennium B.C.E. acquired the ears of an ass and a dagger drawn through the head or body. Most of the twenty or so words that use the Seth-animal as a determinative have negative connotations: "illness," "suffering," "nightmare," and so on.[75]

In these various ways, the writing system of the ancient Egyptians exploits a variety of graphic and phonetic signifiers to produce a multiply determined semantic effect, which might be even more complex in scenes where hieroglyphic writing appears with representational art. The system operates through a number of characteristic features in any given such instance. The hieroglyphs may be oriented toward the right but they could almost as easily be oriented in other directions, including left to right and also bottom to top. Second, the boundary between text and representation is fragile, and the two often complement and interpret each other. Third, the writing explains the artistic representation, identifies the persons in the scene, and records the speeches made by these persons. In addition to these basic features, the hieroglyphic writing system works through its own internal complexities such as the rebus principle in which the phonogrammic interpretation of the character suppresses any semantic trace. Thus, if one were to replace the first word in the English expression "I see you" with the rendering of an eye, one could still with a little difficulty read the expression, provided one suppressed the semantic reference of the drawn eye to an anatomical part. In hieroglyphs, the situation is similar in the case of phonograms, but with the complication that all characters, and not just phonograms, are pictorially based, and that some often serve in more than one capacity in the triad logogram, phonogram, and determinative.[76]

The hieroglyphic inscription generates meaning through the movement

75. See Te Velde 1985–86, 67–71.
76. The transposition of this example into ancient Egyptian leads to a situation that is even more complicated than my remarks suggest. See Hare 1999, 71–72: "The ubiquitous glyph of an eye, for example, can mean "eye" as ideogram, but only with the addition of the feminine termination *t* and the supplementary stroke mentioned earlier. It performs an exclusively phonetic role in the spelling of the word "milk," *jrtt* . . . ; in other words it serves as an unpronounced determinative, as in the words . . . *m33*, "see"; then *rs*, "be wakeful" or "dream"; *dg(j)*, "look"; and *sp*, "be blind." The glyph is commonly used to write the verb *jr(j)*, "do," as well. It may appear alone, or with the supplementary inscription of the phonetic *r* (sometimes doubled in the emphatic and imperfect participial inflections). . . . The problems encountered in trying to understand how the glyph of an eye is used in Egyptian—whether simply phonetically, or whether logographically—have a relevance for understanding, not only Egyptian writing, but figural language in a broader sense. They require the alchemy of metaphor, apostrophe, metonymy, and so on, not merely for the construction of a secondary or ornamental sense, but frequently for the construction of any sense whatsoever."

of these signs. Obviously, practiced Egyptian readers did not always stop to consider individual signs but read them quickly, and probably read groups of signs as units or "logographs."[77] Word division would not have been an obstacle since determinatives terminate most words. "At the same time the regular differentiation of homophonic roots in writing, by the use of differing patterns of phonemic signs and different taxograms [determinatives], helped the logo- or semographic reading of Egyptian."[78] The reader would recognize word units or logographs quickly, and absorb the text divulged by the interaction of the signifiers. This is not to say that the Egyptians themselves were unable to analyze their language in terms of individual signs. The wide flexibility in orientation and combination of signs alone points to the opposite conclusion. One could also add cryptographic examples in hieroglyphic characters that have to derive from comprehension of individual sign units. The cryptographic extreme is reached in two texts from the Roman period in Esna, on one of which only a crocodile sign appears repeated ad infinitum and on the other only a ram.[79] But such evidence is not required to prove that Egyptians readily understood separate signs, and any text from the high classical period will demonstrate the high degree of linguistic sensitivity that was prevalent at the time.

The play of signs in the Egyptian hieroglyphic tradition, then, fundamentally undercuts the Platonic desire for the stability of written language and for linguistic signs that provide unmediated access to extralinguistic

77. For reading of groups of words, see Eyre and Baines 1989, 99.
78. Ibid.
79. Quoted in Eyre and Baines 1989, 98; cf. Sauneron 1982. The range of the Egyptian writing system was grasped by some Greek writers in late antiquity: see e.g. Horapollo, *Hieroglyphica* 1.38: "In order to denote Egyptian letters, or a scribe, or a limit, they draw ink and a sieve and a reed (Αἰγύπτια δὲ γράμματα δηλο-ῦντες, ἢ ἱερογραμματέα, ἢ πέρας, μέλαν καὶ κόσκινον καὶ σχοινίον ζωγρα-φοῦσιν). Egyptian letters, for all writing is done with these among the Egyptians. For they write with a reed and not with anything else. And a sieve, since the sieve first was used for making bread, being made from reeds. Accordingly, they show that everyone who eats or takes nourishment should know his letters. But he who does not, should use another art. For this reason, education among them is called *Sbo*, which being interpreted means 'full nourishment.' And a scribe, since he distinguishes between life and death. And a holy book among the scribes is called 'amber,' by means of which they decide the fate of a sick man lying down, whether he will live or not. This they judge from the position of the sick man. And a limit, since he who knows letters has come into a calm harbor of life, no longer wandering among life's evils." This passage is also a characteristic combination of the authentic and the fraudulent that we find throughout Horapollo's work. See Fowden 1993 for a sensitive evocation of the late antique milieu in which thinkers such as Horapollo lived.

truths. Where Plato claims to champion the transparency of language, fixity of form and meaning, and lexical steadiness, the hieroglyphic system thrives on difference, movement, and the flexible collocation of signs. In foregrounding the materiality of the sign, the Egyptian texts show an astonishing freedom and pliability, thereby making possible the generation of meaning along several different axes. For their part, the scribes continually exploit the size, coloring, location, and iconic element of signs as well as the medium in which signs are marked, in order to present a complicated yet legible hieroglyphic text and an intricate yet assimilable semantic effect. Against Plato, and like the works of certain gifted poets, these writings illustrate the "penetrating insight into language that meaning is itself a formal property of discourse," and they make the case that "[t]o the extent that signification is itself synthetic, language represents a wholly plastic order whose forms of expression and forms of content are equally susceptible to appropriation, recoordination, and exchange." [80] On the question of signification, accordingly, the Egyptian writings present a countertradition to Plato, to his assertion of a referent outside of language, and to his insistence on a linguistic system that allows for the unproblematic passage between sign and referent.

Speech, Writing, Reading

If we turn next to the question of speech and writing—the second area, after modes of signification, deemed to be problematic by Socrates in *Phaedrus*—we find that ancient Egyptians structured this issue differently also. In the first place, writing, and especially hieroglyphic writing, often draws praise and not suspicion, although this is not surprising given the strong scribal control over technologies of the written word. Secondly, however, the texts raise the issue not of speaking and writing, but rather of reading, that is, of the reader of written texts and the reading process in general. The question of reading occurs largely because of the monumentality of hieroglyphic writing, and this monumentality is a factor which needs to be given some thought. While Greek letters were written on such media as wax tablets, vases, and papyrus as well as on monuments, the hieroglyphic texts

80. Selden 1998b, 382. Interestingly, Selden makes these remarks in connection with Callimachus, in the context of an extended discussion of the cohabitation within the poet's work of Egyptian and Greek literary and cultural models. It is significant that a Greek poet who drew so deeply on Egyptian traditions should illustrate this quality of language. For Alexandrian poetry's use of Egyptian and Greek themes, see also Stephens, forthcoming.

are for the most part monumental. The texts appear on monuments of all periods in Egyptian history, on large temple walls, and on small objects; they include religious, legal, and historical themes, as we saw above, and they occur in official and public arenas.

Assmann has pointed out that the act of reading a monumental inscription corresponds more closely to an oral than a written situation, contrary to what may appear intuitively obvious.[81] An oral situation is characterized by the voice and body of the speaker and by a specific physical context or locale. In the case of the hieroglyphic inscriptional situation, when material cosignification is actualized, the script serves as the voice, the monument as the body, and the environs as the particular context. Conversely, with conventional written communication today, such as the text on these pages, the materiality of the script is not activated, and the body of the text is easily translatable into different environments and media without any serious loss of effect; for example, it may copied by hand onto another writing surface, or stored on a computer disk. The text can be passed around, and is not anchored in a particular context. Thus, the three features of the oral situation—voice, body, limited context—are minimally weighted in the written texts of modern everyday life. The hieroglyphic monumental inscription, on the other hand, addresses the reader with all the force of its writing in a fixed, often enclosed, space where the aspects of an oral/aural exchange seem to be present. This interpretation of an Egyptian practice is given support by a text of the Late Period:

> When you meditate on this stela,
> enter into the inscriptions contained thereon,
> when you view the transfigurations of the ancestors in their place in
>   unequaled abundance,
> when you hear those who quarrel, exchanging loud words with their
>   companions,
> when you hear the singing of the musicians
> and the lamentations of those who mourn,
> when you find the name of every man above him in his offices given
>   by name,
> the herds of cattle, the tree, and the herbs
> with their names above them. . . .[82]

81. Assmann 1994, 25–26.
82. The text is quoted in Assmann 1994, 405 n. 2.

The inscription identifies reading letters with hearing them speak, and suggests that readers will be able to listen to the monument.

The hieroglyphic script, with cosignification actualized, acts as the voice in the monumental recreation of the oral situation. Yet if the text is to find fulfillment, it requires a reader, a reading voice, a reader's voice. Reading in ancient Egypt and Greece was in general the act of reading *aloud*.[83] Jesper Svenbro has used this information to argue that the instrumental status of the reader heightens the "question of power" that is raised by acts of reading.[84] The reader lent his or her voice to the written text to allow the text to become meaningful, and the reader's voice was the sonorous instrument necessary for the text to be realized. When the reader chose not to read, the writing lay mute and unheard; but when the reader read out the text, he or she actualized the written words and brought them to life. The reader's voice was at the service of the written text at the instant of reading: the text appropriated the reader's voice and used the sonorous instrument to gain actualization. The reader's voice belonged to the written text and not to the reader during this reading process, and the text exerted a power over the voice. To go back earlier in this process, moreover, the writer of the text understood that it would need a reading voice to be actualized. The writer knew that the text could be read in his or her absence, and accordingly the writer wove the *potential* of the reading voice into the text. Therefore, the potential reading voice is already inscribed in the written text—the reading is part of the text. Accordingly, Svenbro observes, after Derrida, "it is not the writing here that supplements the voice, but the voice that supplements—in both senses of the word—the writing. The writing *lacks* a voice that is added to it to *supplement* it."[85]

Svenbro makes this claim as a modern reader of ancient inscriptions, and his observation, combined with the correspondence between the monumental and oral situations, points to the writers' concern for reading, readership, and readers' response to inscriptions. Egyptian written stories often contain devices that imply a context of reading: line division, formulae, repetition, and episodic structure. In the Egyptian case, these are intended to make reading and recitation easier, and are not indications of a formu-

---

83. This is my position in a large debate about silent reading in antiquity. The main references to works involved in the debate are collected in Detienne 1992, 536–37; for Egypt in particular, see the analysis in Eyre and Baines 1989, 97–103.

84. The phrase is from Pierre Bourdieu and quoted in Svenbro 1993, 47; for this paragraph, see in general his ch. 3.

85. Svenbro 1993, 63.

laic oral poetry transcribed after generational passage, for which there is no evidence in ancient Egypt. It may be true that autobiographical texts derive from orally performed praise poetry, attested in Africa; and some royal inscriptions use a dialogic exchange of praise that may have an oral counterpart. In general, however, it is difficult to trace oral counterparts for the surviving Egyptian literature. "Any attempt to assess the relationship of such genres to oral forms of display must be speculative, as is the assessment of the relationship between oral and written literature in general. . . ."[86] What is less speculative is that the repetition of stock phrases, the use of formulae, division, and so on imply a context of readability.

The point of theorizing along these lines is not to enter into a dispute about oral composition and the like, but to emphasize that the hieroglyphic monumental inscription implies a context of reading, and that many Egyptian texts factor the reader into consideration. In the first place, this attitude alone represents a useful departure from the clear demarcation of speech and writing attested in Plato and other Greek writers. Admittedly, many Greek inscriptional texts survive on monuments; in addition, many of these possibly anticipate their audience and readership. Nevertheless, given the monumentality of Egyptian hieroglyphic writing, the formulation of reading voice as a "supplement" to writing applies more persuasively to the Egyptian than to Greek material. The notion of speech as "supplement," that is, addition and substitute, of writing not only inverts the Platonic hierarchy of speech over writing but comes near to obliterating the hierarchy altogether; as Derrida has shown, the logic of the supplement, of being both an addition and a substitute, puts into question the basis of a binarily oriented metaphysics.

Secondly, Egyptian writing on monuments recreates, performatively, a relationship between reader and inscription that reconfigures the Herodotean association between tyrannic symbolism and Egyptian monumental writing. Many of the Egyptian temple and tomb inscriptions involve the names, formulae, and paraphernalia of royalty, and the reader of these inscriptions often could find himself enacting the role of king for the duration of the reading. The performative enactment of this role would not occur with every inscription, to be sure, and would very according to monumental space and text. But the reenactment is vividly suggested in dozens of cases, including, for instance, the text inscribed on the Iykhernofret Stela which is presented in the first-person voice of the pharaoh: "I had

---

86. Eyre and Baines 1989, 109.

Wepwawet go forth, setting out in the protection of His Father, I drove the enemy away from the Neshmet Barque, I defeated the foes of Osiris. I made the great procession. I had the god's ship set sail with Thoth at the helm. . . ."[87] In a strict sense, the pharaoh is the person carrying out the actions on this stela and making the various gestures of thanksgiving that it records. But Egypt had numerous holy spaces and the spaces had numerous inscriptions and dedicatory texts, so the pharaoh himself would not have been performing the rituals enacted in all the many temples or tombs where these inscriptions were set up. "Here the individual private subject enacts the king," Tom Hare observes, "to set off a chain of giving from himself (or herself) through the king to Osiris. . . . So the filters of identity through which the gift passes come to suggest filters of a subject who enacts the king (whether the living king, Horus, or the dead king, Osiris) even as his private individual identity is preserved."[88] Thus, where Greek sources point to tyrannical power, the Egyptian inscriptions do not quite correspond to the Greek implications of tyranny by delivering injunctions from on high, but reconfigure the relationship so that every reader of the inscription can be a king. Self-identification with the pharaoh follows on "an epistemological stance that is not about usurpation but rather about the framing of the subject within the myth of royal identity: every man a king."[89] Within the indisputable reality of the royal authority, the Egyptian monumental inscription projects a transformative subjectivity for which, in truth, there is no exact Greek correlative. The subjectivity enacted here is neither fully democratic, nor fully autocratic, but it indicates a self-identification on the part of the reader that the Greek sources fail adequately to grasp.

Different Matters

The hieroglyphic script in its various capacities seems to point to an approach to writing that contrasts with Plato's approach in important ways. We have observed how hieroglyphs interact with each other as signs, and how Egyptian texts exploit phonemic and graphemic constituents of the linguistic system to produce an effect of the signified. Such factors as the fluid orientation of characters and the general artistic environment, in

---

87. For a translation of the stela, see Lichtheim 1973, 123–25; this quotation is from Hare 1999, 38.
88. Hare 1999, 42.
89. Hare 1999, 43.

which art blends with hieroglyphs for deliberate effect, indicate an attitude to signification that differs from the Greek. Plato appears to have posited a less elastic and more rigid relationship between sign and object, as his views of the speech / writing dichotomy showed. When we turn to the dichotomy between speech and writing in particular, we see that whereas Plato accepts the dichotomy unconditionally even as he debates the relative merits of each side, the Egyptian sources make the possibility of the dichotomy less easy to maintain. The comprehensive monumentality of hieroglyphic texts needs to be evaluated in the light of the argument that the reading of a monument has affinities with the oral situation. That argument and the supplementary logic on which the speech / writing opposition is predicated question the usefulness of adhering strictly to the dichotomy. The Egyptian hieroglyphic system, then, alters the nature of the debate over writing at the precise places where poststructuralist criticism has mounted its attacks.

The consequences of this divergence can be sketched out in slightly more detail by conceptualizing the Egyptian monument and hieroglyph within the framework of Egyptian notions of matter and soul. The concepts of matter without soul and of soul without matter are foreign to Egyptian thought.[90] The Egyptian soul, or *ba*, is unlike the Greek or Christian *psykhe* since it is unable to live outside a body. The *ba* of a dead person is said to reunite with the body every night in the underworld; the *ba* has desires, it feels hunger and thirst, and it indulges in sexual activity. Conversely, the body's integrity was highly valued too, as the practice of mummification indicates, and its resurrection and rejuvenation also occurred every night in the underworld. When the monument is conceived of as having a life force or spirit, therefore, the suggested parallel between the monumental and oral situation gains support. "One became physically present through monuments and gained speech and voice through hieroglyphs."[91] Monuments, idols, and hieroglyphs are imbued with spirit or soul, and they inhabit a world of such entities. For these reasons, Akhenaten erased all named references to the god Amun, and in other circumstances hieroglyphs may appear with mutilations and daggers drawn through them.

Perhaps the iconic nature of hieroglyphs made it easier for them to be vivified. It is also in this iconic nature, that is, the materiality referred to earlier, that we find the close correspondence between words and things in

90. See Hornung 1992, ch. 9.
91. Assmann 1994, 26.

Egypt, yet this does not lead to the production of a separate transcendental realm where meaning may be found. The gods are everywhere and assume many sensible shapes, including hieroglyphs. Hieroglyphs are thus often called "the writing of the gods," and they can mediate between the divine and human. They draw on a system based on a close correspondence between words and things. Thus, whoever authorizes words also may authorize things. The pharaoh's role as the representative of the gods, and often as the son of the sun god, suggests that his decrees and inscriptions are also invested with the authority of the gods; and this authority contributes to the frequently performative nature of the hieroglyphic monuments.[92]

Plato, on the other hand, habitually posits a transcendental meaning that is separate and distinct from language. That demarcation is harder to make within the Egyptian philosophical tradition where matter and soul are separable, but not without a degree of mutual parasitism. But in the Greek tradition, language stands in for something else, or is mimetic of something else, and truth is always located in this something else, whether it is an essence, a Platonic Form ($\iota\delta\acute{\epsilon}\alpha$), or an Aristotelian Being ($\check{o}\nu$). This is what makes possible an ontological discourse, that is, a discourse that presumes to ponder presence as an essence and as an independent, matterless being. If there is a reality outside of language, however, then language is but a representation of it, and language doubles, replaces, and displaces reality and the truth. Derrida observes that this kind of thinking privileges what is real, true, essential, and imitated as anterior and superior to what imitates or represents; and that truth depends on this hierarchy. "This order of appearance," he claims, "is *the order of all appearance,* the very process of appearing in general. It is the order of truth."[93] This argument leads to complications, since the statement that truth is the order of all appearance itself rests on a notion of truth, but Derrida exploits these complications to produce his deconstructive readings of texts in the Western tradition.

I do not wish to follow Derrida into the deconstruction of truth, but rather I would like to emphasize the shift in perspective afforded by his argument. While Greeks such as Plato conceived of language as material and thought of true meaning as existing in a separate metaphysical realm, the Egyptians lived in a world of "direct signification" where the congru-

---

92. For the performative aspect of hieroglyphic monuments, see Assmann 1990a and Vernus 1991.
93. Derrida 1981, 192, original emphasis.

ence between signs and things was maintained.[94] When the world changed with the advent of Greeks and other foreigners, the number of things in the world increased, but also the number of things that act as signs. Thus, the number of hieroglyphic characters increased from 700 to more than 5000 in the Ptolemaic age, but before the Ptolemaic age the number of characters remained relatively stable at around 700. These characters formed words and other grammatical units, but they did not stand in for something else. As we noted above, the Egyptians did not have a concept of matter and soul, at least not in the Greek or modern sense of inanimate mass or bodyless soul. Similarly, the Egyptians took the iconic hieroglyphs as part of their world and the world as a text of hieroglyphs.[95] They read hieroglyphs, and they even evaluated the iconic elements of the hieroglyphs for metaphorical, symbolic, and abstract meanings, but they did not conceive of a metaphysical realm of true meaning outside of language. Indeed, in the Egyptian view, the gods created many things through language, the inception of which therefore preceded several parts of the world. Thus, both Plato and the Egyptians "interpreted the visible world as the infinite material reproduction of a finite set of immaterial ideas,"[96] but Plato, unlike the

94. Assmann 1994, 27–28.

95. The phenomenon is formulated thus by Tom Hare, in connection with the texts and pictures found in tombs: "The writing and the pictures it accompanies—the two usually cannot be considered separately—are, then, a performance of reality. This same performative nature can be remarked in a great many Egyptian inscriptions, and might be taken further in considerations of the programs of decorations found in a wide variety of tombs. Again and again in reading about tombs, one comes upon the assertion that the articles depicted on the walls have a reality that might not merely supplement offerings made by the family or mortuary endowment of the deceased, but that in the case that such offerings should cease to be made, then the words and pictures alone might suffice" (Hare 1999, 95–96). These remarks are reminiscent of observations about figural meaning and symbolism made by Hegel in "The Oriental World," which is part of his *Philosophie der Weltgeschichte* (see also Hare 1999, 240).

96. Assmann 1997, 115. As Assmann argues, this is one reason why Neoplatonist thinkers turned to Egyptian thought in late antiquity. See e.g. Iamblichus, *On the Mysteries of the Egyptians* 7.1: "They [i.e. the Egyptians] imitate the nature of the universe and the divine creation of the gods when they produce images of the mystical, invisible, and secret notions through symbols, in the same way that nature has expressed the invisible *logoi* by visible forms in a symbolic manner and that the divine creation of the gods has sketched out the truth of the ideas by visible images" (οὖτοι γὰρ τὴν φύσιν τοῦ παντὸς καὶ τὴν δημιουργίαν τῶν θεῶν μιμούμενοι καὶ αὐτοὶ τῶν μυστικῶν καὶ ἀποκεκρυμμένων καὶ ἀφανῶν νοήσεων εἰκόνας τινὰς διὰ συμβόλων ἐκφαίνουσιν, ὥσπερ καὶ ἡ φύσις τοῖς ἐμφανέσιν εἴδεσι τοὺς ἀφανεῖς λόγους διὰ συμβόλων τρόπον τινὰ ἀπετυπώσατο, ἡ δὲ

Egyptians, believed that language seriously distorted a person's grasp of these finite ideas, and he did not quite see the reproductive and imitative powers imputed to it in the Egyptian tradition.

WRITING AND CONTROL

The apprehension about writing in Plato, Herodotus, and Aeschylus occupies a particular position within the sociopolitical circumstances governing the practice and spread of literacy in Greece. These Greek circumstances, in turn, contrast with the sociopolitical factors governing writing in Egypt, where writing stayed within the control of the ruling classes in all historical periods. Greek writing, which was imported from the Semitic Phoenicians, was not restricted just to political and religious elites, as in Egypt, and always had the potential to spread outside elite confines. The ability of writing to circulate beyond the dominant political, religious, and intellectual centers provoked ample anxiety among many of the Greeks who reflected on its consequences. Of course, literacy itself was not widespread in Greece, but the potentially expansive appeal of writing remained a source of unease to intellectuals, most of all to antidemocrats such as Plato. In Egypt, on the other hand, and especially with the hieroglyphic tradition, the elites maintained an extremely fierce grip on the technology and were reluctant to let it disseminate among the wider subject population. But we rarely find among Egyptian writers the suggestion that writing should not be passed along to the larger human society, and we rarely find the notion that writing is somehow deleterious to humans' creative powers. Perhaps since the likelihood of the spread of hieroglyphic technology appeared slim to Egyptian elites, the literate population seldom expressed fears that writing might slip away from their hands and into the hands of the general public. This difference between the Egyptian and Greek background to writing gives us another avenue to understand the issues that we have been exploring in the chapter. When writing is considered from these perspectives, the concerns of Plato and the other Greeks can be interpreted as extensions of their views of politics and their attitudes to regimes of control.

In Egypt, the political, ideological, and administrative developments that accompanied the consolidation of state power were responsible for the introduction of writing. The state developed the Egyptian writing system

---

τῶν θεῶν δημιουργία τὴν ἀλήθεια τῶν ἰδεῶν διὰ τῶν φανερῶν εἰκόνων ὑπε-γράψατο).

indigenously, and put it into service for its own purposes, though it probably took the idea of writing from outside, perhaps from Mesopotamia.[97] Hence, writing appears after the formation of the nation state in Egypt, and as a deliberate innovation by the political forces "controlling and exploiting the resources of the market or the growth of the productive forces in order to maintain and further its rule."[98] Writing is, therefore, inextricably linked to a strong, central, political authority from the earliest phases of Egyptian history, and virtually all samples of early writing are connected to royalty or to persons near royalty. Moreover, the elite's historical control of early Egyptian writing is confirmed by two of the media on which writing occurred, namely, papyrus and monuments of stone. Papyrus, which was invented as a medium for the written word a couple of centuries after writing itself, was expensive and not as widespread in the pharaonic period as it was in the Graeco-Roman, so that its cost and rarity restricted its accessibility to the rich and powerful.[99] Monuments and monumental writing projected on a grand scale the world-view of the dominant elite, subject to the conventions of display and decorum which determined the material appearance of hieroglyphic texts.[100] On monuments, writing and pictorial art were integrated through a complex symbolic system designed to promote elite protocols, and this interdependence between writing and art became integral both to the projection of pharaonic power and the ideology of kingship.[101] Kingship, ideology, and monumental display were related forces, harnessed to further the political authority at the heart of the nation state. Meticulously, Egyptian elites exerted their control of writing technology through materiality, literacy, and political ideology.

Starting from the earliest phases of the Old Kingdom and extending to the end of the Late Period, then, elite groups controlled writing and its proliferation in Egypt, and members of the literate were inevitably drawn from these groups.[102] Success in administrative and political offices depended on literacy: royal figures were depicted as scribes, and officeholders were often

97. Schenkel 1983 and Ray 1986; cf. Schott 1950.
98. Lefebvre 1991, 112; cf. Baines 1988, 194.
99. Baines 1983, 593 n.4.
100. Baines 1985, 68–75, 277–305.
101. See Fischer 1977 and 1986, Brunner 1979, Tefnin 1984, Vernus 1985, and Assmann 1987.
102. For a discussion of writing practices and their relationship to the construction of power in ancient Egypt, see Baines 1983; Ray 1994 (for the Late Period); and Thompson 1994 (for the Ptolemaic era). For estimations of literacy, see Baines and Eyre 1983.

the authors of texts. The scribal class itself numbered a few hundred at any one time in the early periods, but then grew to encompass a wider cross-section of the elite classes. Priests, another elite class, belonged to the ranks of the literate, and literacy was essential to the practice of their several official rituals. Repositories of written knowledge were maintained by priests in the temples in all phases of Egyptian history, and the walls of temples were often covered with written and pictorial representations, exemplifying the interconnection of religion, politics, and the written word in Egypt. During the Late Period, when Greeks and Egyptians enjoyed more contact than before, writing and administration fell more and more to religious establishments, and this development may have restricted widespread literacy, owing to the priests' increasing conservatism. At any rate, writing was a carefully transmitted technology in Egypt, and it was confined to elite circles where it played a crucial role in giving expression to political, religious, and scribal powers.

If we turn from the Egyptian situation to the Greek, the contrast is readily apparent. Writing was rarely in Greece, as it was in ancient Egypt and some parts of the ancient Near East, solely under the control of political, religious, or scribal elites. The spread of writing in the period 750 to 650 B.C.E. is well studied. If literacy spread along trading and commercial routes from Al Mina in the east to Iskhia in the west, this would explain the diffuse and scattered nature of the early evidence and also suggest why writing was not restricted to a scribal class, though Crete may pose an exception to the nonscribal nature of Greek literacy.[103] The increase in the dispersal of writing is thoroughly attested for the subsequent period, when again, unlike the case in Egypt, it appears not to be stimulated or manipulated by elites for political purposes. This is not to deny that writing in Greece could have overt political uses or could function as state-sanctioned propaganda. On the contrary, Athenian public documents from the fifth century include "decrees of the Assembly and council, laws, accounts of the various treasuries and officials, temple inventories and building accounts, calendars, treaties, public dedications,"[104] and the fourth century sees an even greater proliferation in the number of public documents set up in the polis. In fact, there is a great deal of evidence to suggest an increase in the number of written documents in the fifth and fourth centuries in Greece.

103. For Crete, see Jeffery and Morpurgo-Davies 1970.
104. Thomas 1992, 137; and cf. Sickinger 1999.

However, the control of writing was not restricted to a scribal class, nor was it the political and religious elites alone who were literate.

What is noteworthy about the expansion of literacy in these years in Greece is not only that writing fails to be a defining characteristic of the city-state, as the example of Sparta shows,[105] but that writing itself becomes an area of anxiety for many Greeks. Nicole Loraux, following Plutarch, asks *"who* writes in Athens?" and comes to the conclusion "that Athenian democracy distrusted writing—or, what amounts to the same thing, never used it—as an instrument of theoretical reflection."[106] And so, the indisputable growth in the number of written texts from the middle of the eighth century to the end of the fourth century has to be reconciled with the distrust of writing attested in the many contemporary authors of whom Plato serves as but one reminder. Why did the inhabitants of the Greek city-states entrust so much to writing if at the same time they felt deeply anxious about the worth of the practice? One could answer with Socrates that writing per se is not shameful, but what is shameful is speaking and writing in an unacceptable way, that is, shamefully and badly (*Phaedrus* 258d). We ought to differentiate between writing in the public domain, the agora and the *boule*, where treaties and laws may be displayed and may remind viewers of the potential power and privileges that come with life in the democratic polis, and private writing, writing created by individuals for closed groups with hidden and potentially subversive motives. While Athenians used the former kind actively to promote their own civic ideology, they gave a negative charge to the latter kind of private writing. Thus, as Steiner's detailed study shows, individuals who are antidemocratic, ἀπράγμων, or ἀχρεῖος tend to involve themselves with written modes of expression, including, for instance, Orpheus, Anaxagoras, Pythagoras, Empedocles, and Heraclitus.[107] On the other hand, Herodotus' eastern despots treat their kingdoms as their personal property, and hence confuse the distinction between writing that is public, accessible, and democratic, and writing that is private, exclusive, and autocratic.

The general unease connected with writing is the proper background to the remarks we have been examining in Herodotus, Aeschylus, and Plato. What is striking is the almost contrary dynamic that they and some others in the Greek tradition impart to writing in the seventh to the fourth cen-

105. See Cartledge 1978 and Boring 1979.
106. Loraux 1986, 178–79.
107. See Steiner 1994, ch. 5.

turies. These Greeks contribute to the growing number of words being put into writing, and thus provide a basis for activities so central to the polis as legislation, education, public debate, and philosophical thought. At the same time, they deny writing a value, function, or place of its own. They either define writing in opposition to what it is not, the spoken utterance, or they contain writing by limiting its utility, usually in relation to its instrumental capacities, to a carefully policed area of human practices. Writing is denied a place in the life of the polis, or if writing is admitted, it is somehow qualified and supplemented to render it acceptable, useful, and harmless, so that it can no longer be thought of as writing itself, but rather as a law, ballot, decree, resolution, or notice of ownership. Even for its practitioners, therefore, writing is hardly taken for what it is, and it is constrained to pass as something else, whether derivative, instrumental, contingent, or subordinate.

It is within just this movement of denial and displacement that Egypt intervenes in the Greek imagination. For Herodotus, writing is a defining characteristic of the barbarian world, a consideration which must secure Egypt's place among the barbarians since Egyptian priests are the world's best record-keepers. To write is to betray your foreignness, according to the historian's logic, but also to inscribe yourself as a constituent part of despotic megalomania, to proclaim your victim's inferiority by the flash of a woman's genitalia, or to treat your country as you would a sheet of papyrus waiting to suffer the marks of the royal reed. Aeschylus' *Suppliants* dramatizes the difference between Egyptians and Greeks by contrasting writing on tablets and papyrus with the speech of a "free man," although the label "free man" seems odd when applied to the king of Argos. The *Suppliants* also likens the Argives' verdict to a decree posted up in the Athenian agora, and so the play divides Egyptians from Greeks as it distinguishes writing that is acceptable to a democracy from writing potentially subversive to it. Plato follows Herodotus to the extent that his dialogues, too, heighten Egypt's affinity to writing and to the written remembrance of things past. The kind of memory cultivated by Egyptian priests in *Timaeus* and *Critias* preserves the record of Athens' glorious defeat of Atlantis, and thus does not resemble the Platonic *anamnesis* that seeks to know the real, the true, and the divine. For Socrates, moreover, writing is the invention of a Theuth who nonetheless has closer ties to Prometheus, Palamedes, and Orpheus than to his Egyptian namesake. It is difficult for Socrates to mention writing without seeking to tether the written word to its intrinsic meaning and to ascertain its legitimate father. The Greek authors want to assimilate

Egyptians to their own treatment of writing, but the contemplation of hieroglyphs shows that continuous apprehension about the written word falls more within the Greek than the Egyptian tradition.

Thus, the representations and the practices of writing function as a means through which we can cast light on certain ethnographic, philosophical, and political faultlines within ancient Greek thought. In the broad terms deployed in this chapter, our analyses flow along two separate but complementary directions of inquiry. The first considers representations of Egyptian writing or representations of writing in Egyptian contexts, and examines these for what they reveal about Greek ideas of Egypt. In this analysis, Egypt appears to be defined programmatically by its relationship to the written word. The country is subjected to a graphic charge of such intensity, especially by Herodotus and Plato, that it will become inconceivable for Greek intellectuals and writers, after these two, to conceptualize the country outside of its written records, archival papyri, and scribal traditions. These representations assume a further significance through the political differentiation they specify between Greece and Egypt, whereby Egyptian usages of writing involve monumental inscriptions in the service of tyranny and autocracy. Yet even as the Greek representations bind together tyranny and monumental Egyptian writing ever more closely, the sources impute democratic openness and accountability to monumental writing within Greek settings. What is left out by the Greek sources, of course, is the assertion that Greek monumental writing, too, has manifest political functions, and that it, too, projects state ideologies through the use of symbolic and nonsymbolic expression.

A second channel of inquiry evaluates Platonic assumptions about the ways in which language functions, as exemplified in the very same passages where the philosopher considers foreign writing, and finds these assumptions to be countered explicitly by the Egyptian hieroglyphic system in significant respects. Since Plato's assumptions about language are closely linked to his metaphysics, the Egyptian system poses a fundamental challenge both to the validity of his linguistic premises, which connect him to Saussure via Aristotle, and to his metaphysics of presence and absolute ideality, of which he remains the founding figure. To find these Platonic beliefs countered in Egyptian thought is not necessarily to allege their falsity, but it is to expose their tendentiousness and ethnocentrism as well as to interrogate their claims to universality and inevitability. Indeed, the Egyptian writing system both confirms the arbitrariness of Plato's metaphysical principles and unsettles the generative logic that lies at the heart of his technologies of language. On the other hand, it should be conceded that Plato, Herodotus, and Aeschylus, unlike numerous Greeks after them, did not exaggerate the otherness of hieroglyphic writing by emphasizing its iconicity or alleged symbolic value at the expense of its phoneticism. But even if they did not go as far as Horapollo or Ammianus Marcellinus in their misconceptions, they nonetheless allowed themselves to be baffled, all too easily, by a language and a culture that was never further than the brief voyage across the eastern Mediterranean.[108] "Already among the Greeks," Hare comments, "misconceptions about hieroglyphs encouraged a charade, a willful misunderstanding of a language they could have naturally mastered (while there were still millions of native speakers of Egyptian). . . . In general, Egyptian writing was beyond not the capacity of the Greeks but rather their will. They did not open their minds to its principles."[109] Between the two poles marked by this charade and this deficiency of will, Greek intellectuals were able to understand only at a rudimentary level the people that continually fascinated them and, as for many foreign readers of hieroglyphs, their sense of the language and culture was partial and unreliable.[110] In fact, the neglect of Greek intellectuals to learn foreign languages was symptomatic of their failure to arrive at a sympathetic understanding of the otherness of Egyptian culture on its own terms.

108. See Horapollo's *Hieroglyphica* and Ammianus Marcellinus 17.4.8–11.

109. Hare 1999, 45. There may be some exaggeration here, however, since it is doubtful that there were millions of native users of hieroglyphs, with which Hare is concerned in his book, in the Late Period; but exact statistics of ancient Egyptian literacy are impossible: see Baines and Eyre 1983.

110. For Herodotus' conception of foreign languages, see Harrison 1998, with good bibliography.

Figure 1.   Danaus lands in the Argolid. Attic red-figure hydria from Vulci, ca. 460–450 B.C.E. The scene probably shows Danaus and his daughters unloading gifts for Pelasgus on their arrival in Argos. Munich: Staatliche Antikensammlung 2429. Photograph courtesy of the museum.

Figure 2.   Death of Danaus. Lucanian red-figure nestoris, ca. 375–350 B.C.E. See the discussion and bibliography in *LIMC*, "Danaos" no. 5 and "Bousiris" no. 37. The scene probably represents the murder of Danaus by Lynceus. Scholars have also interpreted, less plausibly, the vase painting as the murder of Busiris by Heracles, or the slaying of Aegisthus by Orestes. Bonn: Akademisches Kunstmuseum—Antikensammlung der Universität Bonn 2667. Photograph courtesy of the museum.

Figure 3.   Heracles is led to sacrifice. Attic red-figure cup from Vulci, ca. 440 B.C.E. Heracles is escorted to the sacrificial altar by Egyptian priests, one in front of him and two behind. Berlin: Antikensammlung, Staatliche Museen zu Berlin—Preussischer Kulturbesitz F2534. Photograph courtesy of the museum.

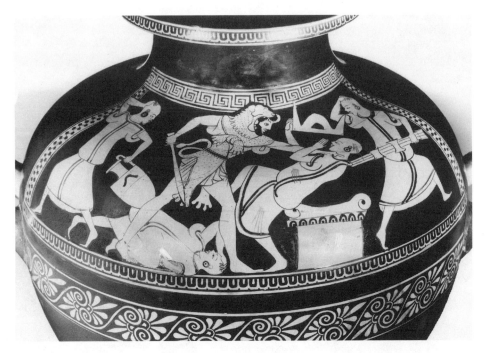

Figure 4. Heracles attacks Egyptians. Attic red-figure hydria from Vulci, ca. 490 B.C.E. Heracles grabs hold of an Egyptian, probably Busiris, by the throat and readies to kill him on an altar. Another Egyptian lies fallen at the feet of the hero. On the far left and right, Egyptian priests run away from the mayhem. Munich: Staatliche Antikensammlung 2428. Photograph courtesy of the museum.

Figure 5.   Heracles attacks Egyptians. Attic red-figure pelike from Thespiae,
ca. 470 B.C.E. Busiris cowers on one side of an altar while Heracles gets ready
to attack him with the body of an Egyptian, whom he is holding by the ankles.
On the right, an Egyptian priest prepares to assault the hero with a mallet.
Athens: National Archaeological Museum 9683. Photograph courtesy of the
museum.

Figure 6.   Heracles attacks Egyptians. Caeretan style hydria from Cerveteri, ca. 510 B.C.E. Heracles, large and unstoppable, attacks the Egyptians who have tried to kill him. The hero tramples on his enemies in a manner reminiscent of triumphant pharaohs. At the foot of the sacrificial altar on the left lies the fallen king Busiris. Vienna: Kunsthistorisches Museum 3576. Photograph courtesy of the museum.

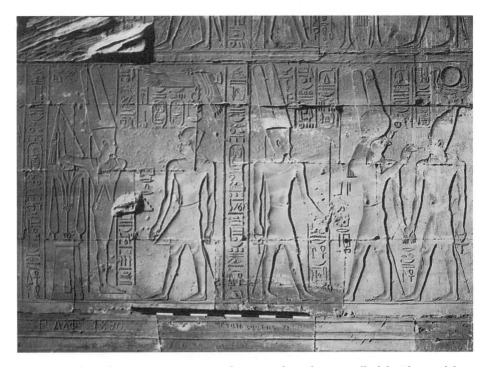

Figure 7.   Alexander in Egypt, Luxor Temple. Scenes from the east wall of the Shrine of the
Bark in the temple of Amun, Mut, and Khons, Luxor. The restoration of the sanctuary dates
to ca. 330–325 B.C.E. On the left, Alexander comes before Amun-Kamutef; on the right, Montu
presents Alexander to Amun. Photograph courtesy of the Oriental Institute of the University
of Chicago P. 38218 / N. 42808.

Figure 8.   Cécile, Frontispiece of the first edition of the *Description de l'Égypte* (1809–26). The *Explication du Frontispice* notes: "In the center of the frieze, the Hero conquering Egypt is depicted on his chariot; before him, the eagle, emblem of the army, crushes the Mamluks as they flee toward the pyramids. The Nile, personified, looks on at these exploits. The Arts and Sciences follow the Hero as he leads them back to a land from which they have for too long been exiled. The two vertical borders show military trophies and standards on which the names of the principal battlefields of Egypt and Syria are inscribed. In the middle of the lower border the Emperor's initial, encircled by a serpent, emblem of immortality, appears. On either side, the conquered form varied groups and lay down their arms. At each end, Egyptian scarabs enclose a bee and a star, a sort of personal symbol of the Emperor." Photograph courtesy of the Getty Research Library.

5 Reading Isocrates' *Busiris*

The rejection of the State in democratic Athens took a particular
form in the admiration of ancient institutions which had remained
unchanged and remote from democratic development; above all
this applied to Egypt, together with the enthusiasm of all oligarchs
for Sparta, seen as modelled on Egypt. This high opinion of Egypt
is expressed not only by Plato, who is famous for it, but occasionally
by Isocrates too. When we find Busiris (15 f.) praising the caste
system as the wise invention of an ancient founding father and
lawgiver of the nation, and also read (*ibid.* 20) that life in Athens
would be happiest if, as in Egypt, some were born to work and the
others (the warrior caste) to guard wealth, we may recall that in
the eighteenth century some Enlightenment thinkers admired
China in much the same way; like Plato, Busiris devotes special
praise to the Egyptians for their piety (*ibid.* 24).

> Jacob Burckhardt, *Griechische Kulturgeschichte*[1]

... Busiris and his Memphian chivalry.

> John Milton, *Paradise Lost*

Busiris is a little-read epideictic exercise composed by the Athenian Isocrates in the first half of the fourth century B.C.E.; its subject is a mythical
king of Egypt who was popular among Athenian vase painters in the late
fifth and early fourth centuries.[2] The speech belongs to the class of speeches
known as "paradoxical" encomia, because it praised a subject that was evidently unworthy of praise: according to Greek myth, Busiris murdered visitors to Egypt. Isocrates' *Busiris* has not received significant scholarly
attention, probably because it is taken for a mere rhetorical exercise, more
lighthearted than serious, although the speech has both truth and aggres-

---

1. Burckhardt 1998, 326.
2. My discussion, in this chapter, is quite distinct from the few available treatments of *Busiris*: see Froidefond 1971, 237–66; Eucken 1983, ch. 5; Bernal 1987,
103–8. References to *Busiris* are to the Teubner edition. I have also consulted the
Budé edition. Translations are modified from volume 3 of the Loeb Isocrates, edited
and translated by Larue Van Hook (1945). I have not been able to consult Niall R.
Livingstone's *Isocrates'* Busiris: *A Commentary* (Mnemosyne Supplement series,
forthcoming).

sion lurking in it. When the speech is read against the background of Greek traditions about Busiris and the genre of parodic rhetoric, then we can understand it as an important contribution to the fourth-century literature on Egypt. It is evident from Isocrates' speech that he was concerned less with the realities of present-day Egypt than with devising a stylized but largely unhistorical portrait of the country. In some ways, he resembles contemporary comic writers who make fun of Egyptians engaged in various trades and professions in Athens and who satirize an Egyptian affinity for zoolatry; but in his attitude, he also marks a break with historical writers such as Herodotus on the one hand, and with the cosmopolitan views of sophists such as Hippias and Antiphon on the other.[3] The parodic context and the largely negative Greek tradition of Busiris ensure the complicity of Isocrates' text with Athenian ethnocentrism and claims to cultural superiority. Thus, Isocrates' work also offers a strong contrast with another epideictic speech, Gorgias' *Helen,* where the categories are so slippery and the exculpatory technique so virtuoso that the paradoxes tend to undermine the conventional logic of praise and blame and to authorize a reading of indeterminacy. The difference between the traditions of Helen and Busiris, among other reasons, means that Isocrates' speech could not be as indeterminate as Gorgias' encomium: Helen's motives are ambiguous from Homer's day onward, while Busiris' actions are seen as murderous by an overwhelmingly large number of authors. Clearly, audiences would bring different expectations to a speech about Helen than they would to a speech about Busiris. No matter how crude some of us might find the picture of alterity that emerges from Isocrates' speech, and no matter how fond some of us might be of finding indeterminacy in ancient texts, Isocrates' *Busiris* re-

3. Hippias = DK 86; Antiphon = DK 87. For some sense of the difference between these writers and Isocrates, see e.g. Antiphon's *On Truth:* "The laws of our neighbors we know and revere: the laws of those who live afar we neither know nor revere. Thus in this we have been made barbarians with regard to one another. For by nature we are all in all respects similarly endowed to be barbarian or Greek. One may consider those natural facts which are necessary in all men and provided for all in virtue of the same faculties—and in these very matters none of us is separated off as a barbarian or as a Greek. For we all breathe into the air by way of our mouths and noses, we laugh when we are happy in our minds and we cry when we are in pain, we receive sounds by our hearing and we see with our eyes by light, we work with our hands and we walk on our feet. . . ." (DK 87 B 44, with *P. Oxy.* 3647, trans. J. Barnes, modified). Antiphon's remarks on biological homogeneity and his point that all humans are similar by nature contrast with the rigid distinction between Greek and barbarian on which much of Isocrates' work depends: see e.g. *Panegyricus* 50.

mains firmly rooted to the authoritative tradition that rarely ceases to refer to the murderous barbarity of the Egyptian king.

BUSIRIS THE EGYPTIAN

We know that Isocrates' audience would have been familiar with the story, since there was a largely invariable tradition concerning the bloodthirsty Egyptian king. The story of Busiris is found in text and art in Athens throughout the fifth and fourth centuries, and it continues to be remembered in Greek and Roman sources into the sixth century C.E., although the artistic representations disappear in the Hellenistic period. A small group of writers attempts to dismiss the idea that an Egyptian would want to sacrifice anyone on his altars, let alone a Greek hero. Nevertheless, definite attempts at rehabilitation are taken only by Herodotus and Eratosthenes, and the persistence of the story in later texts points to the tenacity of this chapter in Egyptian ferocity and Greek heroism. The Egyptian data, it hardly needs to be said, side with Herodotus and Eratosthenes and make clear that the Busiris myth has no basis in fact, since human sacrifice is scarcely evident in Egypt, quite apart from the absence of the king's name among Egyptian personages.

What recurs in the Greek and Latin authors who mention Busiris, from Pherecydes and Panyassis in the fifth century B.C.E., to Lactantius Placidus in the sixth century C.E., is the idea that the Egyptian king regularly seized foreign visitors and sacrificed them on his altars.[4] The relevant passages from the authors just named are representative insofar as they indicate the fragmentary or abbreviated nature of so many of the ancient texts that reveal a knowledge of the myth of Busiris. Even in their spare and meager condition, however, the texts point to a common theme when they disclose the traces of an insidious king who indulged in the practice of human sacrifice, until, of course, he was thwarted by Heracles, who turned *him* into a sacrificial victim. Apollodorus provides a fuller version of the impression made by Busiris on the Graeco-Roman imagination:

4. The main sources are collected in Hiller von Gaertringen 1897, Hopfner 1922–25, Griffiths 1948, and Laurens 1986. Pherecydes: scholiast at Apollonius, *Argonautica* 4.1396. Panyassis: quoted in Athenaeus 4.172d = F 26 (Kinkel) = F 23 (Davies); see Matthews 1974, 126–28, for a discussion of the text. Lactantius Placidus: at Statius, *Thebaid* 12.155. There is also a reference to Pherecydes' treatment of Busiris in *De orthographia* (2), a work once attributed to Apuleius. The work is largely a forgery, written by Caelius Rhodiginus (Ludovico Ricchieri, 1450–1520), in Ferrara, under the name Lucius Caecilius Minutianus Apuleius.

> After Libya, he [Heracles] traversed Egypt. That country was then
> ruled by Busiris, a son of Poseidon by Lysianassa, daughter of Epaphus.
> This Busiris used to sacrifice strangers on an altar of Zeus in accordance
> with a certain oracle. Egypt was then visited with dearth, for nine years,
> and Phrasios, a learned seer, who had come from Cyprus, said that
> the dearth would cease if they slaughtered a stranger in honor of Zeus
> every year. Busiris began by sacrificing the seer himself, and continued
> to slaughter the strangers who landed. So Heracles also was seized, and
> haled to the altars, but he burst his bonds, and slew both Busiris and
> Amphidamas.[5]

With changes here and there, Apollodorus' description of the Busiris story
contains the important details of a tradition that seems to have attracted the
attention of many writers before and after him. The list of authors who exploited the story of Busiris in a context or manner that invariably signals
complicity with this tradition includes Euripides, Cratinus, Cicero, Virgil,
Ovid, and more than a dozen others.[6] To this barrage of evidence must be
added also the names of writers who, without explicitly naming Busiris or
Heracles, suggest that the Egyptians used to sacrifice human beings. These
include Juvenal (who implies anthropophagy), Sextus Empiricus, Porphyry
(who quotes Manetho), Achilles Tatius, and Procopius.[7]

---

5. Apollodorus 2.5.11. James Frazer, whose translation I adapt, makes a claim
that is interesting as an example of the kind of reception accorded to the Busiris
myth even by scholars of the modern period. Frazer asserts that the Greek sources
describe an ancient Egyptian practice in which kings were sacrificed in the interests
of the fertility of the land (an assertion developed further in *The Golden Bough*).
In response to the particular question of fertility, however, it needs to be added that
drought and fertility are first mentioned in connection with the Busiris story only
as late as Ovid, and after Ovid by Apollodorus, Hyginus, and Claudian, and that
most of the Greek writers omit any reference to this aspect of the myth. See Griffiths 1948.

6. Euripides, frs. 313–15 (Nauck); Cicero, *De Republica* 3.15; Virgil, *Georgics*
3.5; Ovid, *Ars Amatoria* 1.647–52, *Epistulae ex Ponto* 3.6.41, *Metamorphoses*
9.182–83, *Tristia* 3.11.39; Statius, *Thebaid* 12.155; Plutarch, *Theseus* 11. See also
Epicharmus, frs. 81.10 and 82, and see fr. 223 (Austin, *CGFP*); Antiphanes frs. 66–
68 *PCG* (= Kock, vol. 2, 37–38); Ephippus fr. 2 *PCG* (= Kock, vol. 2, 251); Cratinus fr. 23 *PCG* (= Kock, vol. 2, 289); Mnesimachus fr. 2 *PCG* (= Kock, vol. 2, 436);
Callimachus, frs. 44–47 (Pfeiffer); Agathon of Samos, *FGrHist* 843 F 3; Aulus Gellius, *Attic Nights* 2.6.3; Hyginus, *Fabulae* 31, 56, 157; Minucius Felix, *Octavius* 30;
Claudian, *In Eutropium* 1.159–62; Macrobius, *Saturnalia* 6.7.5; Servius, at *Georgics* 3.5 and *Aeneid* 8.299; Orosius, *History against the Pagans* 1.11; scholia at Aristophanes, *Wealth* 178. See also Hesiod, fr. 378 (Merkelbach-West, spurious);
Ovid, *Ibis* 399–400; Suetonius, *Nero* 37; Lucian, *True Histories* 2.23; and Dio Chry-
sostom 8.32 and 33.47.

7. Juvenal 15.78–81; Sextus Empiricus, *Outlines of Pyrrhonism* 3.24 (a difficult
passage—he says that most Egyptians considered the practice impious; but the

Against this extensive catalogue of those who appear all too keen to ascribe a story of human sacrifice to one or more Egyptians unfolds the shorter roster of writers who complicate the standard narrative, or even deny it altogether: Herodotus, Eratosthenes, and Diodorus.[8] Nevertheless, even these writers' statements about the Busiris story are not always unequivocal, and we see clear and unambiguous denials chiefly in Herodotus and Eratosthenes. These two writers suggest the possibility of a counter-discourse. Eratosthenes (ca. 275–194 B.C.E.) claims that "by Zeus, no king or tyrant named Busiris ever existed" (οὐ βασιλέως, μὰ Δία, οὐδὲ τυράννου γενομένου τινὸς Βουσίριδος).[9] Herodotus refuses to accept even the hint of human sacrifice in the Busiris story:

> The Greeks tell many stories that show no manner of thought. In particular, there is the tale they tell of Heracles to the effect that he came to Egypt, and that the Egyptians put garlands on his head, and led him in procession, with intent to sacrifice (θύσοντες) him to Zeus; that for a while he held quiet, but when they brought him near the altar itself, and had started the first rites on him, he took himself to his valor, and slaughtered (καταφονεῦσαι) them all. In my opinion, the Greeks who tell this story know absolutely nothing about the nature of the Egyp-

Latin version notes that the practice was considered sacred); Porphyry, *On Abstinence* 2.55 (= Manetho, *FGrHist* 609 F 14); Achilles Tatius 3.15; and Procopius, *The Persian War* 1.19; cf. Plato, *Laws* 953e; Cassius Dio 71.4; and Eusebius, *Preparation for the Gospel* 4.16.4 (a passage from Porphyry).

8. Perhaps, Conon (first century B.C.E. to first century C.E.) and Arrian fall into this class insofar as they remain silent about Busiris' sacrificial grotesqueness when they invoke the king for other reasons in their narratives. In Conon's fragmentary account, preserved by Photius, Proteus gives over "the kingship of Busiris" when the former joins Cadmus in the search for Europa (Photius, *Bibliotheka* 186; *FGrH* 26 F 1, sec. 32). Arrian writes simply that Heracles was said to have consulted the oracle of Ammon at Siwah "when he was journeying into Libya to find Antaeus, and into Egypt to find Busiris" (*Anabasis* 3.3.1). The silence of Conon and Arrian about Busiris' cruelty is noticeable, but their positions are hard to ascertain since they offer no comment on the truth or falsity of the traditional charges made against the Egyptian king.

9. Strabo 17.1.19: "According to Eratosthenes, the expulsion of foreigners is a custom common to all barbarians, and yet the Egyptians are condemned for this fault because of the myths which have been circulated about Busiris in connection with the Busirite nome, since the later writers wish falsely to malign the inhospitality of this place, although, by Zeus, no king or tyrant named Busiris ever existed; and, he says, the poet's words are also constantly quoted 'to go to Egypt, a long and painful journey' [*Odyssey* 4.483]—the want of harbors contributing very much to this opinion, as also the fact that even the harbor which Egypt did have, the one at Pharos, gave no access, but was guarded by shepherds who were pirates and who attacked those who tried to bring ships to anchor there." See Winkler 1992, 33–37.

tians and their customs. Here is a people for whom the sacrifice (θύειν) of beasts themselves is unholy, except for pigs, bulls, bull-calves—that is, such as are pure—and geese; how could they sacrifice (θύοιεν) human beings? And furthermore, since Heracles was still only one, and also a human being, as they themselves say, how can it accord with nature that he should slaughter (φονεῦσαι) that many tens of thousands? That is what I have to say about the matter; as I do so, may both gods and heroes view me kindly![10]

In a later passage, allegedly based on Egyptian sources, Herodotus takes his refutation of the story to the point where he can attribute the sacrifice of human beings to a Greek rather than an Egyptian agent. Menelaus found the winds against him when he retrieved Helen from Egypt, and decided to set sail for Sparta; in order to deal with the problem, he took two native children and sacrificed them (λαβὼν γὰρ δύο παιδία ἀνδρῶν ἐπιχωρίων ἔντομά σφεα ἐποίησε).[11] Herodotus thus reverses the ethnic logic of the story, not only by repudiating the likelihood of human sacrifice in the socioreligious context of Egypt, but also by imputing to a Greek hero the very actions that the canonical narrative, despite his history, represents as characteristically Egyptian.

In the first century B.C.E., Diodorus also betrays some uncertainty about the story of Busiris and recalls again the xenophobia of Egyptians. In book 1, he credits Busiris with the founding of Thebes (1.45) and adds: "The impiety of Busiris was rumored abroad among the Greeks because of the inhospitality of the natives, although the account of this impiety was not actually true, but was placed in the form of a myth because of exceptional disrespect for ordinary customs" (1.67). In book 4, however, he writes in connection with Heracles about "Busiris, who throughout Egypt used to sacrifice to Zeus the strangers who sojourned there" (4.27). This latter comment is not qualified in any useful way and encumbers Diodorus' earlier reluctance to accept the crueler side of the Busiris story. But a further twist is furnished by Diodorus in his discussion of the sacrifice of Typhonian men, a custom that Plutarch claims was also recorded by Manetho.[12] Diodorus writes:

10. Herodotus 2.45.
11. Herodotus 2.119; cf. 3.11; see Plutarch, *On the Malice of Herodotus* 857A–B; and Lloyd 1976, 212–14.
12. Plutarch, *On Isis and Osiris* 73 = Manetho, *FGrHist* 609 F 22: "Many say that the soul of Typhon is dispersed among these animals, and this myth seems to encode the idea that every irrational and bestial soul is a portion of the evil spirit and that men appease and conciliate that spirit by tending and worshipping these

They say that it was agreed to sacrifice red oxen because it seemed that
this was the color of Typhon, who plotted against Osiris and was then
punished by Isis because of the murder of her husband. They say that
men also, if they were of the same color as Typhon, were in ancient
times sacrificed by the kings near the tomb of Osiris. However, of
Egyptians few were found to be red, but of foreigners the majority.
Hence, the story gained currency among the Greeks concerning the
killing of foreigners practised by Busiris, although Busiris was not
the name of the king but of the tomb of Osiris, which is called that
in the native language.[13]

Greeks linked the story of human sacrifice to an Egyptian king called Busiris, Diodorus notes, but Busiris was the name of a place and not of a person; and the name denotes "tomb of Osiris." Diodorus may well be following local tradition in connecting the place-name Busiris to the Egyptian god
Osiris (see below). Nevertheless, he also appears to claim that Egyptians
did in the past sacrifice red men, even if the sacrificer was not a King Busiris. Thus, Diodorus' initial repudiation of Busiris' impiety is compromised
by the counternarratives he furnishes in other parts of his history.

The vase paintings complement what the texts reveal concerning the
expectations that an audience of Isocrates would bring to the speech. The
artistic images, which in all cases depict the king in his encounter with Heracles, leave little doubt about the victory of the Hellenic hero over the exot-

---

animals. If a long and severe drought occurs, bringing many fatal diseases or other
strange and unexplainable disasters, then the priests lead away some of the honored
animals, calmly and by night, and they begin the ritual by threatening and frightening them. If the drought persists, they go on to consecrate and slaughter them.
This is a sort of punishment of the spirit and also a purification for the greatest pol-
lutions. And indeed in the city of Eilethyia they burned living human beings, as
Manetho has recorded, calling them 'Typhonians,' and they winnowed their ashes
and made them vanish by scattering them. But this was done publicly, at a certain
time in the dog days, whereas the consecrations of honored animals take place in secret at irregular times as the need arises, and most people are unaware of them—
except when they hold the funeral of Apis. Then they pick out some of all the animals present and lay them to rest together with Apis, in the belief that this gives
pain back to Typhon and diminishes his pleasure, because Apis, with a few other animals, is deemed worthy to be sacred to Osiris, and they accord the greatest honors
to him." See Griffiths 1970, 551–53.
    13. Diodorus 1.88. For the significance of red in Greek religion, see Wunderlich
1925, with the comparative Egyptian material in Griffiths 1991, 214–15. For Diodorus' treatment of Busiris, see Burton 1972, 204–5, 246–48, 258–59. Stephens,
forthcoming, discusses Egyptian foe-smiting scenes in connection with Diodorus'
handling of the Busiris story; she suggests that Diodorus, like the court poets of the
Ptolemies, matches Greek concept to Egyptian concept within the framework of
pharaonic kingship.

icized, murderous barbarian.[14] The paintings usually emphasize the hero's victorious role and draw attention to the manner in which he dispatches the Egyptian king. Annie-France Laurens has studied the iconographic material and divides the vase paintings, apart from those where the identification is tentative or uncertain, according to the following categories: (a) Heracles is led to the sacrifice by Egyptian priests (fig. 3); (b) Heracles frees himself of his bonds and attacks Busiris and his escort; and (c) Heracles kills Busiris and puts to flight the pharaoh's entourage (figs. 4 and 5).[15] Parody and satire, Laurens suggests, are the defining characteristics of the iconographic evidence. Her interpretation is strenghthened by the fact that Euripides composed a satyr-play on the subject and that the comic playwrights used the story in their plays.[16] Most of the vases heighten the divide between the two sides of the conflict by emphasizing contrasts in number and race: one against many, Greek versus Egyptian. On one hydria from about 510, Heracles even tramples his enemies underfoot in a manner reminiscent of triumphant pharaohs as these appear in Egyptian art: if Heracles, like the pharaoh, represents order and civilized community in the image, this is a paradoxical inversion since the hero's victims are the pharaoh's own subjects (fig. 6).[17] The earliest vase paintings date to the second quarter of the sixth century, but they cease to be produced by the end of the fourth century, with the bulk of the surviving evidence localized to Athens in the last quarter of the fifth century, which was the period of Isocrates' youth (he was born in ca. 436). As far as other milieux are concerned, no artistic representations survive from Hellenistic, Etruscan, or Roman workshops, and this implies that the anxiety over the Egyptian Busiris evaporates, or is otherwise modified, among artists after the fourth century.

In the face of all this evidence from Greece and Rome about the sacrificer-king, the Egyptian sources respond with a profound silence, since the truth is that there was no King Busiris in ancient Egypt. The reticence of the Egyptian sources on the issue means, indeed can only mean, that any figure by the name "Busiris" is a fantasy of Greek myth. The Greek and

14. See the analysis in Raeck 1981, 175–79; and Durand and Lissarrague 1983.
15. Laurens 1986. The most important illustrations may be consulted in the article by Laurens, which supplies bibliographical references for each vase. See also Snowden 1970, 23, 25–26, 103–4, 159–60; Snowden 1976, 152 and figs. 171–72; and Snowden 1983, 15, 48, 82.
16. See n. 6 above.
17. See Stephens, forthcoming, for the suggestion that the vase painter appropriates for Heracles the properties of the pharaoh as the bearer of order and civilized community.

Roman sources make a point of Busiris' Egyptian nationality to so great an extent that Busiris remains inseparable from his Egyptian homeland in the Graeco-Roman tradition. This is one way in which he differs from other diabolical hosts (οἱ ξενοκτόνοι) in Greek myth, such as Phalaris and Procrustes, who are not identified with their home regions as closely as Busiris is with his. But not a single text, picture, or other piece of evidence from Egypt refers to a king with this name. The closest we come to something in Egypt with this name is the Greek place-name "Busiris." This probably applies to the place once known by the Egyptian name '*ndt*, or *Ddw*, and which later became *Pr-Wsir-nb-Ddw*, "house of Osiris, lord of Djedu," and then *pr-Wsir*, "the house of Osiris," and eventually "Abusir."[18]

Even the supposition that the Greek myth conceals a general reality lurking around the subject of human sacrifice in ancient Egypt comes up short against what the country itself tells us, since the evidence for such sacrifices in Egypt is both uncertain and sparse. Neither sacrifices *of* pharaohs nor human sacrifices *by* pharaohs are attested in any Egyptian source; human sacrifices in general, too, are only ambiguously established.[19] Pharaohs are often shown in pictorial art as smiting the enemy, usually with a club, but this cannot be interpreted as evidence for human sacrifice, even if foreigners, from Greece and elsewhere, may have misconstrued these representations.[20] Some scholars have interpreted material remains from the First Dynasty as evidence for mass burial forced upon servants and relatives of the dead man, although this interpretation of the date has been challenged, and it is further debatable whether the practice can be thought of as sacrificial.[21] Again, the tomb of Montu-her-khopeshef in Thebes depicts the death by strangling of Nubians, but these representations need not reflect a real sacrificial background. Also, excavations of a nobleman's tomb dated to the Middle Kingdom at Kerma, in Nubia, have revealed the sacrifice of "well over one hundred," but the line between sacrifice and mass burial is not clearly drawn here too and, strictly speaking,

18. Hiller von Gaertringen 1897, cols. 1077–78; Burton 1972, 258–59; and Lloyd 1976, 269.

19. *LÄ*, s.v. "Menschenopfer." See also Lloyd 1976, 212–14. But cf. Yoyotte 1980–81; and Hoffman 1991, 116, 124, 261–62, 275–79, 284. In the story of King Khufu and the magician Djedi, written in the Middle Kingdom, the king asks the magician to behead a human being, but the magician demands that his victim be a goose rather than a human. See Lichtheim 1973, 217–20.

20. For Hellenistic Greek readings of the standard representations of the Egyptian pharaoh, see Stephens, forthcoming.

21. See Griffiths 1970, 552.

the area in question lies outside Egypt.[22] These few and controversial examples constitute the bulk of the evidence for human sacrifice in Egypt.

In fact, as many examples from Greek literature illustrate, there are better reasons to accept the practice of human sacrifice within Greece than to
suppose that this sort of sacrifice existed within Egypt.[23] Iphigenia, Theseus, the Bacchae, and the cult at Brauron, to name a few, force the realization that human sacrifice could justifiably be attributed to Greeks. Scholars
may be correct to claim that human sacrifice was not practised in the historical period in Greece—this is the current consensus—but it should be
pointed out that Greek texts of many periods and genres repeatedly raise
the subject. It is at least plausible that the Greeks projected onto the Egyptians in the Busiris myth their own psychopolitical anxieties about the role
of sacrificial scapegoats (φαρμακοί) in Hellenic society, given that invariably the king dies because Heracles slays the barbarian Busiris on an altar.
Such a reading would imply that Greeks made an Egyptian king a scapegoat
in their myths in order to accommodate their unease over a phenomenon
that disturbed them, whether or not it ever took place in Greece. And it remains true, in any event, that reports of human sacrifice are more widespread in Greek than in Egyptian literature and thought, whatever the explanation for the persistence of the idea in Greek material.

Let us recall what James Rives has shown, moreover, that Greeks and
Romans used stories of human sacrifice to serve as a marker of difference
to signify the otherness of the group onto which the practice was projected,
and often to differentiate themselves from non-Greeks and non-Romans.[24]
Greek and Latin writers consistently marshaled arguments about human
sacrifice so as to make clear the demarcation between self and other, insider

22. See Reisner 1923, 141 ff., with Hoffman 1991, 275–79. In the Mediterranean region, human sacrifice is attested among the northwest Semitic peoples (see
the arguments over Molech in Weinfeld 1972, Heider 1985, and Day 1989), and
among Carthaginians (see Brown 1991). Passages in the Hebrew Bible relating to
human sacrifice are numerous: see e.g. Exodus 22.29–30; Leviticus 18.21 (Molech);
Judges 11.30–31, 39; 1 Kings 16.34; 2 Kings 3.27 and 21.6. Day 1989, 86–91, translates the main classical and patristic references to Phoenician and Carthaginian human sacrifice.

23. For human sacrifice in Greece and in Greek thought, see Schwenn 1915;
Henrichs 1981; Burkert 1983, 84–7, 114–15; Foley 1985; O'Connor-Visser 1987,
211–30; Hall 1989, 147–48; Hughes 1991; Pucci 1992; Winkler 1992, 18–24, 29–
37; Bonnechere 1994. For theory, see Brelich 1969, Burkert 1983, Girard 1977.

24. Rives 1995, which concentrates on Roman, including early Christian, material. For a study of the problems that arise when one culture (the British colonial
administration) confronts and misunderstands the practice of human sacrifice in
another (tribal villagers in central India), see Padel 1995.

and outsider, or native and foreigner. Depending on the cultural location of the writer, the foreign element consisted of Taurians, Theban women, Alexandrian Jews, Catilinarian conspirators, and pagans, not to mention Egyptians. In this discourse, the perpetrators of human sacrifice were reckoned barbarous, uncivilized, threatening, or marginal to the writer's society; and, similarly, denial of human sacrifice was invoked to recoup the subject's hold on an acceptable identity. The uses to which the discourse of human sacrifice was put are evident in ample detail throughout Graeco-Roman antiquity, quite apart from the recognition that the evidence may or may not have corroborated the claims of writers.

READING ISOCRATES' SPEECH

The parodic force of Isocrates' *Busiris* is apparent from a consideration of the genre to which it belongs and of the contents of its narrative. The speech belongs to the class of texts known in antiquity as "paradoxical" because of the manner in which the texts played against the expectations of the audience. Paradoxical speeches are *parodic* by definition, therefore, since they belong to a genre that consists of speeches that praise or blame subjects unworthy of praise or blame. In addition to being parodic because it is paradoxical, moreover, Isocrates' *Busiris* has particular elements that signal its status as parody to an audience. The most obvious of these elements is the narrative self-reflexivity that inescapably reminds the audience of the kind of speech that it is consuming.

As Philodemus indicated in antiquity, encomia of Busiris belong to this category of "paradoxical" or "adoxographic" treatises, which flourished in nearly all periods of ancient Greek literature.[25] These were speeches written in the encomiastic style on subjects that were immediately recognizable to ancient audiences as vile, trivial, ridiculous, or otherwise unsuited to praise. Inversely, the blame of subjects that were perceived to be good, beautiful, excellent, or worthy of honor also fell into the category of paradoxical speeches. The classification is ancient and typically covers speeches as early as Gorgias' works. Arthur Stanley Pease surveyed the whole class

---

25. Philodemus, *On Rhetoric* 1.216–17 (Sudhaus): Ἀλλ' οἱ ῥητορικοὶ σοφισ-ταὶ Βουσείριδας καὶ Πολυφήμους καὶ τοιούτους ἄλλους ἐγκωμιάζοντες τὰ τῶν ἀγαθῶν ἔπαθλα κοινοποιοῦσι καὶ πολλοὺς εἶναι πονηροὺς προτρέπονται. Cf. Quintilian 2.17.4, and Fraustadt 1909, 51–53. On paradoxical speeches, see Polybius 12.26; Menander Rhetor 2.1.346 (Spengel); Gellius 17.12.1–2; Burgess 1902, 157–66; Pease 1926; Colie 1966, 3–40; Nightingale 1995, 100–102.

of paradoxical speeches, and drew up a list of items praised in paradoxical speeches: Busiris, Thersites, Polyphemus, the presence or absence of hair, quartan fever, gout, blindness, deafness, insomnia, sleep, negligence, adultery, the ass, the horse, the cow, the parrot, the ant, the bumblebee, flies, gnats, fleas, lice, bedbugs, the Dog Star, pots, pebbles, salt, wine, figs, the lyre, dust, smoke, ashes, and dung.[26] Examples from the fifth and fourth centuries include the encomia of Busiris and Helen by Isocrates, the praise of Helen by Gorgias, the praise of the nonlover given to Lysias in Plato's *Phaedrus*, speeches on death and the courtesan Nais by Alcidamas, the eulogy of the courtesan Lagis by Cephalus, the praise of the lyre by Lycophron, and the praise of Polyphemus by Zoilus, who was a student of Polycrates. It is Isocrates who refers to the encomia of bumblebees and salt, and Aristotle who writes of eulogies for dogs, words, Hermes, and Paris.[27]

Polycrates, who is chastised in *Busiris*, wrote several paradoxical speeches.[28] Modern scholars attribute to him encomia of Clytemnestra, mice, poets, pebbles, pouring vessels, beggars, exiles, and possibly salt and Paris, in addition to Busiris.[29] According to Aristotle, the encomium of mice exalted the way in which they gnawed through bowstrings—which may be a reference to a similar feat performed by Egyptian mice in book 2 of Herodotus.[30] Athenaeus claims that Polycrates contrived a "scandalous treatise on love" to damage Philenis, and describes him as "an Athenian by birth, sly of words, and of an evil tongue."[31] Dionysius of Halicarnassus groups Polycrates together with Antiphon of Rhamnus, Thrasymachus of Chalcedon, Critias (the leader of the Thirty), and Zoilus, but finds Lysias more incisive (ἀκριβέστερον) and charming (χαριέστερον) than any of these. Not altogether impressed by the rhetorician, Dionysius observes,

---

26. Pease 1926, 37–41.

27. Death: Cicero, *Tusculan Disputations* 1.48.116; Nais and Lagis: Athenaeus 13.592c; lyre: Aristotle, *On Sophistical Refutations* 15.174b; Polyphemus: scholia at Platonic *Hipparchus* 229d (Radermacher 1951, 200); salt and bumblebees: Isocrates, *Helen* 12, and cf. Plato, *Symposium* 177b; dogs, words, Hermes: Aristotle, *Rhetoric* 1401a13–25; Paris: Aristotle, *Rhetoric* 1401b20–23, and cf. 1398a22. See Nightingale 1995, 100–101. These paradoxical encomia may be compared with the numerous prose encomia, in general, from the fifth and fourth centuries B.C.E., for which see Fraustadt 1909, 42–90, and Buchheit 1960, chs. 1–2.

28. For Polycrates, and especially for his accusation of Socrates, see Markowski 1910; Humbert 1930; Chroust 1957, ch. 4; Dodds 1959, 28–29; Erbse 1961.

29. The references are collected in Chroust 1957, 254 n. 382; some of these are controversial. See also Nightingale 1995, 100–101, esp. n. 25 and n. 29.

30. *Rhetoric* 1401b; Herodotus 2.141.

31. Athenaeus 8.335c–d.

"Polycrates is ineffectual in his speeches for actual lawsuits, frigid (ψυχ-ρός) and vulgar (φορτικός) in his epideictic speeches, and lacking in charm when charm is required."[32] However, Demetrius thinks otherwise and does not fault Polycrates for his levity in an encomium, the name of which is unfortunately lost. "Let jesting be permitted," Demetrius declares.[33] Polycrates was writing in the manner of a plaything (παίγνιον), and in that context his playful style was acceptable.

The paradoxical speech was, as mentioned, also parodical; indeed, in a way it was paradox because it was parody. The speech parodied the encomiastic genre by taking the embellishments of the encomium and applying these to a subject that was, in received opinion (δόξα), unsuited to eulogy. Polycrates' defense of Busiris was manifestly ridiculous since mythological tradition had definitively marked the Egyptian king as a bloodthirsty killer.[34] The speaker in Isocrates' *Busiris* reinforces the point when he says that he is delivering a eulogy on this subject "although it is not serious, and does not call for a dignified style" (καίπερ οὐ σπουδαίαν οὖσαν οὐδὲ σεμνοὺς λόγους ἔχουσαν, 9), and his speech too is a parody of a serious encomium. Similarly, the encomia of Thersites, ashes, dung, flies, gnats, and the rest clearly parody both eulogy and the rules for eulogy formulated so exactly in the rhetorical handbooks. Over the centuries, of course, even paradoxical speeches entered the handbooks, although they retained the element of parody through which they always functioned. Paradoxical speeches, therefore, can be parodic to the extent that they parody both the originary genre and the received tradition concerning a given topic. Further, paradoxical speeches are parodic in another degree because they parody systems of logic. In her study of paradox in the Renaissance, Rosalie L. Colie observes, ". . . can a thing unpraisable in fact be praised? If it can, then it is not unpraisable; if it cannot, then a vast number of pieces of paradoxical prose do not exist."[35] Paradoxical speeches are parodic, then, in at least three modes of functioning, insofar as they parody the originary genres, received traditions, and systems of logic.

Isocrates' epideictic speech is presented as a parodic and paradoxical rival to speeches by Polycrates, who once tried to defend Busiris and condemn Socrates, but managed only to come up with inadequate show-pieces.

32. Dionysius of Halicarnassus, *Isaios* 20.
33. Demetrius, *On Style* 120.
34. See Quintilian 2.17.4 on the ingenuity rather than sincerity of Polycrates' encomium of Busiris.
35. Colie 1966, 5.

Like many epideictic speeches, Isocrates' composition is brief and full of rhetorical flourish. The speaker chastises Polycrates for failing in his exercise and puts forth a paradigmatic speech of his own, so that Polycrates can learn how an epideictic speech should be composed, especially a eulogy. The Isocratean composition enumerates the accomplishments of Busiris, points to the exemplary piety of the Egyptian people, and refers with approval to the caste system instituted in Egypt by the king. Busiris fostered the development of practical wisdom by taking good care of the priests, the speaker maintains, and he ensured the religiosity of his people through various incentives. The speaker says that his own praise of Busiris is more plausible than Polycrates', even as he glosses over the faults of the earlier speech, namely, the king's penchant for sacrificing foreigners. It would be better for Polycrates not to have written such an encomium at all, the speaker concludes, than to have delivered this discourse which will cause the teaching of rhetoric to be scorned even more by contemporaries.

When we look a little more closely at Isocrates' text, we appreciate how this speech in particular functions as an example of parody. The two passages in which Busiris' sacrificial actions are mentioned are of special interest since they give explicit examples of how the narrative frame of *Busiris* upsets its narrative content, and thus they illustrate the self-reflexivity that is characteristic of parody. In these passages the speaker mentions the accusation about Busiris, imputed to Polycrates here with the additional charge of anthropophagy. The speaker appears to play down the king's part in human sacrifice, but he never fully refutes the charge. In the first passage the speaker notes that Polycrates "imputed to him a lawlessness of such enormity that it is impossible for one to invent wickedness more atrocious," and mentions what Polycrates attributed to Busiris:

> Although everyone knows that those who wish to praise (εὐλογεῖν) a person must attribute to him a larger number of good qualities than he really possesses, and accusers (κατηγοροῦντας) must do the contrary, you have fallen so far short of following these principles of rhetoric that, though you profess to defend Busiris, you have not only failed to absolve him of the calumny (τῆς ... διαβολῆς) with which he is attacked, but have even imputed to him a lawlessness of such enormity that it is impossible for one to invent wickedness more atrocious. The other writers whose aim was to malign (λοιδορεῖν) him went only so far in their abuse (βλασφημούντων) as to charge him with sacrificing the strangers who came to his country; you, however, accused (ἠτιάσω) him of actually devouring victims. And when your purpose was to accuse (κατηγορεῖν) Socrates. . . . (4–5)

In the second passage, the speaker observes with respect to Busiris' sacrifices that Polycrates "gave no proof he did these things," and that his charge was less credible since it required "the cruelty of wild beasts."

> When you wished to praise (εὐλογεῖν) Busiris, you chose to say that he forced the Nile to break into branches, and surround the land, and that he sacrificed and ate strangers who came to the country; but you gave no proof he did these things. And yet is it not ridiculous to demand that others follow a procedure which you yourself have not used in the slightest degree? No, your account is far less credible than mine, since I attribute (αἰτιῶμαι) to him no impossible deed, but only laws and political organization, which are the accomplishments of honorable men, whereas you represent him as the author of astounding acts which no human being would commit, one requiring the cruelty of wild beasts, the other the power of the gods. Further, even if both of us happen to be wrong, I, at any rate, have used only such arguments as authors of eulogies (τοὺς ἐπαινοῦντας) must use; you, on the contrary, have employed those which are appropriate to revilers (τοὺς λοιδοροῦντας). Consequently, it is obvious that you have gone astray not only from the truth, but also from the entire pattern which must be employed in eulogy (εὐλογεῖν). (31–33)

In each passage, the comments made by the speaker *in propria persona* are a marker of the self-reflexivity that is typical of Isocrates' parody.

In fact, the speaker draws attention to the kind of speech he is delivering in passage after passage, as above where—"even if both of us are wrong"—he insists on following "the entire pattern which must be employed in eulogy" (33). In an early part of the speech, the speaker says, "I will try briefly to expound the same subject—even though it is not serious, and does not call for a dignified style (καίπερ οὐ σπουδαίαν οὖσαν οὐδὲ σεμνοὺς λόγους ἔχουσαν)—and show out of what elements you ought to have composed the eulogy and the speech in defense" (9). The speaker again intrudes on his parodic rehabilitation of Busiris and reminds his audience of the light-hearted tones that sometimes color representations of the Egyptian king by dismissing the gravity and dignity of the subject. Later, he admits that "my aim in this discourse is . . . to show for your benefit how each of these topics should be treated" (44). Toward the end he adds that he considers the subject to be base and Polycrates' speech a bad advertisement for teachers of rhetoric: "If, then, you will listen to me, you will preferably not deal in future with such base subjects, but if that cannot be, you will seek to speak of such things as will neither injure your own reputation nor corrupt your imitators nor bring the teaching of rhetoric into disrepute" (49). The speaker also observes that he is careful to apply the principles of rhetoric, even though he cannot always vouch for the true state of things concerning Busiris: "If it were manifest that another had done the deeds which I assert were done by him, I acknowledge that I am exceedingly audacious in trying to change men's views about matters of which all the world has knowledge. But, as it is, since the question is open to the judgment of all, and one must resort to conjecture, who . . . ?" (34 – 35). Yet, the reader's assessment of the accuracy of the praise given to Busiris and Egypt is again rendered virtually impossible once the speaker says that "as it is, the question is open to the judgment of all, and one must resort to conjecture" (νῦν δὴ ἐν κοινῷ τῶν πραγμάτων ὄντων καὶ δοξά-σαι δέον περὶ αὐτῶν).

What is noticeable in these and other passages is how frequently the speaker draws attention to the encomiastic parody that is being enacted over the course of his speech, although it is, of course, not surprising that the speaker makes these gestures, since he claims that he composed *Busiris* in order to give an example of an exemplary eulogy. The speaker repeatedly defers to arguments from rhetoric and the encomiastic tradition, and his claims on encomiastic propriety and technical mastery link his assertions about Busiris closely to the genre and style that are being parodied, and hardly at all to reasoned arguments against the plausibility of Busiris' morbid behavior. In the first passage above, he mentions how Polycrates has failed to adhere to the basic principles of eulogy in imputing to Busiris such lawlessness, and he clearly uses the terms that evoke the tradition of speeches of praise and blame, and, to a lesser degree, the legal tradition (εὐ-λογεῖν, διαβολῆς, λοιδορεῖν, βλασφημούντων, ἠτιάσω). Again, in the second passage, the speaker places a greater stress on arguments proper to eulogy and praise than on arguments having to do with mythological proof, and once more the terms he uses are specific to the literary tradition associated with the encomiastic genre (εὐλογεῖν, αἰτιῶμαι, ἐπαινοῦντας, λοιδοροῦντας). Like Agathon in Plato's *Symposium,* the speaker of Isocrates' *Busiris* informs his audience over and again that he is conferring eulogistic praise, even as he is conferring it.

The speaker's appeal to persuasive argument in these passages also reminds us of the audience's complicity in the parody, and we can say, regarding the audience of the parodic text, that part of the function of such a text is to enact an audience that can consume it. When the speaker points to arguments that are, in his opinion, more plausible and hence more persuasive, he says, "Your account is far less credible than mine, since I attribute to him no impossible deed, but only laws and political organization, which are the accomplishments of honorable men." But in this case persuasion is invoked as a nod to the parody, since the speaker has admitted to the levity of the topic, and his arguments cannot be hoped to persuade anyone about the seriousness of his rehabilitation of Busiris. Persuasion is the "superficial ideology" of epideictic rhetoric because the speaker of the epideictic speech may claim persuasion as a determining factor, when he remains aware that his primary goal is display rather than persuasion.[36] Isocrates is aiming more to give a display (ἐπίδειξις) of a skilled oration than to convince anyone about what he is saying about Busiris. The author is hoping to show off his ability to induce pleasure and amazement in his listeners and readers by diction, style, rhythm, euphony, agility with words, and so on. The conceit of Isocrates' parody is, therefore, to posit an audience that will appreciate the plausibility of the speaker's arguments against Busiris' horrifying practices. The expectation is to dazzle the audience by the force of style and language. And the practical effect is to play on the audience's awareness of paradoxical encomia and of the Busiris tradition, and thus to place the audience in a position of deciding how far it wishes to take its own recuperation of the parody and its reassessment of the cruel other.

THE PARADOX OF PARODY

What can the study of parody tell us about otherness? If we look to Isocrates' *Busiris*, we see how parody can be put at the service of an othering process, since the text reaffirms the distinctive alterity of an Egyptian king at the same time that it parodies the tradition of encomiastic speeches. According to the tradition of Greek myth, as we saw above, Busiris was a xenophobic Egyptian in the habit of sacrificing visitors to his country, until he was thwarted by Heracles, who turned the king's world upside down by sacrificing him on his own altar. In Isocrates' text, the speaker crafts a eulogy to the mythical Busiris and his purported achievements, and rejects the stories of the king's homicidal activities. But the speech belongs to the epideictic class of "paradoxical" speeches; it parodies both the encomiastic genre and the conventional tradition of Busiris' activities: what is apparent praise of Egypt and an Egyptian proves to be parody. To acknowledge the parodic nature of the text is, however, to diminish the text's ostensible

36. "Persuasion. . . . is the superficial ideology of rhetoric; it is to be indulged or humored, but not to be taken seriously, whereas the beliefs that sustain (rather than produce) it are" (Porter 1993, 296, with respect to an epideictic speech by Isocrates' teacher, Gorgias); cf. Longinus, *On Sublimity* 1.3–4. For this point in connection with Isocrates in particular, see Cahn 1989.

praise of Egypt, and to situate its claims within a context that leaves any trace of eulogy irremediably corrupted. Far from securing Greece's innocence in relation to barbarian Egypt, the text's parodic rhetoric makes it impossible for the reader to gauge the seriousness of its encomiastic language. And since the praise of Busiris and the repudiation of his cruelty are difficult to read without qualification, the text can be seen to reaffirm the tradition against which it claims to be written.

Given that the pragmatic effect of *Busiris* is to reinforce the traditional portrait of this bloodthirsty barbarian, it should be said that the text is complicit with the tradition of Busiris' cruelty and that Isocrates' parody is largely orthodox in its reinscription of the other. In theory, parody is always a discursive intervention that opens up an existing rhetorical situation, and it may be said to have a dialectical relationship with the authority that is being parodied. The particular nature of the dialectical relationship with authority varies widely, and parody in general has a wide pragmatic range. As Linda Hutcheon has observed, parody may be neutral, respectful, contesting, scornful, or mocking, and it is not necessarily and always limited to the trivializing of an existing tradition or text. What is interesting in the case of Isocrates' text is that the potential for dialectical exchange with anterior authority is realized only in a weak sense, and the inversion of tradition that occurs in the speech colludes with the denigration of the other. Isocrates' *Busiris* perpetuates the cultural stereotype of Egyptians as xenophobic and inclined to human sacrifice, and it shows how a Greek mechanism of otherness can usurp and contain parody for its own attenuated ends. A nuanced reading of the speech needs to consider effects and expectations within the context of a theory of parody as well as to understand narrative content in the light of the traditions to which the text responds.

In discussing the parodic status of Isocrates' speech and in considering the implications of parody for our understanding of Greek thought concerning Egyptians in the fourth century, then, I suggest that any reading of *Busiris* must take into account the complex nature of parody and veer away from treating its parodic aspect as a derisory and linear reworking of some originary object.[37] The text cannot be taken to deny the received view of Busiris,

37. It is a measure of Isocrates' skill at epideictic composition that the parodic eulogy is often taken at face value, so that critics read *Busiris* as a simple denial of the Egyptian's sacrificial activities, describe it as an attempt to defend the king, or say that the speech offers "an extremely flattering picture of Egypt" (Bernal 1987,

not simply because the text is a parody, but also because its parodic quality mediates praise of Busiris and denial of his cruelty in a situation where eulogy and repudiation are difficult to read unreservedly. Once the concept of parody is introduced into the discussion, it is hard for the reader to assess the content of the speech, to estimate the degree and extent of parody, or to reconstruct the precise effects of the speech, given a determinate horizon of expectations. To appreciate better the critical negotiations asked of readers of Isocrates' *Busiris*, I would like to draw on some recent and important discussions of parody, my point of departure being Simon Goldhill's essay on Aristophanes' parody of Aeschylus and Euripides in *Frogs*. Goldhill follows, among others, Margaret Rose in *Parody//Metafiction*, Gérard Genette in *Palimpsestes*, and Hutcheon in *A Theory of Parody*, in order to describe a theory of parody that encompasses "the ambivalent relationship between parodist and object of parody; the problems for interpretation that are produced by parody's self-reflexive 'repetition with a difference'; the function of an audience's complicity in comprehending parody; the disruptive process of reading otherwise that parody evokes."[38] Each of these points, developed from critics of parody, elaborates the kind of parodic writing that is explicit in Isocrates' speech, which, additionally, presents itself not merely as a parody but as a reinscription of a parody. In what follows, I shall briefly develop Goldhill's theory of parody in connection with Isocrates' speech, and then discuss the speech from the perspective of these observations.

In the first place, parody is relational in nature and does not quite repudiate and mock the received tradition or the genre that it parodies. Instead, as August Schlegel observed, "Parody always implies a relationship with and dependence on the parodied object."[39] Parody always acknowledges the originary object that it is parodying, since parody is parasitic on that object and cannot have a meaningful existence without it. The parodist remains

---

103). See also Servius at *Aeneid* 7.11; Hiller von Gaertringen 1897, cols. 1075–76; Griffiths 1948, 410, 415; Brown 1962, 266; and Laurens 1986, 148; and cf. Smelik and Hemelrijk 1984, 1877.

38. Goldhill 1991, 210–11, in "Comic Inversion and Inverted Commas: Aristophanes and Parody," ch. 3 of *The Poet's Voice*. See Rose 1979, Genette 1982, and Hutcheon 1985. Rose 1993 offers a critical and historical survey of the main uses and theories of parody.

39. "Parodie setz immer eine Beziehung auf das Parodierte und Abhängigkeit davon voraus," in his eighth lecture on Aristophanes, in "Vorlesungen über dramatische Kunst und Literatur," in A. W. Schlegel, *Kritische Schriften und Briefe, 1809–11*, new ed. (Mainz, 1966), 132, and quoted from Rose 1979, 34, translation modified.

aware of the originary tradition and is, therefore, crafting a work that is, in Goldhill's phrase, "a licensed transgression," or, in Julia Kristeva's formulation, a principle of "law anticipating its own transgression"—a principle that Hutcheon refers to as the paradox of parody.[40] Isocrates wrote *Busiris* against a background of Busiris as the king who sacrificed human beings, and of the encomiastic genre as the aesthetic institutionalization of the discourse of praise. Within the framework of the standard view of Busiris and of the encomiastic tradition, Isocrates' speech is a parodic transgression, but within the framework of the paradoxical speech, Isocrates' parody is the acceptable norm. Thus, Isocrates' parody works through repetition and difference, since the speech revives the familiar by invoking Busiris and by using terms from eulogy, but renders these different by displacing the tradition about the Egyptian king in a paradoxical mode. In doing this, the text does not so much deny the Busiris story as enlarge the epistemological and hermeneutic statements that can be developed out of and then reflect back on the narrative.

Second, the parodic dynamic of repetition and difference requires recognition on the part of the audience, with the level of recognition fluctuating according to the kind of audience. Isocrates' *Busiris* makes the audience recognize the conditions that make possible the parody of the mythical tradition and the encomiastic genre. Parody allows the audience to recognize the effect of sameness and difference, and even to recognize that parody depends on this possibility, and that parody is constituted by this possibility. By drawing attention to the condition of sameness and difference that makes parody possible, the parodic text exposes to the audience the complex negotiation required by the audience for it to appreciate fully the parody that it is reading or hearing. Parody, thus, reflects back not only on the mythical story and encomiastic genre, but also on parody itself. The self-reflexive nature of literary writing in a text such as *Busiris* is enacted all the more explicitly when the speaker repeatedly intervenes and comments on several parts of his own discourse. This kind of self-reflexivity also makes it harder for the reader to subsume the parodic text within simple or unmediated categories of contempt or ridicule, which an uncritical concept of parody may imply. The categories of the comic or the ridiculous would preclude a simple hermeneutics in any event, of course, but this is especially true in the case of parody.

The theorist of parody also needs to consider the audience's complicity

40. Goldhill 1991, 207; Kristeva 1980, 71; Hutcheon 1985, ch. 4.

in appreciating parody and the complications that may ensue from the critical negotiations elicited by reading parody. Since each audience brings different levels of knowledge to the text or performance, the degree of parodic recognition varies according to the audience's awareness of the originary material, the literary genre being parodied, the literary genre of the parody, and so forth. Given the self-reflexive nature of parody, however, the parodic text also makes its audience question how far it is willing to take its recognition of parody. I noted above that Isocrates' *Busiris* parodies the encomiastic genre, the Busiris tradition, and a system of logic, for example, but another reader may well challenge this identification and posit a different scheme. Part of the pleasure of parody, then, derives from the complicity of the audience. Nevertheless, awareness of the constant interplay between complicity and distance also may produce an unsettling feeling in the audience. When readers appreciate the high level of sophistication required for a nuanced understanding of the parodic text, they also can sense that their own interpretations may be partial or incorrect. "For parody, like irony," Goldhill writes, "establishes an unsettling possibility of *reading otherwise* that becomes finally difficult to control." [41]

A consideration of parody in these terms indicates that *Busiris,* though a parody of an encomium, does not merely mock or ridicule the parodied text and tradition. On a formal level, the parody reinscribes the parodied object and, therefore, ensures the continued survival of the target, in this case, the tradition of the wicked Busiris. Even at a pragmatic level, however, *Busiris* confirms, recognizes, and acknowledges the potency of mainstream opinion, since it transgresses the tradition of the Egyptian's cruelty only within the generic boundaries of the paradoxical encomium, which authorizes the absurdity of Isocrates' claim and its surplus of praise. By circumscribing this reinscription within the confines of the paradoxical genre, the author also marks out the differential status of the parodic text. Yet the anterior text thus not only grants legitimacy to the parodic text, but also has its own legitimating authority reinforced by the parodic text. In this sense, therefore, Isocrates' text is deeply conventional with regard to the tradition of Busiris' turpitude, since his speech invests the tradition with authority even when it purports to deny the charges.

Reading *Busiris* as a parodic text entails a shared code between author and audience. "In parodically encoding a text," Hutcheon observes, "producers must assume both a shared cultural and linguistic set of codes and the familiarity of the reader with the text parodied. . . ."[42] Isocrates' parody would be apprehended as parodic by that section of the population familiar with the Busiris story and with the discourse of praise, but would be regarded as just another text by an unknowing population. In the case of Isocrates' text, however, the shared cultural and linguistic codes are clearly in place, given the strength of the Busiris tradition in the fifth and fourth centuries, the popularity of the encomiastic genre, and the subsequent spread of paradoxical encomia. The evidence from vase painting and literature indicates that the story enjoyed a minor notoriety in the Athens of Isocrates' day. References within the text, moreover, draw attention to both the genre being parodied and the genre of the parody, the former in the course of the speaker's didactic remarks on the composition of eulogy, and the latter in his admission of the topic's levity. The fact of a shared code that makes *Busiris* available to an audience as parody emphasizes that Isocrates' audience is aware of the conditions that make his parody possible, and that it can differentiate the parodic text from the parodied subject. To infer an audience of this sensitivity is, again, to posit an audience that will recognize the parasitic dependence of the parody on the parodied. Isocrates' text, then, cannot be interpreted as the repudiation of Busiris' cruelty at the level of audience-response.

It is important to account for the audience's role in an analysis of the parodic text since some complicity on the part of the audience is essential to the actualization of parody. Even without access to Polycrates' speech, we can assume some intertextual correspondence between Isocrates' and Polycrates' speeches, unless, as is unlikely, the mentions of Polycrates' composition in Isocrates and other writers are literary fictions without an extratextual referent. Whatever the degree of intertextual penetration, however, the speaker's mention of an earlier parody by Polycrates means that the speaker's own work is the rewriting of a parodic text, and this is made clear by the moments when the speaker recapitulates passages from Polycrates in order to castigate and improve upon the earlier speech. Yet it is impossible to ascertain all the places where Isocrates' text imitates, quotes, or alludes to Polycrates' speech, and where it parodies his speech. This difficulty—and this would be true even for a contemporary audience—in separating parody from imitation, quotation, citation, allusion, and burlesque has the consequence of complicating the precise nature of the parodic charge emanating from the text, even though parody shares

42. Hutcheon 1985, 95.

with imitation, quotation, citation, allusion, and burlesque the functional mechanism of repetition with difference. This is the kind of complicated multivalence in Isocrates' text that can make it hard for the audience to make an exact determination of the speech's parody.

"Parody by itself is not subversive," Judith Butler remarks in another context, "and there must be a way to understand what makes certain kinds of parodic repetitions effectively disruptive, truly troubling, and which repetitions become domesticated and recirculated as instruments of cultural hegemony."[43] While it is always true that parody alone is not subversive, Isocrates' speech and its Greek situation illustrate the nicely dichotomous effect of Butler's remark, since, on the one hand, the text reveals the imitative and contingent nature of the parodic work, but, on the other, the resulting disruption is indeed domesticated and recirculated as an indicator, if not an instrument, of cultural hegemony. The factors that we have considered preclude a straightforward reading of Isocrates' text as parody and disrupt any interpretation that tends simply to subvert the received view of the cruel Busiris. It is quite possible that the *Busiris* evoked laughter from the audience, quite possible also that laughter is one of the responses intended by the author—but laughter should not be deemed to challenge the conventional criminality of Busiris. On the contrary, this laughter recognizes the eulogized Busiris as a fictive construct, and thereby also animates the traditional Busiris. This laughter is predicated on the polarity of Greek and Egyptian, Hellene and barbarian, while its ringing tones endorse the values and conceal the anxieties that are contained in the story of the murderous Egyptian king and his Greek nemesis.

Michel Foucault inaugurated *Les mots et les choses (The Order of Things)* with a resounding laugh because he had found a passage by Jorge Luis Borges that made a mockery of the distinction between same and other which lies at the heart of Western epistemology. Isocrates' text generates a laughter that not only needs the same-other distinction to make it possible, but also reaffirms the binary by privileging the same at the expense of the other. As the audience's mirth resonates and circulates in fourth-century Athens, its laughter stands in an indexical relationship to the controlling ethos of Egyptians and Greeks in the parodied story of Busiris. If Isocrates' text were truly disruptive and troubling, the parody would expose to the audience the ideological basis of the Busiris story and suggest how that narrative reifies notions of cultural difference and ethnic typecasting. If Isoc-

43. Butler 1990, 139.

rates' parody were really subversive, it would furnish or demand a true account of the subject of the parody, the Egyptians. Given the relative dearth of challenges mounted against the veracity of the Busiris myth, however, the truth is that Isocrates' parody, so far from contesting this advertisement of Egyptian cruelty, appears instead to channel its eulogy of Busiris into a realm where praise and exaltation are hard to accept unconditionally. And if Isocrates' text misses the opportunity to dispute the bases of the dominant tradition, it too must be said to cohere with and energize the impossible logic which implicates Egyptians as bloodthirsty assassins of visitors to their land and as assailants of the heroic Heracles.

The distinctions introduced by parodic theory prove to be of use in interrogating the rhetoric used in Isocrates' *Busiris*, and, hence, to determine the Hellenocentric bias behind the portrayal of Egypt in Greek literature. When is parody reactionary, and when is it authentically progressive? Parody, for all the sanction that it receives from on high, has the capacity to challenge literary, social, or political authority. The great significance of parody arises when it becomes the site of conflicting intentions, or becomes a double-voiced discourse that engages in an open, unfinalizable dialogue with an authoritative tradition. Even if it is true that parody's transgression is sanctioned by a larger, harder, or more powerful force, parody can show the capacity to smash authority and to undermine officially privileged discourses, as the example of the medieval carnival indicates.[44] But the containment that occurs in Isocrates' speech cannot be thought of as progressive, since the parody fails to offer a "refunctioning" of the parodied, nor is it the case here that his composition "becomes a battlefield for opposing intentions."[45] Isocrates' *Busiris* does not enter into a genuine dialogue with the tradition of Busiris as an Egyptian executioner, and it does not stall the momentum of a hostile perspective on Egypt; rather, the text designates Egypt and the Egyptian as points where parody glides off before approaching its rhetorical mark, and it leaves intact the popular image of Busiris as a bloodthirsty foreigner.

What is nonetheless interesting about Isocrates' parody is the similarity it shares with the cultural stereotype, on which it depends: both parody and the cultural stereotype rely on the notion of fixity, a fixity that in either case frustrates a theoretically informed articulation of difference. The parody takes a fixed tradition and reasserts it, though in the guise of reversing or altering it; the stereotype takes a tradition and never hesitates to repeat it. The stereotype, Homi Bhabha reminds us, "is a form of knowledge and identification that vacillates between what is always 'in place', already known, and something that must be anxiously repeated. . . ."[46] Just as parody moves between the parodied and its own reformulation and reaffirmation of the subject, the stereotype ceaselessly repeats its one representation as part of its denial of difference. Isocrates' parody claims to invert the tradition of Busiris, but assists only in reinforcing it. The stereotype distorts reality, perpetuates a specious representation, and by its incessant repetition, blocks the sign "Busiris" from signifying anything other than murderer, even though the empirical data free Egyptians of this taint. No amount of signification can contribute to an informed view of cultural difference, however, if what is being signified is fixedly absent or false. The fact that so many in antiquity maintained the tradition concerning Busiris points to an apprehension and a fantasy that we have only just begun to uncover.

ISOCRATES, PLATO, ATHENS

The rivalry between Isocrates and Plato haunts *Busiris* and serves as the proper background to some of its central themes. Both these men were followers of Socrates, but they had different opinions about education, rhetoric, and the philosophical life in Athens, as their works reveal. Today, it is Plato whom we associate with Athenian philosophy, but this association was something Plato worked to achieve, often in fierce opposition to other thinkers and writers. Plato attempted to define "philosophy" (φιλοσοφία) in terms of exclusions, boundaries, and limits, and he sought to demarcate it as a new activity practised by men such as Socrates and refined further by the members of the Academy. As Andrea Wilson Nightingale observes, one of the chief rivals to Plato in this appropriation of philosophy was Isocrates, who also determined to integrate "philosophy," as he conceptualized it, into his own political and social plans for the city:

> For Plato and Isocrates both offer detailed descriptions of the program
> of study and education which constitutes "true" philosophy, and they
> both reject all other activities as "false" or "counterfeit" philosophy. It
> should go without saying that these "definitions" of philosophy contain

46. Bhabha 1996, 37.

as much rhetoric as they do description. For the mere description of a given programme of study cannot, by itself, provide a rationale for laying claim to the title of "true" philosophy. Both Plato and Isocrates "define" philosophy, first of all, by explicitly excluding a variety of "imposters" on a number of grounds; in particular, these imposters are identified by their alleged ignorance and/or bad influence. But this is only part of the story. For "philosophy," as Plato and Isocrates conceive it, is not just a mode of discourse or a program of study but rather a way of living and thinking that is based on a specific set of social and political values. A crucial aspect of the "definitions" of philosophy offered by these thinkers is the attempt to articulate the relation of this new cultural practice to the political and social institutions of the Athenian democracy. Each offers a definition that cannot be fully understood outside of the culture of democratic Athens.[47]

For our purposes, what should be emphasized about this rivalry is that these intellectuals incorporated divergent views of rhetoric into their philosophical agendas, and that each earnestly believed that his philosophy related to vital social and political questions of the day in contemporary Athens. It is precisely in these key areas concerning philosophy, the use of a certain kind of rhetorical language, and political rule that the competition between Isocrates and Plato flares up in *Busiris*.

In this speech, as later in his *Antidosis*, Isocrates shows a keen awareness of current practitioners of philosophy and alludes to Plato on different occasions, here both in the frame sections and in the epideictic demonstration.[48] The frame sections of Isocrates' speech refer, significantly, to Socrates, for it turns out that the addressee Polycrates had composed an *Accusation of Socrates* as a companion piece to his *Defense of Busiris* (ἐπί τε τῇ Βουσίριδος ἀπολογίᾳ καὶ τῇ Σωκράτους κατηγορίᾳ, 4), both of which were, of course, characterized by the speaker as failed examples of rhetorical display. Why should the denunciation of Socrates be introduced, and so aposiopetically, as the parallel to this praise of Busiris? One answer, following from the preceding discussion, is that the blame of Socrates was as parodic as *Busiris*, and so also logically and rhetorically vulnerable. But another response, not mutually exclusive, would be to make the chiastic substitution that the juxtaposition of the two titles entails, and so to recall that Polycrates' paradoxical encomia were targeting a *Defense of Socrates* and an *Accusation of Busiris*. To the reader who is willing to make this interpretive sub-

47. Nightingale 1995, 20–21. For Isocrates in this regard, see Wilcox 1943; Eucken 1983; Cooper 1986; and Too 1995.
    48. For φιλοσοφεῖν and its cognates, see *Busiris* 1, 17, 22, 28, 30, 48, and 49.

stitution, the speech's frame sections especially, which not coincidentally also refer to "philosophy," assume profoundly interesting implications, as Busiris stands in for Socrates, Polycrates for Plato, and Isocrates is seen to be admonishing his rival for the discipline of philosophy itself. In the last sections, which are part of the narrative frame and not directly part of the epideictic demonstration, Isocrates assails Polycrates / Plato for the inanity of his defense of Busiris / Socrates, and says that it is not right "to compose discourses such that they will do the most good if they succeed in convincing no one among those who hear them" (47). But perhaps Polycrates / Plato will say that he wished to give to "philosophers" (φιλοσόφοις) an example of how defenses (τὰς ἀπολογίας) should be made against shameful and difficult charges? Nevertheless, Isocrates thinks that defenses of this kind will be of no help, and further that "philosophy (τῆς φιλοσοφίας), which is already in mortal jeopardy and is hated, will be detested even more because of such discourses" (49). Without pushing the consequences of such a substitutive logic too far, it is evident that this particular conjunction of philosophy, Socrates, and defensive apologia inevitably recalls the Platonic situation, and moreover suggests that Isocrates is here attempting to strengthen his claims to superiority over Plato in matters of rhetoric and philosophy.

Turning to remarks made within the epideictic demonstration, we see that the speaker refers specifically to "philosophy" (φιλοσοφία) or its cognates, in various additional passages, including one in which he observes that Pythagoras of Samos studied the religion of the Egyptians, and as a result brought "all philosophy" (τὴν τ'ἄλλην φιλοσοφίαν) to the Greeks (28). This "practice of philosophy" (φιλοσοφίας ἄσκησιν), first introduced by Egyptian priests for the souls of human beings, had the power "not only to establish laws, but also to investigate the nature of the universe" (22). Of course, Isocrates' claim about the Egyptian origin of philosophy can be considered a direct affront to Plato, who self-consciously was trying to give shape and definition to what he considered a new discipline. At another point in the speech, moreover, Isocrates says that "with respect to the system which enables them [i.e. Egyptians] to preserve royalty and their political institutions in general, they have been so successful that philosophers (τῶν φιλοσόφων) who undertake to discuss such topics and have won the greatest reputation prefer above all others the Egyptian form of government" (17). Many scholars have taken this comment, which is discussed further in the following chapter, to be a reference to Plato and his *Republic*, which, in their view, was perceived by some in antiquity to be based on an Egyptian caste system. Whether or not Isocrates is referring to

Plato's *Republic,* the Busiris of his speech certainly offers an alternative to the philosopher-king of Plato's work. Briefly put, this ruler, who is both an inventor and a lawgiver, divides up his people into classes, encourages them to cultivate a practical wisdom (τὴν φρόνησιν, 21), tends to the priestly system, and establishes religious practices for the Egyptians. In the course of his encomiastic demonstration, then, Isocrates gives a broad definition of philosophy, makes it encompass several other disciplines, and simultaneously credits its invention to Egyptian priests.

How does the rhetorical context of these remarks about philosophy affect our understanding of the rivalry between Isocrates and Plato? With the figure of Busiris in particular, a substantial and indisputably negative tradition indicates that Isocrates' remarks about the Egyptian king do not have to be taken at face value in this paradoxical encomium. But there was no unified tradition about philosophy in early fourth-century Athens, and in fact philosophy was a site of contestation between Isocrates and Plato. It is unlikely, given this contestation, that Isocrates meant his remarks about philosophy in *Busiris* to be considered wholly parodic or completely irrelevant. What we can affirm, nevertheless, is that this use of the epideictic context itself is indicative of the state of the dispute between Isocrates and Plato. As scholars have shown, Plato's attitude to paradoxical encomia and to most genres other than dialogue was largely adversarial, even if he incorporated other genres in his works to develop particular philosophical arguments. Plato did not write paradoxical encomia outside of his philosophical dialogues and was disturbed by the implications of the encomiastic genre; for him, despite his fondness of irony, *Busiris* would be a trivialization of questions of central importance to life in Athens. For Isocrates, however, such encomia were evidently acceptable exercises in rhetoric and, furthermore, they provided a fertile location for the definition of philosophy.

To the extent that *Busiris,* like all paradoxical encomia, implied a relativization of values and provided an occasion for inaccurate exaggeration, Isocrates' eulogy of the Egyptian king would have troubled Plato, who vehemently rejected the destabilization of ethical values in his philosophical works as he did the tendency of demagogues to sway the public with rhetorical excess. Of course, Plato himself manipulated rhetoric in general and eulogy in particular with the skill of a master, but he nonetheless remained deeply skeptical of the uses to which this art and this specific genre were put by his contemporaries. "While Plato was clearly concerned with rhetoric in all its aspects," Nightingale writes, "there was one genre that he found especially pernicious: the rhetoric of praise. . . . Again and again, Plato sets the encomium in diametrical opposition to the discourse of the philosopher: philosophy is defined by the 'otherness' of eulogy."[49] If Plato distrusted eulogy, this distrust stemmed from an anxiety over its misuses in the public spaces of the democratic city-state and from a worry that expertise in such genres as the paradoxical encomia might inculcate the wrong values in students preparing for careers in politics and the law courts. "The foolish use of the language of praise, he reminds us, poses a very real danger for the city as a whole."[50] In short, Plato was highly critical of the false values and the fictive judgments endemic to paradoxical encomia such as Isocrates' *Busiris*. But where Plato remained wary of paradoxical encomia, Isocrates went so far as to give rules for it in his *Busiris*, thus making this speech antithetical to Plato's philosophical program in a very real way.[51]

From a Platonic perspective, moreover, it is no compensation to say that Isocrates' work does not overwhelm the widespread and negative view of Busiris as a murderous Egyptian. The speechwriter cannot hope to persuade any Hellene of the moral worthiness of the Egyptian king or the seriousness of his praise. He in no way diminishes the general tradition against Busiris, although he brings to bear arguments ranging from the historical to the ahistorical, the plausible to the implausible, and the credible to the incredible in the course of his eulogy. Although Isocrates' *Busiris* realizes only in an attenuated sense the unsettling of values that Plato worries about in his philosophical writings, this attenuated relativization would confirm further for someone like Plato the folly of paradoxical encomia. Thus, on the one hand, Isocrates indulges in the kind of rhetorical exercise that Plato finds extremely dangerous; and on the other hand, Isocrates' speech itself is misguided for Plato also because it attempts to relativize values concerning Busiris and Socrates, but for Plato these are figures about whom one cannot make ambiguous, indeterminate, or trivial judgments.

In the light of the rivalry between Isocrates and Plato, therefore, *Busiris* shows that even when the speech purports to be about a foreign king it also, like many Athenian writings about Egypt, reflects back on Greece and on internal anxieties and tensions within the city-state of Athens. I have just drawn attention to the ways in which Egypt was part of Isocrates' struggle against Plato to define philosophy by opposition and to demarcate the role

49. Nightingale 1995, 93.
50. Nightingale 1995, 127.
51. Rules for composing encomia are provided, in the fourth century, by Isocrates' *Busiris*, Aristotle's *Rhetoric* (1366a–1368a), and the *Rhetoric to Alexander* (1425b–1426b).

of rhetoric in public spaces, and I will turn to Plato's appropriation of Egypt for domestic purposes in the following chapter. Others have already commented on the ways in which Isocrates' speech was implicated in contemporary Athenian discussions about politics and democratic government. For instance, Christian Froidefond has observed in the context of *Busiris* that the turn to Egypt afforded Athenian intellectuals of the fourth century "an original solution to the great problems of the moment," which he characterizes as political stability, legitimate government, the role of religion in the city, the function of elites, and the very basis of the polis itself.[52] Certainly, Isocrates' speech adverts to these issues through the course of a meandering text in which political reflection, philosophical commentary, rhetorical display, and parodic energy are part and parcel of the demonstration. Some have argued that Athenian intellectuals such as Isocrates and Plato were worried about the nature of their city's political system and thought that the Egyptian political system, credited to Busiris by Isocrates, was an attempt to present a better *politeia.* This was not so much a new constitution as an ancient one, which Isocrates made all the more respectable and attractive for certain segments of the Athenian aristocracy through association with a perceived Egyptian antiquity and conservatism, on the one hand, and austere Lacedaemonian traditions of Hellenism, on the other (17). As Isocrates weaves together these different themes in his work, Egypt appears less as the subject of the speech and more as a locus for responses to the political concerns of fourth-century Athenians.

It is worthwhile to observe, regarding the text's implication in Athenian politics, that Plato, too, in one of his last works, turned to an Egyptian practice in order to make the case for a legal model that was different from the Athenian one. In his *Laws,* Plato proposes a law-code that the citizen body of Magnesia will have to read, learn, and memorize with meticulous care: this law-code consists of a set of "sacred" written texts that are fixed and binding. Unlike the citizens of contemporary Athens, the citizens of the Platonic state are made to know their laws so well that they will be able to internalize, acknowledge, and follow the laws with little trouble. Further, the Athenian Stranger says specifically that he would like the citizens of Magnesia to behave like doctors (857d-e). Scholars have demonstrated that he is referring in particular to Egyptian doctors, and this is also evident from supporting evidence about Egyptian doctors in Aristotle and Diodorus, where Egyptian doctors and patients are said to be experts at following

52. Froidefond 1971, 234–35.

fixed, written rules.[53] Although he is historically inaccurate,[54] it is not surprising that Plato appeals to the conservatism of Egyptian medical practices, since elsewhere in *Laws* he also points to the stability of Egyptian art over a span of ten thousand years and to the success of Egyptians in preventing innovations in music and dance; in these cases, stability and conservatism is linked to the Egyptians' ability to follow sacred, written texts.[55] Of course, Plato's representation of Egyptian practices also concurs with the

53. I am simplifying the more complicated argument made in Nightingale 1999. See Aristotle, *Politics* 1286a, and Diodorus 1.82.

54. Medical papyri from Egypt indicate that ancient Egyptians adopted a holistic approach to medicine in which magical incantations, ritual practices, and practical prescriptions were all important to the patient's health. The range of Egyptian medical knowledge and practice is represented by the Edwin Smith Medical Papyrus, the Kahun Medical Papyrus, the Berlin Papyrus, the Ebers Medical Papyrus, the Hearst Papyrus, the Chester Beatty VI Papyrus, and the London Papyrus (which exemplifies the holistic method). For ancient Egyptian medicine, see Leca 1971 and Nunn 1995; for doctors in the pharaonic period, see Ghalioungui 1983.

55. See *Laws* 656d–657a and 799a–b. The former passage is especially revealing in this respect: "Long ago, apparently, they [Egyptians] realized the truth of the principle we are putting forward only now, that the movements and tunes which the children of the state are to practise in their rehearsals must be good ones. They compiled a list of them according to style, and displayed it in their temples. Painters and everyone else who represent movements of the body of any kind were restricted to these forms; modification and innovation outside this traditional framework were prohibited, and are prohibited even today, both in this field and the arts in general. If you examine their art on the spot, you will find that ten thousand years ago (and I'm not speaking loosely: I mean literally ten thousand), paintings and reliefs were produced that are no better and no worse than those of today, because the same artistic rules were applied in making them" (trans. T. J. Saunders). By saying in *Laws* that Egyptians are good at following sacred written texts, Plato is not contradicting the views about writing that he set forth in *Phaedrus*, where he distinguishes between beneficent and harmful kinds of writing (see chapter 4). In *Laws*, Plato seeks to invoke a good use of writing, and he describes the writings of the law-code as "antidotes" (ἀλεξιφάρμακα, 957d) to other kinds of discourses, rather than as a drug (φάρμακον). As Nightingale notes, ". . . the drug is now beneficial, since it provides non-philosophers with an 'antidote' to bad discourse. According to the *Phaedrus*, written logos is ambiguous and easily misunderstood; it therefore needs the presence of its father to defend it (275d–e). In the *Laws*, Plato set out to create a new kind of text in which interpretative ambiguities are minimized. . . . A law-code, moreover, differs from other written texts in that it gains authority precisely by the disappearance of its author (Solon, Lycurgus, etc.). Plato constructs in the *Laws* a text which both anticipates and accommodates his own imminent death. He thus builds the voice of the father—and indeed, of god—right into his dialogue, thereby creating a text which claims for itself the authority of ancestral and divine wisdom" (Nightingale 1999, 122). It is, of course, precisely when Plato arrogates to himself an authority which is both ancient and divine that Egypt is made to enter and sanctify the discussion.

inflection given to Egyptian history and custom by Herodotus in his work (see chapter 3 above), and Plato appears to be taking over for himself what seems to have become a canonical designation for Egyptian temporality.[56] So, in order to construct a model law-code for his city of Magnesia, Plato has recourse to what he says are Egyptian approaches to medicine. At different times in the fourth century, then, both Plato and Isocrates appeal to Egypt in order to reflect on important constitutional and legal questions. And, given that Plato, like Isocrates, is making an intervention in the domestic affairs of the city-state, it can be said that, despite significant differences in philosophy and outlook, both Plato and Isocrates also evince a need to formulate their discussions of local Athenian politics out of an engagement with purported Egyptian customs and beliefs.

François Hartog asks concerning *Busiris*, Why this political fiction against a thousand declarations that oppose barbarians?[57] Hartog himself suggests that the antiquity of Egypt, the heavily Asiatic connotation of the barbarian, and the Persian domination of Egypt all played a role in making possible the connection between Egypt and the just monarchy that occurs in Busiris. It is entirely plausible that, despite the parodic nature of the speech, Isocrates really was attempting to intervene in Athenian debates about the viability of governments and types of constitution, even if for someone like Plato the parody gets in the way of these interventions. Given that *Busiris* is so intensely parodic, however, one might refine Hartog's question and ask instead, Why did Isocrates, who wrote so voluminously against barbarians, choose to write about Egyptian barbarians in this manner and in this context? This is a hard question to answer, and in response, I first repeat myself, observing that the speech is not solely about Egyptians, and that it uses Egypt and the figure of Busiris to address the great issues of the day, whether in the realm of philosophy, rhetoric, or politics. Thus, the use of Egypt is a feint by which Isocrates can slip in his views on the issues that he cares about. But secondly, without contradiction or tautology, I remark only that Isocrates wrote about Egyptians in the context of a parody because that was how he chose to write about them, from all the many subjects, contexts, and genres available to him. Outside of *Busiris*,

56. Interestingly, Herodotus calls Egyptians the healthiest people in the world after the Libyans, and he attributes their good health to the stability of the climate and the seasons (2.77).

57. Hartog 1996, 70. On Isocrates' Athenocentrism and his attitude to barbarians, see Usher 1994 with Cartledge 1994.

Egypt and Egyptians scarcely figure in Isocrates' surviving works.[58] The Athenian could bring himself to deliver an encomium to an Egyptian king in the context of parody, and he left his readers to understand the implications of this action. And we may well wonder about a text that seldom troubles to grasp the realities of contemporary Egypt, that treats and handles ethnocentrism as if it were anti-ethnocentrism, that reeks of both condescension and arrogance, that retards rather than advances ethnic understanding, and that ultimately takes for granted the most pernicious of cultural stereotypes.

58. See the brief mentions in *Helen* 68; *Panegyricus* 140, 161; *Archidamus* 63; *On the Peace* 86; *Philippus* 101; and *Panathenaicus* 159.

6 Plato's Egyptian Story

An Egyptian priest is reported to have said that the Greeks
remain eternally children. We may say, on the contrary, that the
Egyptians are vigorous *boys,* eager for self-comprehension, who
require nothing but clear understanding of themselves in an ideal
form, in order to become *Young Men.* . . . This mandate [clear self-
understanding] was given to the Greeks, and in the Greek Spirit
humanity exhibits itself in its clear and developed condition.

   G. W. F. Hegel, *Vorlesungen über die Philosophie der Geschichte*

Egypt recurs as an archaic origin in the works of the Greeks, but nowhere
so spectacularly as in Plato's *Timaeus* and *Critias.* When we look to Egypt
in these dialogues, we find indications of the cultural anxiety that under-
pins what we now call Orientalism lurking in the founding texts of philosophy. In these dialogues, Plato makes Egypt the source for his descriptions
of the lost city of Atlantis and the activities of its inhabitants. During its
most arrogant phase, he writes, this island city threatened to conquer the
whole of the Mediterranean region, and especially the two ancient civilizations of Egypt and Greece. It was the Athenians who came to the rescue
and pushed the invaders back to their homeland, just beyond the Pillars
of Heracles, outside the Mediterranean. That Athens saved the civilized
world from barbarian invaders is clear, Plato says, from Egyptian annals
which contain historical descriptions that reach further back in time than
any Athenian archive. In reflecting on the originary role of Egypt in Plato's
work, we need to take into consideration the manner in which the country
is integrated into a narrative of past Athenian glory.

   What I would like to discuss in this chapter are the consequences of
Plato's locating the source for his Atlantis story in Egypt. At a basic level,
Plato's characters turn to Egypt's written records in order to give credibility to an early Athenian success story. But the historical preference given
to Egypt in the dialogues is triangulated through the speakers' philosophical concerns and their anxiety over the status of Athens. In Plato, native
points of view and the exaltation of Egyptians suffer displacement away
from the issue of Egypt to domestic prerogatives. In order to understand
the role of the foreign in the dialogues, one needs to appreciate that Plato
is creating a discourse that borrows from Egypt in order to serve his own

political, philosophical, and social programs. And, although his characters insist on the veracity of their tales, Plato's work seems instead to designate Egypt as the site where his discourses of truth glide off into utopian fantasy before they approach their political and philosophical marks.

If Egypt is the point at which it nonetheless becomes possible for an Athenian philosopher to praise a more ancient Athens, this is due in part to Egypt's position outside the structures of mainstream Athenian politics. Plato was openly antagonistic to the perceived excesses of the democracy in Athens, and nowhere in *Timaeus* and *Critias* did he exalt the government of the city in his own day.[1] He saw Egypt as an other-place where his own visions for society could be actualized, and his construction of Egypt was part of a counterdemocratic process in which Egypt was desired as an alternative to the sociopolitical constraints that were current in fourth-century Athens.[2] Thus, although the author figures Egypt in different ways, he represents it as a utopian space and the antithesis of contemporary Athenian society and culture. According to one report from antiquity, Plato even based the imaginary republic of his famous dialogue on existing Egyptian institutions, and was later chastised for passing himself off as the inventor of ideas that he merely copied from Egypt.[3] As was the case with the fascination for Mao and China among many French intellectuals in the late 1960s and early 1970s, the concern with Egypt in these narratives is presented more within the terms of a Western debate over theoretical, philosophical, and social problems than from a desire to understand a contemporary native culture with a different ethos and history.[4] Like these modern European intellectuals, Plato appears to fetishize Egypt, in both the Freudian (substitution) and Marxist (mystification) senses of the word. Egypt serves as the substitute location for the realization of his philosophy and politics; at the same time, his texts mystify the country by stripping it bare of historical practice and change. Even this dynamic of substitution and mystification is somewhat muddled, however, since the Greek courtship of Egypt is matched by reluctance, denial, and self-affirmation from within.

1. There is some debate whether Plato and Socrates were anti-democratic or pro-democratic: see e.g. Vlastos 1983 with Wood and Wood 1986; and Ober 1998, ch. 4. For Athenian critics of democracy, see Jones 1957, ch. 3; Roberts 1994; and Ober 1998; and for fifth-century perceptions of democracy, see Raaflaub 1989.

2. It may be helpful to distinguish Plato's handling of Egypt here from the attempts he made to establish his ideal city elsewhere: he says, in his *Seventh Letter*, that he tried and failed to realize his ideal polis in Syracuse, during the rule of Dionysius II, with the latter as philosopher-king.

3. Crantor, in Proclus, *Commentary on Timaeus*, at *Timaeus* 24a, quoted below.

4. See the discussion in Lowe 1991, 136–89.

The following pages, then, may be read as an index to the displaced status of Egypt and Egyptians in these works by Plato, and alongside the other chapters of this book as an attempt to foreground the uneasy figuration of Egypt in Greek thought. In tracing Plato's apprehension over contemporary Athenian democracy as well as his efforts to stake out a space where he can theorize an alternative political scenario, I would like, first, to examine how Plato archaizes Egypt in order to render the Egyptians distinct from the Greeks in *Timaeus* and *Critias*. In this regard, as suggested in chapter 4 above, the concern with written discourses and Egyptian graphomania will emerge as central to Plato's mechanism of otherness. And, second, I lay out the implications of this particular portrayal of the other by analyzing the imaginary Egypt that Plato constructs in his dialogues and by exploring the anxiety that this imaginary country conceals. In setting forth my argument along these lines, I am conscious that I am both contributing to and skirting around the countless debates aroused by Plato's Egyptian story ever since its appearance in the dialogues. While I cannot take into account all those debates in this chapter, I wish to underline the story's usefulness in helping to create nationalist propaganda. In his detailed article on "Atlantis and the Nations," Pierre Vidal-Naquet has shown how various nationalistic ideologies—in countries ranging from Spain and Sweden to the former Soviet Union—have drawn on the tradition of Atlantis as a way of making a claim on this peculiar and remote origin.[5] I hope to complement this analysis by demonstrating that nationalist, or at least ethnically prejudiced, features have been present in the story since its initial unveiling in Plato's works.

A GRAPHIC HISTORY

"Listen then, Socrates, to a tale which though very unusual, is yet wholly true. . . ."[6] Plato's story of Atlantis is recounted by the character Critias over two separate dialogues, *Timaeus* and *Critias*. Evidently set the day after the conversation in the *Republic*,[7] the dialogue in *Timaeus* includes Critias' tale of a proto-Athens (which, according to him, corresponds explic-

5. Vidal-Naquet 1992.
6. Translations of *Timaeus* and *Critias* are adapted, with changes, from the edition of R. G. Bury in the Loeb Classical Library.
7. The opening sections of *Timaeus* offer a summary of books 2 to 5 of *Republic*. Even if we are not to believe that the exact conversation in *Republic* took place the previous day, the opening sections of *Timaeus* certainly recapitulate these parts of the dialogue: see Cornford 1937, 4–5. The relationship between *Timaeus* and *Republic* is treated in Taylor 1928, 27–34. There is no sure way of knowing the order

itly to Socrates' imaginary city in the *Republic*) and of Atlantis. One day at the festival of the Apaturia, Critias says, he heard a story from his grandfather Critias, who heard it from his father, who heard it from Solon. When Solon traveled to Saïs, in Egypt, the story goes, he questioned the priests there about ancient matters and learned how shallow was Greek knowledge concerning antiquity. For, after Solon's narration about Phoroneus, Niobe, Deucalion, Pyrrha, and the flood, one of the Egyptian priests responded by saying, "O Solon, Solon, you Greeks are always children: there is not such a thing as an old Greek" (22b), and went on to inform him how the Earth had undergone numerous cataclysms and natural disasters, of which Solon had merely mentioned the latest in the series. Egypt was immune to these cycles of destruction because of the Nile, however, so that the country's written records remained unaffected by the disasters that ravaged other lands, and afforded more complete accounts of human history than any Greek source. The Greeks themselves had no grasp of events from long ago because, every time a flood swept through the land, it carried away the lettered and the civilized folk, and left behind only the ignorant and the uncultured in the mountains. But the citizens of Athens of nine thousand years ago were the bravest and best organized of any state at that time, the Egyptian priest continued, and the social structure of this proto-Athenian state, including its caste system, closely resembled the society of contemporary Saïs. It was this same great state that at one time repulsed the invaders from the island of Atlantis beyond the Pillars of Heracles, and thereby saved itself, Egypt, and all the countries in the Mediterranean, many of which had been enslaved by the enemy. At a later stage, of course, another round of nature's upheavals swallowed up both Atlantis and proto-Athens, and this is why Solon had to journey to Egypt to learn about the courage of his magnificent ancestors.

Timaeus moves on from this subject to a consideration of such weighty matters as the construction of the universe, but the younger Critias continues his tale of the two cities, Athens and Atlantis, in *Critias*. Still repeating what he remembers from his grandfather's account of Solon's story, he now describes the roles of Hephaestus and Athena in the establishment of proto-Athens, the autochthonous origin of its citizens, the nature of the military class (which, Critias claims, resembles Socrates' guardians), the evolution of the city's geographical orientation, and its renown through-

in which Plato wrote any of his works. Scholars generally place Plato's *Republic* among the middle dialogues, and *Timaeus* and *Critias* among the late.

out all Europe and Asia. Then, Critias begins to relate the story about the
city that proto-Athens vanquished, and he mentions Poseidon's role in
the founding of Atlantis, the island's great wealth, its buildings and layout,
the kings who ruled over the whole, and, lastly, the inhabitants' moral decline. The dialogue *Critias* breaks off in midsentence at this point, however,
so that the text as it stands today gives the appearance of being incomplete.
It is impossible to give a definitive explanation for the appearance of the
text, and we have to make to do with what we have—for our purposes,
what remains may be sufficient.

A crucial and defining emphasis is placed on the written word in Critias'
account of Atlantis, and this emphasis is what Plato uses to distinguish between Egyptians, with their amazing historical memories, and Greeks, who
remember events merely from the recent past. From this perspective, it is
instructive to see how *Timaeus* and *Critias* conjoin written texts, Egyptian
priests, and the incredible antiquity of Egyptian civilization. When Solon
traveled to Egypt, Critias says in the former dialogue, he questioned priests
in Saïs who "were most versed in ancient lore about their early history"
(22a). As I just remarked, Solon discovered from these priests how inadequate was his own sense of the past, since the Egyptians told him that his
stories about Phoroneus, Niobe, Deucalion, Pyrrha, and the flood were
concerned with relatively recent events. "You are young in soul, every one
of you. For therein you possess not a single belief that is ancient and derived from old tradition, nor yet one science that is hoary with age" (22b).
The priest who uttered these words continued by narrating to Solon the
story of the cataclysms that repeatedly destroyed civilization, effaced the
literate records of the Greeks, and left behind only unlettered folk on
mountain sides. As we have already seen, the priest explained that Egypt
was spared the obliteration of its written records thanks to the Nile, the
country's savior in this as in so many other respects:

> Hence it is, for these reasons, that what is here preserved is reckoned
> to be most ancient (παλαιότατα); the truth being that, in every place
> where there is no excessive heat or cold to prevent it, there always ex-
> ists some human stock, now more, now less in number. And, if any
> event has occurred that is noble, or great, or in any way conspicuous,
> whether it be in your country, or in ours, or in some other place of
> which we know by report (ἀκοῇ), all such events are written down
> from of old and preserved here in our temples (πάντα γεγραμμένα ἐκ
> παλαιοῦ τῇδ' ἐστὶν ἐν τοῖς ἱεροῖς καὶ σεσωσμένα); whereas your
> people and the others are but newly equipped, every time, with letters
> (γράμμασι) and all such arts as civilized states require; and when, after

the usual interval of years, like a plague, the flood from heaven comes sweeping down afresh upon your people, it leaves none of you but the unlettered and uncultured (τοὺς ἀγραμμάτους τε καὶ ἀμούσους), so that you become young as ever, with no knowledge of all that happened in old times (ὅσα ἦν ἐν τοῖς παλαιοῖς χρόνοις), in this land or in your own. Certainly, the genealogies which you related just now, Solon, concerning the people of your country, are little better than children's tales; for, in the first place, you remember but one deluge, though many had occurred previously; and next, you are ignorant of the fact that the noblest and most perfect race among men were born in the land where you now dwell, and from them both you yourself are sprung and the whole of your existing city, out of some little seed that chanced to be left over; but this has escaped your notice because for many generations the survivors died with no power to express themselves in writing (γράμμασιν . . . ἀφώνους). (22e–23c)

All the astonishing truths that Solon discovered in Egypt converge on this prodigious written archive, which both conceals and reveals Athens' own identity as Athens by knowing its origins better than its citizens do. These same sacred writings (τοῖς ἱεροῖς γράμμασιν) disclose the facts of eight thousand years of Egyptian civilization and also nine thousand years of Athenian history, the actual texts of which (αὐτὰ τὰ γράμματα) Solon was invited to inspect later at his leisure (23e–24a). "For it is related in our writings (τὰ γεγραμμένα)," the priest said to Solon, "how once upon a time your state stayed the course of a mighty power, which, starting from a distant point in the Atlantic ocean, was insolently advancing to attack the whole of Europe and Asia" (24e).

Critias, like *Timaeus,* also raises the subjects of written record and archival memory in connection with Egypt. With this dialogue and concerning these subjects, however, let us concentrate for the moment on what Critias indicates about names. Even before he begins his description of the two cities, Critias feels obliged to explain why the names of the Athenians' predecessors are preserved, but not the record of their achievements and laws. Since the people who survived each successive upheaval were mountaineers without knowledge of writing, they transmitted names from one generation to the next, but not the accomplishments or the institutions of the earlier Athenians. The proof of this, for Critias, is the evidence given to Solon by the Egyptian priests, who ascribed Hellenic names such as Cecrops, Erechtheus, Erichthonius, and Erysichthon to the heroes who fought for proto-Athens in the war against Atlantis (110a–b). These simple, unlettered folk gave little heed to the past, Critias further claims, because they were concerned more with survival and life's essentials than with the enterprise of history: "For mythology (μυθολογία) and research into the past (ἀναζήτησίς ... τῶν παλαιῶν) are visitants that come to cities in company with leisure, when they see that men are already furnished with the necessities of life, and not before" (110a).

The topic of names emerges again when Critias embarks on his description of Atlantis, and he is now constrained to account for the presence of Greek names among the barbarians of Atlantis (βαρβάρων ἀνδρῶν, 113a). The cause of this is that Solon, intending to use the story for his poetry, inquired into the meaning of the names, and found that the Egyptians who first wrote down (γραψαμένους, 113a) the names had turned them into their own language. Solon in turn retrieved the sense of each name, and he himself wrote them down (ἀπεγράφετο, 113b) in Greek translation.[8] Grandfather Critias had these very writings of Solon (καὶ ταῦτά γε δὴ τὰ γράμματα, 113b) in his keeping, we learn, and now they are in the possession of the younger Critias, who committed them to memory when he was a child. This is the reason why the barbarians have Hellenic names, Critias says, and his listeners should not marvel at the anomaly of the situation.[9]

As Marcel Detienne has observed, Plato's use of the issue of writing to differentiate between the Egyptians and the Greeks may explain why each *ethnos* bears a separate affiliation to the remembered past.[10] Critias depicts

---

8. It is intriguing that Plato uses Solon in a situation in which he emphasizes the written word, since Solon was famous for having created written laws, for Athens, in about 600 B.C.E.: "I wrote (ἔγραψα) laws alike for good and bad, fitting straight justice to each" (fr. 36 West). The implications of Solon's claim are discussed in Loraux, "Solon et la voix de l'écrit," in Detienne 1992, 95–129.

9. Svenbro 1993, 79, argues that within the Greek tradition "a name functioned as a memorial to a parent or an ancestor, indeed, as an 'inscription,' proclaiming the ancestral *kléos*, in particular that of fathers and grandfathers."

10. See Detienne 1981, 155–89 and Detienne 1989, 167–86. Detienne, whose presentation of the use of writing in *Timaeus* and *Critias* I have been loosely following, asks further whether these Platonic dialogues really link the issues of writing and memory in so adhesive a manner. In fact, the dialogues admit of ambiguity on this point, but they nevertheless do not contravene the basic schema of graphic Egypt, on the one hand, and oral Greece, on the other. The dialogues' ambiguities tend to obscure the too clean association between writing and recollection, as Detienne agrees, rather than between writing and the Egyptians. The interconnection of written and oral tradition is complicated by Critias, who in *Critias* contradicts the claim made by him in *Timaeus* about his recollection of the story: whereas in *Timaeus* he emphasizes how well he has rehearsed his tale and how firm is his grasp on the turns of the narrative, in *Critias* he repeatedly asks his audience's indulgence as he attempts to recall the details in all their fullness. Moreover, Critias refers in *Critias* to written texts of which no mention is made in *Timaeus*.

in these dialogues two societies, each defined in relation to the technology of the written word: one is the deeply literate society of Egyptian priests, whose holy papyri contain the authentic beginnings of Athens' history, and the other is the graphically impoverished community of Athenians, whose memories are so slender that they look for their origins only in the immediate past. One kind of research into the past is that found among the Egyptian priests in the *Timaeus*, who live in a society permeated by the written word. Writing always seems to have existed in this Egypt, and it seems to be current there from the foundation of the state. The true history of Athens is relayed in Egypt entirely by means of a graphic activity and by the written preservation of past events. Exact and exhaustive on the subject of the Athenian victory (τὸ δ' ἀκριβὲς περὶ πάντων ἐφεξῆς, 24a), the sacred writing of Egypt thus divulges what Critias terms the authentic "mythology" of the Greeks.

Against the graphic space of Critias' Egypt may be placed the interrupted history of the Athenians, themselves analphabetic, uncultured, and lacking written memorials of their own glorious antiquity. The only Greeks who survive after each deluge, Critias reminds us, are the illiterate peasants in the mountains who are too occupied with staving off poverty to concern themselves with "mythology" and "researches into the past." As civilization and its inscribed markers fall victim to nature's cataclysmic ravages, each new cycle brings with it a society beginning anew, a society without an historical memory or a sense of its prior achievements, so that even the stories of Solon's generation seem laughably childish to the Egyptian priest. According to Critias, thus, without knowledge of writing, a society's sense of the past is inaccurate as well as flat and one-dimensional: historical time, as such, does not exist without writing.

Let me enlarge upon Plato's use of writing by observing that it is precisely when Critias *speaks* to the others, during the festival of the Apaturia in Athens, that Plato's lesson, inscribed for all time in Egypt's annals, travels to the fifth-century Athens of *Timaeus* and finds its intended and proper audience. In short, the written text of Atlantis comes to life only when it satisfies the description of the kind of writing that Socrates favors in Plato's *Phaedrus*. Nicole Loraux observes that the narrative has to take "refuge *elsewhere*," and adds that when the narrative reappears, as Critias' eulogy of ancient Athens, it is "endowed with all the qualities that, in the *Phaedrus*, the philosopher attributes to the animated logos."[11] Unlike the

---

11. Loraux 1986, 456, 300. For a slightly different interpretation, see Derrida 1995, 123–27. On the critique of writing in *Phaedrus*, see chapter 4 above.

writing that Socrates deprecates in *Phaedrus*, this story of Atlantis does not stand in need of its father and is not silent, but rather is the result of repeated questions from Critias to his old relative, "so that the story is stamped firmly on my mind like the encaustic designs of an indelible painting" (26c). Critias' invocation of painting in *Timaeus* contrasts with Socrates' in *Phaedrus*, where writing is deprecated through a comparison with silent painting. Critias seems to use writing here in the manner in which Socrates advocates in the other dialogue, and his comments point to the sort of discourse that, in *Phaedrus*, "goes together with knowledge, and is written in the soul of the listener, which can defend itself, and knows to whom it should speak, and to whom it should say nothing" (276a). This is a story, after all, that at first said nothing for centuries, but then at later moments in its transmission was subject to interrogation and dialogue, whether by Solon, who questions the priest in Saïs, by Amynander, who questions Solon in Athens (21c–d), or by the interlocutors who question Critias.

A corollary way of approaching this issue of writing is to say that Plato uses the Egyptian writings in *Timaeus* and *Critias* to set proto-Athens apart from the contemporary Athens of his era. The story of Atlantis is preserved in the holy archives of Egyptian priests in Saïs, not in fifth-century Athens, because the political structure that Socrates has advocated only the day before in the *Republic*, can be found there, in the Egyptian city, just as it could have been found once in proto-Athens. But contemporary Athens has come to represent the failure of political ideals, for Plato, Socrates, and his interlocutors, and this renders it unsuitable as a space for the realization of the Platonic polity. Contemporary Athens, indeed, is a city in need of Plato's philosophy and politics. It is, accordingly, not a coincidence that an Egyptian story—the famous anecdote of Theuth and Thamus—also features in the critique of writing in *Phaedrus*, where Socrates appears to advocate the sort of writing that is much like Plato's own dialectic, though nothing like the static annals of the Egyptian priests in Saïs. With the aid of Socrates' Egyptian anecdote, the critique of writing in *Phaedrus* is directed, in part, at the fashion in which certain written texts were being used in fourth-century Athens.

Against this background, moreover, the choice of these particular characters in the philosopher's work takes on a politically charged significance. None of the participants in the conversations in *Timaeus* and *Critias* could be counted among the supporters of the Athenian democracy, and at least two of them actively contrived to overthrow it. The historical Critias was one of those responsible for the overthrow of the Athenian democracy and achieved notoriety as one of the Thirty Tyrants.[12] Hermocrates led Syracuse against Athens in military engagements, after which he spent part of his life in exile in Sparta and in Asia; he was a tyrant and an antidemocrat.[13] Timaeus was from Locri in Sicily.[14] As for Socrates himself, it is sufficient, if crude, to sum up his complicated relationship with the democratic polis by observing that it was the city that condemned him to death. It is these counterdemocratic figures who are privy to the political lesson that Plato delivers to his fellow Athenians through the Egyptian story of Atlantis.

Further, the representation of Egyptian history that follows from his use of writing is remarkable. We could scarcely find a clearer basis for the postcolonial lament that " 'Europe' remains the sovereign, theoretical subject of all histories," including the history of Egypt, than we do in *Timaeus* and *Critias*.[15] The Egyptian annals that Solon consults in Saïs appear to have waited for a Greek wise man to have arrived in Egypt, so as to divulge to him the fabulous account of the Athenian defeat of Atlantis. Nowhere do the annals or the Egyptian priests reveal to Solon what might have occurred in Egyptian history, nor do they dwell upon the role that Egypt might have played in the encounter with Atlantis, other than to point out that Athens saved the region from slavery. Egypt is the point at which the bad writing of *Phaedrus* begins to turn into good writing, and it is the point through which the philosopher's narrative passes before making a return to its home in Athens.[16] Egypt becomes useful to the Greek philosopher when

12. A few scholars argue, on chronological grounds, that Plato is referring not to the Critias who was one of the Thirty Tyrants, but to the grandfather of that tyrant: see Cornford 1937, 1–2, and Taylor 1928, 23–25. See also the intricate discussion in Davies 1971, pp. 322–26. The name of Critias would certainly evoke the tyrant in an Athenian audience in the early fourth century, when Plato was writing, whether or not the philosopher was precise about chronology in the dialogue.

13. See esp. Thucydides 4.58–65; 6.33–35, 72–80; 7.73–74; 8.85; Xenophon, *Hellenica* 1.1.27, 1.3.13.

14. On Timaeus, see Cornford 1937, 2–3. The fourth, unnamed person in *Timaeus* is, perhaps, also an outsider: he may be from Sicily, as commentators argue, since Socrates asks Timaeus about his whereabouts, and the latter agrees to stand in for him (17a–b): see Taylor 1928, 25, following Proclus.

15. Chakrabarty 1992, 1.

16. Derrida 1995, 114–15: "As the myth of its origin, the memory of a city is seen to be entrusted not only to a writing but to the writing of the other, to the secretariat of another city. It must thus *be made other* twice over in order to be saved, and it is indeed a question of salvation, of *saving* a memory (23a) by writing on the walls of temples. The living memory must be exiled to the graphic vestiges of *another place*, which is also another city and another political space. But the technographic superiority of the Egyptians is nonetheless subordinated to the service of the Greek *logos*: you Greeks, 'you surpassed all men in all sorts of qualities, as befits

its experience and its history intersect with Greek experience and Greek history, or when one of its cities can serve as a space for him to accommodate so Platonic an entity as the ideal republic: in a word, Egypt enters the philosopher's realm of debate and discussion only when it enables him to carry forward the particular philosophical and political lecture that he wishes to give to fourth-century Athens. To the implications of this role of Egypt for Plato's thought, I wish to turn in the remainder of this chapter.

FROM ISOCRATES TO CRANTOR

The Egypt described by Plato occupies an imaginary space within the philosopher's dialectic and overlaps only partially with historical realities. Owing to his own cultural and political uneasiness, Plato is more concerned with how Egypt may serve him in his disenchantment with the Athenian democracy than he is to give an accurate or sensitive description of the country. Part of Egypt's allure lay in the fact that it was a much older and more accomplished civilization than Greece, and its historical stature lent itself to appropriation and transformation by the philosopher. What was left out of Plato's description was the political collapse of Egypt's pharaonic civilization, its occupation by Nubian, Assyrian, Libyan, and Persian invaders, the decline of temple culture, and a contemporary scribal tradition looking back to models from the Middle and New Kingdom for its monumental inscriptions. As the dialogues make clear, to be sure, Plato did not set out either to write Egyptian history, or to give analyses of contemporary Egyptian culture and society. Nevertheless, the recourse to Egypt and its particular construction in his work betoken an anxiety that calls out for analysis.

Why does Plato depict Egypt as the repository of "history," and why

---

the scions and the pupils of the gods. Numerous and great were your exploits and those of your city: they are here by writing *[gegrammena]* and are admired' (24d). The memory of a people inspected, appropriated by another people, or even by another culture: a phenomenon in the history of cultures well known as the history of colonization. But the fact appears highly significant here: the memory is deposited, entrusted to a depot on the shores of a people which declares, here at least, its admiration, its dependence, its subordination. The Egyptian is supposed to have appropriated the culture of the Greek masters, who now depend on this *hypomnesis*, on this secretariat's writing, on these monuments: Thoth or Hermes, whichever you prefer. For this discourse of the priest—or Egyptian interpreter—is uttered here and interpreted in Greek, for the Greeks. Will we ever know who is holding this discourse *on* the dialectic of the master and the slave and on the two memories?"

does he show Egyptians divulging information from their superior records to a Greek statesman? In order to begin formulating a response to these questions, let us take a short detour through a passage from Isocrates' *Busiris* and then to a passage pertaining to Crantor of Soli. As we saw in the last section of chapter 5, the works of Isocrates and Plato and their references to Egypt were written out of a contestation over politics and philosophy. While both men often wrote in opposition to the city's democracy and its democratic politicians, each of them claimed to be the true exponent of "philosophy." Within the locus of these Athenian struggles, Egypt's precise place is complicated by its displacement in Greek philosophy, history, and politics. The ancient and originary status of Egypt in Plato's dialogues is obscured by his desire to think of the country as paternal in the sense I have been describing, while the apparently flattering picture of Egyptians in Isocrates' work is vexed by the complexities arising from genre and aesthetic response that were mentioned in the previous chapter.

Of particular interest here is the passage in which the speaker in Isocrates' work refers to Busiris' role in the formation of the country's caste system and to his organization of political institutions:

> Including in all classes the right numbers for the best administration
> of the commonwealth, he [King Busiris] gave orders that the same in-
> dividuals should always engage in the same pursuits, because he knew
> that those who continually change their occupations never achieve pro-
> ficiency in even a single one of their tasks, whereas those who apply
> themselves constantly to the same activities perform each thing they
> do surprisingly well. Hence, we shall find that in the arts the Egyptians
> surpass those who work at the same skilled occupations elsewhere more
> than artisans in general excel laymen; also, with respect to the system
> which enables them to preserve royalty and their political institutions
> in general, they have been so successful that philosophers who under-
> take to discuss such topics and have won the greatest reputation prefer
> above all others the Egyptian form of government, and the Lacedaemo-
> nians, on the other hand, govern their own city in admirable fashion
> because they imitate certain of the Egyptian customs. (16–17)

Familiarity with the Egyptian caste system among Greek authors dates back at least to Herodotus (2.164–68),[17] but the speaker makes the further

---

17. For references to the Egyptian caste system in Greek writers of the fifth and fourth centuries, in addition to Herodotus, Isocrates, and Plato's *Timaeus*, see Aristotle, *Politics* 1329a40 ff. and Aristagoras, *FGrHist* 608 F 1 (with the commentary by Fornara to *FGrHist* III C). Aristotle was the first to attribute the caste system to

claim, in the second half of the passage, that eminent philosophers who have discussed political organizations find the Egyptian system (τὴν ἐν Αἰγύπτῳ . . . πολιτείαν) most appealing. Scholars have identified these philosophers in various ways, and Christian Froidefond, for instance, has argued that Isocrates has the Pythagoreans in mind and that he is drawing on a Pythagorean idea or written treatise concerning Egyptian politics.[18] Attempting to identify the philosophers to whom Isocrates is referring is a difficult task, however, and we shall approach the question here from another perspective.

I do not say that I am about to craft the solution to the problem related to the identity of the philosophers implicated by Isocrates. Instead, I would like to reconfigure the question and try to place besides Isocrates' text Plato's *Timaeus* and *Critias*, texts which also show Greeks borrowing the caste system from Egypt and which describe a similar epistemic trajectory through which learning and wisdom come from Egypt to Greece.[19] My juxtaposition of the two Greek authors, it must be admitted, dates back in the modern era to Karl Marx, who writes that "Plato's *Republic*, in so far as the division of labour is treated in it as the formative principle of the state, is merely an Athenian idealization of the Egyptian caste system, Egypt having served as the model of an industrial country to others of his contemporaries, e.g. Isocrates."[20] It should be noted that Marx is not suggesting that Isocrates is referring to Plato's work, despite the admittedly clear parallels in the two works. One obstacle to affirming Plato's *Republic* as the philosophical work intended by Isocrates' *Busiris* is that the exact dates of the two works are uncertain, and it can be added that Plato makes only brief reference to Egypt in the dialogue (436a). These considerations explain the careful formulation of Marx's remark and also weaken any notion that Isocrates is necessarily alluding to Plato's *Republic*, even if it is allowed that Isocrates knew of Plato's opinions by word of mouth or from oral debate and conversation before the publication of the *Republic*.

Sesostris. See, too, Dicaearchus, *FGrHist* 665 F 120, as a slightly later example of the same attribution.

18. Froidefond 1971, 237–48. This view is also followed by Bernal 1987, 104–6; cf. Isocrates, *Busiris* 28: "On a visit to Egypt, he [Pythagoras] became a student of the religion of the people, and was first to bring to the Greeks all philosophy. . . ."

19. Eucken 1983, ch. 5, offers a detailed evaluation of Isocrates' *Busiris* alongside Plato's *Republic* and *Timaeus*, but his emphases are quite distinct from mine in what follows; see also Morgan 1998.

20. Karl Marx, *Capital: A Critique of Political Economy*, vol. 1, trans. B. Fowkes (New York, 1977), 488–89.

The material from Isocrates does not answer the problem concerning the turn to Egypt in Plato, but allows us to reformulate it in the following way. Why do both Plato and Isocrates appear so ready to say that Greek philosophers and wise men such as Solon visited Egypt? What does it mean for Egypt to be the place where the Greeks refined their wisdom and the place where they acquired new learning? As far as Plato is concerned, it is interesting to remark on the place of Egypt in the genealogy he constructs in his narratives. Socrates' initial recapitulation of his imaginary city from *Republic* is followed by Critias in *Timaeus* with a story brought to Greece from Egypt in which both proto-Athens and contemporary Saïs share the same class system as that imaginary Socratic city. With respect to Plato, then, we are prompted to ask questions of a more specific nature. Why does Critias' story of two cities, with its lengthy pedigree, originate in records that are found in Saïs, where a native priest discloses his archival material to the Greek Solon? How is it significant that the imaginary city of Plato's *Republic* is said to have an actual counterpart in proto-Athens and contemporary Saïs? What does it mean to refer the story of proto-Athens and Atlantis to Egyptians? In his monumental commentary on *Timaeus*, the Neoplatonist Proclus (412–85 C.E.) long ago reported the answers given by Crantor of Soli to these questions:

> With respect to the whole of this discourse about the Atlantians, some say that it is pure history (ἱστορίαν), which was the opinion of Crantor, the first interpreter of Plato. He says that Plato was mocked by his contemporaries on the grounds that he was not the inventor of the Republic (πολιτείας) but copied that of the Egyptians; and that he attached so much importance to these mockers that he attributed to the Egyptians this history (ἱστορίαν) about the Athenians and the Atlantians to make them say that the Athenians once lived in conformity with this Republic (πολιτείαν). This is attested, he says, also by the prophets of the Egyptians who assert that these matters were written on pillars which were still preserved. Others again say that this narration is a tale (μῦθον), a fictitious account of the least reality but which gives an indication of natures that are perpetual or are generated in the cosmos; but these people are not listening to Plato [*Timaeus* 20d], who exclaims that "the narration is extremely strange, yet absolutely true."[21]

---

21. Τὸν περὶ τῶν Ἀτλαντίνων σύμπαντα τοῦτον λόγον οἱ μὲν ἱστορίαν εἶναι ψιλήν φασιν, ὥσπερ ὁ πρῶτος τοῦ Πλάτωνος ἐξηγητὴς Κράντωρ· ὃς δὴ καὶ σκώπτεσθαι μέν φησιν αὐτὸν ὑπὸ τῶν τότε, ὡς οὐκ αὐτὸν ὄντα τῆς πολιτείας εὑρετήν, ἀλλὰ μεταγράψαντα τὰ Αἰγυπτίων· τὸν δὲ τοσοῦτον ποιήσασθαι <τὸν> τῶν σκωπτόντων λόγον, ὥστε ἐπὶ Αἰγυπτίους ἀναπέμψαι τὴν

Proclus goes on to give the explanations of other writers on the significance of the Atlantis story, but it is remarkable that Crantor (ca. 335–275 B.C.E.)[22] should make these claims about Plato's story. Crantor says that he believes in the historicity of Atlantis and that Plato imputed the narrative to Egyptian priests because he was mocked by those who claimed he had plagiarized the political system of the Egyptians. As I understand the passage, Crantor is suggesting that Plato was meeting the charge of plagiarism by making Egyptians themselves say that Plato's ideal republic was already in place in proto-Athens, even before a similar political system developed in Egypt. Thus, Crantor's remarks both emphasize the priority of Athens over Egypt in the development of the Platonic polity and insist on the truth of the story of Atlantis.

Concerning the important issue of cultural priority and dependence, Crantor may have been drawing on earlier debates: such appears to be the case with the particular relationship between Saïs and Athens, a subject about which there was some speculation among Greek writers. It is plausible, for example, that Crantor consulted the Egyptian history of Hecateus of Abdera, given the status quickly attained by Hecateus' work (which was published probably between 320 and 315, and at the latest before 305 B.C.E.), and its stated reliance on Egyptian priestly sources.[23] Hecateus' writings do not survive—a full consideration lies beyond the scope of this book—but we can form some conception of his work from Diodorus, who relied extensively on Hecateus in book 1 of his history. Reconstructing Hecateus from Diodorus, we can say that Hecateus argued for at least the following: Athens was a colony of Saïs, and the origins of three Athenian classes *(eupatrids, geomoroi,* and *demiourgoi)* lay in Egypt.[24] Significantly, these two

---

περὶ Ἀθηναίων καὶ Ἀτλαντίνων ταύτην ἱστορίαν, ὡς τῶν Ἀθηναίων κατὰ ταύτην ζησάντων ποτὲ τὴν πολιτείαν· μαρτυροῦσι δὲ καὶ οἱ προφῆταί φησι τῶν Αἰγυπτίων ἐν στήλαις ταῖς ἔτι σῳζομέναις ταῦτα γεγράφθαι λέγοντες. οἳ δέ φασιν αὐτὴν μῦθον εἶναι καὶ πλάσμα γενόμενον μὲν οὐδαμῶς, ἔνδειξιν δὲ φέρον τῶν ἀεὶ ὄντων κατὰ τὸν κόσμον ἢ γιγνομένων, οὐδὲ τοῦ Πλάτωνος ἐπακούοντες οὗτοι βοῶντος, ὅτι μάλα μὲν ἄτοπος ὁ λόγος, παντάπασί γε μὴν ἀληθής *(Commentary on Timaeus,* 1.75.30–76.14, ed. Diehl). I have based my translation on Taylor 1820 and Festugière 1966, and on the suggestions in Cameron 1983.

22. For Crantor's fragments and testimonia, see Mette 1984. There is a brief life in Diogenes Laertius 4.24–27.

23. *FGrHist* 264; *FHG,* vol. 2, 384–96; DK 73. For the date of Hecateus' Egyptian work, see Jacoby in *RE* 7, 2750–69, and Murray 1970, 143–44.

24. Diodorus 1.28. Hecateus also seems to have made similar claims about points not directly mentioned by Plato in the context of Atlantis, since Diodorus writes that "certain rulers of Athens were originally Egyptians" (1.28.6), and that

claims fly in the face of the Egyptian priest's statements about the greater age of Athens in *Timaeus*, though it is impossible to say whether Hecateus was directly refuting Plato in his history, catering to the official propaganda of Ptolemy, or serving some other purpose. Nevertheless, one sees that Hecateus, like several Greek writers, held to the symbolic importance of Egypt for the question of cultural transmission, and he also, along with Plato, Plutarch, and Proclus, referred to Solon's visit to Egypt.[25]

Was Athens a colony of Saïs, or was Saïs a colony of Athens? Plato's remarks in his dialogues appear to have sparked a controversy about the nature of the "'genetic' cultural relationship" between Athens and Saïs, for Greek writers other than Hecateus also seem to have developed the implications of *Timaeus* in deliberating over the putative historical kinship between the two cities.[26] Plato said that Athens was a thousand years older than Saïs (23e), and not that Saïs was a colony of Athens, but after him different opinions on this question were given by Callisthenes, Phanodemus, and pseudo-Theopompus, along with Hecateus. Proclus writes, "Callisthenes and Phanodemus record that the Athenians were the ancestors of the Saïtes, but Theopompus says in contrast that Athens was a colony of Saïs."[27] It is not clear in what context Callisthenes, the historian executed by Alexander in 327, and Phanodemus, a fourth-century Atthidographer, made these remarks about Athens and Saïs; perhaps Phanodemus was reflecting on Saïs in his treatment of early Athenian history. As for Theopompus, Proclus' statement refers not to the historian of that name, but to the rhetor Anaximenes of Lampsacus, who published a pamphlet, *Trikaranos*, under the name of Theopompus, to get him into trouble. At any rate, the view of this pseudo-Theopompus agrees with the view of Hecateus of Abdera, who also said that Athens was a colony of Saïs, as we just saw

"the Athenians observed their sacrifices and ancient ceremonies in the same way as the Egyptians" (1.29.4).

25. Diodorus 1.69, 98.
26. The phrase comes from Bernal 1987, 108.
27. Proclus, *Commentary on Timaeus* 1.97.27 ff. (Diehl), on *Timaeus* 21e and ties between Saïs and Athens. This text appears variously as *FGrHist* 124 F 51 (Callisthenes), *FGrHist* 325 F 25 (Phanodemus), and *FGrHist* 72 F 20b (pseudo-Theopompus, or Anaximenes). For the view that Saïs or Egypt was older than Athens, see also Charax of Pergamum, *FGrHist* 103 F 39, and Ister, *FGrHist* 334 F 43–46. For the view that Athens was older than Saïs, see also Philochorus, *FGrHist* 328 F 93, and Pseudo-Pherecydes, *FGrHist* 333 F 3 (= *FGrHist* 3 F 178). On these passages, see especially Jacoby's commentary in *FGrHist* IIIb (supplement) vols. I and II, and the index therein s.v. "Athens and Attica—and Egypt"; "Egypt, Egyptians"; and "Sais."

above. The works of these three intellectuals, who were active well before Hecateus, suggest that Greek writers of the fourth century were actively discussing the question whether Athens was older than Egypt or Egypt was older than Athens.[28] When Crantor arrived at the conclusion that the Atlantis story was factually based and that the Greek details in Plato's account were true, he must have been taking the side of those who preferred to advocate the greater age of Athens over Saïs. The remarkable thing about Plato's story, then, is that it succeeded in inspiring this debate about the relationship between Athens and Saïs, and even in persuading subsequent writers such as Crantor and Callisthenes (against others such as Hecateus of Abdera) that the Athens was indeed the mother city of Saïs.

Concerning the authenticity of Atlantis, Crantor stands alone among Athenian intellectuals in holding to his opinion about the story, since no other surviving writer of his era believes in the existence of the island. It is true that writers of subsequent eras held divergent opinions about the truth of Plato's story, but, in his own day, few if any Greeks believed it.[29] Aristotle made the point that the island's maker and the person responsible for wiping it out were one and the same.[30] The Athenian orators and the

28. In book 5, Diodorus reverses what he says about the kinship between Saïs and Athens in book 1: "Likewise, the Athenians, although they were the founders of the city in Egypt men called Saïs, suffered from the same ignorance because of the flood" (5.57). Given the context, however, Diodorus' source here must be Zeno of Rhodes, who was writing in the second century, and not Hecateus of Abdera.

29. Already in the fourth century, Aristotle said that Plato had invented the story (implied in Strabo 2.3.6 and 13.1.36, but not certain). Ancient writers who mention Atlantis include Posidonius (quoted by Strabo) and Strabo (2.3.6), the elder Pliny (*Natural History* 2.92.205), Philo of Alexandria (*On the Eternity of the World* 26.141), Diodorus (3.54, 3.56–61), Plutarch (*Life of Solon* 26), Tertullian (*On the Ascetics' Mantle* 2 and *Apology* 40.4), Athenaeus (14.640e), Aelian (*On the Characteristics of Animals* 15.2), and Ammianus Marcellinus (17.7.13). In addition, Proclus refers to Amelius, Origen, Numenius, Porphyry, Iamblichus, Syrianus, Longinus (*Commentary on Timaeus* at 24a-d), and Marcellus (*Commentary on Timaeus* at 55a). The story of Atlantis is also mentioned by Cosmas Indicopleustes, *Christian Topography* (12.456D), who repudiates the authenticity of Plato's account. See Ramage 1978, 20–27. The relevant passages are conveniently assembled in de Camp 1954, 278–311.

30. Strabo 2.3.6: "On the other hand, he [Posidonius] correctly sets down in his work the fact that the earth sometimes rises and undergoes settling processes, and undergoes changes that result from earthquakes and the other similar agencies, all of which I too have enumerated above. And, on this point, he does well to cite the statement of Plato that it is possible that the story about the island of Atlantis is not a fiction. Concerning Atlantis, Plato relates that Solon, after having made inquiry of the Egyptian priests, reported that Atlantis did not exist, but disappeared—an island no smaller in size than a continent; and Posidonius thinks that it is better to put the matter in that way than to say of Atlantis that its inventor caused it to

Atthidographers remain silent about a version of Athenian history that was so richly suitable for them to use and to consider. As Alan Cameron points out in his revealing article on Crantor and Atlantis, "Not only did the orators and Atthidographers not regard Plato's account of the struggle between antediluvian Athens and Atlantis as history; they did not even regard it as genuine legend."[31] On the question of Atlantis, it seems, Plato's fellow thinkers believed that he had fabricated the story of Athens' conquest as well as the very existence of the distant island.

As far as proof is concerned, it can be said that despite numerous attempts scholars have failed to offer persuasive evidence for either an Egyptian source of the kind detailed by Plato, or an island of Atlantis to suit his description.[32] The references to Saïs and Neïth in *Timaeus* indicate that Plato was drawing not on Egyptian accounts of real antiquity, but on gleanings from a more recent tradition. Saïs became the capital of Egypt as late as the Twenty-sixth Dynasty (664–525 B.C.E.), which is the period when Greece and Egypt developed closer ties and when the Greek settlement of Naukratis was founded in the Delta. The goddess Neïth became important in Egypt at this time, although she is attested in material from the First Dynasty and the Old Kingdom. Her identification with Athena, presumably linked to her martial qualities, also points to the influence of relatively late developments in Egypt; it is first implied by Herodotus among Greek writers.[33] Out of these details, one can say that Plato, contrary to the implications of his texts, is reflecting a relatively recent state of contact between Egyptians and Greeks, and it would be foolish to infer that he was privy to an Egyptian tradition of genuine antiquity. At any rate, there are

---

disappear, just as did the Poet the wall of the Achaeans." The phrase "its inventor caused it to disappear" is attributed to Aristotle on the basis of Strabo 13.1.36; it indicates that Aristotle believed that the story was Plato's creation. Unlike Aristotle and Crantor, Posidonius (ca. 135–50 B.C.E.), is not reported to have taken a stand concerning the existence of Atlantis; however, he appears to have said that Plato's explanation for its destruction was plausible given his own meteorological observations.

31. Cameron 1983, 84–85.

32. There are good bibliographies in Luce 1969, 217–18; Ramage 1978, 196–200; and Gill 1980, xxv–xxvii. Schenkel 1979, posits an Egyptian etymology for "Atlantis": *jw.tt rn = s,* "whose name exists not, who has no name." Alternatively, Griffiths 1985, reprinted in *Atlantis and Egypt with Other Selected Essays* (Cardiff, 1991), 3–30, proposes *'3t rn = s,* "'Great One' is its name," and also sketches "the extent of the conceptual debt to Egypt" in Plato's story. There is additional discussion on Atlantis and Egyptian etymology in Bernal 1991, 35, 248, 274–319.

33. Herodotus 2.28. Plutarch observes that Egyptians often call Isis by the name of Athena (*On Isis and Osiris* 62).

no Egyptian sources, from the earliest historical period to Plato's day, that validate the Greek story of Atlantis. Of course, the lack of corroborative evidence has not stopped scholars and other writers from ascribing a deep knowledge of Egypt to Plato, or from claiming that he visited Egypt. Thus, one scholar, who is by no means atypical in his attitude, writes: "In his Egyptian journey, financed, perhaps as Plutarch says (*Life of Solon* 2.8), by a cargo of olive oil from his Attic estate, Plato was following in the footsteps of illustrious predecessors. . . . By inspection of monuments and by conversation with temple-spokesmen, Plato can hardly have failed to learn something about Egypt in the Bronze Age."[34] I shall return to the question of Plato's travels in Egypt, and I note for the moment that these travels and the Egyptian learning are highly problematic readings of themes generated by the philosopher's own texts.

Incidents contemporary or nearly contemporary with Plato indicate that he may have been alluding to Greek rather than Egyptian details in his story of Atlantis. The island of Atalante, near the coast of Opuntian Locris, was inundated by tidal waves caused by earthquakes in 426; the destruction of Athenian fortifications there was recorded by Thucydides (3.89), who in the same passage gives a description of the inundation at Orobiae in Euboea. The fact that the island was called Atalante must be relevant. In the fifth century, Eastern Locris was probably an oligarchy based in the capital of Opus, which today is called Atalanti.[35] Moreover, in 373 the city of Helice was completely wiped out, also by tidal waves. The exact cause was much debated among writers contemporary with or slightly later than Plato, including Aristotle, Heraclides of Pontus (who was also at the Academy), and Callisthenes.[36] Heraclides' comments, in particular, show telling parallels with the destruction of Atlantis: Helice was destroyed at night, and its destruction was the result of the gods' wrath.[37] (On the other hand, the island of Santorini, which was covered up by volcanic eruption, cannot be considered a candidate for Plato's Atlantis, since the latter was destroyed by an earthquake and tidal waves, according to the philosopher, and not by

34. John V. Luce, in Ramage 1978, 61, 63. I refer to these claims precisely because they are made in an otherwise useful survey of "The Sources and Literary Form of Plato's Atlantis Narrative."

35. For the topography of Opuntian Locris, see Fossey 1990.

36. Aristotle, *Meteorology* 343b2, 344b34 ff., 368b7 ff.; Heraclides, in Strabo 7.7.2, 8.7.2; Callisthenes, *FGrHist* 124 F 19–21 (= Seneca, *Natural Questions* 6.23, 6.26.3, 7.5.3 –5). Unlike Heraclides, Aristotle and Callisthenes favored meteorological or natural explanations.

37. Strabo 7.7.2; 8.7.2; Gottschalk 1980, 94–95.

seething lava.) Thus, Plato's story resonates in several important respects with events that had recently occurred in or near the mainland of Greece.

Leaving these significant details, we might return to Crantor and use his claims to reflect on the two questions about the authenticity of Plato's story and the relationship between Athens and Egypt. On the subject of authenticity, enough has been said to show that there is little, if any, proof for the Egyptian records mentioned by Plato and for the existence of Atlantis, though there are several contemporary incidents which Plato may be invoking in his narration. Secondly, the subject of the relationship between Athens and Saïs is linked to important questions of cultural priority and dependency, questions which were then picked up and discussed by later Greek intellectuals. Plato makes the claim in his dialogues that Athens, being about nine thousand years old in his day, is older than Saïs. It scarcely needs to be said that "the Athens which Plato describes could not have existed in 9500 B.C. or thereabouts. At that time Greece was in the late Paleolithic period and man was still living in caves or rock shelters and was hunting and gathering his food. Settlement was not to begin for another 3,000 years, and even then the process of civilization was a slow one."[38] If we read Plato's claims for their symbolic rather than their historical value, we still need to ask why he makes Athens older than an Egyptian city, but at the same time sets up a relational position between Athens and Saïs. The philosopher appears to be creating a chiastic situation where political knowledge proceeds from Athens to Egypt and then back again to the Athens of his own times. Egypt's function as the pivot of this chiasmus is to sanctify and authorize Plato's political philosophy. Thus, Plato stakes out the priority of the Greek invention of political philosophy, but nevertheless chooses to link it to Egypt before he reintegrates it into Athenian history. Like the biographical tradition that has Greek philosophers, eventually including Plato, spend some part of their lives in Egypt, the philosopher himself in these dialogues has political philosophy relayed from proto-Athens to Egyptian Saïs to contemporary Athens. The alien culture of Egypt is, hence, regulated and incorporated by Plato into his works, so as to allow him to deliver political and philosophical prescriptions to the fourth-century city. Somewhat like elite thinkers of other societies, Plato takes whatever resources he deems suitable, whether material, symbolic, or of another kind, to help him make the strongest possible intervention in "the universe of possible discourse."[39] Egyptian culture, for Plato, represents a

38. Ramage 1978, 19.
39. Bourdieu 1977, 169.

hallowed, ancient, conservative, and authoritative alternative to the world of contemporary Athens, and the philosopher uses this Hellenized version of Egypt, regardless of any immanent characteristics, features, or qualities, in order to advocate and to augment his own political and philosophical position in contemporary society.

ATHENS AND ATLANTIS

In contrast to Crantor, I have been saying that Plato is using Egypt as an all too convenient source for a political narrative targeted at his contemporary Athenians. By praising a proto-Athens that is also an anti-Athens, Plato is attempting to direct his contemporaries away from the present condition of the city to a possible ideal, a model city that present-day Athens can become, or a proto-Athens to which it can return, if only its citizens were to contemplate his story and open their eyes to the folly of their imperialist excess. This is one of the main points of the story recounted by Critias, as scholars ranging from Giuseppe Bartoli (in 1779–80) to Pierre Vidal-Naquet have claimed.[40] Vidal-Naquet, in particular, offers a sensitive discussion of the structure and meaning of Plato's story, and surmises that "Plato's Athens meets and vanquishes Atlantis; in so doing, she really overcomes herself."[41] What this means is that Plato is presenting a lesson to his fellow Athenians by conjuring up for them two different perspectives on their own city: "the city of Athena and the olive tree is identified with proto-Athens, and the city of Poseidon, lord of horses and the sea, is realized in Atlantis."[42] The land-based nature of proto-Athens, its unity, changelessness, and correspondence with the Same of *Timaeus* imply that Plato's proto-Athens is the inverse of contemporary Athens, namely, "an anti-Athens," perhaps even a Sparta, although Vidal-Naquet does not explicitly infer this.[43] But in contrast to this anti-Athens there stands Atlantis, which is almost "the political expression of the Other," and "an imita-

40. Giuseppe Bartoli, *Essai sur l'explication historique que Platon a donnée de sa "Republique" et de son Atlantide et qu'on n'a pas considérée jusqu'à maintenant* (Stockholm, 1779–80); and Pierre Vidal-Naquet, "Athènes et l'Atlantide," *REG* 77 (1964): 420–44, translated as "Athens and Atlantis: Structure and Meaning of a Platonic Myth," in Vidal-Naquet 1986, 263–84. Plato's story is located within a fourth-century context in Morgan 1998. For a discussion of the political frame of Timaeus, see Sallis 1999. See also Brisson 1982, and Gill 1977 and 1993.
41. Vidal-Naquet 1986, 268.
42. Ibid.
43. Vidal-Naquet 1986, 270.

tion of the model."[44] The coexistence of earth and water on Atlantis, its mixed constitution, movement toward disunity, division into ten parts, naval strength, and imperial power suggest that Atlantis is close to the Athens of the late fifth and early fourth centuries, the Athens of Plato's day. *Timaeus* and *Critias* are celebrations of the proto-Athenian city that exemplifies the excellence of human achievement, and saves the world from being dominated by the Atlantians. The fact that even the idealized city of proto-Athens is destroyed by a natural upheaval and effaced like Atlantis indicates not that the story is unserious, according to Vidal-Naquet, but that human affairs are difficult to understand, and so Plato's Atlantis story is to be construed as a tale about mortals to be contemplated by mortals.

If the dialogues are eulogizing proto-Athens, moreover, then they also appear to be bestowing praise on Egypt, since they invite comparison between the proto-Athenian city and Saïs. The same Egyptian priest who tells Solon that proto-Athens was the bravest of all states, "supremely well organized also in all other respects" (23c), and characterized by "the finest accomplishments and the finest political organizations (πολιτεῖαι) of any nation" (23c) also says to the Greek traveler, "To get a view of their laws, look at the laws here [in Saïs]; for you will find existing here at the present time many examples of the laws which then existed in your city" (24a). The priest then outlines an Egyptian caste system that resembles the system found in both proto-Athens and Socrates' ideal city. The best constitution (ἀρίστη πολιτεία) of *Republic*, and perhaps also *Laws*, is thus brought to fruition in Critias' proto-Athens and in turn seems to exist in Egyptian Saïs. Further, the appeal of Egypt in the dialogues derives from its position as a repository of knowledge that extends back millennia and as the source of narratives which exalt an ancestral Athens and which portray it as the liberator of the Mediterranean peoples. It should also be mentioned that the static nature of the Egyptian state mentioned in *Timaeus* and the conservatism of the Egyptians in *Laws* (656–57)[45] would add to the appeal of Egypt for those Athenian politicians, including possibly the historical Critias, who wanted to revive the ancestral constitution (πάτριος πολιτεία). At more than one level, therefore, Egypt may appear to be cast in approving terms in the two dialogues.

44. Vidal-Naquet 1986, 272. For a discussion of the philosophical categories of same and other in Plato's *Timaeus*, see Brisson 1994.
45. The passage in book 2 of *Laws* is discussed in Davis 1979. See also the concluding pages of chapter 5 above.

But the designation attached to Egypt by Plato in these dialogues is hardly formulated out of a discursive innocence. Herodotus had affirmed the veracity of Helen's presence in Egypt by referring the episode to Egyptian priests (2.113–20), and Plato is following Herodotus to the extent that Critias too insists on the truth of a narrative obtained from an Egyptian priest.[46] Nevertheless, Plato presents his story in a context of ambiguity that generates suspicion concerning the claims to truth insisted upon by Critias, whereas Herodotus did nothing to undermine the truth of what he heard from Egyptian priests. Whatever the status of Herodotus' narrative, Plato's story is presented in a dialogue which is constructed in a manner so self-consciously clever that the reader also recognizes the fictitiousness of the story.[47] The fictional quality of the story is emphasized by its presentation as an illustration of Socrates' ideal city, the coincidence between the social institutions of proto-Athens and Saïs, displacement in time, participation of gods, and Timaeus' remarks on truth and likelihood (29c). Further, the authenticity of the story is put into doubt by Critias' ambiguous recollection of the story in the two dialogues. In *Timaeus*, Critias told the story the previous day to Hermocrates and Timaeus just after they heard Socrates expatiate about his ideal city, then he rehearsed it during the night, then repeated it to his friends after daybreak, and now he claims that he remembers the whole story in every detail, and that it is stamped firmly in his mind "like the encaustic designs of an indelible painting" (25e–26c). He adds, "I am ready to tell my tale, not just in summary outline only, but in full detail just as I heard it" (26c). In *Critias*, however, he asks for his audience's indulgence since it is difficult to tell a story about mortals to other mortals (107) and says, "to an account given now on the spur of the moment indulgence must be granted, should we fail to make it a wholly fitting representation" (107e). Socrates then compares Critias and Timaeus to poets speaking before an audience in a theatre, and Critias again expresses hesitation as he calls upon the Muses, and especially Mnemosyne, since "if I can sufficiently remember and report the tale once told by the priests and brought here by Solon, I am convinced that I shall appear to have fulfilled my task adequately" (108b–d).

If the status of the Atlantis story is ambiguously fictional, we are left

46. See *Timaeus* 20d7–8 and cf. 21a4–5, 26e4–5; also 17c–20c.
47. See Socrates' remarks about the truth of his account of Theuth and Thamus in *Phaedrus* 274c1–3, 275b3–c2. Plato does not use the word *muthos* to refer to the Atlantis story, and refers to it as a *logos:* for the distinction between *muthos* and *logos* in Plato's work, see Brisson 1982, 114–43. For Plato's use of myths, see Wright 1979, 364–71; Detienne 1981 and 1989, 167–86; and Gill 1993.

with a mythopoetic discourse that stimulates the reader to engage the questions raised by Plato, but also a discourse in which the authenticity of various statements concerning proto-Athens, Atlantis, and Egyptian Saïs is impossible to register. Even as the conflict between proto-Athens and Atlantis, the same and the other, the idealized city and the obstructing state is abstracted outward on to philosophical dialectic, Egypt abides as the surplus referential pressure that is unabsorbed and unaccommodated. Egypt remains the home of an avowedly Athenian narrative, a narrative which transmits moral paradigms, which romanticizes an ancestral polity now long since destroyed, and which folds back in reflecting upon the historiography of the city. Egypt is merely there *for* the philosopher. In his texts, Egypt is a Greek topos—intellectualized into existence and in turn good to think with—and is simultaneously an object of academic appropriation for Greeks.[48] Plato appropriates Egypt—he submits his lessons about proto-Athenian glory to a Saïtic priest, he ascribes his charter myth to an Egyptian speaker, he enacts the working of historiographical writing by devising a story told by a Nilotic holy man, he forges a moral tale from Egyptian archives for contemporary Athenians—and marks it as the point in his text from which his thought-exercises are written out. His use of Egypt is such as to essentialize it, to make it suffer an objectification, and to place it at the service of Hellenic philosophy. For Plato, Egypt is signified within an intellectualized dialectic, and perhaps can only be signified within such an intellectualized effort.

It is necessary to stress that Plato's Egypt must exist in the dialectic's imaginary because, as noted earlier, the country that Solon visits does not correspond to historical reality. Egypt never had a caste system and the government in Saïs did not resemble the system outlined in the beginning of *Timaeus* and in *Republic*, although there was division of labor, as in several other countries. Recorded history in Egypt never reached back eight thousand or nine thousand years, even if Egypt had an older and richer culture than Greece in the fifth century. From 525 to 404, Egypt was under Persian rule (and again from 343 to 332, after the philosopher's death), which Plato neglects to mention in erecting the image of a "pure" Egypt. As for the journey itself, it is not easy to pinpoint the date at which Plato has Solon travel to Egypt, since he is unreliable about chronology and genealogy: he is wrong by two generations, at least, with Solon's genealogy.[49] But it is perverse to seek precision in such a matter, despite a frame narra-

48. See the related discussion in Brisson 1987.
49. Thomas 1989, 170–71.

tive with pretensions to historical realism. Herodotus had earlier described Solon's visit to Egypt, yet his account admitted of anachronisms, and the visit was elaborated on by other writers. Plutarch gives the names of the priests with whom Solon conversed, Sonkhis of Saïs and Psenophis of Heliopolis, and quotes a line of verse from a Solonian poem that used Egyptian material. On the other hand, Proclus remarks that the name of the priest at Saïs was Pateneït.[50]

From the perspective of these observers within the Western tradition, the hold of Egypt on Greek thinkers such as Solon appears to be unquestioned, and the country reproduces itself as a school for Hellas. In this connection, it is revealing that, beginning in the first century B.C.E., writers add Plato's name to the list of those who journeyed to Egypt.[51] The sources assert variously that Plato sold oil to pay for the passage, that Euripides was his companion on the voyage, and that he studied theology under Moses, Jeremiah, or Hermes Trismegistus in Egypt. Strabo can point to the house where Plato and Eudoxus lived for thirteen years, and Clement names Sechnuphis of Heliopolis as the source for the story of Theuth and Thamus in *Phaedrus*. In a document that comes from the ancient epistolary tradition, the eponymous Phaedrus writes a letter to Plato, while the latter is in Saïs, and inquires about the Pyramids and Egyptian animals.[52]

In the face of these claims about Egypt's symbolic authority, I find it

---

50. Herodotus 1.30; Plutarch, *Life of Solon* 26; Proclus at *Timaeus* 21e. See Griffiths 1985, 5–7.

51. The first notices appear in Diodorus 1.96 and Cicero, *De Republica* 1.10.16 and *De Finibus* 5.29.87. See also Plutarch, *On Isis and Osiris* 10 and *Moralia* 578F–579D; Quintilian 1.12.15; and the references in the next note. See F. Daumas in Godel 1956, 73–83; Griffiths 1970, 285–86; Riginos 1976, 64–69; Davis 1979, 121–22; Luce in Ramage 1978, 60–66; and Lefkowitz 1996, 81–84. In a curious crossing of different traditions, two Neoplatonist thinkers, Olympiodorus and the author of the *Anonymous Prolegomena to Platonic Philosophy*, claim that Plato was imitating his "ancestor" Solon in writing his *Republic* and *Laws:* see Riginos 1976, 186–87.

52. Oil: Plutarch, *Life of Solon* 2.4; Euripides: Diogenes Laertius 3.6. For Moses: see Aristobulus (quoted in Eusebius, *Praeparatio evangelica* 13.12.1 and 13.13.3–8); Philo, *On the Creation* 6.25; and Josephus, *Against Apion* 2.36.257. For Jeremiah, see Ambrose, in Augustine, *On Christian Teaching* 2.107–8 and Epistle 34 (cf. *City of God* 8.11); and cf. Lactantius, *Divinae Institutiones* 4.2.4. For Hermes Trismegistus, see Tertullian, *On the Soul* 2.3. The remaining details come from Strabo 17.1.29 and Clement of Alexandria, *Stromateis* 1.15.69; and Phaedrus' letter is Epistle 28 of the *epistula Socraticorum*, in *Epistolographi Graeci* (ed. R. Hercher), 627–28. For the putative dependence on figures from the Hebrew Bible, see Momigliano 1978, 93, 115–16; Schürer 1973–87; as well as Riginos 1976, 64–65; and Lefkowitz 1996, 84–90.

more useful to think in terms of European cultural anxieties than of evidence that begins with simplistic detail and ends in convoluted, self-canceling contortion. Hegel insisted that history traveled from East to West, and that Europe was "the absolute end of history." In his account, "self-consciousness" and freedom were the characteristics of European Man at the end of history.[53] Critias, or Plato, renders Egypt as the pivot of the chiastic arrangement through which glorious history returns to Greece after nine thousand or more years, but in this narrative, too, there is little doubt that Europe emerges as the sovereign subject. It is, ultimately, the heroic savior of the known world against the barbarian invaders of Atlantis. To point to the privileged status of Europe in the discourse of universal history, nevertheless, is merely to reinforce a self-sustaining ideology. The truth is that the Hegelian master-narrative is not really one of heightened "self-consciousness," but of the increasing apprehension felt by the European intellectual through the growing awareness of non-European societies; it is about the effect of the encounter of the European with the non-European. "Western Man," Rey Chow writes, "henceforth became 'self-conscious,' that is, uneasy and uncomfortable, in his 'own' environment."[54] Universal history is not a grand narrative that culminates in Greece, Germany, or Europe, but the record of an unsettling, or the disturbing of a self-complacency, dislocations caused by the European's experience of the gaze of the non-European. The preposterous excess of history in *Timaeus* and *Critias* is thus not just an homage to Egypt's past, although it may in part be so; it also points to the anxiety about the other. The anxiety over Egypt's monumental history is the anxiety of Greece's shortage of history; it is a testimony to the unsettling experience felt by Greek intel-

---

53. Hegel believed that Hellenic clarity, reason, and self-consciousness responded to, and supplanted, the enigmas and symbolism of Egyptian tradition. Thus, the Egyptian sphinx posed the riddle or the problem, but the Greek Oedipus was the one who answered it. The central Egyptian figures in this Hegelian narrative were the Egyptian priest in the Saïs of Plato's *Timaeus;* the sphinx; and the goddess Neith, in whose sanctuary was the inscription: "I am that which is, that which was, and that which will be; no one has lifted my veil." This inscription comes from Plutarch, *On Isis and Osiris* 9, and from Proclus, who modified it slightly and also supplied the additional line: "The fruit which I have produced is Helios" (*Commentary on Timaeus* 21e3–7, see Festugière 1966, 140). Hegel knew of Proclus' supplement, and found it congenial to his philosophy of history: "In the Egyptian Neith, Truth is still a problem. The Greek Apollo is its solution; his utterance is: Man, know thyself." On the Saitic inscription, see Assmann 1997, 118–25; on Hegel's treatment of Egypt in his lectures on the philosophy of history, see Harten 1995.

54. Chow 1994, 145.

lectuals as they came into contact with one of the most accomplished civilizations of the Mediterranean. In Egypt, hence, the Greeks sought to find their own lost origins and to authenticate their rewriting of history.

One day, perhaps, we shall learn whether Solon, Plato, Pythagoras, Thales, and the rest really touched the shores of Egypt to consult with Egyptian priests and bring home their ideas. There are numerous texts that inform us of these "theoretical"[55] pilgrimages to the originary homeland of learning and wisdom—but it happens that they are written by Greeks and in Greek, at least until the end of the fourth century B.C.E. By dispatching Solon to a Saïs where Egyptians can divulge to him the fragments of an unrivalled archive, and by assigning to Egypt the responsibility of teaching many Greeks, not excluding the Pythagoreans, the rudiments of philosophy, Plato is merely one among the many Hellenes who transmit evidence for this kind of intercontinental traffic. But between the silence of the Egyptian records and the ascriptions of the Greek there is a discrepancy that compels us not to accept meekly these notional salutes to the country that every brilliant Hellene must visit, and instead to ask after the reasons behind the signification of this originary locale. There emerges the suspicion that Egypt is appreciated, not so much for what it is, as for what it can be said to be. To adapt Edward Said's words, Egypt exists "as a set of values attached, not to its modern realities, but to a series of valorized contacts" it has had with Greece.[56] And after Plato, we know, Egypt becomes increasingly important as the site of epistemological dissemination, the place to ally one's history with, and the necessary way-station for Greek wise men. To discover one's wisdom along the shores of the Nile is not only to make Egypt a theatre where one may represent oneself to one's own, but also to betray the anxious symptoms of a lack.

Echoing other scholars who write about Greek perceptions of Egypt, Froidefond asks, "Was Plato, ultimately, an admirer of Egypt?" and then goes on to remark that the number of responses to the question almost equals the number of scholars who have attempted to answer it.[57] At some

---

55. Herodotus 1.30: αὐτῶν δὴ ὧν τούτων καὶ <u>τῆς θεωρίης</u> ἐκδημήσας ὁ Σόλων εἵνεκεν ἐς Αἴγυπτον ἀπίκετο παρὰ Ἄμασιν κτλ. And cf. the notion in Isocrates' *Busiris* of the Egyptian priest as ὁ ἀνὴρ θεωρητικός; but this type of person stands in contrast to the kinds of philosophers represented by Plato and Aristotle. For Greek travelers in Egypt from Menelaus to Herodotus, see Müller 1997.

56. Said 1978, 85.

57. Froidefond 1971, 337.

level, Plato's characters express admiration for Egyptian customs and practices, as in *Laws*, and if we want to extend these feelings to the author, then we can say that Plato as well was an admirer of Egypt. On the other hand, Froidefond also says about Plato, "Without doubt he was always, in the last analysis, persuaded by the superiority of the Greek λόγος."[58] Thus, it appears that there are definite limits to Plato's Egyptophilia and that his admiration for Egypt is always circumscribed by certain boundaries. As Froidefond well understands, the question of admiration hits against these limits and is useful only up to a point. One is prompted further to inquire into the conditions that allow Plato to express his many comments, admiring or otherwise, about Egypt in his dialogues. And one might also ask after the things that Plato does not even discuss, that are beyond question for him, that he takes for granted, and that are yet at the heart of his radical critique of democracy and political philosophy. These are harder issues than the question of "admiration," which itself depends on, and is limited by, the Hellenic rhetoric of praise and blame,[59] but they may still need to be addressed, to the extent that it is possible to do so, and to the extent that they relate to the subject of this book. What matters, for example, is not just Plato's belief in the superiority of Greek logos, or his acceptance of the opposition as such between Greeks and barbarians, though these issues are clearly important. The difference between Plato's and Isocrates' uses of Egypt suggest that we should also examine the specific appropriations into their works of phenomena that are identified as Egyptian. We need to consider what is at stake in this mobilization of Egypt as a resource in the competing political and philosophical programs of Athenian aristocrats. From what we have seen so far, it appears that Plato's antidemocratic stance, his hostility to figures such as Isocrates, and the writing of his political philosophy all draw on the symbolic capital represented by Egypt.[60] Thus our interests are directed not only to the issue of whether Plato admired Egypt, but also to an analysis of why admiring (and other) uses of Egypt figure in his works and to an explanation of what function they assume in his narratives.

One of the features of Plato's work is how it skirts around any engagement with contemporary Egypt at the same time that it mobilizes representations of Egypt to intervene in domestic disputes and struggles for power. To the extent that Egyptian culture was "admired," it was less for any fea-

---

58. Froidefond 1971, 341.
59. See chapter 5 above.
60. See the basic study of symbolic capital in Bourdieu 1977, 171–83.

tures of contemporary life and society than for its capacity to serve in Greek struggles for power and legitimacy among rivals with different political orientations. It seems incredible to us that the Greeks were able to get away with the claims they made about Egypt in the face of ever increasing knowledge about and contact with the country and especially the Delta. In the middle of the fifth century, for instance, the Athenians dispatched and lost about two hundred ships when they tried to help Egyptians rebel against Persia, and in the beginning of the fourth century, the city entered into an alliance with Akhoris, an Egyptian ruler, and Evagoras, from Cyprus, against Persia. For many Greeks, Egyptian culture was no longer what it used to be because Egypt was now under Persian domination. It may be that Egypt's political and military subjugation by Persia enhanced its appeal for anti-Persian discourses. Perhaps, the Persian rule indicated to Greeks that Egypt itself was unlikely to pose a real threat to Greece and was, therefore, a "safe" culture to appropriate, or even promote, in Greek elite circles. Whether Egypt was invoked because of its potential to collude with anti-Persian sentiment, or because of rivalry among Athenian elites, or even because of a Greek cultural inferiority complex, the country seems to assume a value in Greek texts that has to do less with an appreciation of Egypt as such than with symbolic mobilization to serve other ends. Plato gives this valuation to Egypt repeatedly in his dialogues, and his work encapsulates some of the chief themes associated with Egypt in the Greece of this period: the emphasis on writing and archival records, the antiquity of the country, conservatism in arts and laws, and the caste system. He refers more often to Egypt than to any other non-Greek country and more substantially to it than to any country other than Persia.[61] Given this degree of attention to Egypt, the deployment and manipulation of Egyptian culture in his work, with all its evasions and imaginary constructions, should be seen as part of a deliberate strategy designed to boost the persuasiveness of his own claims.

If the Greek treatment of Egypt is both deceptive and self-serving, Egypt nonetheless has the potential to unsettle thinkers such as Plato—but it is a potential they are keen to suppress. Plato is anxious to insist on the Greek origins of the discipline of philosophy as he defines it, and to subordinate Egypt's antiquity and learning to Greece's in his *Timaeus*. Thus, Plato's philosophy both appropriates Egypt and distances itself from the country in

61. Froidefond 1971, 267. I have not seen O. Neuman, *De locis Aegyptiacis in operibus Platonicis*, Breslau, 1874.

his work. In this respect, the Platonic invention of philosophy through the symbolic and imaginative use of Egypt poses an interesting contrast with the colonial origins of the modern discipline of Egyptology. It is evident beyond doubt that Europe's militarism and colonialism contributed directly to the founding and subsequent institutionalization of the discipline. One need only recall the Rosetta stone and Napoleon's expedition in connection with the development of modern Egyptology. What occurs in the case of Plato is interesting not just because Egypt is, by the hindsight of history, in a precolonial situation with respect to Greek rule, but that he carries out his invention of philosophy through his engagement with an imaginative and Hellenized version of a real contact zone inside Egypt. It is not irrelevant that *Timaeus*, which was so influential in philosophical circles from antiquity to the Renaissance, begins with a lengthy exhibition of Egyptian priests and annals, for it is over and against the archival nature of Egyptian knowledge that Plato's great meditation on the construction of the universe follows. One of the effects of this text, then, is to show that Egyptian "archaeography,"[62] though it contains evidence for such events as Athens' defeat of Atlantis, differs from Platonic thought, which, at its fullest, subsumes historical narrative as part of a much larger, more challenging, and more rigorous philosophical enterprise. But this picture of Egyptian knowledge is very much a Greek construction that is at once partial and tendentious. Thus, to use the distinctions drawn by François Hartog and discussed in the introduction, it is the "Egyptian voyage" of Plato, and not a "voyage in Egypt," that informs the creation of his new and singular discipline.

Since there were those who had undertaken "voyages in Egypt," however, and since the country as an historical and geographical entity could not be dismissed, Plato and other Greek intellectuals also had to learn how to negotiate the undeniable reality of the place. The Greeks' contact with Egypt brought them face to face with a rich historical culture, whose chronological immensity they could only begin to fathom. In comparison with Greek history and with the Greeks' sense of their own history, Egyptian history seemed astonishingly vast, and it was the realization of its vastness that made Herodotus, for instance, reject the Milesian Hecateus' preferment of Greek saga and made Herodotus foreground instead the extent of Egyptian history. It is not surprising, then, that Solon's genealogy in Plato's work recalls the genealogy given to Hecateus by Herodotus, since both the Platonic Solon and the Herodotean Hecateus are working within

62. See Hartog 1996, 66.

a tradition that associates genealogy and Greek antiquity. It was a belief in Greece's antiquity that was completely upset by contacts with Egypt and Near Eastern civilizations, and it was the sizeable histories of these non-Greek nations that Herodotus made a point of stressing. Hegel, for his part, preferred to measure cross-cultural comparisons on a different scale, and he said that the Egyptians, being boys, lacked full self-understanding, which was attained first by the Greeks, and that it was the Greeks who first moved from Nature to Spirit, as he defined these terms. But as I remarked apropos of Hegel above, the great extent of Egyptian history produced an unsettling effect among Greek intellectuals as they came to awareness of it. The self-understanding of which Hegel speaks, then, is better reinterpreted as the acknowledgment of other cultures and other traditions that may be older and no less valid than one's own. Benjamin Jowett, Plato's most famous English translator, joined the dialogue *Timaeus* to another remark made by Hegel in this way: "There is nothing in Plato grander and simpler than the conversation between Solon and the Egyptian priest, in which the youthfulness of Hellas is contrasted with the antiquity of Egypt. Here are to be found the famous words, 'O Solon, Solon, you Hellenes are ever young, and there is not an old man among you'—which may be compared to the lively saying of Hegel, that 'Greek history began with the youth Achilles and left off with the youth Alexander.'"[63] But Hegel also noted, as Jowett does not, that both Achilles and Alexander appeared in contests with non-Greeks, so that Greek history is something that was forged from beginning to end by opposition to the barbarian states of Egypt and Asia. For the Greeks and for Plato, the newness of Greek history was impressed upon them by their contacts with non-Greek civilizations, and it remained a source of wonder and anxiety. Ultimately, Plato shares with Hegel his Eurocentrism and he misses the opportunity presented by the gaze of the old Egyptian priest in Saïs. It is this priest who, in conversation with Solon, assures the lawgiver both that Athens is a thousand years older than Saïs, and that the Greek city once had a polity just like the one described in *Republic*. In this story, then, an old Egyptian looks at the face of Greek wisdom and offers to its bearer the sentiment that Athens really is the birthplace of philosophy, and that if Saïs is the copy, "the originary and the original are in Greece."[64] Thus, Plato's writings on Egypt present both the awareness of a culture much older than Greece and the strategy for its philosophical containment.

63. B. Jowett, *The Dialogues of Plato*, 5 vols., 3d ed. (Oxford, 1892), vol. 3, 435.
64. Hartog 1996, 66.

It is appropriate, lastly, to conclude this part of the book with Plato because he prefigures the conquest of Egypt by Alexander as well as represents the tensions relating to the Hellenizing of the country. Indirectly, he informed the conquest of Egypt through his student Aristotle, who was Alexander's tutor for a period in his youth. And it is also Jowett who reminds us vividly of the uses to which Plato's philosophy could be put, since it is he, after all, who tutored his students in Plato's dialogues and then advised them to go forth and act as guardians of the British Empire, a mission they discharged with great success in such organizations as the Indian Civil Service.[65] This is the same man who once wrote that in Alexandria "the genius of Plato and Greek philosophy reacted upon the East, and a Greek element of thought and language overlaid and partly reduced to order the chaos of Orientalism."[66] Such comments tell us more about Jowett than Plato or Alexander, but they are nonetheless important for the history of the philosopher's reception. As we shall see in the following chapter, Alexander was acutely aware of the Greek traditions concerning Egypt in which Plato's writings, together with other texts discussed above, played a significant and powerful role.

65. See Symonds 1991, with Said 1993, 109.
66. Jowett, 342–43.

7 Alexander's Conquest and the Force of Tradition

Alexandria. At last. Alexandria, Lady of the Dew. Bloom of white
nimbus. Bosom of radiance, wet with sky-water. Core of nostalgia
steeped in honey and tears. . . .
  Alexandria, I am here.

Naguib Mahfouz, Miramar

Would Alexander ever have dreamed of conquering Egypt if it had not
haunted and fascinated the Greeks for years before his invasion?

This book has considered the politics that informed Greek representations of Egypt in the fifth and fourth centuries B.C.E. It ends with the study
of a tangible and material realization of this politics, namely, Alexander's
invasion of 332/1, when the country came under Greek-Macedonian rule
for the first time in its history. Egypt was ruled by Ptolemy and his successors for the next three hundred years, until the death of Cleopatra VII in
30 B.C.E., when Octavian brought the country under Roman rule. It is my
design in this concluding chapter to read Alexander's invasion in the light
of the Greek discourse on Egypt that we have been considering above. The
Greek tradition on Egypt provided the discursive and ideological framework to the Alexandrian conquest; it facilitated the invasion and it influenced the agents who planned and carried out the mission. The association
of politics and literature thus attains a dramatic and sensational actualization in Alexander's imperializing actions.

The power that I am ascribing here to the Greek tradition about Egypt
has its parallels in other moments in Greek and world history. One might
recall that for Greeks in the archaic and early classical periods the myths of
Odysseus and other heroes were implicated in "protocolonial perceptions,
friendly mediating contacts, justification of expansion and annexation, and
failure and decolonization."[1] Or one might point to a figure whom I mentioned in the introduction, al-Biruni, who quotes from a range of sources—

---

1. Malkin 1998, xi. See the caution expressed by Malkin about the use of analogies to explain the archaic and early classical Greek material (16–20).

including, to mention only a few Greeks, Plato, Ptolemy, Proclus, Galen, Porphyry, and the scholia to Dionysius Thrax—in his account of India.[2] When Mahmud of Ghazna was invading India in the early eleventh century C.E., al-Biruni was at the same time crafting his work on the country; his *Ta'rikh al-Hind* was part of the background tradition to invasions of India by later figures. Or one might point, with Anthony Grafton, to the European discovery of the Americas, which was so heavily informed by the Hebrew Bible and by Greek and Roman works, no less influential for being so ancient.[3] It was these ancient texts, as they were understood in the early Renaissance, which helped shape the intellectual frame and worldview of European explorers, navigators, and colonizers, even though the texts made no mention of American regions. Christopher Columbus, from reading Ptolemy, felt that he might sail to the coast of India via western sea routes, and during and after his voyages, he mistakenly insisted that he had reached the country, even when the evidence suggested otherwise. Later, as the encounter between the old world and new wore on, the understanding of Greek and Latin texts and of the world itself went through important changes.

A similar process took place in the Mediterranean world when a whole production of knowledge preceded Alexander's conquest of Egypt. The Greek tradition, in all its variety and multiplicity, opened up a space in which it was possible and acceptable to make certain claims about Egypt and to take certain actions concerning it. The discursive tradition was an enabling and transformative force on the Greek and Macedonian interaction with Egypt. The tradition shaped a specific reality, or series of realities, about Egypt; it influenced the preconceptions and prejudices that the Greeks and Macedonians brought with them to the country and to their dealings with its inhabitants; and it created expectations with lasting consequences for Greeks, Macedonians, and Egyptians. From this perspective, Alexander's invasion of Egypt should be considered as part of the reception-history of the discourse, and his actions can be said to constitute a specific "reading" of the existing tradition. Incidentally, the theoretical framework entailed by this claim of discourse driving empire is also not alien to the ancient world. The theory is explicit in the biography of the Macedonian soldier whose tutor in his youth was none other than Aristotle. It is also evident to a limited extent in a self-professed digression in Polybius, who refers to Alexander (3.57–59); perhaps it is no coincidence that someone who re-

2. Sachau 1992.
3. Grafton 1992.

flected on the phenomenon, namely, Polybius himself, was the first historian to offer a different model of ethnographic writing after the historians
of the Hellenistic era who were influenced by Herodotus.

The continuity in the tradition breaks down somewhat in the time after
Alexander, when new accounts of Egypt were fashioned by such figures as
Hecateus of Abdera and Manetho that overlapped only in part with older
ideas and visions. Epistemological adjustments of this kind are not surprising since the sociopolitical realities had changed, and the newer writers
were working in altered circumstances and in the light of additional knowledge available to them. Alexander himself was heavily responsible for the
reshaping of the older tradition, since his expeditions increased the amount
of empirical and scientific data possessed by Greeks. Still, at least until Polybius, the changes seem to be empirical and annalistic rather than theoretical and methodological: as Oswyn Murray has shown, Herodotus remained
the model for many of the Hellenistic historians long after the death of Alexander.[4] How the existing tradition made an impact on Alexander and his
imperialism nonetheless remains to be examined.

I shall sketch out the case for the claim that this discursive production is
the proper ideological background to the Alexandrian invasion. Other factors not treated here—such as military ambition, the war against Persia,
the desire to travel, and personal greed—are admittedly of consequence,
and I do not wish to minimize them. Alexander also relied on native informers and sources, and not just on the Greek tradition, when he reached
distant places that were not well known to his Greek or Macedonian col-
laborators—but the phenomenon seems to have been more common the
further east he journeyed from Greece. Communications from foreign informers, in any event, would have been filtered through the ideas and preconceptions that were shaped, to a large extent, by the discursive tradition.
The claim that I am making for Egypt can possibly be extended to Alexander's invasions of Persia, India, and other regions east of Greece. Such an
extension of this claim may well be valid, since the Greek traditions on
these regions had a role to play in Alexander's interaction with them. Brian
Bosworth has partly discussed India from this perspective in *Alexander
and the East*.[5] But to extend the argument so widely as to encompass Per-

4. Murray 1972.
5. Bosworth 1996. For a discussion of Alexander and Arabia from this perspective, see Högemann 1985.

sia and India cannot be justified in this book, with its more restricted ethnographic focus, and I shall concentrate on the case of Egypt.

Alexander himself stayed for about six months in Egypt, which he conquered in 332, after he had subjugated the Greek city-states and before his important conquests of Persia and India. Interestingly, he marched into Memphis from West Asia, the site of Egypt's traditional enemies during the years of pharaonic power and imperialism in the Middle and New Kingdoms. But Egypt was now under Persian rule, and the Persian satrap Mazakes, getting no support from Darius III, is reported to have handed over the satrapy to Alexander without a struggle. The Greek sources dwell on two events in connection with Alexander's Egyptian conquest—his consultation of the oracle at Siwah and the founding of Alexandria—although he must have done much else in the six months he remained in the country. He continued the Persian system of administration and delegated real political and military power to his own officers. In May 331, he left Memphis in order to squash a revolt in Samaria and never returned to Egypt.

After his death, however, Alexander's body proved important to the fate of Egypt. At his demise in 323, a contest broke out among his successors over the appropriate burial place. Ptolemy managed to secure the body after a struggle and directed the cortège to Egypt. Some sources say that this was where the king had wished to be buried, in order to be close to the god Ammon, but other writers interpret this wish as a play by Ptolemy.[6] Both the corpse and Egypt were of symbolic importance, so that in the end the body was laid out on display, first in Memphis and then in Alexandria, in a coffin made of gold and crystal, and buried in the mausoleum known as the Sema.[7] Ptolemy exploited the memory of Alexander in many ways, and he went on to secure a place in the country for himself and his dynasty. Alexander's Egyptian burial place symbolized not only his ties to the region, but the dramatic changes in relations between Greeks and foreigners that was brought about by his extensive conquests. Thanks to these conquests, it was possible for a ruler of Greece to be buried and honored in an Egyptian city founded and named by him. The tomb was a memorial both to a fu-

---

6. Diodorus (18.3.5), Curtius (10.5.4), and Justin (12. 15.7) say that Alexander wished to be buried near Ammon. For a discussion of Alexander's hearse and the struggle over his body, see Stewart 1993, 214–25.

7. Diodorus 18.26.3, 28.2–4; Pausanias 1.6.3; Strabo 17.1.8; Aelian, *Historical Miscellany* 12.64; Curtius 4.6.29.

ture of Ptolemaic control and to a period in which earlier notions of ethnicity and otherness were being radically transformed.

GREEKS AND MACEDONIANS

One reason it is appropriate to think about a Greek tradition in connection with Macedonians in the fourth century is that the Hellenization at the royal court is well attested in Alexander's early days.[8] While the differences between Macedonians and Greeks are stressed by some scholars, it is also irrefutable that there were significant continuities between the two cultures, and increasingly so by the time of Alexander's birth, when his father Philip was consolidating Macedonian control over the mainland. Thanks to Philip, there were growing numbers of Greeks in Macedon, some as part of his cosmopolitan court and some as soldiers in his army. It appears from Herodotus that the Hellenization of Macedonians had begun already in the fifth century, since he says that the royal family was Argive and was allowed to take part in the Olympic Games (5.22, 8.137–39). The Macedonian kings traced their Greek ancestry back to Zeus. By Polybius' era, Macedonians were accepted as Greeks (9.37). The Macedonian language, it is true, was unintelligible to Greeks in the fifth and early fourth centuries. The Greeks would also have found the Macedonian monarchy anachronistic, to say the least, since most of Greece consisted of city-states administered by oligarchic or democratic governments. Demosthenes refers to Philip as a barbarian (3.17). But Isocrates, whose politics are different from Demosthenes', accepts the royal family's Greekness, and calls Philip a Greek ruling over barbarians (5.107), an identification that roughly corresponds with Herodotus'. Claims at least as strong as Herodotus' and Isocrates' can be made for the presence of a Greek culture in royal circles in Macedon during the fourth century.

Among the Greeks who were supported or patronized by the Macedonian court in the fifth and fourth centuries were men of letters, such as Euripides, Pindar, Bacchylides, and Hippocrates.[9] The court even invited Socrates to come to Pella after he was tried and sentenced in Athens. Euripides produced his *Archelaus* for King Archelaus in Pella and was also perhaps

---

8. Lane Fox 1973, ch. 3.
9. Euripides, *Archelaus* frs. 228–64 (Nauck); Pindar, frs. 120–21 (Maehler); Bacchylides, fr. 20 B (Snell); *Suda*, s.v., "Hippocrates." Many of the stories told about Alexander are invention and propaganda, and should be handled with caution.

given the title of Companion.[10] It is recorded that Alexander knew all of
Euripides by heart, was able to quote lines of his plays from memory, and
that he asked for plays by Aeschylus, Sophocles, and Euripides, in order to
read them during spare moments in his eastern conquests.[11] He was also a
patron of Lysippus, the sculptor, and Apelles, the painter.[12] According to
one story, Alexander asked Apelles to paint his mistress Campaspe in the
nude. Apelles did the painting, and then fell in love with his model, and so
in return from his patron, he received the gift of Alexander's first mistress,
Campaspe herself.

Let us turn from the evidence for a court versed in Greek art and letters
to the issue of Alexander in Egypt. Did Alexander and his generals really
read and consider the Greek authors who wrote about Egypt? I just brought
up Alexander's reputed reading of the three tragedians, and his ability to
quote from at least one of them. It is not known whether he read Aeschylus' *Suppliants*, Euripides' *Helen*, or any of the lost plays involving Egypt,
and what impact, if any, these plays had on him or his soldiers and plan-
ners. But there are three other authors, Homer, Herodotus, and Aristotle,
who need to be considered in this discussion and to whom we can refer at
somewhat greater length. The evidence that Alexander or members of his
expedition read their works is, if occasionally circumstantial, at least plausible. In the case of these three, and above all in the case of Aristotle, the
general link to Alexander is well documented. For the purpose of this discussion, it will be helpful to relate these writers and their works specifically
to the Alexandrian invasion of Egypt.

HOMER AND ALEXANDER

He was also by nature a lover of learning and a lover of reading.
And since he thought and called the *Iliad* a journey-book of the
military art, he took with him Aristotle's recension of the poem,
called the *Iliad of the Casket*, and always kept it lying with his
dagger under his pillow, as Onesicritus (*FGrHist* 134 F 38) reminds
us; and when he could find no other books in the interior of Asia,
he ordered Harpalos to send him some.

Plutarch, *Alexander* 8

10. See the testimonia in Harder 1985, 145–47.
11. Plutarch, *Alexander* 8; Athenaeus 537d = Nicobule, *FGrHist* 127 F 2.
12. Lysippus: Arrian, *Anabasis* 1.16.4; for Apelles and the following story,
see Pliny, *Natural History* 35.86; Lucian, *Imagines* 7; Aelian, *Historical Miscellany* 12.34.

From Homer, Alexander, like any careful reader, would come away with an exaggerated sense of Egyptian wealth, which was surely a topic to catch the eye of a prospective conqueror. The *Iliad* associates Egypt with great treasures, while the *Odyssey* contains stories of Greeks receiving valuable gifts from Egyptians, or trying to plunder the country for its riches. In either poem, Egypt's material affluence is undeniable.[13] The import of such passages would not have been lost on Alexander and his soldiers, who seldom refrained from helping themselves to the spoils of war, and Alexander's concern with the funds in his treasury is noticeable in the standard accounts of his campaigns.

Alexander read Homer and professed a love for the two epic poems, especially the *Iliad*.[14] He believed that he was descended from Achilles on his mother's side, as also from Heracles and Perseus, and seemed to want to emulate Achilles and the other heroes in their accomplishments. The mixture of admiration and rivalry that Alexander felt in connection with Achilles in particular is known from his historians. Alexander appears to have made a detour, from the point of view of military strategy, to Troy. At Troy, he is related as having crowned the tomb of Achilles, while Hephaistion placed a wreath on Patroclus' tomb: "and Alexander, so the story goes, blessed Achilles for having Homer to proclaim his fame to posterity" (Arrian, *Anabasis* 1.12.1). Moreover, like the Greeks at Troy, Alexander believed he was involved in a panhellenic expedition against the Asian enemy; the Persian Wars in the fifth century had been portrayed in a similar fashion by Herodotus (1.1–5). And, soon after crossing into Asia, Alexander had sacrificed at the tomb of Protesilaos, the first of the Greeks to disembark in Asia at the start of the Trojan War and the first Greek casualty there; he wanted, Arrian notes, his own arrival on Asian soil to be more auspicious than that of Protesilaos (*Anabasis* 1.11.5).

Given Alexander's intense identification with Homer and his hero, it is not a wanton assumption that he was familiar with Achilles' speeches

13. For Homer and Egypt, see Froidefond 1971, 15–68.

14. For Alexander and Homer, see Lane Fox 1973, ch. 3, and Brunt 1976–83, appendix 4. For Alexander as a new Achilles, see Stewart 1993, 78–86. Strictly speaking, Homer and the archaic period lie outside the scope of this book. But, for the argument made in this chapter, the continuities between the Homeric poems and the later texts that I am considering are strong, and accordingly I refer, if briefly, to the *Iliad* and *Odyssey* in this discussion. At the least, Plutarch, in the passage quoted, neatly connects Homer to Aristotle, an author who does fall inside the chronological frame of this book, and gives some support to the political interpretation I am attempting here. For the recension of the Casket, see also Strabo 13.1.27 = Callisthenes, *FGrHist* 124 T 10.

in the *Iliad*, especially in the longer speeches that unfold in crucial and famous points in the poem. In book 9, Achilles refuses to accept Agamemnon's gifts and rejoin the war, and insists that he will continue to refuse Agamemnon's offer "even if he offered me ten times or twenty times all he possesses now, and others' wealth besides, not even all the wealth that pours into Orchomenus, or Thebes in Egypt, where the houses are piled high with treasure, and the city has a hundred gates, and through each gate two hundred men drive out with horses and chariots."[15] The effect of this Homeric reference to Egyptian wealth is magnified by the mention of large gifts in context and, as noted below, also by Aristotle's reference to it.

Egypt's prosperity in the *Iliad* is complemented by the riches that are also mentioned in the *Odyssey*. The country has citizens who make gifts of finely crafted wares to Menelaus and Helen; its earth is very fertile farmland, and it is said to yield a wealth of drugs (4.123–32, 227–32). In two passages that are roughly similar, the disguised Odysseus seems to fabricate an account of a voyage to Egypt in which his crew plunders the country; the crew members are then killed or enslaved, but Odysseus is spared; he lives among the Egyptians, and before he moves on, he says "[I] gathered much wealth among the men of Egypt, because they all made me gifts."[16] The overwhelming impression in this passage and others in Homer, is of a country teeming with riches available for possession, either through plunder or the generosity of the natives. In this regard, let us note that only one of Alexander's dreams is recorded, but it is entirely becoming that he be the person to have dreamt it. When Alexander was in Egypt, he dreamt that an old man who resembled Homer appeared to him, and the old man recited lines from the *Odyssey* so as to suggest to him where to lay the foundations for the new city of Alexandria.[17] "Even in his dreams," writes Robin Lane Fox, "Alexander was later believed to be living out the poems he loved. . . ."[18] That view may be correct; but one might say in addition that the poems he loved must have influenced his conscious perceptions of the world and of the rewards that the world held out to its heroes.

15. See *Iliad* 9.379–87; since *Iliad* 9.382 is the same as *Odyssey* 4.127 ("in Egypt, where the houses are piled high with treasure"), editors sometimes suggest that the line from the *Iliad* is an interpolation from the *Odyssey*, where it seems to fit the context more intricately.

16. *Odyssey* 14.285–86. See 14.245–86; 17.424–44.

17. Plutarch, *Alexander* 26.3–7; the lines are *Odyssey* 4.354–55: "Now there is an island in the surging sea in front of Egypt, and men call it Pharos. . . ."

18. Lane Fox 1973, 66.

HERODOTUS AND ALEXANDER

Herodotus exerted an influence on Alexander and his friends that affected their view of the world as well as their conquest of large parts of it.[19] His relevance to Alexander is easy to see: he wrote about the Persian Wars, which the Macedonian felt he was re-enacting at some deep level; he described the Persian satrapies, including Egypt, that Alexander also conquered; he provided ethnographic and geographical information that was useful to military strategists and campaigners; and in many ways he offered a theoretical frame for experiencing and connecting with the Eastern world and its peoples. Glen W. Bowersock notes that some of Alexander's "most important symbolic gestures point directly to Herodotean prototypes": they include the pouring of libations into the sea at the Hellespont, the inspection of the royal horses in the Nesaean plain, and the receiving of "Amazon" women from a satrap in Media.[20] Moreover, the high-ranked men who campaigned with Alexander, such as Ptolemy, Nearchus, and Callisthenes, had read Herodotus, and drew on his work for their ethnographic descriptions.[21] A frequently used model is the Egyptian account in book 2; this account is used not only to describe Egypt, but also other places such as India, which the Alexandrian campaign reached after subjugating Egypt and Persia.

I have already discussed Herodotus' Egyptian writings in chapters 2 and 3 above, and shall not repeat those analyses here. I will say that Herodotus, like Homer and Aristotle, gave Alexander the overall impression of a historical, and historically rich, civilization, and an important country in the cultural system formed by Europe, Asia, and Africa. He had incorporated the Persian conquest of Egypt into his narrative of the Persian Wars, as part of his account of Persia's rise and subsequent humiliation by Greeks. Alexander, though Macedonian, reinflicted a defeat on the Persians, and he determined to strip the Persian empire of its satrapies, and situate these within his own, new empire. Egypt had to be part of it, especially when a writer such as Herodotus had underscored the central position of the country in the world empire of the Persians.

19. The influence of Herodotus on Alexander and the Alexander historians is discussed, briefly, in Murray 1972; Hartog 1988, 357–59; and Bowersock 1989.

20. Bowersock 1989, 410.

21. Ptolemy, *FGrHist* 138 F 2; Nearchus, *FGrHist* 133 F 8, 17, 18, 20; Callisthenes, *FGrHist* 124 F 38; and see my discussion below. These and other lost historians of Alexander are discussed in Pearson 1960 and Pédech 1984; the fragments are collected in *FGrHist* nos. 117–53.

Alexander quotes from Herodotus' work at least twice, in ways that reveal awareness of context.[22] He could have had contact with Herodotus' works at an early age, perhaps, though not necessarily, through some such intermediary as Theopompus. Theopompus had visited Philip's court in Macedon and worked there, and he was later restored to his homeland of Chios by Alexander's intervention. Among his writings is an *Epitome of Herodotus*, in two books.[23] Theopmpus was known to fill his writings with Herodotean digressions, but the charge would not have fazed him, since he said that "he would write stories in his histories more marvellous than Herodotus and Ctesias and Hellanicus and all those who write on India."[24] Given the importance of Herodotus' work in Greece, and given the king's reputation as a lover of learning, however, it is even likely that Alexander read the whole work, in detail rather than in an epitome.

Nearchus and the Rivers

The Níl al-Mubárak itself—the Blessed Nile,—as notably fails too
at this season to arouse enthusiasm. . . . To me there was double
dulness in the scenery: it seemed to be Sind over again—the same
morning mist and noon-tide glare; the same hot wind and heat
clouds, and fiery sunset, and evening glow; the same pillars of dust
and "devils" of sand sweeping like giants over the plain; the same
turbid waters of a broad, shallow stream studded with sand-banks
and silt-isles, with crashing earth slips and ruins nodding over a
kind of cliff, whose base the stream gnaws with noisy tooth. . . .
The boats, with their sharp bows, preposterous sterns, and lateen
sails, might have belonged to the Indus. So might the chocolate-
skinned, blue-robed peasantry. . . .

> Richard F. Burton, *Personal Narrative of a*
> *Pilgrimage to al-Madinah and Meccah*

The person and work of Nearchus offer a remarkable confluence of the divergent streams we are considering here.[25] Nearchus was reputedly one of the boyhood friends of Alexander, as well as his admiral and fellow

---

22. See Plutarch, *Alexander* 21.10 and 34.3, with Herodotus 5.18 and 8.47 respectively.

23. For the *Epitome of Herodotus*, see Theopompus, *FGrHist* 115 F 1–4. The recipient or patron of this work is not recorded, but he can have been Philip or Alexander, given their dealings with Theopompus: see Theopompus, *FGrHist* 115 T 8, 31 and F 250–56.

24. Theopompus, *FGrHist* 115 F 381.

25. For an historical assessment of Nearchus' voyages, see Brunt 1976–83, vol. 2, 518–25.

campaigner.[26] His historical account of Alexander survives only through quotations, largely in Arrian and Strabo. It is said that he read a preliminary version of this history to Alexander a few days before the king's death in Babylon—hence, the surviving fragments may be from a work written while Alexander was alive and not necessarily from a work revised later.[27] Nearchus' history is one of the main sources for Arrian's *Indica*, which is written in Ionic. If Nearchus' book was also in Ionic, as historians believe, the choice of dialect may well have to do with emulation of Herodotus, since he was from Crete and since literary Ionic was not practised in his day.

In his book on the lost histories of Alexander, Lionel Pearson showed how the fragments of Nearchus reveal the pervasive influence of Herodotus in form and conception.[28] Pearson's work enumerates in such great detail the linguistic and thematic parallels between Nearchus' history and Herodotus' that it would be impracticable to list them all here. But I would like to consider the correspondences between book 2 and Nearchus' work, insofar as these will help establish the influence of Herodotus' Egyptian account on a person intimately involved in the planning and execution of Alexander's campaigns. Several of the fragments of Nearchus' work come from his lost description of India. What is noticeable about these fragments is how deeply they seem to respond to Herodotus' remarks about Egypt, and how clearly they indicate that Nearchus used Herodotus' Egyptian account as his model for writing about India, even though he himself made the journey to India as a member of Alexander's campaign.[29] What is striking in the fragments is the recourse to Egypt and the Nile as a touchstone for the analysis of India and Indian rivers. Again and again, in Nearchus as well as in other accounts of Alexander by fellow campaigners, the Nile reappears as the point of comparison for the behavior of Indian rivers. These writers see the world through Herodotean eyes, the concepts that they use are Herodotean concepts—and the part of Herodotus to which they often defer for their inquiries is the work on Egypt.

In one example, Nearchus' discussion of the formation of the alluvial plain of the Indus draws on parallels and logic that show the influence of

26. For a biography, with bibliography, see Heckel 1992, 228–33.

27. See Plutarch, *Alexander* 76.3, and Hamilton 1969, 211; cf. Arrian, *Anabasis* 7.25.4.

28. Pearson 1960.

29. No evidence points to Nearchus' presence in Egypt with Alexander. He was appointed satrap of Lycia and Pamphylia by Alexander in 334/3, and remained in office until 330 (Arrian, *Anabasis* 3.6.6, with 1.24.3–4; but cf. Justin 13.4.15); Alexander was in Egypt in 332/1. See Heckel 1992, 228–29.

Herodotus. According to Nearchus, just as Egypt is the gift of the Nile, and just as the Nile is responsible for the formation of the Deltaic plain, so India is the gift of the Indus and the Indian plain is created by the silting up of its river.[30] The details are significant: like Herodotus, Nearchus refers to Egypt as the gift of the Nile, he also speaks of the silting up of rivers, he also brings in the rivers of Asia Minor for comparison, and he also says that these rivers of Asia Minor are small in contrast to a much larger river (Indus / Nile).[31] It should be noted, further, that Nearchus' account is preserved by both Strabo and Arrian, and that the linguistic parallels between Nearchus and Herodotus are especially revealing in the excerpt in Arrian, since Arrian wrote his *Anabasis* in an Atticizing style, not in Ionic, and the Herodotean phrases are more likely to have come from Nearchus than to have been his own invention.[32] If the language is Nearchus', he is expressing a literary kinship with his ethnographer predecessor, Herodotus.[33]

A second example from Nearchus draws on Herodotus' famous consideration of the Nile's behavior, high in summer, low in winter. Before giving his own view, Herodotus had supplied three explanations that he had

30. Strabo 15.1.16 = Nearchus, *FGrHist* 133 F 17; and Arrian, *Anabasis* 5.6.5–8. As Pearson indicates, Nearchus' reliance on Herodotus is evident in the train of thought, which follows passages in book 2.

31. Herodotus 2.5, 2.10.

32. Arrian, *Anabasis* 5.6.5–8: "For that Aegyptus was the old name of the river which the Egyptians and men outside Egypt now call the Nile, Homer is ample evidence, when he says that Menelaus stationed his ships at the mouth of the river Aegyptus. If, then, these quite small rivers (and a single river in each instance) were able to make a large area of land by silting up on their way down to the sea, whenever they brought down slime and mud from the uplands where their sources were, there is no reason to doubt what is said concerning the land of the Indians—that most of it is plain and that it has this plain thanks to the soil deposited by the river. After all (as they point out) the Hermus, the Cayster, the Caicus, and the Maeander or any other rivers of Asia that empty into this inner sea, even if all put together, cannot compare with a single one of the Indian rivers for volume of water; not to mention the Ganges, the greatest of all, with which neither the waters of the Nile in Egypt nor the Ister in Europe can be compared; those rivers all put together certainly would not equal the Indus, which is a large river right from its source, receives the waters of fifteen tributaries (all greater than the rivers of Asia), prevails over them with its name, and so reaches the sea."

33. As the fragments indicate, Nearchus is also appealing to Homer's authority in claiming that the river was referred to by the name Aegyptus: the reference is *Odyssey* 4.581 (ἂψ δ᾽ εἰς Αἰγύπτοιο διιπετέος ποταμοῖο), which was also used by Eudoxus of Cnidus and Aristotle (scholia to *Odyssey* 4.477 = Eudoxus F 287) to argue that summer rainfall caused the Nile's annual inundation—see the section on the search for the Nile's sources in this chapter below. Unlike Eudoxus and Aristotle, Nearchus is using the Homeric line to argue that alluvial silt caused the formation of the Indus plain. For Eudoxus' fragments about Egypt, see the appendix.

heard and found unsatisfactory: the etesian winds cause the Nile's flooding; the Nile flows out of the river Ocean, which flows around the world; or the Nile comes from melting snow. Nearchus in turn addresses the behavior of the Indian rivers, and manages to introduce all three of Herodotus' reported explanations for the Nile's behavior.[34] It seems that Nearchus is picking up the old controversy from Herodotus' Egyptian writings and trying to come up with an explanation based on his observations in India. According to him, the summer rains are responsible for the flooding of the rivers in India, and therefore summer rains are also the cause of the Nile's flooding. It may be the case that Nearchus actually saw the monsoon rains and gave an accurate account of them, but it is clear that his point of reference is the Nile. There is, also, some circularity here: Nearchus uses Herodotus' description of the Nile's behavior as an ethnographic model to describe the nature of the Indian rivers; he then uses the behavior of the Indian rivers to devise a solution to a problem in the Herodotean model, and transfers the solution back to the Egyptian phenomenon at the center of the original model.

Despite the difficulties posed by Nearchus' scheme, the interplay with Herodotus' Egyptian account in his writings is indisputable. His references to floating islands and crocodiles in Indian rivers find parallels in Herodotus. Nearchus' "Egyptian bean" is intelligible in the light of a reference to the Egyptian sacred lotus by Herodotus (2.92), after which the expression was customarily used by Greek writers for the seeds of the plant.[35] A description of tigers recalls Herodotus' words about the phoenix in Egypt.[36] Nearchus also discusses the famous large ants that Herodotus locates in India. Nearchus says that he did not see these creatures himself, but saw their skins brought into the Macedonian camp, and that they were like leopard skins. It is significant that he does not choose to dispute Herodotus' story of the gold-digging ants, but rather chooses to accommodate what he sees in India to what he has read: he shapes his experience to fit the cognitive framework that he has acquired from Herodotus.[37]

---

34. See Strabo 15.1.18 = Nearchus, *FGrHist* 133 F 18; and Strabo 15.1.25 = Nearchus, *FGrHist* 133 F 20; and see also Arrian, *Indica* 6.5–8, which complements the fragments in Strabo.

35. Theophrastus, *Inquiry into Plants* 4.8.8. See Lloyd 1976, 372–75, and Bosworth 1996, 70–71.

36. Arrian, *Indica* 15.1–3 = *FGrHist* 133 F 7; Herodotus 2.73; cf. Megasthenes' impression of the Indian tiger, Strabo 15.1.37 = *FGrHist* 715 F 21a.

37. Arrian, *Indica* 15.4, Strabo 15.1.44 = *FGrHist* 133 F 8; Herodotus 3.102. See also Megasthenes' report on the ants, Arrian, *Indica* 15.5–7, Strabo 15.1.44 =

Moreover, Nearchus is not the only member of Alexander's expedition to demonstrate the influence of Herodotus. The cumulative evidence suggests that Herodotus' history, and in particular the account of Egypt, made an impact on the campaign. If the campaigners were looking at India and its rivers through eyes accustomed to Herodotus' account of Egypt, it must follow that these same campaigners were familiar with his account during their earlier invasion of Egypt. The heavier attention to India than to Egypt in the histories of Alexander may be due to two reasons: Egypt was a less exotic country to Greeks by the end of the fourth century, while India was still the land of the fabulous and the unknown; and the campaign spent more time in the eastern satrapies and in India than in Egypt. Again, it is possible that some of Alexander's marshalls read Herodotus only after they returned from the campaign and when they started writing down their accounts; it is also possible that some Herodotean elements are due to later authorities such as Arrian and Strabo, and not to the records of Alexander's contemporaries. But the preponderance of data that establishes Herodotus' influence is significant and comes from a spectrum of professionals; it cannot be easily dismissed. Callisthenes of Olynthus, the historian, speculates about the cause of the Nile's behavior; he may have been part of the team that went to discover the river's source (as I will discuss later). Onesicritus of Astypalaea, a pilot and philosopher, entertains comparisons between the Indian rivers and the Nile, and tells of an Indian island, called Delta, which is equal in size to the Egyptian Delta. Aristobulus of Cassandreia, an engineer and architect, compares the Indian rivers to the Nile; he may have also compared the Euphrates to the Nile.[38] In the writings of these men and others who accompanied Alexander on his conquests, the presence of Herodotus' most famous ethnographic chapter is undeniable.

ARISTOTLE AND ALEXANDER

Yes, the equipment that he had from Aristotle, his teacher, when he crossed over into Asia, was more than what he had from his father, Philip.

Plutarch, *On the Fortune of Alexander* 327E

FGrHist 715 F 23; Megasthenes' account has Herodotean overtones. On these passages in Nearchus and Megasthenes, see Pearson 1960, 124–25; Murray 1972, 206; and Bosworth 1996, 83–84.

38. Callisthenes, *FGrHist* 124 F 12; Onesicritus, *FGrHist* 134 F 7, 22, 26; Aristobulus, *FGrHist* 139 F 35, 38, 39, 56.

The relationship between Aristotle and Alexander[39] exemplifies the general argument that I making in this chapter, concerning the coalescence of knowledge and power. Much of the evidence for the relationship is circumstantial and of dubious value, however, so we are unable to form a wholly reliable judgment about the influence of Aristotle on Alexander. It is clear that the philosopher served as the young Alexander's tutor, but the precise impact this education had on Alexander is difficult to ascertain. Aristotle's remarks on Egypt are mostly derivative, gleaned from earlier writers and travelers. On the other hand, it can be said that Aristotle makes prejudicial comments against barbarians in his writings, and was restrained by his own biases from using Egypt and Egyptian material as a point of departure for his philosophical, scientific, or theoretical work. The exception to this attitude are his comments on the Nile, to which I shall return below in connection with Alexander's search for the river's sources.

The biographical details, which are widely recorded, indicate an intimate relationship between Aristotle and Alexander's family.[40] Philip invited Aristotle in 343 to serve as tutor for the thirteen-year-old Alexander in Mieza. There were several Greeks who wanted the post and actively sought it, including Theopompus, the historian, but it was Aristotle who received the appointment, and who stayed for about a year.[41] Personal connections might have helped him get the job, for his father, Nicomachus, was a physician to an earlier king of Macedonia, Philip's father, Amyntas III.[42] And Philip had maintained contact with Plato's other students. Aristotle also taught the prince's friends, such as Nearchus, and was able to get a position for his relative Callisthenes on Alexander's expedition.[43] In his surviving works he does not directly mention Alexander or his stay in Macedonia, but there are passing references to such events as Philip's assassination; later authors have him dispensing advice to Alexander in letters.[44] In his will Aristotle appointed as his executor Antipater, who had

39. On this subject, see in general Ehrenberg 1938, 62–102; Jaeger 1948, 105–23; Hamilton 1969, 16–20.

40. The ancient evidence concerning Aristotle's relationship with Philip and Alexander is assembled and discussed in Düring 1957, 284–99.

41. This is the implication of Theopompus' panegyric of Philip: *FGrHist* 115 F 255–56.

42. Diogenes Laertius 5.1.

43. Diogenes Laertius 5.5.

44. Plutarch, *Alexander* 7.6–9.

been Alexander's representative in Macedonia while he was away on his conquests.[45]

Aristotle wrote pamphlets for Alexander that are lost, but the surviving titles are revealing: for example, *In Praise of Colonies* and *On Kingship,* and perhaps *The Glories of Riches.*[46] Later Alexander may have served as patron to his philosophical and scientific investigations. According to one report of doubtful authenticity, "Alexander the Great was so inflamed by a desire to know the natures of animals that he asked for several thousand men throughout the whole of Greece and Asia to be at the learned Aristotle's disposal—everyone who lived by hunting or falconry or fishing, or who looked after parks, herds, apiaries, fishponds, or aviaries—so that no living creature should escape his notice."[47] The story is probably fictitious, but it again illustrates the collusion between knowledge and imperialism that characterized Alexander's campaigns. Aristotle *had* speculated on the Nile, like many other Greek writers, and later may have been a beneficiary of an Alexandrian expedition to the Nile, as we shall see below.

It may be reckless to believe that Alexander was familiar with his teacher's works written before and after his tutelage. They are so varied and so many, and Alexander was young at the time of his schooling with Aristotle. But if Alexander did absorb Aristotle's thoughts, he would not have found in them much that was considerate of barbarians as a category. There is the infamous doctrine of natural slavery, according to which Greeks were "naturally" free and barbarians "naturally" servile.[48] The idea comes from his *Politics,* a work written after Aristotle left Macedonia, but it is not distant from the advice he once gave Alexander, as Plutarch alleged, to "deal with Greeks in the manner of a leader, with foreigners in that of a master, caring for the former as friends and relatives, treating the latter as animals or plants."[49] Whether Alexander followed this suggestion in his dealings with non-Greeks is a matter of considerable speculation and debate.

On the other hand, Aristotle does not always denigrate Egypt and the

45. The will is preserved in Diogenes Laertius 5.11–16, and in two Arabic texts, Ibn an-Nadim's *Kitab al-Fihrist* and Ibn Abi Usaibia's *Tabaqat al-atibba'.* For the Arabic works, see Düring 1957, 193–96, 213–46.
46. Hamilton 1969, 18–19. Diogenes Laertius gives a lengthy catalogue of Aristotle's works (5.22–27). Usaibia supplies the contents of another catalogue made by a Neoplatonist Ptolemy of Aristotle's writings: Düring 1957, 221–31.
47. Pliny, *Natural History* 8.16.44.
48. *Politics* 1253b–1255b30; see Cartledge 1993, 120–28, and Rosivach 1999.
49. Plutarch, *On the Fortune of Alexander* 329B.

Egyptians in his writings, but offers more varied views.[50] In this regard, Aristotle's work is interesting for a history of the Greek reception of Egypt because it thematizes exactly the features that we have been considering. He adds little that is new to the Greeks' statements about Egypt, apart from his contribution to the Nile controversy, and much of what he says about Egypt can be found in earlier authors, or is an elaboration of their remarks. Like other Greeks, he reminds his readers of the great antiquity of Egyptian civilization, and calls Egyptians the most ancient of men, and Sesostris the earliest of legislators.[51] He claims that Egypt at all times has had its laws and political systems, and attributes the invention of the caste system to Sesostris,[52] who is one of several Egyptian rulers mentioned by Aristotle. Given his political philosophy, and his observation that the old laws were simple and barbarous,[53] Aristotle must have disapproved of tyranny, but he does devote part of his *Politics* to a consideration of a subject which held some fascination for him: in this context, he mentions the Egyptian pyramids as examples of projects that allowed rulers to keep their subjects perpetually at work and in poverty.[54] Egypt was the birthplace of mathematics because of the leisure time of the priests, he notes, and he both credits Egyptians (and Babylonians) with the invention of astronomy and expresses admiration for their astronomical observations.[55] For him, the Egyptian priests are the first examples of the contemplative life. Despite, or because of, the faithfulness with which he reinscribed these now canonical features of the Greek discourse on Egypt, Aristotle was, as Christian Froidefond remarks, ultimately unable to draw important consequences for his own philosophical or political plans from Egypt or its priestly tradition.[56] With his views about foreigners and slaves, how could he?

From his scattered remarks about Egypt, we can say that Aristotle held to the broad picture of an ancient civilization, with its tyrannical pha-

---

50. For Aristotle's treatment of Egypt, see Froidefond 1971, 343–53.
51. See *Meteorology* 352b20 ff., quoted in ch. 1, and the next note.
52. *Politics* 1329a40 ff.
53. *Politics* 1268b31 ff.
54. *Politics* 1313b16 ff.; cf. Herodotus 2.124. Like Herodotus, Aristotle also remarks on the effects of climate, and he situates Greeks midway between Europeans, who are full of spirit, but lacking in skill and intellect, and Asiatics, who have intellect and skill, but lack spirit and therefore remain enslaved and subject. The Greeks, he writes, are spirited, intelligent, free, live under the best constitution, and, given one constitution, are capable of ruling over all other peoples (*Politics* 1327b18 ff.).
55. *Metaphysics* 981b; *On Heaven* 292a; *Meteorology* 343b; cf. Seneca, *Natural Questions* 7.3, who questions Egyptian skill at detecting comets.
56. Froidefond 1971, 353.

raohs, monumental structures, and priestly culture. This set of ideas may have impressed upon Alexander, if he imbibed any of it, the historical appeal of the country he invaded. In many respects, he had a mind more curious and inquisitive about the non-Greek world than did his teacher, and he used it skillfully while he was realizing his favorite themes of conquest and empire.[57]

THE CONQUEST OF EGYPT

Alexander conquered Egypt in November 332. If the conquest of Egypt was simple enough for so skilled an imperialist as Alexander, it needs to be asked why he came to Egypt at all. Alexander could have pursued Darius III east to Babylon, after he inflicted an humiliating defeat on the Persian army in Issus, but he chose not to follow the Persians and made a long and time-consuming journey to the south. "Why, instead," asks Peter Green, "did he march over three hundred miles out of his way down the coast of the Mediterranean, spend seven months besieging Tyre and a long winter in and around the Nile Valley, and not resume his career of conquest until late April of 331?"[58] In truth, Alexander was surely making conquests as he traveled down the Mediterranean coast and into Egypt, but it is nonetheless pertinent to ask why he came to Egypt in the first place when his quarry, the Persian king, had fled to the east. Green suggests that Alexander, being concerned with Persian naval operations in the eastern Mediterranean, wanted to secure the ports and sea routes against Persian attack, and hence to seize Phoenicia and Egypt from the Persians. It may well be that Alexander was worried about naval operations in the eastern Mediterranean when he chose not to pursue Darius after Issus. Equally, the answer must lie in the fascination exerted on him by the country, a fascination that was sparked and stimulated by the Greek writers and writings that we have been considering. Alexander wanted to get to Egypt at any cost, and to capture for himself the ancient land of the Nile. Although Egypt's strategic importance to military operations was incontrovertible, its hold on Alexander's mind and imagination was also irresistible. As much as military

57. The themes of this chapter converge strikingly in a later Islamic tradition, according to which Aristotle built two pyramids (usually ascribed to Cheops and Chephren) in Egypt as tombs for Alexander and for himself: Haarmann 1996, 609–10. No less striking is the story behind the Arabic "sayings of the philosophers," that is, the laments offered by famous Greek philosophers, including Aristotle and Plato, over Alexander's coffin: Rosenthal 1975, 120–24.

58. Green 1996, 6.

strategy, everything that he had heard and seen about Egypt made it too enticing for him to ignore.

Unlike Napoleon, whose invasion of Egypt was bloody and vicious, Alexander conquered the country with a minimum of resistance. The relative ease may have to do with the fact that the country was under Persian occupation prior to the invasion. "The rapid conquest of Alexander," Edward Gibbon wrote, "was assisted by the superstition and revolt of the natives; they abhorred their Persian oppressors, the disciples of the Magi, who had burnt the temples of Egypt, and feasted with sacrilegious appetite on the flesh of the God Apis."[59] Gibbon's remark is an exaggeration, but after the end of the first occupation in 404, the Persians had tried repeatedly to regain control of Egypt, and it was not until Artaxerxes III Ochus defeated Nectanebo II in 343 that they were successful.[60] Even after Artaxerxes' victory and Nectanebo's defeat, the Persians were not able entirely to prevent native uprisings, so that Darius had to squash a revolt led by Khabash just three years before Alexander's arrival. Given these years of Persian domination and native unrest, Greek sources are possibly right to say that the Egyptians welcomed Alexander as a liberator, although some scholars have doubted the truth of this claim.[61] At any rate, the Persian satrap, Mazakes, could get no help from Darius on this occasion, since Alexander had dealt the Persian army a crushing defeat at the battle of Issus, in September 333, and put the Great King to flight. Accordingly, the satrap surrendered his powers to Alexander without a struggle at the frontier fort of Pelousion, and Alexander marched on to seize Memphis and the eight hundred talents contained in its treasury. When he reached Memphis, Alexander held athletic and musical games in the Greek style.[62]

In Memphis, Alexander secured his position as ruler of Egypt by showing respect to the local gods and temples and to priestly traditions.[63] He made public sacrifices to the Apis bull, for example, which was part of the most prominent cult of the Saqqara necropolis in the city of Memphis.[64]

---

59. Edward Gibbon, *The History of the Decline and Fall of the Roman Empire*, ch. 51. For Greek distortions of the Persian treatment of Apis, see the introduction.
60. Olmstead 1948, 437–40; Kienitz 1953, 102 ff.; Ray 1987.
61. Diodorus 17.49.1–2; Curtius 4.7.1; cf. Burstein 1995, ch. 4, reprinted from *Achaemenid History* 8 (1994), who casts doubt on the Greek sources.
62. Arrian, *Anabasis* 3.1.4.
63. As Plato (*Politicus* 290d) wrote earlier for a Greek audience, "In Egypt, it is not possible for a king to rule without the art of the priests; if he has forced his way to power from another class, then he must be enlisted into the priestly class before he can rule."
64. For Memphis and Apis, see Thompson 1988, 190–211.

His care with Apis is reflected further in his instructions found on a papyrus from Saqqara concerning the protection of the sanctity of temple precincts.[65] Memphis was the home of shrines to Apis and the closely associated god Ptah, and the Memphite temples enjoyed substantial holdings of agricultural land. Cambyses had specifically exempted the Ptah temple of Memphis from financial constraints imposed on other temples, a reflection of the temple's importance. Of the many cults that proliferated in the Late Period in Memphis, the most important was that of Apis, and of the many shrines in North Saqqara, the largest was the House of Osiris-Apis. Therefore, Alexander was making a gesture of symbolic importance to his Egyptian subjects by showing his interest in the bull.

His treatment of the sacred Apis bull was also guided by the Greeks' exaggeration of Persian blasphemy in Egypt. Certainly, from the perspective of Greek stories about the Persians and Apis, it is no surprise that Alexander was careful in paying his respects to Egyptian deities during his conquest. According to Greek writers such as Herodotus, the Persians had acquired a reputation for sacrilege in Egypt, especially in connection with the Apis bull (3.27–29). Cambyses and Artaxerxes were said to have slaughtered the Apis bull, and Artaxerxes actually to have roasted and eaten the flesh.[66] Herodotus adds, "It was directly as a result of this, say the Egyptians—this deed of wrong—that Cambyses went mad, though indeed he was not in true possession of his wits previously" (3.30). Alexander's sacrifices "to other gods and especially to Apis,"[67] in Memphis, indicate that he was aware of the Persian reputation for sacrilege, perhaps even from Herodotus. At the same time, these efforts show the importance he placed on making widely known his status as the king of Egypt.

Both the seriousness with which he took his sovereignty over Egypt and the Egyptian priests' acquiescence to his rule are also apparent in Alexander's restorations of sanctuaries in the temple of Thothmes III at Karnak, and Amenhopis III at Luxor.[68] The restorative work undertaken by the priests, who were in charge of the temples, assumes greater significance in the light of their refusal to honor the Persians with titles similar to those bestowed on Alexander. The work at Luxor, dated to the early 320s, especially stands out for the detail on the Shrine of the Bark in a temple dedi-

---

65. Turner 1974.
66. Plutarch, *Moralia* 363C, 355C; Aelian, *Animal Peculiarities* 10.28; see Thompson 1988, 106.
67. Arrian, *Anabasis* 3.1.
68. See the discussion in Stewart 1993, 174–78.

cated to the Egyptian pharaoh and to the cult of the royal *ka* (fig. 7).[69] Alexander's shrine, in this temple to *ka*, has a canonical form, as some eighteen carved panels and fifty-two images of the ruler emphasize still today.[70] In the shrine, he appears in the divine company of Amun-Ra, Amun-Ra Khamutef, Monthu, Waset, Ipet, and Khonsu, and he is depicted with pharaonic symbols, ankhs, cartouches, and crowns, including the white, blue, red, double, Nemes, Atef, horned, double-feather, and gold-ribbon. A socle frieze portrays him as the leader of the nineteen nomes of Upper Egypt and the sixteen nomes of Lower Egypt. The evidence points to the priests' desire for cosmic continuity, to their recognition of Alexander as legitimate ruler of Egypt, and to the weight he placed on manifesting his power over the old civilization.

Alexander's fascination with Egypt is evident at every level: he went out of his way to get to the country; he took great care in paying his respects to local gods and priestly traditions; and he commissioned expensive restorations in the southern temples that depict him as the legitimate successor to the pharaonic kings of the past. As his treatment of the Apis bull makes especially clear, he was influenced in his actions by the Greek traditions concerning Egypt. As an imperialist of boundless ambition and prowess, Alexander did much else during the six months he spent in Egypt, in addition to seeing to the organization of the administration, before he left in May of 331. It is instructive to look at three of his activities in Egypt from the perspective of this study: the founding of Alexandria, the journey to the oracle of Ammon at Siwah, and his investigation of the Nile. Each of these can be explained by a variety of factors, but in each case it is obvious that Greek traditions on Egypt were also influential in shaping his actions and determining his plans.

Alexandria

The founding of a city[71] in Egypt that bridged the divide between East and West was the perfect realization of Herodotus' notion, discussed in chap-

69. For the cult of the royal *ka*, see further Bell 1985.
70. The material is gathered in Abd el-Raziq 1984.
71. Ancient accounts for the foundation of Alexandria are: Diodorus 17.52; Curtius 4.7.27–28; Justin 11.11.13; Plutarch, *Alexander* 26.2–6; and Arrian, *Anabasis* 3.1.5–2.2. The foundation is also related in the *Alexander-Romance* 1.25–33, with many fictitious details. In the ninth century C.E., part of this material was reworked by al-Mas'udi in his *Murûj ad-Dhahab wa Ma'âdin al-Jawhar*, completed in about 947: for al-Iskandar as the founder of Alexandria in this work, see Doufikar-

ter 2, of Egypt as an in-between country. The foundation was ordered by Alexander while he was in Egypt, and he himself left indications for the evolution and shape of the site.[72] Since the king was responsible for the plan and layout of the city from an early stage, it is safe to say that he specifically envisioned the port city as an heterogeneity, a place where under the Ptolemies, "diverse ethnic groups enjoyed independent and competing sets of civil rights that enabled them to remain grounded in their hereditary cultures."[73] There is no reason to assume that Alexander directly applied only Herodotus' words to the planning of a city; nevertheless, his vision and its realization do rework the important theme of "in-betweenness" in Herodotus' Egyptian histories.

How did Alexander come to choose the site for his city? This, too, has its origins in the Greek discourse on Egypt. He already had a site in mind where he planned to build a city as a memorial to himself. Then one night, as remarked above, an old, white-haired man appeared to him in his sleep and recited lines about the island of Pharos from book 4 of the *Odyssey*.[74] When he awoke, Alexander decided to follow the dream, even to the extent that he planned to build his city on the island itself, but changed his mind when he perceived that the island was not large enough for his intended city. So he chose for his city the nearby harbor settlement of Rhakotis, about forty-five miles north-west of Naukratis, at the western end of the Delta, and then linked it to the island of Pharos by a causeway known as the Heptastadion.[75] "He himself marked out where the city's *agora* was to be built, how many temples there were to be, and the gods, some Greek, and Isis, the Egyptian, for whom they were to be erected, and where the wall was to be built round it."[76] Other features ascribed to Alexander's own plans are the streets, which were laid out in a ninety-degree grid formation, the vast ramparts, the large royal palace, and the sewer system.[77] The ex-

---

Aerts 1994; for the Arabic and Iranian evidence concerning Alexander's foundations in general, see Fraser 1996, ch. 2.

72. Green 1996.

73. Selden 1998b, 294.

74. Plutarch, *Alexander* 26.3–7, with *Odyssey* 4.354–55.

75. See Arrian, *Anabasis* 3.1.5; Plutarch, *Alexander* 26; and the *Alexander-Romance* 1.31 ff. For the founding, see Cavenaile 1972; Fraser 1972, ch. 1. See also Strabo 17.1.6, esp. for Rhakotis and the Heptastadion, with commentary in Yoyotte, Charvet, and Gompertz 1997.

76. Arrian, *Anabasis* 3.1.5.

77. Diodorus 17.52.2–3; *Alexander-Romance* 1.31; with Green 1996, 10.

tent to which he actively contributed to these items is not known, but the ancient sources do mention the help he received from the architect Deinocrates of Rhodes.[78]

The location of the city, in the Delta, also suggests a Greek influence behind the foundation, since the pharaohs historically had been reluctant to encourage major coastal developments.[79] Naukratis was a relatively recent creation in Egyptian history, but was a Greek entrepot, and some of the impetus for Alexandria may have come from Greek residents such as Cleomenes in the trading post who were seeking a commercial boost. Moreover, the strategic importance of the Delta and of the northern cities was reinforced by Greek writers from Herodotus to Thucydides.[80] Of course, in addition to keeping an eye out for his own military and economic interests, Alexander did cater to Egyptian feelings in this location, and he dedicated an Egyptian temple to Isis, Osiris, and Horus. A hieroglyphic text of 311 describes the new city thus: "The fortress of the King of Upper and Lower Egypt, beloved of Amun, and selected of Ra, son of Ra, Alexandros, on the shore of the great sea of the Ionians; Rhakotis was its earlier name."[81]

What is additionally arresting about the founding of the city is the efforts taken to give it its in-between status, to make it both Egyptian and non-Egyptian.[82] Everything necessary for the city was brought in from outside, including the supplies, the equipment, the workers, and even the people who were going to inhabit the city.[83] As early as Alexander's day, Egyptians were being brought to the city by force and deviousness, especially by characters such as Cleomenes, who amassed a fortune from bribes and outright robbery.[84] Alongside the Egyptians, however, there lived Greeks, Macedonians, and others, many of whom were given financial incentives to migrate there. Eventually the Ptolemies succeeded in attracting residents from more than fifty Greek city-states and more than twenty different non-Greek ethnic groups.[85] Initially the government of Egypt itself was headed by an Egyptian, a Persian, and a Greek, all appointed by Alex-

---

78. Vitruvius 2 *praefatio* 1–4; Pliny, *Natural History* 5.62; *Alexander-Romance* 1.31.

79. Nibbi 1975, 7–34, and Mokhtar 1993.

80. Herodotus 2.30, 3.91; Thucydides 1.104; Cavenaile 1972.

81. Quoted by Wilcken 1967, 119, and adapted here.

82. This point is elaborated more fully in Selden 1998b, 289–300.

83. Strabo 17.1.6; Curtius 4.8.5; Fraser 1972, chs. 1–2.

84. [Aristotle], *Oeconomica* 2.2.33.

85. Heichelheim 1925.

ander before he left for West Asia, and the languages of the official bureau-
cracy in the country were demotic, Aramaic, and Greek.[86]

Contrasting Alexandria with the city-states of classical Greece, Daniel L.
Selden aptly notes that in the former "neither the rulers nor their subjects
were indigenous" and that "the term *metoikos* was not in use."[87] The
situation in Alexandria thus offers a deliberate comparison with the city-
states where, as Aristotle implied, there was the fear that "foreigners and
immigrants" would take over the polis.[88] For instance, in Athens, whose
founding myth was autochthony, first the Cleisthenic and then the Periclean reforms made it more and more difficult for foreigners to become citizens. Athens did have a large population of non-Athenians and foreigners
who were employed or enslaved in a variety of capacities.[89] Of these, even
free resident aliens had few if any political or legal rights, and they needed
to have citizens as guardians for official transactions. In Alexandria, however, the situation was completely different. Paradoxically, given the impact of the Greek tradition on the Alexandrian campaign in Egypt, it appears that the city was designed to counter the political model of the Greek
city-states. Not so paradoxically, on the other hand, this "doubly eccentric
site,"[90] with centers on Pharos and the mainland, but really neither in
Egypt nor outside of it, conformed in spirit to the in-between status given
to the country in Herodotus' influential history.

If Alexandria "by" Egypt, as it was often called in Roman times (not
Alexandria "in" Egypt), was in a sense the fulfillment of the discourse, it
was also the one of his foundations to which Alexander seems to have given
the most attention.[91] P. M. Fraser has cut down Plutarch's list of seventy
cities founded by Alexander to exactly six: of these, Alexandria by Egypt
was very probably the first city that he founded, and the one that gives
us the most information concerning his intentions and the method of
construction.[92] He did not build another foundation until after he won the
battle of Granicus and marched into the so-called Upper Satrapies of Per-

86. For the men and their names, see Arrian, *Anabasis* 3.5, with H. Smith in
Johnson 1992, 296, and Burstein 1995, 43–49.
87. Selden 1998b, 292.
88. Aristotle, *Politics* 1326b20–21.
89. Rosivach 1999.
90. Selden 1998b, 290.
91. Arrian, *Anabasis* 7.23.7.
92. Plutarch, *Moralia* 328E; Fraser 1996: the six are Alexandria in Egypt, Alexandria in Aria, Alexandria Eschate, Alexandria in Susiana, Alexandria-Bucephala,
and Alexandria among the Oreitai (Rambakia). For a general assessment of Alexander's foundations, see Fraser 1996, ch. 6.

sia. Extravagantly, Victor Ehrenberg said that Alexander intended to make Egyptian Alexandria the capital city of his empire.[93] It was the most successful of Alexander's foundations, and appears to be the only one still flourishing. The care and interest he showed in this city suggest that from the earliest stages it was positioned between different cultures, between diverse traditions.

Alexander and Ammon

Alexander's journey to Siwah is one of the oddest and least understood pieces of his life. About this much-analyzed event, I am concerned here only to underscore the Greek traditions that explain the significance of Ammon's oracle and to note the importance of Alexander's Egyptian visit to his self-image.

In a few weeks after the founding of Alexandria,[94] Alexander journeyed west along the coast to Paraetonium (Mersah Matruh) and then southwest on the caravan road to Siwah, near the Libyan border. After a challenging journey, he reached the oracle of Zeus Ammon, which was well known throughout the Greek world, as Herodotus and others said.[95] It appears likely that, although he had arrived in the land only recently, the local population received him as the ruler of Egypt and the son of Ammon (the Egyptian god Amun). The priests from the temple met him and escorted him into the precinct after the appropriate rituals, and once he was inside the sanctuary, they let him put his questions to the god. According to one reconstruction of events, priests hiding in a secret chamber above the sanctuary would have registered his words.[96] He would then have proceeded to a congregation of the higher clergy, the eldest of whom would have dictated Amun's response to Alexander. The response would have taken the form of a written letter composed in hieroglyphs or perhaps demotic. It may have been at the start of this recital that the priest greeted the

93. See Green 1996, 18.

94. Plutarch (*Alexander* 26) and Arrian (*Anabasis* 3.3.1) say that Alexander made the journey to Siwah after founding Alexandria; Diodorus (17.51.4–52.1), Curtius (4.7.5), and Justin (11.11) say that he made the journey before founding the city.

95. 1.46; 2.18, 32, 55. For the journey to Siwah, see Arrian, *Anabasis* 3.3.3–4 (= Aristobulus, *FGrHist* 139 F 13–15); Diodorus 17.49–51; Curtius 4.7.5–32; Plutarch, *Alexander* 26–27; Justin 11; Strabo 17.1.43 (= Callisthenes, *FGrHist* 124 F 14a).

96. Kuhlmann 1988; for a brief treatment, in English, by the same author, see *Ancient History* 18 (1988) 65–85.

king with the words, "Rejoice son; take this form of address as from the god also."[97] Alexander never disclosed what the oracle revealed to him, but he said that "he had heard what pleased him."[98]

There is no question that the journey to the oracle at Siwah and the events that transpired there had a profound impact on his life and his legend. Although he did not disavow his father Philip,[99] he is said to have invoked Ammon as his father on various occasions from then on, for example, in central Persia when his lover Hephaistion died, or at the mouth of the Indus in India. His belief in divine ancestry disaffected many of the Macedonian soldiers, who interpreted Alexander's actions as sacrilegious and an insult to the memory of Philip. But Alexander never gave up his ties to Zeus Ammon and the Egyptian desert, and the connection with Ammon persisted even after his death, when it was proclaimed that he had asked to be buried in Egypt, ostensibly to be close to the god.[100] Ptolemy I Soter depicted him with the ram-god's curved horn on his early coinage.[101] In the *Alexander-Romance*, he sends emissaries to Tyre with a letter that is written by "King Alexander, son of Ammon."[102] The Islamic tradition made him Iskandar Dhu'l-Qarnein, Alexander the Two-Horned, the Quranic prophet of Surah 18 who repels Yuj (Gog) and Majuj (Magog), and so he is spoken of still in a literature that has been repeated and embellished over centuries.[103]

Alexander's motives for the trip to Siwah remain controversial and have inspired a large debate. But in discussing the question, it is helpful to stress the favorable reputation of Ammon's oracle in the Greek-speaking world. Ammon's fame had been spreading in Greece after 500, thanks partly to the importance of the Greek colony of Cyrene on the Libyan coast, not far from Siwah.[104] Pindar is said to have made a voyage to Cyrene to compose his poem in honor of King Arcesilas IV, the winner of a chariot race in 462, and then to have returned home and composed a poem for Zeus Ammon;

97. See Diodorus 17.50.6–51.2.
98. Arrian, *Anabasis* 3.4.
99. This is the view of many modern scholars; cf. Plutarch, *Alexander* 28, and Bosworth 1996, ch. 4.
100. Curtius 10.5.4; Justin 12.15.7; cf. Diodorus 17.117.3.
101. Stewart 1993, 231, 434–35.
102. 1.35.
103. In the Quran (Surah 18.83 ff.), Dhu'l-Qarnein is not identified with Iskandar, but the identification with him begins to be discussed in Quranic commentaries from a very early date.
104. Ammon in Greece: Parke 1967, ch. 9; Lloyd 1976, 195–96.

he also dedicated an image made by the sculptor Calamis for Ammon's temple in Greek Thebes.[105] Cimon, the Athenian general, consulted the shrine when he was laying siege to Citium; and during Alcibiades' time, before the Sicilian expedition, the oracle declared to Athenian envoys that every Syracusan would fall into Athenian hands.[106] Athens itself had forged connections with Ammon some years before Alexander's day, for a temple to Zeus Ammon had been built in the Piraeus; moreover, Athenians had sent gold to Siwah and Athenian playwrights like Euripides and Aristophanes invoked Ammon's name in their works. A sanctuary to Ammon is attested as well in Sparta, which was said to consult the oracle more than any other Greek city. The Spartan Lysander dreamed that the god advised him to raise the siege of Aphytis in Pallene, an action which made the god especially popular among the besieged population.[107] If Herodotus' remarks about the oracle of Ammon in his histories are also recalled, then it can be said that Greek reports, no less than Egyptian ones, shaped Alexander's desire to make the journey to Siwah.

If Greek knowledge about Ammon appears from these remarks to have been predominantly about the general importance of the god's oracular function, it should be noted that Ammon's cult sites in places such as Athens had specifically Egyptian connotations in Greek eyes. Ammon was presented and conceived of in some city-states more as a foreign and Egyptian deity and less as a local one, and Alexander was making a pilgrimage to a place that for Greeks had a recognizably Egyptian part to its history. When Alexander arrived in Egypt, the connection with the Egyptian god Amun would have been easy to make in any case. Once he was in Egypt, the impetus for going to Siwah could have come from Greek, Egyptian, or Libyan traditions, but with different overtones. From an Egyptian perspective, since no pharaoh before Alexander had visited the temple in person, he was not required to make the journey. It is true, of course, that Amun was regularly worshipped by Egyptian pharaohs, and that Amasis and Nectanebo II had commissioned buildings in Siwah not long before Alexander's time.[108] But for the reigning pharaoh to make the grueling expedition to Siwah was without precedent. The weight of mainland Greek lore about the

105. Pindar, *Pythian* 4, is composed for Arcesilas; and see fr. 36 (Maehler) for a poem to Ammon. For the image, see Pausanias 9.16.1, who claims that he saw Pindar's hymn to Ammon "still carved on a triangular slab by the side of the altar dedicated to Ammon by Ptolemy."

106. Plutarch, *Cimon* 18 and *Nikias* 13.

107. Pausanias 3.18.3.

108. Fakhry 1944, 77–79; Lane Fox 1973, 202, 212.

foreign god Ammon, combined with whatever Alexander learned in and around Egypt and with whatever personal desires he nurtured inside himself, helped propel the new ruler to Siwah.

The Search for the Nile's Source

Alexander dreamed about finding the sources of the Nile and of discovering the answer to the problem of the river's behavior.[109] His imperialism in Egypt made it possible for him to investigate the river's sources, and to attempt to bring to an end a line of scientific enquiry stretching back to the pre-Socratic philosophers. The Greek scientific tradition, which had set up the Nile's behaviour as an intellectual problem to be solved, was both an enabling discourse and a beneficiary of this particular Alexandrian mission in the non-Greek world. Only someone who had encountered the Nile first as Greek discourse, not as fact, would have conceived of it as a problem to be solved; only someone who had heard of the Greek tradition about the Nile, and had not actually seen the river firsthand, would have desired to tame the river in this way. Alexander's was an example not of a native trying to ascertain the solution to the river's inundations, but of a foreign conqueror making his contribution to a problem posed within his own cultural and intellectual background. If the river and its mystery were part of Egypt's appeal for Alexander, it is also true that the Greek tradition about the river assumed a directly colonial function.

To understand the implications of Alexander's ambition, therefore, we should read his actions and attitudes in the light of the Greek tradition concerning the river's inundation. While Herodotus had written about the Nile and was certainly the model for Nearchus' reports on Indian rivers, he was not the only Greek to have reflected on the river, its nature, and its sources. It needs to be kept in mind, when Alexander's invasions are considered, that the Nile was a subject of discussion among several Greek writers, including the pre-Socratic philosophers and Aristotle. A particular concern of these writers was to explain why the river flooded in summer and not in winter; it was often believed that the sources of the Nile in southern Egypt and Ethiopia held the key to the solution. This speculation of Greek writers about the Nile forms the discursive background to Alexander's actions and to the expedition that he sent up the river.

Further, the contrast between the Greek and Egyptian traditions concerning the Nile is striking, for the desire to explain the Nile's behavior is

109. The annual inundation of the Nile has not occurred since the construction of the Aswan High Dam in 1971.

more a Greek than an Egyptian obsession. There is no search for the river's origins or for the cause of the annual inundation in the Egyptian texts comparable to that found in the Greek and Latin texts. Even the texts written after the time when the Egyptians had first ventured south beyond the vicinity of Aswan continue to regard subterranean caverns at Elephantine as the river's source.[110] It seemed natural to ancient Egyptians that the river rose and inundated the land in one season every year; there are no Egyptian texts that try to analyze the inundation. But the Egyptians did have an explanation for the phenomenon; they believed that the inundation had a divine cause: the god who personified the Nile flood was Hapy, the god of the inundation; and the ram god Khnum was patron of the first cataract and of the mythical underground caverns at Elephantine. The river was merely called *iterw* in Egyptian and not itself deified, though the inundation was, in the figure of Hapy. Both Hapy and Khnum had major cult-centers in the region of Aswan in southern Egypt. The *Hymn to the Nile*, a text that dates to the Middle Kingdom, offers the following thought about Hapy: "No one knows the place he's in, his cavern is not found in books." In her study of the river in Greek and Roman antiquity, Danielle Bonneau calls this the most explicit textual response on the part of the Egyptians to the inundation of the Nile.[111]

The Greek obsession with the Nile starts long before Alexander. The earliest speculation goes back at least to the sixth century, when Thales is said to have claimed that "the Nile floods when its streams are checked by the contrary etesian winds."[112] His view was not far from Democritus', who said that torrential rains were produced by clouds that were driven from the north to the south of Egypt by etesian winds; Thrasyalces gave roughly the same explanation.[113] On the other hand, Anaxagoras of Clazomenae argued that the cause of the inundation was the melting snow in Ethiopia.[114] Oenopides of Chios said that the cause was subterranean waters, which were warm in winter and cold in summer, while the historian Ephorus said that the Egyptian soil absorbed water during the winter and released it during the summer months like a body's sweat.[115] Herodo-

---

110. Hornung 1982, 79.

111. Bonneau 1964, 136; for a translation of the hymn, see Lichtheim 1973, 204–10.

112. Diogenes Laertius 1.37 = DK 11 A 1.

113. DK 68 A 99; DK 35 F 1.

114. DK 59 A 91. This view is repeated in Euripides, *Archelaus* fr. 228 (Nauck); on this passage, see Harder 1985, 179–90.

115. DK 41 F 11; *FGrHist* 70 F 65.

tus, who criticized others' theories, did not fail to give his own explanation, which held the action of the sun responsible for dispersing wind-bearing rains (2.20–25). There were, in short, numerous Greeks who deliberated on the reasons for the Nile's behavior; Bonneau describes them at some length and divides them into six different categories.[116]

The Nile was also a subject of discussion among the men who knew Alexander or campaigned with him, as my remarks about Herodotus' influence on Nearchus have already indicated. Unable to resist the challenge of the Nile problem, Aristotle himself championed the theory of summer rainfall as the cause of the annual inundation.[117] He also absorbed Herodotean and Homeric reflections about the river in his early writings. In his *Meteorology*, for example, Aristotle considers the whole country of Egypt as the deposit of the Nile and then refers to the passage from the *Iliad*, mentioned above in connection with Achilles, where Homer refers to Egyptian Thebes.[118] He notes that Egypt was once merely the place that was occupied by Egyptian Thebes, since if Homer did not mention Memphis, it could not have existed in his day, or could not have been as important as it was in the fourth century. (Incidentally, *Meteorology*, which was written before Alexander's campaign, underscores the importance of Achilles' remarks in the *Iliad*, where Egypt's material wealth is played up.)

In these observations, however, Aristotle's main focus is on the Nile, which seems to have concerned him no less than Herodotus, and which he, like Herodotus, Aeschylus, and others, described as an exceptionally fecund river.[119] Aristotle may also be following Herodotus in saying that Egypt was once called Thebes, and in stating that Memphis did not exist in Homer's time, since Herodotus, too, had claimed that the land north of Memphis was once a gulf of the sea. As for the general argument about the silting of the river, this too was mentioned by Herodotus and would be mentioned again by Nearchus. Thus, the precedent for consulting Herodotus on the subject of Egypt and the Nile was laid down for Alexander and Nearchus by their teacher Aristotle.

Against the Egyptians' attitude, the Greek texts seem so obsessed with accounting for the Nile that a response from Alexander about the river

---

116. Bonneau 1964, 137–214.

117. This follows from a remark made by Eratosthenes and subsequently quoted by Proclus, *Commentary on Timaeus* 22e (1.121, ed. Diehl) = *FGrHist* 646 T 2c.

118. *Meteorology* 351b28 ff.

119. Aristotle, frs. 283–85 (Rose); *History of Animals* 562b, 584b, 606a; *Generation of Animals* 770a35.

seems an inevitable consequence. Once the occurrence of the inundation had been posed as a question by Greek intellectuals, it was likely that the tradition would not cease referring to the problem until some authority would intervene with information about the river's southern stretches. From this perspective, there could be no better authority than the most successful of all Greek campaigners and explorers. And so it was that Alexander on two occasions grappled with the issue of the Nile's behavior. The first time was in Egypt, where he dispatched an expedition to the south of the country to investigate the sources. What came of this expedition is not clear, and it is not known whether any information from it reached Alexander during his lifetime, although writers who lived long after the king did exaggerate in their accounts. Indeed, it appears unlikely that any concrete information emerged from this expedition, since much later Alexander tried again to account for the river's behavior. This second attempt to answer the question of the Nile's source and its annual inundations came, incredibly, when Alexander was in India, where he even believed for a brief while that he had come up with a definitive solution—only to discover that he was deluded by misleading similarities between the landscapes of India and Egypt. It should be noted, however, that argument and debate about the Nile does come to a halt by 325: after this no Greek appears to have forwarded new theories about the river, and it was assumed by writers and intellectuals that the cause of the river was the summer rains in the southern stretches of Egypt. If the reason for the end to speculation was information trickling back to Greece from Alexander's campaigns in Egypt, India, and elsewhere, as the evidence strongly suggests, then it can be asserted that Alexander's imperialism and scientific knowledge reinforced each other with real and observable consequences.

Given the king's exceptional curiosity about the Nile, and given that Aristotle, Nearchus, and Callisthenes, to mention only a few men whom he knew personally, had all evinced interest in accounting for the inundation, it is not surprising that Alexander, probably while in Egypt, dispatched an expedition to the south in search of the river's sources, as I stated above.[120] A member of Alexander's campaign is said to have traveled south and discovered the cause from personal observation.[121] What actually emerged

120. The strongest case for the expedition is made in Burstein 1995, ch. 6 = *Greek, Roman, and Byzantine Studies* 17 (1976): 135–46.

121. John the Lydian identifies the person as Callisthenes: see *De mensibus* (*On months*) 4.107 = *FGrHist* 124 F 12a. Although the expedition is attested by several writers, it is unlikely that Callisthenes himself went on such an expedition, since he would have barely had the time to take part in the expedition, and then rejoin the

from the expedition is hard to say, since Alexander sent another expedition looking for the river's source while he was campaigning in India. It may be that nothing definitive came from this expedition, or that its results became known only after the Indian campaigns or even after Alexander's death. Nevertheless, there are brief comments in ancient writers that allude to a mission in the south of Egypt.[122] The expedition also lies behind what Lucan writes in a passage of his *Civil War*, namely, that Alexander, because of "jealousy" with the Nile, sent explorers through the furthest parts of Ethiopia.[123]

With the passing of time, interestingly, this expedition appears to have been magnified and embellished by writers. Their remarks may reflect the general reality of an Alexandrian expedition, but they also play to expectations arising from within the twin Greek traditions of speculation about the Nile and speculation about Alexander. In an anonymous *Life of Pythagoras*, summarized by Photius, the author discusses the inundation and says that Aristotle, too, studied the phenomenon firsthand: "He personally examined the facts on the spot, when he decided to accompany Alexander of Macedon to those regions and witness the cause of the Nile's flood. So he speaks of it as a problem solved, since the rise in the water level had been observed after the rains." [124] This author is boldly taking the tradition even further, since there is no other record of Aristotle going in person to the south of Egypt to investigate the source of the Nile. On the other hand, the

---

campaign in its eastern phase, before his execution. If Callisthenes had already found out the cause of the inundation, moreover, Alexander would not have contemplated looking for the source of the Nile in India, nor would Nearchus have attempted to explain the river's nature by analogy with Indian rivers. The most likely scenario is that the expedition proceeded without Callisthenes, and that its findings reached Alexander, if at all, after the campaign in India when he was deluded enough to connect the Indus to the Nile: see Bosworth 1993, 418–19, against Burstein 1995, ch. 6.

122. According to Eratosthenes, "there is no longer a need to investigate the Nile's inundation because clearly voyagers have gone to the sources of the Nile and seen the rains, so as to confirm Aristotle's explanation." See Proclus, *Commentary on Timaeus* 22e (1.121, ed. Diehl) = *FGrHist* 646 T 2c. In the *Alexander-Romance*, the king establishes contact with Kandake, the queen of Meroe, in the deep south, and it just may be possible that the story reflects the tradition of some kind of Alexandrian penetration into the Nile's southern regions. On the historical reliability of the *Romance*, see Fraser 1996, chs. 1–2, and appendix 2.

123. *Civil War* 10.272–75.

124. Photius 441a = *FGrHist* 646 T 2a. Since the passage in Photius seems to be only loosely connected with what precedes it, and since codex 250 of Photius, about Agatharchides' *On the Erythraean Sea*, deals with similar subject matter, it is possible that this passage in Photius also comes from Agatharchides.

author's claim is consistent with Alexandrian ideology, informed as it was by Greek thought and culture, and it may be even be interpreted as its logical conclusion. For the perfect fusion of Greek knowledge and power, there could be no better actors than Alexander and Aristotle, and no better subject than the Egyptian Nile.[125]

Long after Alexander left Egypt, he waged war in India and once again came to address the question of the Nile's sources. How did Alexander believe that he had found the sources of the Nile in India? The details of this amazing situation are described by Nearchus.[126] Alexander saw crocodiles and "beans" in the Indian rivers, and connected these with the crocodiles and "beans" he had seen earlier in Egypt. Perhaps he was following Herodotus, who also felt that the crocodiles in the Indus resembled the crocodiles in the Nile,[127] and who described the "beans" as the seeds of the lotus which was found in the Nile.[128] On the basis of parallels such as these, Alexander formed the idea that he had discovered the origin of the Nile. His belief was that the river rose somewhere in India, flowed through a vast desert, where it lost the name Indus, and then again flowed through inhabited regions, namely, Ethiopia and Egypt, where it took on the name Nile and then emptied out into the Mediterranean Sea. The king was so excited about this discovery that, in a breathtakingly Freudian twist, he wanted to write to his mother, Olympias, that he had discovered the sources of the Nile. He also prepared for a voyage to Egypt, with the mistaken notion that he could sail there down the river. When he had investigated the Indian river systems and spoken to the natives, however, he learned that the Indus had nothing to do with the Nile. He abandoned the plan of sailing to Egypt on the river and cancelled the part of the letter to his mother that dealt with the Nile.[129] Soon afterward, the campaigners experienced the monsoon and decided that the cause of the Nile's inundation was summer rainfall after all.

125. Some scholars, taking this line of thinking further, have suggested that all the evidence for the expedition should be dismissed because it consists of remarks made by overeager ancient authors trying to connect together Alexander and the Nile. This argument is forcefully refuted by Burstein 1995, ch. 6.

126. Strabo 15.1.25 = Nearchus, *FGrHist* 133 F 20; Arrian, *Anabasis* 6.1.1–6 = *FGrHist* 133 F 32.

127. Herodotus 4.44; see also Aristobulus *FGrHist* 139 F 38.

128. Herodotus 2.92. According to scholars, the lotus was introduced by Persian rulers into Egypt from India in about 500 B.C.E.: see Lloyd 1976, 372–75. Bosworth writes, "Aristotle could well have informed his royal pupil about the rarity of the sacred lotus and its apparent uniqueness to Egypt." See Bosworth 1993, 414–15.

129. For Alexander's knowledge of Indian rivers, see in general Bosworth 1993 and Bosworth 1996, 186–200.

In understanding why Alexander arrived at the false supposition that he had found the Nile's source in India, it should be pointed out that the ideas mentioned in an Aristotelian treatise could have aided the conqueror in this belief. The treatise, which surveys various views about the river, is lost, but an abstract survives in a medieval Latin translation.[130] The author of the treatise writes that summer rains are the established and true cause of the inundation, but also gives other views that scholars attribute to the fourth century. Artaxerxes III Ochus, the king of Persia and ruler of Egypt, had investigated information about a connection between the Nile and the Indus, the treatise notes, and had thought about diverting the course of the Indus to dry up the Nile. Whether or not Artaxerxes actually considered this action, the treatise seems to be divulging information about fourth-century views that hold out a possibility of there being a connection between the Nile and the Indus. It may have been the prospect of discovering this riverine connection that made Alexander believe he had actually done so.

Eventually, Alexander gave up the idea, as we know, and the members of the campaign made another "discovery" in India. Nearchus and others experienced the monsoon rains in the summer of 326, and Nearchus, in particular, argued by analogy that the cause of the Nile's inundation was also summer rainfall. But Nearchus was not the only person to hold the theory. This view was also held by Aristotle, as we saw above, and the theory of summer rainfall certainly appears in the Aristotelian treatise just mentioned, where the summer rain is attributed to eyewitness reports.[131] In his *Meteorology*, written before Alexander's conquests, Aristotle mentioned Ethiopia and Arabia as areas that receive much rain in the summer. Nearchus, in India, appears to have been verifying Aristotle's theory about the summer rainfall, and Aristotle elaborated the theory with greater confidence in his later work.[132] This explanation of the inundation is also attributed to Callisthenes,[133] the historian who campaigned with Alexan-

---

130. Text, French translation, and discussion in Bonneau 1971, who accepts the Aristotelian authorship of the treatise. The text also appears as *FGrHist* 646 F 1, but Jacoby denies the Aristotelian authorship, and dates the treatise to about 125– 100 B.C.E. However, the *Vita Menagiana* attributes a work *On the Rising of the Nile* to Aristotle (*FGrHist* 646 T 1a). And a work entitled on "The Egyptian Nile" does appear in a Neoplatonist catalogue (recorded in Arabic by Usaibia) of Aristotle's writings: Düring 1957, 224 = *FGrHist* 646 T 1b.

131. *Liber Aristotelis de inundatione Nili* 12 = *FGrHist* 646 F 1.10.

132. Aristotle, *Meteorology* 349a5–9; and see n. 117, above.

133. See *FGrHist* 124 F 12c (from an anonymous Florentine), and n. 121 above on John the Lydian; and cf. *FGrHist* 124 F 19–21 = Seneca, *Natural Questions* 6.23; 6.26.3; 7.5.3–5.

der, and Callisthenes is said to have borrowed the theory from Aristotle.[134] At various times, three men who were in a position directly to influence Alexander—Aristotle, Nearchus, and Callisthenes—worked out explanations for the behavior of the Nile, and two of these even accompanied him on parts of his conquests. Thus, Alexander's interest in the river's sources exemplifies the collusion of science and imperialism that characterized much of his campaign.

The Nile investigations are perfectly intelligible from within the lengthy tradition of speculation about the inundation, a tradition with roots going back to Ionian thinkers in the sixth century, if not earlier. It is clear that the discursive history about the Nile influenced Alexander, his worldview, and his conquests. It may even be that Aristotle was the beneficiary of information gathered on the campaigns, as some believe, and that he later composed the Aristotelian treatise in which the inundation is attributed to the summer rains; certainly, the expedition confirmed the theories that he had hinted at earlier in his *Meteorology*. If he did receive such eyewitness information, the force of his reputation combined with the observers' accounts was responsible for ending the debate. After Ephorus, as Stanley M. Burstein has noted, new theories for the inundation were not forthcoming.[135] At any rate, no clearer evidence can be found of the conjunction of discourse and power than Alexander's speculations and investigations. This patron of poets, scientists, and philosophers wanted to know the truth about the Nile while in the region, and he dispatched a mission up the river to ascertain it. Later, he was excited when he reached India, the exotic land of marvels; for a dizzying period, he was even more excited at the thought of making the journey back to Memphis on waters, at once Indian and Egyptian, that would reveal to him the source of the Nile. But he was mistaken in this supposition; and eventually the campaigners settled on the notion of summer rainfall, and the idea made its way back to Greece as the accepted explanation for the annual inundation.

EPILOGUE

"Cultural, material, and intellectual relations between Europe and the Orient have gone through innumerable phases, even though the line between East and West has made a certain constant impression upon Europe. Yet

134. Callisthenes, *FGrHist* 124 F 12b = Strabo 17.1.5, who traces it back to Homer.
135. Burstein 1995, 70; for Ephorus, see Diodorus 1.39.7.

in general it was the West that moved upon the East, not vice versa."[136] In July 1798, Napoleon sailed up to Alexandria and stormed the city gates. This event marked the beginnings of the French occupation of Egypt, which lasted until the English forced the French surrender two years later. The French and the English were fighting for the "Orient," and the French attack on Egypt was also intended as a blow against the English and their access to India. Napoleon himself arrived in Egypt as both the chief of the Army of the Orient and, as a member of the National Institute, at the head of more than 150 scholars, engineers, draughtsmen, and artists. This group of *savants* went around Egypt surveying the country, making drawings of sites and places, and carrying out extensive fieldwork. In 1808, Napoleon, now emperor in France, received the first installment of their labors as the inaugural volume of the *Description de l'Égypte* (fig. 8), which eventually filled twenty-three massive tomes.[137]

The scholars and soldiers who made possible this monument to science and learning had relied in turn upon earlier writers and sources for truth, guidance, and inspiration. These earlier writers included Claude Étienne Savary, whose *Lettres sur l'Égypte* was published in 1785–86, and Constantin François de Chasseboeuf Volney, the author of the *Voyages en Syrie et en Égypte* of 1789.[138] More arresting for our purposes are the frequent appeals to Greek and Roman antiquity made by the French in connection with Egypt. Although European writers such as Savary and Volney had been sending back accounts of Egypt and West Asia in the centuries immediately preceding, the impact of the ancient texts seems not to have diminished. Exemplary in this regard is Jean-Baptiste-Joseph Fourier's preface to the *Description*. Noting that Egyptian palaces and temples are the very ones described by Hecateus, Diodorus, and Strabo, Fourier adds that "there can be nothing more valuable for the history of the arts than a

136. Said 1978, 73, in response to Michelet's observation that "the Orient advances, invincible, fatal to the gods of light by the charm of its dreams, by the magic of its *chiaroscuro.*"

137. *Description de l'Égypte*, 23 vols., Paris, 1809–26; 2d ed., Panckoucke, 1821–26. References below are to the first edition. For details concerning the French invasion, I have consulted Herbold 1962; Thiry 1973; Beaucour, Laissus, and Orgogozo 1990; and the nineteenth-century account in al-Jabarti's *Tarikh muddat al-Faransis bi-Misr* (see Jabarti 1993). For background to the *Description*, see also Gillispie's introduction to Gillispie and Dewachter 1987, 1–29.

138. Claude Étienne Savary, *Lettres sur l'Égypte*, 3 vols., Paris, 1785–86; and Constantin François de Chasseboeuf Volney, *Voyages en Syrie et en Égypte, pendant les années 1783, 1784 et 1785*, 2 vols., Paris, 1789. For a study of otherness and gender issues in these texts, see Le Coat 1997.

knowledge of the great models that fired the imagination of the Greeks and helped develop their genius."[139] The "discovery of Egypt," it appears, is made more meaningful for the French scholar by this invocation of the ancient Greeks.

But Fourier's use of Greek and Roman antiquity is more than mere invocation. He introduces the Herodotean trope of an "in-between" Egypt on the very first page of his preface to the *Description*: "Placed between Africa and Asia, and communicating easily with Europe, Egypt occupies the center of the ancient continent." After referring to the country as the land of "great memories" *(grands souvenirs)* and "innumerable monuments" *(monumens innombrables)*, Fourier writes that "Homer, Lycurgus, Solon, Pythagoras, and Plato all went to Egypt to study the sciences, religion, and the laws." But it was not only these Greeks who went to Egypt, since Alexander himself established an opulent city there, and this city witnessed Caesar, Mark Antony, and Augustus determining the fate of the world. Therefore, Fourier argues, it is appropriate for Egypt to attract the attention of princes who rule the destinies of nations.[140] After scores of pages on this and other subjects, he ends his preface with another touch worthy of Herodotus, by commenting that history will "preserve from oblivion all the circumstances of this extraordinary event" *(préserve de l'oubli toutes les circonstances de cet évènement extraordinaire).*[141] Egypt's position as a foothold to other regions, its historical value, its service as a school for Greece, its importance to Greek and Roman generals: even as he enters into more recent events and political justifications for the French intervention in Egypt, Fourier revalidates the old themes via a direct appeal to Greek

139. *Description de l'Égypte*, "Préface Historique," lxxx.

140. "L'Égypte, placée entre l'Afrique et l'Asie, et communiquant facilement avec l'Europe, occupe le centre de l'ancien continent. Cette contrée ne présente que de grands souvenirs; elle est la patrie des arts et en conserve des monumens innombrables; ses principaux temples, et les palais que ses rois ont habités, subsistent encore, quoique les moins anciens de ces édifices aient été construits avant la guerre de Troie. Homère, Lycurge, Solon, Pythagore et Platon, se rendirent en Égypte pour y étudier les sciences, la religion et les lois. Alexandre y fonda une ville opulente, qui jouit long-temps de l'empire du commerce, et qui vit Pompée, César, Marc-Antoine et Auguste, decider entre eux du sort de Rome et de celui du monde entier. Le propre de ce pays est d'appeler l'attention des princes illustres, qui règlent les destinées des nations" (*Description de l'Égypte*, "Préface Historique," i). Said 1993, 33–35, contrasts Fourier's preface with the anguished remarks of the roughly contemporary work by the Egyptian Jabarti, *Aja'ib al-athar fi al-tarajim wa al-Akhbar*, a part of which dealt with the French occupation.

141. *Description de l'Égypte*, "Préface Historique," xcii; and cf. the proem to book 1 of Herodotus.

and Roman antiquity, and to the country's most famous Greek chronicler, Herodotus.

Napoleon himself took copies of the *Iliad*, Xenophon's *Anabasis*, and Plutarch's *Lives* with him on his expedition, and he had the particular example of Alexander in mind when he conquered Egypt.[142] At Brienne, as a student, he had studied Plutarch more than once. From this source and others, he remembered that Alexander knew the "mentality" of Egyptians, and supposed that this was why he visited the temple of Ammon and was welcomed as a liberator.[143] In fact, the visit to Siwah recurs in Napoleon's writings and recollections about the Egyptian campaign. "It was most politic of him to go to Amon: it was thus he conquered Egypt. If I had stayed in the Orient, I probably would have founded an empire like Alexander's by going on pilgrimage to Mecca."[144] But instead of going to Mecca or Siwah, Napoleon actually went to the mosque of Al Azhar in Cairo and held discussions with the ulemas and muftis there. He may not have been the son of a god, like Alexander, but did not the Quran prophesy his great revolution?[145] Yet Napoleon found these religious leaders harder to win over than Alexander did the priests of Ammon in Siwah, and his turn to Islamic authority was less sincere than Alexander's to Ammon.[146] Ultimately, he was unable to maintain French superiority in Egypt for even the duration of his stay and he left without fanfare for France in August 1799.

In other ways as well, Napoleon circles us back to Alexander. Both leaders brought with them to Egypt writers and scientists, and both expeditions changed the home country's knowledge of Egypt. Under Alexander, the Greeks gained a better grasp of the Nile's behavior; after him, relations between Greeks and Egyptians were profoundly changed, and new ways of speaking and thinking about Egypt were opened up. Owing to Napoleon's expedition, the Rosetta stone was looted out of Egypt and made available

142. For the texts, see Bernal 1987, 185.

143. *Correspondance de Napoléon 1ᵉʳ publiée par ordre de l'Empereur Napoléon III*, 32 vols. (Paris, 1858–70) vol. 29, 478.

144. G. Gourgaud, *Sainte-Hélène: Journal inédit*, 2 vols. (Paris, n.d.) vol. 2, 435–36.

145. *Correspondance de Napoléon 1ᵉʳ publiée par ordre de l'Empereur Napoléon III*, 32 vols. (Paris, 1858–70) vol. 29, 481.

146. "I never followed any of the tenets of that religion. I never prayed in the mosques. I never abstained from wine, or was circumcised, neither did I ever profess it. I said merely that we were the friends of the Mussulmans, and that I respected Mahomet their Prophet, which was true; I respect him now. I wanted to make the Imaums cause prayers to be offered up in the mosques for me, in order to make the people respect me still more than they actually did, and obey me more readily" (quoted in Jabarti 1993, 164–65).

to scholars in France and elsewhere. Through the offices of his brother Jacques-Joseph Champollion-Figeac, Jean-François Champollion had the opportunity to meet Fourier, when Fourier was *prefet* of Isère, and the decipherment of hieroglyphs soon followed.[147] After Napoleon, knowledge of ancient and modern Egypt in the West was altered dramatically, even as European imperialists continued to intervene on its behalf. In the cases of both Alexander and Napoleon, earlier traditions shaped the attitudes and actions of the invaders, and from the interaction between knowledge and power there emerged, at different times and in different ways, cultural understanding and the imperialism that comes from a shortage of it.

Egypt was a special place for these men, partly because of its multiple significances in discursive traditions. For the Greeks, by Alexander's day, Egypt was known to have the oldest civilization in the Mediterranean, its fabulous wealth had been described by Homer, it was a putative school or place of pilgrimage for famous sages such as Solon, it was a land of mysterious immensities such as the Pyramids and the Nile, and it was a bridge between Europe and Asia. Although commercial, military, and political interests often brought Greeks to the country in the fifth and fourth centuries, and there were even Greek-speakers living in cities in the Delta, its discursive valences invariably exceeded the hardness of these real-world experiences and encounters. The relationship between Greek representations of Egypt and the country itself was nonmimetic, especially, and incredibly, even after Herodotus' extended tour de force. The literature was never a mirror of life in the cities of the Delta or along the Nile, but rather one that, in looking less at the present than at symbolic values fashioned out of the past, solicited and demanded a response from a Greek reader sensible enough to interpret its constitutive tropes and creative enough to link them to his own ambitions.

For Alexander and the Greeks, the Egypt of this discursive tradition and the Egypt that was a real country with a politics and history of its own were not incompatible entities. As with their other myths, the Greeks used and believed in their "myths" of Egypt as long as they were interested in doing so and up to the point where their interests in such conceptualizations reached.[148] Alexander could read about Egypt in authors from Homer to

147. For the colonial and scientific importance of Napoleon's expedition, see Gillispie 1994. There are many accounts of Champollion's life and the decipherment: see e.g. Iversen 1993, 136–45.

148. Veyne 1988, 83–84: "The Greeks believe and do not believe in their myths. They believe in them, but they use them and cease believing at the point where their interest in believing ends."

Aeschylus to Isocrates, but he never forgot that its present-day rulers were Persians whom he would have to defeat if he wished to take over the country. Nor did he forget about Greek allies in the Delta such as Cleomenes, or forget that the power of the temples lay in the hands of the priests, whom he would have to placate if he wished to be accepted as the next pharaoh. For him, as for Greek-speakers after him, the discursive Egypt and the real one were able to coexist, and we never find the kinds of laments in the literature as we do later in Europe after the Middle Ages. For instance, in August 1843, some four decades after Napoleon's expedition, Gérard de Nerval wrote to his friend Théophile Gautier, "I have already lost, Kingdom after Kingdom, province after province, the more beautiful half of the universe, and soon I will know of no place in which I can find a refuge for my dreams; but it is Egypt that I most regret having driven out of my imagination, now that I have sadly placed it in my memory."[149] With Nerval, the memory of his own voyage to Egypt had a demystifying effect, and destroyed the dreams that had lived in his imagination prior to his travels: the country that he visited and lived in was simply unable to match the Egypt that he had created for himself by his readings and in his dreams. Such a lament is never adumbrated in the Greek literary tradition.

At some point, nevertheless, these Greek writings and traditions brought about certain processes and produced transformations in the field of actions and events. The relationship between the works analyzed in this book and the contexts in which they were created is not simple to define. But at some level in Greek antiquity these texts and representations came to constitute a field of possibilities in which specific statements and actions could seem acceptable and concrete when realized. There is no way of knowing how Alexander, one morning, may have read the second book of Herodotus, or Isocrates' *Busiris,* or Plato's *Timaeus,* and decided there and then to conquer Egypt. If there is no such data, however, there is the reality of the authors' words and the reality of the Alexandrian conquest of Egypt. "Herodotus does not make things happen," François Hartog writes; "he does not cause the war or the peace or the extension of the democracy." As Hartog goes on to say, Herodotus does affect his audience and his readers, whoever they may be, and he engenders certain effects "at the level of whatever

149. Gérard de Nerval, *Oeuvres,* ed. A. Béguin and J. Richet (Paris, 1960), vol. 1, 933, quoted in Said 1978, 100. Gautier himself visited Egypt in 1869, three years before he died, but it informed several of his works, including *Une nuit de Cléopatre* (1842), *Le pied de la momie* (1840), *La mille et deuxième nuit* (1842), *Nostalgies d'obélisques* (1851), and *Le roman de la momie* (1857).

it is that provides the structure of the narrative—whatever makes it possible for the narrator to construct it, but also whatever makes it possible for the addressee to 'read' it, to calculate the meaning of the statements or even of the implicit codes that organize it."[150] In the case of Herodotus' histories, one code that is operative throughout the work is that of power, and another is the distinction between Greek and barbarian; it follows that questions of identity, otherness, power, and political control are organizing principles of the text. No ancient reader of his work could have come away from the text without confronting these issues, least of all such a one as Alexander, whose very actions raised issues of power and Greekness. In similar ways and for similar effects, one could read the works of such authors as Isocrates, Plato, Euripides, and Aeschylus, who refer to Egypt in their writings. With Alexander's conquest, as again with Napoleon's, Egypt was simultaneously the imaginative territory in which the European mind revisited its most basic anxieties of otherness and a geographical space that was subjected to European imperialism.

150. Hartog 1988, 318.

Fragmentary Greek Historians on Egypt, to 332 B.C.E.

Several Greeks wrote accounts of Egypt before Alexander and the Ptolemies inaugurated Greek rule in the country. These accounts took the form of an *Aegyptiaca* (or *History of Egypt*), or were part of a larger ethnographic or geographic treatise such as a *Periodos ges* (or *Journey around the World*). Only Herodotus' work survives intact, as book 2 of his histories; the works of the remaining writers have to be pieced together from quotations in other sources. The following are translations of the most important of these fragmentary Greek accounts, composed between the late sixth century and 332, when Alexander invaded. The authors are Hecateus of Miletus, Hellanicus of Lesbos, Aristagoras (of Miletus?), and Eudoxus of Cnidus.[1]

HECATEUS OF MILETUS

Hecateus, from Miletus in Asia Minor, was active around 500 and probably died after 476. His works include a *Periegesis* (or *Periodos ges*) and *Genealogies* (or *Histories* or *Herologia*); the latter included a section on the Danaids and their arrival in Greece from Egypt (F 19–22). His work was discussed, famously, by Herodotus. See *FGrHist* 1 for the full testimonia and the fragments; the numbers of the fragments below correspond to that text.

Fragments

Periegesis

300. Herodotus 2.143–45: Once upon a time Hecateus, the historian, was in Thebes and was tracing his family tree and connecting his descent

---

1. In the fourth century, Ctesias of Cnidus may also have referred to Egyptians in his *Periplus* or *Periodos:* see *FGrHist* 688 F 55, with Jacoby's note on the text. See also Lyceas of Naucratis, *FGrHist* 613.

to a god in the sixteenth generation. The priests of Zeus there did for him what they did for me, too—though I was not tracing my family tree. They brought me into a great hall and showed me the huge wooden figures there, counting them up to the number they had already given. For each high priest, in his own lifetime, sets up in that place an image of himself. The priests counted up and showed me each son succeeding his father, from the image of the most recently dead, going right through all of them, until they had traced through all. Hecateus had traced his family tree and connected himself with this god in the sixteenth generation; but the priests countered by constructing a family tree by their method of reckoning, because they would not take it from him that a man had been born from a god. As they established their rival family tree, they declared that each one of these huge figures was a "piromis" succeeding a "piromis," until they had gone through the entire line of 345 figures, and they failed to connect any one of these with either a god or a hero. A "piromis" (πίρωμις) is in Greek a "gentleman" (καλὸς κἀγαθός).

So, those whose images were there the priests have shown to be all human and quite different from gods; but, they say, before these men there were gods who were rulers of Egypt, who lived not at the same time as these men; and, of these gods, one was always supreme ruler. The last of these divine beings to rule Egypt was Horus, the son of Osiris, whom the Greeks call Apollo. He, they say, deposed Typhon and became the last god to rule Egypt. Osiris, in the Greek language, is Dionysus.

Among the Greeks, Heracles and Dionysus and Pan are thought to be the youngest of the gods, but among the Egyptians Pan is the oldest and is one of the first gods, those who are called the Eight. Heracles is of the second group, those called the Twelve, and Dionysus is of the third, who were born of the Twelve. I have already made clear the number of years the Egyptians themselves say stretch between Heracles and King Amasis (2.43). Pan is said to be still earlier; and though the number of years between Dionysus and King Amasis is the smallest, even it is reckoned as being fifteen thousand. The Egyptians claim that they know these matters absolutely because they are making their calculations and continually writing down the number of years. (T 4.)

301. Arrian, *Anabasis* 5.6.5: And as for Egypt, the historians Herodotus (2.5) and Hecateus, although possibly the work on Egypt is not by Hecateus (T 15c), both call it similarly "the gift of the river," and Herodotus has shown by very clear proofs that this is so.

302. (a) Diodorus 1.37.1–7: Since there is great difficulty in explaining the swelling of the river, many philosophers and historians have under-

taken to set forth the causes of it. . . . Hellanicus (4 F 173) and Cadmus (489 F 1), for instance, as well as Hecateus and all the writers like them, belonging as they do one and all to the early school, turned to the answers offered by the myths. . . . And as for the sources of the Nile and the region where the stream arises, not a man, down to the time of the writing of this history, has ever affirmed that he has seen them, or reported from hearsay an account received from any who have maintained that they have seen them. The question, therefore, resolves itself into a matter of guesswork and plausible conjecture; and when, for instance, the priests of Egypt assert that the Nile has its origin in the ocean which surrounds the inhabited world, there is nothing sound in what they say, and they are merely solving one perplexity by substituting another.

(b) Herodotus 2.19–23: I was not able to find out anything at all about this from the Egyptians, despite my inquiries of them, as to what peculiar property the Nile possesses that is the opposite of every other river in the world. . . . But some of the Greeks who want to be remarkable for their cleverness have advanced three explanations about the river. Two of them I do not consider worthy of commenting on, save for simply indicating the position they advance. One of these says that it is the etesian winds that cause the Nile's flooding by preventing the Nile from flowing to the sea. . . . The second opinion, which has even less knowledge to it than the aforesaid but is certainly more wonderful in the telling, is the one that speaks of the Nile effecting this thing itself—because it flows from Ocean—and of Ocean as flowing round the whole world. . . . The person who urged the theory about the Ocean has carried his story, which is indeed only a tale, back to where it vanishes and so cannot be disproved. For myself, I do not know that there is any river Ocean, but I think that Homer or one of the older poets found the name and introduced it into his poetry.

(c) Scholia to Apollonius of Rhodes 4.259: Hecateus of Miletus relates that the Argonauts went from the Phasis into Ocean, then from there to the Nile, from there to our sea.

303. Stephanus of Byzantium, s.v. "Phakousa" (Φάκουσα): village between Egypt and the Red Sea. Strabo 17 (1.26). Hecateus says Phakoussai (Φάκουσσαι) and Phakoussais (Φακούσσαις). Also islands of Phakousai (Φάκουσαι) and Phakaioi (Φάκαιοι).

304. Stephanus of Byzantium, s.v. " Atharrabis" (Ἀθάρραβις): city in Egypt, as Herodian in book 4: 'Atharrabites (Ἀθαρραβίτης) nome in Egypt and Atharrabis (Ἀθάρραβις) city.' Hecateus in book 2 of *Periegesis* uses one ρ and the letter μ: "Atharambites (Ἀθαραμβίτης) nome and Atharambe (Ἀθαράμβη) city." The ethnic is Atharambitai (Ἀθαραμβῖται).

305. Stephanus of Byzantium, s.v. "Khemmis" (Χέμμις): city in Egypt . . . there is also the island Khembis (Χέμβις), with the letter β, in Boutoi, as Hecateus says in his *Periegesis* of Egypt: "in Boutoi, near the temple of Leto is the island named Khembis, sacred to Apollo, and the island is afloat and it sails around and moves on the water." The islander is called Khemmites (Χεμμίτης) and Khembios (Χέμβιος).

306. Stephanus of Byzantium, s.v. "Bolbitine" (Βολβιτίνη): city in Egypt. Hecateus. The citizen is called Bolbitinites (Βολβιτινίτης). The possessive is Βολβίτινος, hence also 'Bolbitine chariot' (Βολβίτινον ἅρμα).

307. Herodian, *On Anomalous Words* 36.26: Pharos . . . masculine. For this is what the helmsman of Menelaus was called. But there is also a feminine, for the island that takes the name from him, as Hecateus says.

308. Aristides 36.108: The name Canopus is from Menelaus' helmsman, as Hecateus the historian says and also common report, and when he died, the name was left behind around this place.

309. Stephanus of Byzantium, s.v. "Heleneion" ('Ελένειον): place near Canopus. Hecateus in the *Periegesis* of Libya. The ethnic is Heleneieus ('Ελενειύς).

310. Stephanus of Byzantium, s.v. "Ephesos" ("Εφεσος): . . . in the Nile, there is an island Ephesos as well as a Chios and a Lesbos and a Cyprus and a Samos and others, as Hecateus says.

311. Stephanus of Byzantium, s.v. "Senos" (Σῆνος): city in Egypt. Hecateus in the *Periegesis* of it. The citizen is called Senikos (Σηνικός).

312. Stephanus of Byzantium, s.v. "Suis" (Σύις): city in Egypt, as Hecateus in the *Periegesis* of it. Also the nome Suites (Συίτης).

313. Stephanus of Byzantium, s.v. "Abotis" ("Αβοτις): Egyptian city, as Hecateus, which Herodian says is marked with the grave accent. The citizen, according to the local fashion, is called Abotites (Ἀβοτίτης) . . . but, according to Hecateus, Abotieus (Ἀβοτιεύς).

314. Stephanus of Byzantium, s.v. "Kramboutis" (Κράμβουτις): city in Egypt. Hecateus in the *Periegesis* of Libya. . . . Herodian writes with the letter o Krambotis (Κράμβοτις), proparoxytone, like Abotis ("Αβοτις).

315. Stephanus of Byzantium, s.v. "Kros" (Κρῶς): city in Egypt. Hecateus in the *Periegesis* of Asia. The citizen is called Kroites (Κρωίτης). Also nome Kroites (Κρωίτης). There is also Krois (Κρῶις), a city of Arabians.

316. Stephanus of Byzantium, s.v. "Liebris" (Λίηβρις): city of Phoenicians, as Herodian. The ethnic is Liebrites (Λιηβρίτης), like Sybarites (Συβαρίτης). Hecateus in the *Periegesis* of Egypt.

317. Stephanus of Byzantium, s.v. "Magdolos" (Μαγδωλός): city in Egypt. Hecateus in *Periegesis*.

318. Stephanus of Byzantium, s.v. "Mulon" (Μύλων): city in Egypt. Hecateus.

319. Stephanus of Byzantium, s.v. "Nile": city in Egypt. Hecateus in *Periegesis* of it: "also a temple of the river Nile."

320. Stephanus of Byzantium, s.v. "Oneibatis" ('Ονείβατις): city in Egypt. Hecateus in *Periegesis* of Libya.

321. Stephanus of Byzantium, s.v. "Tabis" (Τάβις): city in Arabia. Hecateus in *Periegesis* of Egypt.

322. Athenaeus 3.114c: Egyptians call their sourish bread *kyllastis* (κυλλᾶστιν). Aristophanes (1.457 Kock) mentions it in *Danaids*, "sing also of the *kyllastis* and Master Petosiris." Hecateus and Herodotus (2.77) and Phanodemus, in book 7 of his *Atthis*, also mention it. Nikandros of Thyateira says that the bread made from barley is called *kyllastis* by the Egyptians.

323. (a) Athenaeus 10.447c: Hecateus in the second book of his *Periegesis*, after saying of the Egyptians that they were bread-eaters, continues: "They grind up the barley to make the drink."

(b) Athenaeus 10.418e: Hecateus says the Egyptians were bread-eaters, eating *kyllestis* (κυλλήστιας), while they ground up their barley to make a drink.

324. (a) Porphyry in Eusebius, *Praeparatio evangelica (Preparation for the Gospel)* 10.3.466b: And why should I say to you that the *Barbarika Nomima (Barbarian Customs)* of Hellanicus (4 F 72) was put together from the works of Herodotus and Damastes? Or that Herodotus in his second book took many passages almost verbatim from the *Periegesis* of Hecateus of Miletus, the description of the phoenix (2.73), for example, and the hippopotamus (2.71) and the method of hunting crocodiles (2.70)?

(b) Herodotus 2.70–73: There are many ways of hunting the crocodile, and of every sort. I will tell you about the one that seems most worthwhile relating. The hunter puts his bait, the back of a pig, on a hook and lets it go out into the middle of the stream; he himself stays on the river-bank, where he has a young pig, alive, and he hits the pig. As soon as the crocodile hears the squeal of the pig, he makes for the sound and meets the bait (the dead pig's back) and swallows it down. Then they draw him in. When he has been hauled to land, first of all the hunter smears his eyes with mud. After he has done that, he masters the animal, for the rest, right easily; but if this is not done, he does so only with trouble.

The hippopotamuses are sacred in the province of Papremis but not so among the rest of the Egyptians. This is the kind of form they have: four feet, cloven hooves like cattle, a snub nose, and with the mane of a horse; they show tusks, a horse's tail and voice, and are of the bigness of the greatest ox. Hippopotamus skin is so thick that, when it is dried, men make spearshafts out of it.

In the river there are also otters, which the people think are sacred. They also regard as sacred the fish they call the *lepidotos* and the eel; these, they say, are sacred to the Nile, as, among birds, is the fox-goose.

There is another sacred bird, the name of which is the phoenix. I never saw one myself, except in pictures; for indeed it comes but rarely—the people of Heliopolis say only every five hundred years. They say that he comes at the time his father dies. If he is indeed like his pictures, he would be of this kind and this size: he has gold on his wings, which are otherwise mostly red, and the outline and size of him are most like an eagle. The people say that this bird manages the following contrivance, though for my part I do not believe it. He sets out from Arabia and conveys his father to the shrine of the Sun, and he carries his father emplastered in myrrh and buries him in the Sun's shrine. The manner of his conveyance is this; first he forms an egg of myrrh, of a weight that he is able to carry, and after that he tries carrying it; and when the trial of it is over, he hollows out the egg and stows his father into it, and with more myrrh he plasters over the place he had hollowed out and stowed his father within. When his father lies within it, the weight is then the same as at first; and so, having plastered it over, he carries his father to the shrine of the Sun in Egypt. This is what the bird does, they say.

327. (b)[2] Photius, *Lexicon* (ed. C. Theodoridis) α 3352: "Aphthos" (Ἄφ-θος): a god among Egyptians, like Isis and Typhon. Hecateus in *Periegesis* of Egypt.

See *Suda* φ 477 "Phthas" (Φθάς): Hephaestus among the inhabitants of Memphis. Also a proverb: Phthas talked to you. Others say Aphthas (Ἄφ-θας), like staphis (σταφίς), astaphis (ἀσταφίς), and stakhus (στάχυς), as-takhus (ἄσταχυς).

HELLANICUS OF LESBOS

Hellanicus lived from about 480 to 395. He composed works of mythography, ethnography, and chronicles, and is most famous for his *Atthis*, a history of Attica. See *FGrHist* 4 for the full testimonia and fragments. Felix Jacoby reprinted the Egyptian fragments as *FGrHist* 608a, and the numbers of the fragments below correspond to that text.

2. For this fragment, which is not in *FGrHist*, see H. J. Mette, *Lustrum* 27 (1985) 34, and West 1991, 145.

Fragments

Aegyptiaca

1. (*FGrHist* 4 F 53) Athenaeus 11.470d: Hellanicus writes as follows in his *Aegyptiaca:* "In the houses of Egyptians are kept a bronze phiale, a bronze ladle, and a bronze strainer."

2. (4 F 54–55) Athenaeus 15.679f–680c: Concerning the ever-flowering wreaths of Egypt, Hellanicus in his *Aegyptiaca* writes as follows: "A city by the river named Tindion; this is a meeting-place of all the gods, and there is a large and holy temple of stone in the middle of the city, with stone portals. Within the temple grow acacias, white and black. Upon them wreaths are laid high above, twined with blossoms of the acanthus, pomegranate, and grape-vine; they are ever-flowering; these the gods deposited in Egypt when they learned that Babys, who is Typhon, was king." . . . (Followed by Demetrius 643 F 1.)

Hellanicus, whom we have just quoted, says also that Amasis, who was an ordinary man of humble rank in the first part of his career, came to be ruler over Egypt through the gift of a wreath which he had sent, after having it twined with the most beautiful flowers of the season, in observance of the birthday of Patarmis, who was ruling over Egypt at that time. For he, delighted with the beauty of the wreath, invited Amasis to dinner, and treating him thereafter as one of his friends, sent him out on one occasion as commander of his forces when the Egyptians went to war against him; and they, in their hatred of Patarmis, proclaimed Amasis king.

3. (4 T 25) Arrian / Epictetus, *Discourses* 2.19: "Of the things that exist, some are good, some bad, some indifferent. . . ."—"What is your authority"—"Hellanicus says so in his *Aegyptiaca.*"

4. (4 F 173) Diodorus 1.37.2–3: For on the general subject of the rise of the Nile and its sources, as well as on the manner in which it reaches the sea and the other points in which this, the largest river of the inhabited world, differs from all others. . . . Hellanicus and Cadmus (489 F 1), for instance, as well as Hecateus (1 F 302) and all the writers like them, belonging as they do one and all to the early school, turned to the answers offered by the myths.

5. (4 F 174) Antigonus, *Historiarum mirabilium collectio* 126: Concerning Egyptian Thebes, Hellanicus of Lesbos relates that there is a cave on the town side in which there is calm on the thirtieth day of the month and wind on the other days.

6. (4 F 175) Athenaeus 1.34a: Theopompus of Chios (115 F 277) relates that the vine was discovered in Olympia, on the banks of the Alpheus. . . .

but Hellanicus says that the vine was first discovered in the city of Plinthine, in Egypt. (Followed by Dion 665 F 81.)

7. (4 Γ 175) Plutarch, *On Isis and Osiris* 34: . . . and Dionysus the Greeks call also Hyes, since he is lord of the nature of moisture (ὑγρᾶς); and he is no other than Osiris. In fact, Hellanicus seems to have heard Osiris pronounced Hysiris by the priests, for he regularly spells the name in this way, deriving it, in all probability, from the nature of Osiris and the ceremony of finding him.

FGrHist 645a

Journey to the Temple of Ammon (ΕΙΣ ΑΜΜΩΝΟΣ ΑΝΑΒΑΣΙΣ)

1. (4 F 56) Athenaeus 14.652a: The phoenix-fruit is so mentioned by Hellanicus in his *Journey to the Temple of Ammon,* if the work be genuine.

ARISTAGORAS

Aristagoras may have come from Miletus in Asia Minor. He was a slightly younger contemporary of Plato and composed his work before 332. The numbers of the testimonia and fragments below correspond to *FGrHist* 608.

Testimonia

1. Diogenes Laertius 1.72: Aristagoras of Miletus (F 11).
2. Stephanus of Byzantium, s.v. "City of women" (Γυναικόσπολις): . . . . Aristagoras, who is not much younger than Plato.
3. Pliny, *Natural History* 1.36: Marvellous structures in various countries: Egyptian Sphinx; pyramids; Pharos; labyrinths. . . . Foreign authorities:. . . . Alexander Polyhistor (273), Apion Plistonicus (616), Duris (76), Herodotus, Euhemerus (63), Aristagoras (F 6), Dionysius (653), Artemidorus (V), Butoridas (654), Antisthenes (655), Demetrius (643), Demoteles (656), Lyceas (613).

Fragments

Aegyptiaca

Book 1

1. Stephanus of Byzantium, s.v. "Hermotumbieis" (Ἑρμοτυμβιεῖς): part of the warriors in Egypt, as Aristagoras in his *Aegyptiaca,* book 1. These are also called Labareis (Λαβαρεῖς).[3]

---

3. The text is uncertain here: an alternative reading has Kalasiries, rather than Labareis. See also Herodotus 2.164–66; Fornara 1994, 22–23.

2. Stephanus of Byzantium, s.v. "Takompsos" (Τάκομψος): town on the border of Egyptians and Ethiopians near the island of Philai, as Aristagoras in his *Aegyptiaca,* book 1.

Book 2

3. Stephanus of Byzantium, s.v. "Nikiou town" (Νικίου κώμη): in Egypt: Aristagoras in his *Aegyptiaca,* book 2. The inhabitant is called Nikiotes (Νικιώτης), as Oros says in his *Peoples,* book 1.

Without Book Number

4. Aelian, *On the Nature of Animals* 11.10: Among the Egyptians, Apis is believed to be the god whose presence is most manifest. He is born of a cow on which a flash of light from heaven has fallen and caused his engendering. The Greeks call him Epaphus and trace his descent from his mother the Argive Io, daughter of Inachus. The Egyptians however reject the story as false and appeal to time as their witness, for they maintain that Epaphus was born late down the ages, whereas the first Apis visited mankind many, many thousands of years earlier. Herodotus (3.28.3) and Aristagoras adduce evidence and tokens of this; but the Egyptians do not acknowledge them.

5. Diogenes Laertius 1.11: They hold that the universe is created and perishable, and that it is spherical in shape. . . . that rain is caused by change in the atmosphere; of all other phenomena they give physical explanations, as related by Hecateus (264 F 1) and Aristagoras.

6. Pliny, *Natural History* 36.79: Those who write about these (the Pyramids)—they are Herodotus (2.124 ff.), Euhemerus (63 F 10), Duris of Samos (76 F 43), Aristagoras, Dionysius (653), Artemidorus, Alexander Polyhistor (273 F 108), Butoridas (654), Antisthenes (655), Demetrius (643), Demoteles (656), and Apion (616 F 17)—among all these, there is no agreement as to who was responsible for the construction, since chance, with the greatest justice, has caused the persons responsible for such monuments of vanity to be forgotten. Some of these writers have recorded that sixteen hundred talents were spent on radishes and garlic and onions.

7. Plutarch, *On Isis and Osiris* 5: The priests feel such repugnance for things that are of a superfluous nature that they not only eschew most legumes, as well as mutton and pork, which leave a large residuum, but they also use no salt with their food during their periods of holy living. For this they have various reasons, but in particular the fact that salt, by sharpening the appetite, makes them more inclined to drinking and eating. To consider salt impure because, as Aristagoras has said, when it is crystallizing

many minute creatures are caught in it and die there, is certainly silly. (Followed by 665 F 109a.)

8. Stephanus of Byzantium, s.v. "Gynaikospolis" (Γυναικόσπολις, "City of women"): city of Phoenicians. . . . There exists also another city in Egypt. Aristagoras, who is not much younger than Plato, says that it was given this name for three reasons: because enemies fell upon the city, while the men were away in the fields, and the women won the war; or because the wife of a nomarch, whose children were kidnapped by the king, took up arms along with her children, attacked the king, and was victorious; or because, when the inhabitants of Naukratis sailed upstream on the river and were prevented from disembarking by the rest of the Egyptians, these people were stricken with unmanly cowardice and did not stop them. Artemidorus also gives these reasons.

9. (a) Stephanus of Byzantium, s.v. "Hellenikon and Karikon": ('Ελληνικὸν καὶ Καρικόν): places in Memphis, from where are Hellenomemphites ('Ελληνομεμφῖται) and Caromemphites (Καρομεμφῖται), as Aristagoras says.

(b) Stephanus of Byzantium, s.v. "Karikon" (Καρικὸν): special place in Memphis, where Carians lived, and after they entered into marriages with Memphites were called Caromemphites (Καρομεμφῖται). 665 F 200.[4]

10. Stephanus of Byzantium, s.v. "Psebo" (Ψεβώ): land deep inside of Ethiopia, about which Aristagoras writes as follows: "These people say that there is a land that is a five-day journey from Ethiopia called Psebo." Artemidorus says it is a lake in book 8 of his *Geography*.

Doubtful

11. Diogenes Laertius 1.72 (*Suda* s.v. χίλων): He was a man of few words (βραχυλόγος); hence Aristagoras of Miletus calls this style of speaking Chilonean (Χειλώνειον). . . . is of Branchus, founder of the temple at Branchidae.

12. Stephanus of Byzantium, s.v. "Momemphis" (Μώμεμφις): city in Egypt; Herodotus, book 2 (2.163.2; 2.169.1). Inflected Μωμέμφεως, as Aristagoras.

EUDOXUS OF CNIDUS

Eudoxus, from Cnidus on the coast of Asia Minor, lived from about 390 to 340. He was the author of works on mathematics, astronomy, philosophy,

---

4. This is a reference to Polyainos, *Strategemata* 7.3.

and geography. His writings about Egypt come principally from his *Ges periodos*. For the full testimonia and fragments, see Lasserre 1966, the numbering of which is used below.

Testimonia

7. Diogenes Laertius 8.86–91: Eudoxus of Cnidus, the son of Aeschines, was an astronomer, a geometer, a physician, and a legislator. . . . After spending two months there [in Piraeus and Athens], he went home and, aided by the liberality of his friends, he proceeded to Egypt with Chrysippus the physician, bearing with him letters of introduction from Agesilaus to Nectanabis, who recommended him to the priests. There he remained one year and four months with his beard and eyebrows shaved, and there, some say, he wrote his *Octaeteris*. From there he went to Cyzicus and the Propontis, giving lectures; afterwards he came home to the court of Mausolus. . . .

Eratosthenes in his writings addressed to Baton tells us that he also composed *Dialogues of Dogs*; others say that they were written by Egyptians in their own language and that he translated them and published them in Greece. . . .

He died in his fifty-third year. When he was in Egypt with Chonuphis of Heliopolis, the sacred bull Apis licked his cloak. From this the priests foretold that he would be famous but short-lived, so we are informed by Favorinus in his *Apomnemoneumata (Memorabilia)*.

There is a poem of our own upon him, which runs thus:

> It is said that at Memphis Eudoxus learned his coming fate
> from the bull with beautiful horns. No words did it utter: for
> whence comes speech to a bull? Nature did not provide the
> young bull Apis with a chattering tongue. But, standing
> sideways by him, it licked his robe, by which it plainly
> prophesied "you shall soon die." Whereupon, soon after, this
> fate overtook him, when he had seen fifty-three risings of the Pleiades.
> (*Palatine Anthology* 7.744)

Eudoxus used to be called "Endoxos" (illustrious) instead of Eudoxus by reason of his brilliant reputation.

11. Philostratus, *Life of Apollonius* 1.34: Moreover, they tell of how Eudoxus of Cnidus once arrived in Egypt, and both admitted that he had come there in quest of money and conversed with the king about the matter.

12. Strabo 17.1.29: In Heliopolis I also saw large houses in which the priests lived; for it is said that this place in particular was in ancient times

a settlement of priests who studied philosophy and astronomy; but both this organization and its pursuits have now disappeared. At Heliopolis, in fact, no one was pointed out to me as presiding over such pursuits, but only those who performed the sacrifices explained to strangers what pertained to the sacred rites. When Aelius Gallus, the prefect, sailed up into Egypt, he was accompanied by a certain man from Alexandria, Chaeremon by name, who pretended to some knowledge of this kind, but was generally ridiculed as a boaster and ignoramus. However, at Heliopolis the houses of the priests and schools of Plato and Eudoxus were pointed out to us; for Eudoxus went up to that place with Plato, and they both passed thirteen years with the priests, as is stated by some writers; for since these priests excelled in their knowledge of the heavenly bodies, albeit secretive and slow to impart it, Plato and Eudoxus prevailed upon them in time and by courting their favor to let them learn some of the principles of their doctrines; but the barbarians concealed most things. However, these men did teach them the fractions of the day and the night which, running over and above the 365 days, fill out the time of the true year. But at that time the true year was unknown among the Greeks, as also many other things, until the later astrologers learned them from the men who had translated into Greek the records of the priests; and even to this day they learn their teachings, and likewise those of the Chaldaeans.

13. Strabo 17.1.30: Now Heliopolis is in Arabia, but the city Kerkesoura, which lies near the observatories of Eudoxus, is in Libya; for a kind of watchtower is to be seen in front of Heliopolis, as also in front of Cnidus, with reference to which Eudoxus would note down his observations of certain movements of the heavenly bodies. The Letopolites nome is here.

14. Cosmas Indicopleustes, *Christian Topography* 3.1: When for the first time men, after the Deluge and during the construction of the tower in their war with God, reached a great height, they made regular observation of the stars and, being led astray, gave consideration to the idea that the heaven was spherical. Since the city where they had erected the tower was among Babylonians, this discovery must have originated with the Chaldaeans, who subsequently elaborated the barbarian theory of the sphere. Then those who were of the race of Abraham, being Chaldaeans in origin, went into Egypt and transmitted this idea to the Egyptians. The Egyptians themselves, taking hold of this starting point with curiosity, also developed this idea, until the Greeks journeyed to Egypt, the philosophers Pythagoras, Plato, and Eudoxus of Cnidus, and altered it some more and elaborated it, taking their starting point from the preceding discoverers.

15. Seneca, *Natural Questions* 7.3.2: Democritus, the most accurate of

all the ancients, says that he suspects there are more stars on the move, but he does not give their number or their names, since the orbits of the five planets had not yet been comprehended (DK 68 A 92). Eudoxus was the first one to bring knowledge of these orbits from Egypt into Greece. Yet he says nothing about comets, from which it appears that this part of astronomy had not been worked on even by the Egyptians, who had a very great interest in the sky.

16. Diodorus 1.96.2–98.4: For the priests of Egypt recount from the records of their sacred books that they were visited in early times by Orpheus, Musaeus, Melampus, and Daedalus, also by the poet Homer and Lycurgus of Sparta, later by Solon of Athens and the philosopher Plato, and that there also came Pythagoras of Samos and the mathematician Eudoxus, as well as Democritus of Abdera and Oenopides of Chios. As evidence for the visits of all these men they point in some cases to their statues and in others to places or buildings which bear their names, and they offer proofs from the branch of learning which each one of these men pursued, arguing that all the things for which they were admired among the Greeks were transferred from Egypt. . . .

Like the others, Eudoxus studied astrology with them [i.e. Egyptians] and acquired a notable fame for the great amount of useful knowledge which he disseminated among the Greeks.

17. Plutarch, *On Isis and Osiris* 10: Witness to this are also the wisest of the Greeks: Solon, Thales, Plato, Eudoxus, Pythagoras, who came to Egypt and consorted with the priests; and in this number some would include Lycurgus also. Eudoxus, they say, received instruction from Chonuphis of Memphis, Solon from Sonkhis of Saïs, and Pythagoras from Oenuphis of Heliopolis.

18. Clement of Alexandria, *Stromateis (Miscellanies)* 1.15.69: Pythagoras, it is recorded, studied with Sonkhis the Egyptian high priest, Plato with Sechnuphis of Heliopolis, and Eudoxus of Cnidus with Conuphis, also himself an Egyptian.

19. Iamblichus, *On the Mysteries of the Egyptians* 1.1: As for me, supposing quite reasonably that the letter sent to Anebo, my student, was written for me, I shall respond to your inquiries with the truth itself. It would not be appropriate for Pythagoras, Plato, Democritus, Eudoxus, and many others of the ancient Greeks to have obtained suitable instruction from the sacred scribes (ἱερογραμματέων) of their own times, and for you, my contemporary, who have the same learning as these men, to fail to obtain guidance from living and so-called public teachers.

20. Philostratus, *Lives of the Sophists* 1.1: Eudoxus of Cnidus, though

he devoted considerable study to the teachings of the Academy, was nevertheless placed on the list of sophists because his style was ornate and he improvised with success. He was honored with the title of sophist in the Hellespont and the Propontis, at Memphis, and in Egypt beyond Memphis where it borders on Ethiopia and the region inhabited by those wise men who are called naked philosophers (οἱ Γυμνοί).

Fragments

Ges periodos

Book 2

286. Stephanus of Byzantium, s.v. "Asdynis" (Ἄσδυνις): Island in lake Moeris. Eudoxus in his second book: "They were seized on Asdynis the island." The islander is called Asdynites (Ἀσδυνίτης), like Memphites (Μεμφίτης).

287. Scholia to Homer, *Odyssey* 4.477: Although many have written about the rising of the Nile, Homer was the first to state the true reason by calling it διιπετῆ ("fallen from Zeus"),[5] since it is filled up by continuous and heavy rainfall during the summer in Ethiopia, as Aristotle and Eudoxus say they learned from the priests in Egypt.

See Aristotle, *Meteorology* 349a4: For the same reason in Arabia and Ethiopia rain falls in the summer and not in the winter, and falls with violence and many times on the same day; for the clouds are cooled quickly by the reaction due to the great heat of the country.

288. Aetius, *De placitis philosophorum (Philosophers' Views of Nature)* 4.1: Eudoxus relates that the priests say that the rain waters vary according to the alternation (ἀντιπερίστασις) of the seasons. For, whenever we who live below the summer tropic are in summer, at that time those who live opposite us and below the winter tropic are in winter, in consequence of which the rising water rushes down.

289. Diodorus 1.40.1–4: [The editor reprints here a lengthy passage from Diodorus about the explanations given by the wise men in Memphis to account for the behavior of the Nile. Eudoxus is not explicitly mentioned, but he may be Diodorus' source.]

290. Plutarch, *On Isis and Osiris* 12–18: [The editor reprints here a lengthy passage from Plutarch concerning the story of Isis and Osiris. Eudoxus is not explicitly mentioned, but he may be Plutarch's source.]

291. Plutarch, *On Isis and Osiris* 21: Eudoxus says that, while many

5. The translation of this expression is discussed in Griffith 1997.

tombs of Osiris are spoken of in Egypt, his body lies in Busiris; for this was the place of his birth; moreover, Taphosiris requires no comment, for the name itself means "the tomb of Osiris."

292. Plutarch, *On Isis and Osiris* 18–20: [The editor reprints here a lengthy passage from Plutarch that continues the story of Isis and Osiris, with details about the help that Osiris receives from Horus. Eudoxus is not explicitly mentioned, but he may be Plutarch's source.]

293. Plutarch, *On Isis and Osiris* 30: It is plain that the adherents of Pythagoras hold Typhon to be a daemonic power; for they say that he was born in an even factor of fifty-six; and the dominion of the triangle belongs to Hades, Dionysus, and Ares, that of the quadrilateral to Rhea, Aphrodite, Demeter, Hestia, and Hera, that of the dodecagon to Zeus, and that of a polygon of fifty-six sides to Typhon, as Eudoxus has recorded.

294. Plutarch, *On Isis and Osiris* 33: But the wiser of the priests call not only the Nile Osiris and the sea Typhon, but they simply give the name of Osiris to the whole source and faculty creative of moisture, believing this to be the cause of generation and the substance of life-producing seed; and the name of Typhon they give to all that is dry, fiery, and arid, in general, and antagonistic to moisture.

295. Plutarch, *On Isis and Osiris* 36: There is another tale current among the Egyptians that Apopis, brother of the Sun, made war upon Zeus, and that because Osiris espoused Zeus' cause and helped him to overthrow his enemy, Zeus adopted Osiris as his son and gave him the name of Dionysus. It may be demonstrated that the legend contained in this tale has some approximation to truth so far as Nature is concerned; for the Egyptians apply the name "Zeus" to the wind, and whatever is dry or fiery is antagonistic to this. This is not the sun, but has some kinship with the sun; and the moisture, by doing away with the excess of dryness, increases and strengthens the exhalations by which the wind is fostered and made vigorous.

296. Plutarch, *On Isis and Osiris* 38–40: [The editor reprints here a lengthy passage from Plutarch concerning various details in the story of Isis and Osiris. Eudoxus is not explicitly mentioned, but he may be Plutarch's source.]

297. Plutarch, *On Isis and Osiris* 52: . . . and Eudoxus asserts that Isis is a deity who presides over love affairs.

298. Plutarch, *On Isis and Osiris* 64: Further, we shall put a stop to the incredulity of Eudoxus and his questionings how it is that Demeter has no share in the supervision of love affairs, but Isis has; and the fact that Dionysus cannot cause the Nile to rise, nor rule over the dead.

299. Plutarch, *On Isis and Osiris* 62: Moreover, Eudoxus says that the

Egyptians have a mythical tradition in regard to Zeus that, because his legs were grown together, he was not able to walk, and so, for shame, tarried in the wilderness; but Isis, by severing and separating those parts of his body, provided him with means of rapid progress.

300. Plutarch, *On Isis and Osiris* 6: As for wine, those who serve the god in Heliopolis bring none at all into the shrine, since they feel that it is not seemly to drink in the day time while their lord and king is looking upon them. The others use wine, but in great moderation. They have many periods of holy living when wine is prohibited, and in these they spend their time exclusively in studying, learning, and teaching religious matters. Their kings also were wont to drink a limited quantity prescribed by the sacred writings, as Hecateus (*FGrHist* 264 F 5) has recorded; and the kings are priests. The beginning of their drinking dates from the reign of Psammetichus; before that they did not drink wine nor use it in libations as something dear to the gods, thinking it to be the blood of those who had once battled against the gods, and from whom, when they had fallen and had become commingled with the earth, they believed vines to have sprung. This is the reason why drunkenness drives men out of their senses and crazes them, inasmuch as they are then filled with the blood of their forbears. These tales Eudoxus says in the second book of his *Periodos* are thus related by the priests.

301. Aelian, *On the Nature of Animals* 10.16: But Eudoxus asserts that the Egyptians refrain from sacrificing sows, because when the corn has been sown they drive in herds of them, and they tread and press the seed into the soil when moist so that it may remain fertile and not be consumed by the birds.

302. Proclus, *Commentary on Timaeus* 22b3–5 (1.102, ed. Diehl): If what Eudoxus says is true, that Egyptians call the month "year," the count of all these years would not be very extraordinary.

Without Book Title

331. Antigonus, *Historiarum mirabilium collectio* 147: Eudoxus says that the spring in Chalcedon has in it little crocodiles that are like the ones in Egypt.

333. Antigonus, *Historiarum mirabilium collectio* 162: Eudoxus also says about the wells in Pythopolis that they are very nearly like the Nile; for, during the summer, they fill up and overflow, but during the winter, they are such that it is not easy to dip into them.

TEXTS

The texts of the fragments of Eudoxus are available in Lasserre 1966; the texts of the remaining fragmentary authors are available in *FGrHist*. On very few occasions, I have followed readings different from the ones given in these editions.

TRANSLATIONS

Passages from the following sources appear above in my own translation: Aetius, Antigonus, Aristides, Cosmas Indicopleustes, Epictetus (in Arrian), Herodian, Iamblichus, Porphyry (in Eusebius), Photius, Proclus, scholia (to various authors), *Suda,* and Stephanus of Byzantium. Translations of Herodotus are modified from Grene 1987. The remaining translations are modified from editions in the Loeb Classical Library.

SELECT BIBLIOGRAPHY

Gutschmid 1855, Ginsinger 1921, Pearson 1939, Brown 1962, Lasserre 1966, Fritz 1967, Froidefond 1971, Drews 1973, Lloyd 1975, West 1991, Fornara 1994, Burstein 1996, and the relevant entries by Jacoby and others in *RE*.

Abbreviations

CGFP   C. F. L. Austin, ed., *Comicorum Graecorum Fragmenta in papyris reperta*, Berlin, 1973.

DK   H. Diels and W. Kranz, eds., *Die Fragmente der Vorsokratiker*, 3 vols., 6th ed., Berlin, 1951–52.

FGrHist   F. Jacoby, ed., *Die Fragmente der griechischen Historiker*, Berlin and Leiden, 1923–.

FHG   C. Müller, ed., *Fragmenta Historicorum Graecorum*, 5 vols., Paris, 1841–70.

FJW   H. Friis Johansen and E. W. Whittle, eds., *Aeschylus: The Suppliants*, 3 vols., Copenhagen, 1980.

GGM   C. Müller, ed., *Geographi Graeci Minores*, 2 vols., Paris, 1855–61.

IG   *Inscriptiones Graecae*, Berlin, 1873–.

LÄ   W. Helck, E. Otto, and W. Westendorf, eds., *Lexikon der Ägyptologie*, 7 vols., Wiesbaden, 1975–92.

LIMC   *Lexicon Iconographicum Mythologiae Classicae*, 8 vols., Zurich, 1981–97.

LSJ   H. G. Liddell, R. Scott, and H. S. Jones, eds., *A Greek English Lexicon, with a Revised Supplement*, 9th rev. ed., 1996.

ML   R. Meiggs and D. M. Lewis, eds., *A Selection of Greek Historical Inscriptions to the End of the Fifth Century B.C.*, rev. ed., Oxford, 1988.

OCT   Scriptorum Classicorum Bibliotheca Oxoniensis (Oxford Classical Texts).

PCG   R. Kassel and C. Austin, eds., *Poetae Comici Graeci*, Berlin,
           1983 –.

RE   A. Pauly, G. Wissowa, and W. Kroll, eds., *Real-Encyclopädie
           der klassischen Altertumswissenschaft*, Stuttgart, 1890 –
           1980.

SEG   *Supplementum Epigraphicum Graecum*, 1923 –.

TrGF   B. Snell, S. Radt, and R. Kannicht, eds., *Tragicorum Graeco-
           rum Fragmenta*, Göttingen, 1971–.

Bibliography

Abd el-Raziq, M. 1984. *Die Darstellungen und Texte des Sanktuars Alexanders des Grossen im Tempel von Luxor.* Deutsches Archäologisches Institut Kairo, Archäologische Veröffentlichungen 16. Cairo.

Algra, K. 1995. *Concepts of Space in Greek Thought.* Leiden.

Alloula, M. 1986. *The Colonial Harem.* Translated by M. and W. Godzich. Minneapolis.

Armayor, O. K. 1978. Did Herodotus Ever Go to Egypt? *Journal of the American Research Center in Egypt* 15:59–71.

———. 1985. *Herodotus' Autopsy of the Fayoum.* Amsterdam.

Arnold, D. 1999. *Temples of the Last Pharaohs.* Oxford.

Asante, M. K. 1990. *Kemet, Afrocentricity, and Knowledge.* Trenton.

Assmann, A., J. Assmann, and C. Hardmeier, eds. 1983. *Schrift und Gedächtnis: Beiträge zur Archäologie der literarischen Kommunikation.* Munich.

Assmann, J. 1970. *Der König als Sonnenpriester: Ein kosmographischer Begleittext zur kultischen Sonnenhymnik in thebanischen Tempeln und Gräbern.* Glückstadt.

———. 1975. *Zeit und Ewigkeit im alten Ägypten: Ein Beitrag zur Geschichte der Ewigkeit.* Heidelberg.

———. 1983. Schrift, Tod, und Identität: Das Grab als Vorschule der Literatur im alten Ägypten. In A. Assmann, J. Assmann, and C. Hardmeier, eds. 1983, 64–93.

———. 1985. Die Entdeckung der Vergangenheit: Innovation und Restauration in der ägyptischen Literaturgeschichte. In *Epochenschwellen und Epochenstrukturen in Diskurs der Literatur- und Sprachhistorie,* edited by H. U. Gumbrecht and U. Link-Heer, 484–99. Frankfurt am Main.

———. 1987. Heirotaxis: Textkonstitution und Bildkonstitution in der altägyptischen Kunst und Literatur. In *Form und Mass: Beiträge zur Literatur, Sprache und Kunst des alten Ägypten: Festschrift für Gerhard Fecht zum 65. Geburtstag am 6. Februar 1987,* edited by J. Osing and G. Dreyer, 18–42. Wiesbaden.

————. 1990a. Die Macht der Bilder. Rahmenbedingungen ikonischen Handelns im alten Ägypten. *Visible Religion* 7:1–20.

————. 1990b. Guilt and Remembrance: On the Theologization of History in the Ancient Near East. *History and Memory* 2:5–33.

————. 1992. Inscriptional Violence and the Art of Cursing: A Study of Performative Writing. *Stanford Literature Review* 9 (spring): 43–65.

————. 1994. Ancient Egypt and the Materiality of the Sign. In *Materialities of Communication*, edited by H. U. Gumbrecht and K. L. Pfeiffer, translated by W. Whobrey, 15–31, 405–6. Stanford.

————. 1997. *Moses the Egyptian: The Memory of Egypt in Western Monotheism.* Cambridge, Mass.

Astour, M. C. 1965. *Hellenosemitica: An Ethnic and Cultural Study in West Semitic Impact on Mycenaean Greece.* Leiden.

Atkinson, K. M. T. 1956. The Legitimacy of Cambyses and Darius as Kings of Egypt. *Journal of the American Oriental Society* 76:167–77.

Austin, M. M. 1970. *Greece and Egypt in the Archaic Age.* Proceedings of the Cambridge Philological Society, suppl. vol. 2. Cambridge, Eng.

Austin, N. 1994. *Helen of Troy and Her Shameless Phantom.* Ithaca.

Backhaus, W. 1976. Der Hellenen-Barbaren-Gegensatz und die hippokratische Schrift περὶ ἀέρων ὑδάτων τόπων. *Historia* 25:170–85.

Bacon, H. H. 1961. *Barbarians in Greek Tragedy.* New Haven.

Baines, J. 1983. Literacy and Ancient Egyptian Society. *Man,* n.s., 18:572–99.

————. 1985. *Fecundity Figures: Egyptian Personification and the Iconology of a Genre.* Warminster.

————. 1988. Literacy, Social Organization, and the Archaeological Record: The Case of Early Egypt. In *State and Society*, edited by J. Gledhill, B. Bender, and M. T. Larsen, 192–214. London.

————. 1989. Ancient Egyptian Concepts and Uses of the Past: 3rd to 2nd Millenium B.C. Evidence. In *Who Needs the Past? Indigenous Values and Archaelogy*, edited by R. Layton, 131–49. London.

————. 1996. Contextualizing Egyptian Representations of Society and Ethnicity. In *The Study of the Ancient Near East in the Twenty-first Century*, edited by J. S. Cooper and G. M. Schwartz, 339–84. Winona Lake, Ind.

Baines, J., and C. J. Eyre. 1983. Four Notes on Literacy. *Göttinger Miszellen* 61:65–96.

Bakhtin, M. M. 1968. *Rabelais and His World.* Translated by H. Iswolsky. Cambridge, Mass.

————. 1978. Discourse Typology in Prose. In *Readings in Russian Poetics: Formalist and Structuralist Views*, edited by L. Matejka and K. Pomorska, 176–96. 1971. Reprint, Ann Arbor.

————. 1984. *Problems of Dostoevsky's Poetics.* Edited and translated by C. Emerson. Minneapolis.

Ball, J. 1942. *Egypt in the Classical Geographers.* Cairo.

Barthes, R. 1986. *The Rustle of Language.* Translated by R. Howard. New York.

Basch, L. 1977. Trières grecques, phéniciennes et égyptiennes. *Journal of Hellenic Studies* 97:1–10.

———. 1980. M. le Professeur Lloyd et les trières: quelques remarques. *Journal of Hellenic Studies* 100:198–99.

Bassi, K. 1993. Helen and the Discourse of Denial in Stesichorus' Palinode. *Arethusa* 26:51–75.

Baxter, T. M. S. 1992. *The Cratylus: Plato's Critique of Naming.* Leiden.

Beaucour, F., Y. Laissus, and C. Orgogozo. 1990. *The Discovery of Egypt.* Translated by B. Ballard. Paris.

Bell, L. 1985. The Luxor Temple and the Cult of the Royal Ka. *Journal of Near Eastern Studies* 44:251–94.

Benardete, S. 1969. *Herodotean Inquiries.* The Hague.

Berlinerblau, J. 1999. *Heresy in the University: The Black Athena Controversy and the Responsibilities of American Intellectuals.* New Brunswick.

Bernal, M. 1987. *Black Athena: The Afroasiatic Roots of Classical Civilization,* vol. 1, *The Fabrication of Ancient Greece, 1785–1985.* New Brunswick.

———. 1991. *Black Athena: The Afroasiatic Roots of Classical Civilization,* vol. 2, *The Archaeological and Documentary Evidence.* New Brunswick.

Bernand, A. 1970. *Le delta égyptien d'après les textes grecs,* vol. 1, *Les confins libyques,* 4 pts. Cairo.

———. 1985. *La carte du tragique: la géographie dans la tragédie grecque.* Paris.

Bernand, A., and O. Masson. 1957. Les inscriptions grecques d'Abou-Simbel. *Revue des études grecques* 70:1–46.

Bhabha, H. 1996. The Other Question. In *Contemporary Postcolonial Theory,* edited by P. Mongia, 36–54. London. Originally published in *Screen* 24 (1983): 18–36.

Bianchi, R. S. 1988. Tattoo in Ancient Egypt. In *Marks of Civilization: Transformations of the Human Body,* edited by A. Rubin, 21–28. Los Angeles.

Bickerman, E. 1952. Origines gentium. *Classical Philology* 47:65–81.

———. 1980. *Chronology of the Ancient World.* 2d ed. Ithaca.

Bleeker, C. J. 1973. *Hathor and Thoth.* Leiden.

Boardman, J. 1978. *Greek Sculpture: Archaic Period.* London.

———. 1980. *The Greeks Overseas.* New ed. London.

———. 1994. *The Diffusion of Classical Art in Antiquity.* Princeton.

Bochi, P. A. 1994. Images of Time in Ancient Egyptian Art. *Journal of the American Research Center in Egypt* 31:55–62.

Bonneau, D. 1964. *La crue du Nil.* Paris.

———. 1971. Liber Aristotelis de inundatione Nili. *Études de Papyrologie* 9:1–33.

Bonnechere, P. 1994. *Le sacrifice humain en Grèce ancienne.* Athens and Liège.

Boone, J. A. 1995. Vacation Cruises; or, The Homoerotics of Orientalism. *Proceedings of the Modern Language Association* 110:89–107.

Boring, T. A. 1979. *Literacy in Ancient Sparta.* Leiden.

Borthwick, E. K. 1963. The Oxyrhynchus Musical Monody and Some Ancient Fertility Superstitions. *American Journal of Philology* 84:225–43.

Bosworth, A. B. 1993. Aristotle, India, and the Alexander Historians. *Topoi. Orient-Occident* 3:407–24.

———. 1996. *Alexander and the East: The Tragedy of Triumph.* Oxford.

Bothmer, B. V. 1960. *Egyptian Sculpture of the Late Period, 700 B.C. to A.D. 100.* Brooklyn.

Bourdieu, P. 1977. *Outline of a Theory of Practice.* Translated by R. Nice. Cambridge, Eng.

Bowersock, G. W. 1989. Herodotus, Alexander, and Rome. *The American Scholar* 58:407–14.

Bowersock, G., W. Burkert, and M. Putnam, eds. 1979. *Arktouros: Hellenic Studies Presented to Bernard M. W. Knox on the Occasion of His 65th Birthday.* Berlin.

Bowman, A. K., and G. Woolf, eds. 1994. *Literacy and Power in the Ancient World.* Cambridge, Eng.

Boylan, P. 1922. *Thoth the Hermes of Egypt.* London.

Brady, T. A. 1935. *The Reception of the Egyptian Cults by the Greeks (330–30 B.C.).* Columbia, Mo.

Braun, T. F. R. G. 1982. The Greeks in Egypt. In *The Cambridge Ancient History,* 2d ed., vol. 3, pt. 3, edited by J. Boardman and N. G. L. Hammond, 32–56. Cambridge, Eng.

Breasted, J. H. 1906. *Ancient Records of Egypt,* vol. 4, *The Twentieth to the Twenty-sixth Dynasties.* Chicago.

Brelich, A. 1969. Symbol of a Symbol. In *Myths and Symbols: Studies in Honor of Mircea Eliade,* edited by J. M. Kitagawa and C. H. Long, with G. C. Brauer and M. G. S. Hodgson, 195–207. Chicago.

Bresciani, E. 1958. La satrapia d'Egitto. *Studi classici e orientali* 7:132–88.

———. 1968. Egypt and the Persian Empire. In *The Greeks and the Persians from the Sixth to the Fourth Centuries,* edited by H. Bengtson, 333–53. New York.

———. 1984. Egypt, Persian Satrapy. In *The Cambridge History of Judaism,* vol. 1, edited by W. D. Davies and L. Finkelstein, 358–72. Cambridge, Eng.

Brillante, C. 1990. History and the Historical Interpretation of Myth. In *Approaches to Greek Myth,* edited by L. Edmunds, 93–138. Baltimore.

Brisson, L. 1982. *Platon, les mots et les mythes.* Paris.

———. 1987. L'Égypte de Platon. *Les études philosophiques* 153–68.

———. 1994. *Le même et l'autre dans la structure ontologique du* Timée *de Platon: Un commentaire systématique du* Timée *de Platon.* 2d ed. Sankt Augustin, Germany.

Brown, S. 1991. *Late Carthaginian Child Sacrifice and Sacrificial Monuments in Their Mediterranean Context.* Sheffield.

Brown, T. S. 1962. The Greek Sense of Time in History as Suggested by Their Accounts of Egypt. *Historia* 11:257–70.

Brunner, H. 1970. Zum Verständnis der archaisierenden Tendenzen der ägyptischen Spätzeit. *Saeculum* 21:150–61.

———. 1979. Illustrierte Bücher im alten Ägypten. In *Wort und Bild,* edited by H. Brunner, R. Kannicht, and K. Schwager, 201–18. Munich.

Brunt, P. A., ed. 1976–83. *Arrian: History of Alexander and Indica.* 2 vols. Loeb Classical Library. Cambridge, Mass.

Buchheit, V. 1960. *Untersuchungen zur Theorie des Genos Epideiktikon von Gorgias bis Aristoteles.* Munich.

Burckhardt, J. 1998. *The Greeks and Greek Civilization.* Edited by O. Murray, translated by S. Stern. New York.

Burger, R. 1980. *Plato's Phaedrus: A Defense of a Philosophic Art of Writing.* University, Ala.

Burgess, T. C. 1902. Epideictic Literature. *The University of Chicago Studies in Classical Philology* 3:89–261.

Burkert, W. 1976. Das hunderttorige Theben und die Datierung der Ilias. *Wiener Studien* 10:5–21.

———. 1983. *Homo Necans: The Anthropology of Ancient Greek Sacrificial Ritual and Myth.* Translated by P. Bing. Berkeley.

———. 1985. *Greek Religion.* Translated by J. Raffan. Cambridge, Mass.

———. 1992. *The Orientalizing Revolution: Near Eastern Influence on Greek Culture in the Early Archaic Age.* Translated by M. Pinder and W. Burkert. Cambridge, Mass.

Burstein, S. M. 1995. *Graeco-Africana: Studies in the History of Greek Relations with Egypt and Nubia.* New Rochelle, N.Y.

———. 1996. Images of Egypt in Greek Historiography. In A. Loprieno, ed. 1996, 591–604.

Burton, A. 1972. *Didodorus Siculus Book I: A Commentary.* Leiden.

Butler, J. 1990. *Gender Trouble: Feminism and the Subversion of Identity.* New York.

Cahn, M. 1989. Reading Rhetoric Rhetorically: Isocrates and the Marketing of Insight. *Rhetorica* 7:121–44.

Caldwell, R. 1974. The Psychology of Aeschylus' *Supplices. Arethusa* 7:45–70.

Cameron, A. 1983. Crantor and Posidonius on Atlantis: *Classical Quarterly* 33:81–91.

Carbonell, C. O. 1985. L'espace et le temps dans l'oeuvre d'Hérodote. *Studi storici per l'antichità classica* 7:138–49.

Carr, D. 1987. *Time, Narrative, and History.* Bloomington.

Cartledge, P. 1978. Literacy in the Spartan Oligarchy. *Journal of Hellenic Studies* 98:25–37.

———. 1993. *The Greeks: A Portrait of Self and Others.* Oxford.

———. 1994. Response. In *The Birth of the European Identity; The Europe-Asia Contrast in Greek Thought 490–322 B.C.,* edited by H. A. Khan, 146–55. Nottingham.

Cavenaile, R. 1972. Pour une histoire politique et sociale d'Alexandrie. Les origines. *L'Antiquité Classique* 41:94–112.

Cerny, J. 1948. Thoth as Creator of Languages. *Journal of Egyptian Archaeology* 34:121–22.

Chakrabarty, D. 1992. Postcoloniality and the Artifice of History: Who Speaks for "Indian" Pasts? *Representations* 37:1–26.

Chow, R. 1994. Where Have All the Natives Gone? In *Displacements: Cultural Identities in Question,* edited by A. Bammer, 125–51. Bloomington.

Chroust, A.-H. 1957. *Socrates, Man and Myth: The Two Socratic Apologies of Xenophon.* Notre Dame.

Clader, L. L. 1976. *Helen: The Evolution from Divine to Heroic in Greek Epic Tradition.* Mnemosyne suppl. 42. Leiden.

Classen, C. J. 1959. The Libyan God Ammon in Greece Before 331 B.C. *Historia* 8:349–55.

Cleary, J. J., ed. 1986. *Proceedings of the Boston Area Colloquium in Ancient Philosophy,* vol. 1 (1985), New York.

Coleman, J. E., and C. A. Walz, eds. 1997. *Greeks and Barbarians: Essays on the Interactions between Greeks and Non-Greeks in Antiquity and the Consequences for Eurocentrism.* Bethesda, Md.

Colie, R. L. 1966. *Paradoxia Epidemica: The Renaissance Tradition of Paradox.* Princeton.

Conacher, D. J. 1996. *Aeschylus: The Earlier Plays and Related Studies.* Toronto.

Cooper, J. M. 1986. Plato, Isocrates, and Cicero on the Independence of Oratory from Philosophy. In J. J. Cleary, ed. 1986, 77–96.

Copenhaver, B. P. 1992. *Hermetica: The Greek* Corpus Hermeticum *and the Latin* Asclepius *in a New English Translation, with Notes and Introduction.* Cambridge, Eng.

Cornford, F. M. 1937. *Plato's Cosmology: The Timaeus of Plato Translated with a Running Commentary.* London.

Cowley, A. E. 1923. *Aramaic Papyri of the Fifth Century B.C.* Oxford.

Craik, E. M. 1984. Marriage in Ancient Greece. In *Marriage and Property,* edited by E. M. Craik, 6–29. Aberdeen.

Csapo, E., and M. Miller 1998. "Democracy, Empire, and Art: Toward a Politics of Time and Narrative." In *Democracy, Empire, and the Arts in Fifth-Century Athens,* edited by D. Boedeker and K. Raaflaub, 87–125. Cambridge, Mass.

Dale, A. M. 1967. *Euripides: Helen.* Oxford.

Darbo-Peschanski, C. 1987. *Le discours du particulier: Essai sur l'enquête hérodotéene.* Paris.

———. 1989. Les barbares à l'épreuve du temps (Hérodote, Thucydide, Xénophon). *Metis* 4:233–50.

Davies, J. K. 1971. *Athenian Propertied Families 600–300 B.C.* Oxford.

Davies, M., and J. Kathirithamby. 1986. *Greek Insects.* London.

Davis, S. 1951. *Race Relations in Ancient Egypt: Greek, Egyptian, Hebrew, Roman.* London.

Davis, W. M. 1979. Plato on Egyptian Art. *Journal of Egyptian Archaeology* 65:121–27.

———. 1981. Egypt, Samos, and the Archaic Style in Greek Sculpture. *Journal of Egyptian Archaeology* 67:61–81.

———. 1989. *The Canonical Tradition in Ancient Egyptian Art.* Cambridge, Eng.

Dawson, W. 1928. References to Mummification by Greek and Latin Authors. *Aegyptus* 9:106–12.

Day, J. 1989. *Molech: A God of Human Sacrifice in the Old Testament.* Cambridge, Eng.

de Camp, L. S. 1954. *Lost Continents: The Atlantis Theme in History, Science, and Literature.* New York.

de Certeau, M. 1988. *The Writing of History.* Translated by T. Conley. New York.

Derrida, J. 1976. *Of Grammatology.* Translated by G. C. Spivak. Baltimore.

———. 1981. *Dissemination.* Translated by B. Johnson. Chicago.

———. 1995. *Khôra.* In *On the Name*, by J. Derrida, edited by T. Dutoit, 89–127. Stanford.

Description de l'Égypte. 1809–26. Paris. 2d ed., 1821–26.

Des Places, É., ed. 1996. *Jamblique: Les mystères d'Égypte.* Rev. ed. Paris.

Detienne, M. 1981. *L'invention de la mythologie.* Paris.

———. 1989. *L'écriture d'Orphée.* Paris.

———. 1996. *The Masters of Truth in Archaic Greece.* Translated by J. Lloyd. New York.

———. ed. 1992. *Les savoirs de l'écriture. En Grèce ancienne.* 2d ed. Lille.

De Vries, G. J. 1969. *A Commentary on the* Phaedrus *of Plato.* Amsterdam.

Dewald, C. 1981. Women and Culture in Herodotos' *Histories.* In *Reflections of Women in Antiquity,* edited by H. P. Foley, 91–125. New York.

Dilke, O. A. W. 1985. *Greek and Roman Maps.* London.

Dodds, E. R., ed. 1959. *Plato: Gorgias.* Oxford.

Donadoni, S., ed. 1997. *The Egyptians.* Chicago.

Donadoni, S., S. Curto, and A. M. Donadoni Roveri, 1990. *L'Egitto dal mito all' egittologia.* Milan.

Doniger, W. 1999. *Splitting the Difference: Gender and Myth in Ancient Greece and India.* Chicago.

Doufikar-Aerts, F. C. W. 1994. A Legacy of the *Alexander Romance* in Arab Writings: Al-Iskandar, Founder of Alexandria. In *The Search for the Ancient Novel,* edited by J. Tatum, 323–43. Baltimore.

Dow, S. 1937. The Egyptian Cults in Athens. *Harvard Theological Review* 30:183–232.

Drews, R. 1973. *The Greek Accounts of Eastern History.* Cambridge, Mass.

Drioton, E., and J. Vandier. 1975. *L'Égypte des origines à la conquête d'Alexandre.* 5th ed. Paris.

Driver, G. R. 1957. *Aramaic Documents of the Fifth Century B.C.* Oxford.

Dumortier, J. 1935. *Les images dans la poésie d'Eschyle.* Paris.

Durand, J.-L., and F. Lissarrague. 1983. Héros cru ou hôte cuit: histoire quasi cannibale d'Héraclès chez Busiris. In *Image et céramique grecque,* 153–67. Rouen.

Düring, I. 1957. *Aristotle in the Ancient Biographical Tradition.* Göteborg.

Eagleton, T. 1983. *Literary Theory: An Introduction.* Minneapolis.

Edwards, A. 1877. *A Thousand Miles up the Nile.* London.

Ehrenberg, V. 1938. *Alexander and the Greeks.* Oxford.

Eisner, R. 1980. Echoes of the *Odyssey* in Euripides' *Helen. Maia* 32: 31–37.

Elgood, P. G. 1951. *The Later Dynasties of Egypt.* Oxford.

Erbse, H. 1961. Die Architektonik im Aufbau von Xenophons Memorabilien. *Hermes* 89:257–87.

Erdmann, W. 1934. *Die Ehe im alten Griechenland.* Munich.

Erman, A. 1937. *La religion des Égyptiens.* Translated by H. Wild. Paris.

Eucken, C. 1983. *Isokrates: Seine Positionen in der Auseindandersetzung mit den zeitgenössischen Philosophen.* Berlin.

Eyre, C., and J. Baines. 1989. Interactions between Orality and Literacy in Ancient Egypt. In *Literacy and Society,* edited by K. Schousboe and M. T. Larsen, 91–119. Copenhagen.

Fabian, J. 1983. *Time and the Other: How Anthropology Makes Its Object.* New York.

———. 1991. Of Dogs Alive, Birds Dead, and Time to Tell a Story. In *Chronotypes: The Construction of Time,* edited by J. Bender and D. E. Wellbery, 185–204. Stanford.

Fakhry, A. 1944. *Siwa Oasis: Its History and Antiquities.* Cairo.

Fehling, D. 1989. *Herodotus and His "Sources," Citation, Invention, and Narrative Art.* Translated by J. G. Howie. Leeds.

Ferrari, G. R. F. 1987. *Listening to the Cicadas: A Study of Plato's Phaedrus.* Cambridge, Eng.

Festugière, A. J. 1966. *Proclus: Commentaire sur le Timée.* Vol. 1. Paris.

Finlay, J., 1983. Flaubert in Egypt. *The Hudson Review* 36:496–509.

Fischer, H. G. 1959. An Example of Memphite Influence in a Theban Stela of the Eleventh Dynasty. *Artibus Asiae* 22:240–52.

———. 1977. *Egyptian Studies II: The Orientation of Hieroglyphs,* pt. 1, *Reversals.* New York.

———. 1986. *L'écriture et l'art de l'Egypte ancienne.* Paris.

Flaubert, G. 1972. *Flaubert in Egypt: A Sensibility on Tour.* Translated by F. Steegmuller. Harmondsworth.

Foley, H. P. 1985. *Ritual Irony: Poetry and Sacrifice in Euripides.* New York.

———. 1992. *Anodos* Dramas: Euripides' *Alcestis* and *Helen.* In *Innovations of Antiquity,* edited by R. Hexter and D. Selden, 133–60. New York.

Fornara, C. W. 1994. *FGrHist IIIC. Fascicle 1. Commentary on Nos. 608a-608.* Leiden.

Fossey, J. M. 1990. *The Ancient Topography of Opountian Lokris.* Amsterdam.

Foucault, M. 1970. *The Order of Things: An Archaeology of the Human Sciences.* New York.

Fowden, G. 1993. *The Egyptian Hermes: A Historical Approach to the Late Pagan Mind.* Cambridge, Eng., 1986. Reprint, Princeton.

Franci, G. R. 1980. Sita e l'εἴδωλον. *Paideia: Rivista Letteraria di Informazione Bibliografica* 35:71–74.

Frankfort, H., H. A. Frankfort, J. A. Wilson, and T. Jacobsen. 1949. *Before Philosophy: The Intellectual Adventure of Ancient Man.* Harmondsworth.

Frankfurter, D. 1994. The Magic of Writing and the Writing of Magic: The Power of the Word in Egyptian and Greek Traditions. *Helios* 21:189–221.

Fraser, P. M. 1972. *Ptolemaic Alexandria.* 3 vols. Oxford.

———. 1996. *Cities of Alexander the Great.* Oxford.

Fraustadt, G. 1909. *Encomiorum in Litteris Graecis usque ad Romanam Aetatem Historia.* Leipzig.

Frazer, J. G., ed. 1921. *Apollodorus: The Library.* 2 vols. Loeb Classical Library. London.

Friis Johansen, H. 1970. *Aeschylus: The Suppliants.* Copenhagen.

Fritz, K. von. 1967. *Die griechische Geschichtsschreibung.* 2 vols. Berlin.

Froidefond, C. 1971. *Le mirage égyptien dans la littérature grecque d'Homère à Aristote.* Aix-en-Provence.

Gantz, T. 1978. Love and Death in the *Suppliants* of Aeschylus. *Phoenix* 32: 279–87.

Gardiner, A. H. 1957. *Egyptian Grammar.* 3d ed. Oxford.

———. 1959. *The Royal Canon of Turin.* Oxford.

Garland, R. 1985. *The Greek Way of Death.* Ithaca.

Garvie, A. F. 1969. *Aeschylus' Supplices: Play and Trilogy.* Cambridge, Eng.

Geertz, C. 1980. *Negara: The Theatre State in Nineteenth-Century Bali.* Princeton.

Gendron, C. 1986. Lucie Duff Gordon's "Letters from Egypt." *ARIEL: A Review of International English Literature* 17 (April): 49–61.

Genette, G. 1982. *Palimpsestes: la littérature au second degré.* Paris.

Ghalioungui, P. 1983. *The Physicians of Pharaonic Egypt.* Cairo.

Ghosh, A. 1992. *In an Antique Land.* New Delhi.

Gianotti, G. F. 1988. Ordine e simmetria nella rappresentazione del mundo Erodoto e il paradiso del Nilo. *Quaderni di storia* 14:51–92.

Gilbert, P. 1949. Souvenirs de l'Égypte dans l'Hélène d'Euripide. *l'Antiquité Classique* 18:79–84.

Gill, C. 1977. The Genre of the Atlantis Story. *Classical Philology* 72:287–304.

———. 1979. Plato's Atlantis Story and the Birth of Fiction. *Philosophy and Literature* 3:64–78.

———. 1980. *Plato: The Atlantis Story.* Bristol.

———. 1993. Plato on Falsehood—not Fiction. In *Lies and Fiction in the Ancient World*, edited by C. Gill and T. P. Wiseman, 38–87. Exeter.

Gillispie, C. C. 1994. The Scientific Importance of Napoleon's Egyptian Campaign. *Scientific American* (September): 78–85.

Gillispie, C. C., and M. Dewachter, eds. 1987. *Monuments of Egypt: The Napoleonic Expedition*. Princeton.

Ginsinger, F. 1921. *Die Erdbeschreibung des Eudoxos von Knidos*. Leipzig and Berlin.

Girard, R. 1977. *Violence and the Sacred*. Translated by P. Gregory. Baltimore.

Godel, R. 1956. *Platon à Héliopolis d'Égypte*. Paris.

Goedicke, H.1971 *Re-Used Blocks from the Pyramid of Amenemhet I at Lisht*. New York.

Goldhill, S. 1991. *The Poet's Voice: Essays on Poetics and Greek Literature*. Cambridge, Eng.

Goossens, R. 1935. L'Égypte dans l'*Hélène* d'Euripide. *Chronique d'Égypte* 10: 243–53.

Gordon, L. D. 1969. *Letters from Egypt 1862–1869*. Edited by G. Waterfield. New York.

Gottschalk, H. B. 1980. *Heraclides of Pontus*. Oxford.

Gould, J. 1989. *Herodotus*. New York.

Graf, F. 1993. *Greek Mythology: An Introduction*. Translated by T. Marier. Baltimore.

Grafton, A., with A. Shelford and N. Siraisi. 1992. *New Worlds, Ancient Texts: The Power of Tradition and the Shock of Discovery*. Cambridge, Mass.

Green, P. 1996. Alexander's Alexandria. In *Alexandria and Alexandrianism*, 3–25. Malibu.

Greenblatt, S. 1991. *Marvelous Possessions: The Wonder of the New World*. Chicago.

Gregory, D. 1999. Scripting Egypt: Orientalism and the Cultures of Travel. In *Writes of Passage: Reading Travel Writing*, edited by J. Duncan and D. Gregory, 114–50. London

Grelot, P. 1972. *Documents araméens d'Égypte*. Paris.

Grene, D., trans. 1987. *Herodotus: The History*. Chicago.

Griffith, R. D. 1997. Homeric διιπετέος ποταμοῖο and the Celestial Nile. *American Journal of Philology* 118:353–62.

Griffiths, J. G. 1948. Human Sacrifices in Egypt: The Classical Evidence. *Annales du Service des Antiquités d'Egypte* 48:409–23.

———. 1985. Atlantis and Egypt. *Historia* 34:3–28.

———. 1991. The Symbolism of Red in Egyptian Religion. In *Atlantis and Egypt with Other Selected Essays*, edited by J. G. Griffiths, 208–16. Cardiff. Originally published in *Ex Orbe Religionum*, Festschrift G. Widengren. Vol. 1, 81–90. Leiden, 1972.

———, ed. 1970. *Plutarch's De Iside et Osiride*. Cardiff.

Grosrichard, A. 1998. *The Sultan's Court: European Fantasies of the East*. Translated by L. Heron. London.

Guépin, J.-P. 1968. *The Tragic Paradox: Myth and Ritual in Greek Tragedy*. Amsterdam.

Guérin Dalle Mese, J. 1991. *Égypte: la mémoire et le rêve: itinéraires d'un voyage, 1320–1601*. Florence.

Guralnick, E. 1997. The Egyptian-Greek Connection in the 8th to 6th Centuries B.C.: An Overview. In J. E. Coleman and C. A. Walz, eds. 1997, 127–54.

Gutschmid, A. v. 1855. De rerum Aegyptiacarum scriptoribus Graecis ante Alexandrum Magnum. *Philologus* 10:522–42, 636–700.

Gyles, M. F. 1959. *Pharaonic Policies and Administration, 663 to 323 B.C.* Chapel Hill.

Haarmann, U. 1996. Medieval Muslim Perceptions of Pharaonic Egypt. In A. Loprieno, ed. 1996, 605–27.

Hackforth, R. 1952. *Plato's Phaedrus.* Cambridge, Eng.

Hall, E. 1989. *Inventing the Barbarian: Greek Self-Definition through Tragedy.* Oxford.

Hall, J. 1997. *Ethnic Identity in Greek Antiquity.* Cambridge, Eng.

Hamilton, J. R. 1969. *Plutarch: Alexander.* Oxford.

Harder, A. 1985. *Euripides' Kresphontes and Archelaos: Introduction, Text and Commentary.* Leiden.

Hare, T. 1999. *ReMembering Osiris: Number, Gender, and the Word in Ancient Egyptian Representational Systems.* Stanford.

Harrell, J. A., and V. M. Brown. 1992. The Oldest Surviving Topographical Map from Ancient Egypt: Turin Papyri 1879, 1899, and 1969. *Journal of the American Research Center in Egypt* 29:81–105.

Harrison, T. 1998. Herodotus' Conception of Foreign Languages. *Histos* 2. http://www.dur.ac.uk/Classics/histos/1998/harrison.html.

Harten, S. 1995. Archaeology and the Unconscious: Hegel, Egyptomania, and the Legitimation of Orientalism. In *Egypt and the Fabrication of European Identity,* edited by I. A. Bierman, 3–33. UCLA Near East Center Colloquium Series. Los Angeles.

Hartigan, K. V. 1981. Myth and the *Helen. Eranos* 79:23–31.

Hartog, F. 1988. *The Mirror of Herodotus: The Representation of the Other in the Writing of History.* Translated by J. Lloyd. Berkeley.

———. 1996. *Mémoire d'Ulysse: Récits sur la frontière en Grèce ancienne.* Paris.

Heckel, W. 1992. *The Marshals of Alexander's Empire.* London.

Heichelheim, F. 1925. *Die auswärtige Bevölkerung im Ptolemäerreich.* Leipzig.

Heidel, W. 1937. *The Frame of the Ancient Greek Maps.* New York.

Heider, G. C. 1985. *The Cult of Molek: A Reassessment.* Sheffield.

Henige, D. 1974. *The Chronology of Oral Tradition: Quest for a Chimera.* Oxford.

Henrichs, A. 1981. Human Sacrifice in Greek Religion: Three Case Studies. In *Le sacrifice dans l'antiquité,* 195–242. Entretiens Fondation Hardt 27. Geneva.

Herbold, J. C. 1962. *Bonaparte in Egypt.* New York and London.

Herrmann, S. 1957. Isis in Byblos. *Zeitschrift für ägyptische Sprache und Altertumskunde* 82:48–55.

Heubeck, A., S. West, and J. B. Hainsworth, eds. 1988. *A Commentary on Homer's Odyssey,* vol. 1, *Introduction and Books I-VIII.* Oxford.

Hexter, R., and D. Selden, eds. 1992. *Innovations of Antiquity.* New York.

Hiller von Gaertringen, Fr. 1897. Busiris. *RE* 4:1073–77.

Hoffman, M. A. 1991. *Egypt Before the Pharaohs: The Prehistoric Foundations of Egyptian Civilization.* Rev. ed. Austin.

Högemann, P. 1985. *Alexander der Grosse und Arabien.* Zetemata 82. Munich.

Hopfner, T. 1922–25. *Fontes historiae religionis aegyptiacae.* 2 vols. Bonn.

Hornung, E. 1966. *Geschichte als Fest: Zwei Vorträge zum Geschichtsbild der frühen Menschheit.* Darmstadt.

———. 1982. *Conceptions of God in Ancient Egypt: The One and the Many.* Translated by J. Baines. Ithaca.

———. 1992. *Idea into Image: Essays on Ancient Egyptian Thought.* Translated by E. Bredeck. New York.

Hornung, E., A. Brodbeck, H. Schlögl, E. Staehelin, and G. Fecht. 1982. *Der ägyptische Mythos von der Himmelskuh: Eine Ätiologie des Unvolkommenen.* Freiburg.

Hughes, D. 1991. *Human Sacrifice in Ancient Greece.* London.

Humbert, J. 1930. *Polycratès: l'accusation de Socrate et le Gorgias.* Paris.

Humbert, J.-M., M. Pantazzi, and C. Ziegler. 1994. *Egyptomania: Egypt in Western Art, 1730–1930.* Ottawa and Paris.

Hutcheon, L. 1985. *A Theory of Parody.* New York.

Immerwahr, H. R. 1966. *Form and Thought in Herodotus.* Cleveland.

Irwin, E. 1974. *Colour Terms in Greek Poetry.* Toronto.

Iversen, E. 1957. The Egyptian Origin of the Archaic Greek Canon. *Mitteilungen des deutschen archäologischen Instituts, Abteilung Kairo* 15: 134–47.

———. 1975. *Canon and Proportions in Egyptian Art.* Warminster.

———. 1993. *The Myth of Egypt and Its Hieroglyphs in European Tradition.* Copenhagen, 1961. Reprint, Princeton.

Jabarti, 'Abd al-Rahman. 1993. *Napoleon in Egypt: Al-Jabarti's Chronicle of the French Occupation, 1798.* Translated by S. Moreh, with an introduction by R. L. Tignor. Princeton and New York.

Jacob, C. 1992. Inscrire la terre habitée sur une tablette. Réflexions sur la fonction de la carte géographique en Grèce ancienne. In M. Detienne, ed. 1992, 273–304.

Jaeger, W. 1948. *Aristotle.* 2d ed. Oxford.

James, G. G. M. 1985. *Stolen Legacy: The Greeks Were Not the Authors of Greek Philosophy, but the People of North Africa, Commonly Called the Egyptians.* New York, 1954. Reprint, San Francisco.

James, T. G. H. 1991. Egypt: The Twenty-fifth and Twenty-sixth Dynasties. In *The Cambridge Ancient History,* 2d ed., vol. 3, pt. 2., edited by J. Boardman, I. E. S. Edwards, N. G. L. Hammond, and E. Sollberger, with C. B. F. Walker, 677–747. Cambridge, Eng.

Jameson, M. H. 1990. Domestic Space in the Greek City-State. In *Domestic Architecture and the Use of Space: An Interdisciplinary Cross-Cultural Study,* edited by S. Kent, 92–113. Cambridge, Eng.

Jeffery, L. H. 1967. Ἀρχαῖα γράμματα: Some Ancient Greek Views. In *Europa: Studien zur Geschichte und Epigraphik der Frühen Aegaeis. Festschrift für Ernst Grumach*, edited by W. C. Brice, 152–66. Berlin.

Jeffery, L. H., and A. Morpurgo-Davies. 1970. Ποινικαστάς and Ποινικάζειν. BM 1969 4–2.1, a New Inscription from Crete. *Kadmos* 9:118–54.

Jenkins, I. 1983. Is There Life after Marriage? A Study of the Abduction Motif in Vase Paintings of the Athenian Wedding Ceremony. *Bulletin of the Institute of Classical Studies* 30: 137–46.

Jesi, F. 1965. L'Egitto infero nell' *Elena* di Euripide. *Aegyptus* 45:56–69.

Johnson, J. H., ed. 1992. *Life in a Multicultural Society: Egypt from Cambyses to Constantine and Beyond*. Chicago.

Jones, A. H. M. 1957. *Athenian Democracy*. Oxford.

Jones, C. P. 1987. Stigma: Tattooing and Branding in Graeco-Roman Antiquity. *Journal of Roman Studies* 77:139–55.

Jouanna, J. 1981. Les causes de la défaite des barbares chez Eschyle, Hérodote, et Hippocrate. *Ktema* 6:3–15.

Junge, F. 1973. Zur Fehldatierung des sog. Denkmals memphitischer Theologie oder: Der Beitrag der ägyptischen Theologie zur Geistesgeschichte der Spätzeit. *Mitteilungen des deutschen archäologischen Instituts, Abteilung Kairo* 29:195–204.

Jüthner, J. 1923. *Hellenen und Barbaren: aus der Geschichte des Nationalbewusstseins*. Leipzig.

Kákosy, L. 1964a. Ideas about the Fallen State of the World in Egyptian Religion: Decline of the Golden Age. *Acta Orientalia Academiae Scientiarum Hungaricae* 17:206–16.

———. 1964b. Urzeitmythen und Historiographie im alten Ägypten. In *Neue Beiträge zur Geschichte der alten Welt*, vol. 1: *Alter Orient und Griechenland*, edited by E. C. Welskopf, 57–68. Berlin.

———. 1995. Egypt in Ancient Greek and Roman Thought. In *Civilizations of the Ancient Near East*, edited by J. M. Sasson, vol. 1, 3–14. New York.

Kannicht, R. 1969. *Euripides Helena*. 2 vols. Heidelberg.

Kapadia, B. H. 1964–65. The Adhyatmaramayana. *Journal of the Oriental Institute* (Baroda) 14:164–70.

Keimer, L. 1948. *Remarques sur le tatouage dans l'Égypte ancienne*. Cairo.

Keuls, E. 1974. *The Water Carriers in Hades: A Study of Catharsis through Toil in Classical Antiquity*. Amsterdam.

Khan, H. A., ed. 1994. *The Birth of the European Identity; The Europe-Asia Contrast in Greek Thought, 490–322 B.C.* Nottingham.

Kienitz, F. K. 1953. *Die politische Geschichte Ägyptens vom 7. bis zum 4. Jahrhundert vor der Zeitwende*. Berlin.

Kitchen, K. A. 1973. *The Third Intermediate Period in Egypt (1100–650 B.C.)*. Warminster.

Knox, B. M. W. 1989. Books and Readers in the Greek World: From the Beginnings to Alexandria. In *The Cambridge History of Classical Literature*, vol. 1, pt. 4: *The Hellenistic Period and the Empire*, edited by P. E. Easterling and B. M. W. Knox, 154–69. Cambridge, Eng. Originally published with different pagination in ch. 1 of the 1985 ed.

Kock, T., ed. 1880–88. *Comicorum Atticorum Fragmenta*. 3 vols. Leipzig.

Kraeling, E. 1953. *The Brooklyn Museum Aramaic Papyri: New Documents of the Fifth Century B.C. from the Jewish Colony at Elephantine*. New Haven.

Kranz, W. 1988. *Stasimon: Untersuchungen zu Form und Gehalt der griechischen Tragödie*. Berlin, 1933. Reprint, Hildesheim.

Kristeva, J. 1980. *Desire in Language*. Translated by T. Gora, A. Jardine, and L. S. Roudiez. Oxford.

———. 1991. *Strangers to Ourselves*. Translated by L. S. Roudiez. New York.

Kuhlmann, K. P. 1988. *Das Ammoneion: Archäologie, Geschichte und Kultpraxis des Orakels von Siwa*. Mainz.

Kurke, L. 1999. *Coins, Bodies, Games, and Gold: The Politics of Meaning in Archaic Greece*. Princeton.

Kurtz, D. C., and J. Boardman. 1971. *Greek Burial Customs*. Ithaca.

Lacau, P. 1913. Suppressions et modifications de signes dans les textes funéraires. *Zeitschrift für ägyptische Sprache und Altertumskunde* 51:1–64.

Lachenaud, G. 1980. Connaissance du monde et répresentations de l'espace dans Hérodote. *Hellenika* 32:42–60.

Lane, E. W. 1954. *Manners and Customs of the Modern Egyptians*. 1836. Reprint, London.

Lane Fox, R. 1973. *Alexander the Great*. London.

Lant, A. 1992. The Curse of the Pharaoh; or, How Cinema Contracted Egyptomania. *October* 59:86–112.

Lasserre, F. 1966. *Die Fragmente des Eudoxos von Knidos*. Berlin.

Lateiner, D. 1989. *The Historical Method of Herodotus*. Toronto.

Laurens, A.-F. 1986. Busiris. *LIMC* 3:147–52.

Leca, A.-P. 1971. *La médecine égyptienne au temps des pharaons*. Paris.

Le Coat, N. 1997. Allegories Literary, Scientific, and Imperial: Representation of the Other in Writings on Egypt by Volney and Savary. *Eighteenth Century: Theory and Interpretation* 38:3–22.

Lefebvre, H. 1991.*The Production of Space*. Translated by D. Nicholson-Smith. Oxford.

Lefkowitz, M. 1996. *Not Out of Africa: How Afrocentrism Became an Excuse to Teach Myth as History*. New York.

———. 1997. Some Ancient Advocates of Greek Cultural Dependency. In J. E. Coleman and C. A. Walz, eds. 1997, 237–53.

Lefkowitz, M. R., and G. M. Rogers, eds. 1996. *Black Athena Revisited*. Chapel Hill.

Lesko, L. H. 1991. Ancient Egyptian Cosmogonies and Cosmology. In *Religion in Ancient Egypt*, edited by B. E. Shafer, 88–122. Ithaca.

Lévêque, P., and P. Vidal-Naquet. 1996. *Cleisthenes the Athenian: An Essay on the Representation of Space and Time in Greek Political Thought from the End of the Sixth Century to the Death of Plato*. Translated by D. A. Curtis. Atlantic Highlands, N.J.

Lévi-Strauss, C. 1962. *La pensée sauvage*. Paris.

———. 1992 *Tristes Tropiques*. Translated by J. and D. Weightman. London, 1973. Reprint, Harmondsworth.

Lévy, E. 1985. "Inceste, mariage, et sexualité dans les *Suppliantes* d'Eschyle." In *La femme dans le monde méditerranéen*, 29–45. Lyon.

Libourel, J. M. 1971. The Athenian Disaster in Egypt. *American Journal of Philology* 92:605–15.

Lichtheim, M. 1973. *Ancient Egyptian Literature: A Book of Readings*, vol. 1, *The Old and Middle Kingdoms*. Berkeley.

———. 1976. *Ancient Egyptian Literature: A Book of Readings*, vol. 2, *The New Kingdom*. Berkeley.

———. 1980. *Ancient Egyptian Literature: A Book of Readings*, vol. 3, *The Late Period*. Berkeley.

Lloyd, A. B. 1972. Triremes and the Saïte Navy. *Journal of Egyptian Archaeology* 58:268–79.

———. 1975. *Herodotus, Book II, Introduction*. Leiden.

———. 1976. *Herodotus, Book II, Commentary 1–98*. Leiden.

———. 1980. M. Basch on Triremes: Some Observations. *Journal of Hellenic Studies* 100:195–98.

———. 1982. The Inscription of Udjahorresnet: A Collaborator's Testament. *Journal of Egyptian Archaeology* 68:166–80.

———. 1988a. *Herodotus, Book II, Commentary 99–182*. Leiden.

———. 1988b. Herodotus' Account of Pharaonic History. *Historia* 37:22–53.

———. 1994. Egypt, 404–332 B.C. In *The Cambridge Ancient History*, 2d ed., vol. 6, edited by D. M. Lewis, J. Boardman, S. Hornblower, and M. Ostwald, 337–60. Cambridge, Eng.

Lloyd, G. E. R. 1966. *Polarity and Analogy: Two Types of Argumentation in Early Thought*. Cambridge, Eng.

Lloyd-Jones, H. 1990. The *Suppllces* of Aeschylus: The New Date and the Old Problems. In *Greek Epic, Lyric, and Tragedy: The Academic Papers of Sir Hugh Lloyd-Jones*, 262–77. Oxford. Originally published in *L'Antiquité classique* 33 (1964):356–74.

Lochner-Hüttenbach, F. 1960. *Die Pelasger*. Vienna.

Long, T. 1986. *Barbarians in Greek Comedy*. Carbondale.

Longo, O. 1986. Idrografia erodotea. *Quaderni di storia* 12:23–53.

Loomba, A. 1993. Dead Women Tell No Tales: Issues of Female Subjectivity, Subaltern Agency, and Tradition in Colonial and Post-Colonial Writings on Widow Immolation in India. *History Workshop Journal* 36:209–27.

Loprieno, A. 1988. *Topos und Mimesis: zum Ausländer in der ägyptischen Literatur*. Wiesbaden.

———. 1995. *Ancient Egyptian: A Linguistic Introduction*. Cambridge, Eng.

———. 1998. Zeichenkonzeptionen im Alten Orient. In *Semiotik: Ein Handbuch zu den zeichentheoretischen Grundlagen von Natur and Kultur*, edited by R. Posner, K. Robering, and T. A. Sebeok, vol. 2, 1785–99. Berlin.

———, ed. 1996. *Ancient Egyptian Literature: History and Forms*. Leiden.

Loraux, N. 1986. *The Invention of Athens: The Funeral Oration in the Classical City*. Translated by A. Sheridan. Cambridge, Mass.

———. 1987. *Tragic Ways of Killing a Woman*. Translated by A. Forster. Cambridge, Mass.

———. 1993. The *Children of Athena: Athenian Ideas about Citizenship and the Division between the Sexes*. Translated by C. Levine. Princeton.

———. 1995. *The Experiences of Tiresias: The Feminine and the Greek Man*. Translated by P. Wissing. Princeton.

———. 1998. *Mothers in Mourning*. Translated by C. Pache. Ithaca.

Lowe, L. 1991. *Critical Terrains: French and British Orientalisms*. Ithaca.

Luce, J. V. 1969. *Lost Atlantis*. New York.

MacKinnon, J. K. 1978. The Reason for the Danaids' Flight. *Classical Quarterly* 28:74–81.

Malkin, I. 1998. *The Returns of Odysseus: Colonization and Ethnicity*. Berkeley.

Mallet, D. 1922. *Les rapports des Grecs avec L'Égypte (de la conquête de Cambyse, 525, à celle d'Alexandre)*. Cairo.

Manetti, G. 1993. *Theories of the Sign in Classical Antiquity*. Translated by C. Richardson. Bloomington.

Marestaing, P. 1913. *Les écritures égyptiennes et l'antiquité classique*. Paris.

Markowski, H. 1910. *De Libanio Socratis defensore*.

Marx, K. 1977. *Capital: A Critique of Political Economy*. Vol. 1. Translated by B. Fowkes. New York.

Matthews, V. J. 1974. *Panyassis of Halikarnassos*. Mnemosyne suppl. 33. Leiden.

McAlister, M. 1996. "The Common Heritage of Mankind": Race, Nation, and Masculinity in the King Tut Exhibit. *Representations* 54:80–103.

McNeal, R. A. 1985. How Did Pelasgians Become Hellenes? Herodotus I, 56–58. *Illinois Classical Studies* 10:11–21.

Meeks, D., and C. Favard-Meeks. 1996. *Daily Life of the Egyptian Gods*. Translated by G. M. Goshgarian. Ithaca.

Mette, H. J., ed. 1959. *Die Fragmente der Tragödien des Aischylos*. Berlin.

———. 1984. Zwei Akademiker heute: Krantor von Soloi und Arkesilaos von Pitane. *Lustrum* 26:7–94.

Mikalson, J. D. 1998. *Religion in Hellenistic Athens*. Berkeley.

Miller, M. 1966. Herodotus as Chronographer. *Klio* 46:109–28.

Miller, M. C. 1997. *Athens and Persia in the Fifth Century B.C.: A Study in Cultural Receptivity*. Cambridge, Eng.

Mitchell, F. 1956. Herodotus' Use of Genealogical Chronology. *Phoenix* 10: 48–69.

Mitchell, T. 1988. *Colonising Egypt*. Cambridge, Eng.

Mokhtar, G. 1993. Pre-Alexandria. In *Alexandria: The Site and the History*, edited by G. L. Steen, 21–31. New York.

Momigliano, A. 1966. Time in Ancient Historiography. *History and Theory*, suppl. 6:1–23.

———. 1978. *Alien Wisdom: The Limits of Hellenization.* Cambridge, Eng., 1975. Reprint.

Montserrat, D. 1996. *Sex and Society in Graeco-Roman Egypt.* London.

———. 1998. Unidentified Human Remains: Mummies and the Erotics of Biography. In *Changing Bodies, Changing Meanings: Studies on the Human Body in Antiquity,* edited by D. Montserrat, 162–97. London.

Morenz, S. 1968. *Die Begegnung Europas mit Ägypten.* Berlin.

———. 1973. *Egyptian Religion.* Translated by A. E. Keep. Ithaca.

Morgan, K. 1998. Designer History: Plato's Atlantis Story and Fourth-Century Ideology. *Journal of Hellenic Studies* 118:101–18.

Morson, G. S. 1989. Parody, History, and Metaparody. In *Rethinking Bakhtin: Extensions and Challenges,* edited by G. S. Morson and C. Emerson, 63–86. Evanston.

Müller, C. W. 1997. Fremderfahrung und Eigenerfahrung. Griechische Ägyptenreisende von Menelaos bis Herodot. *Philologus* 141:200–214.

Müller, K. E. 1972. *Geschichte der antiken Ethnographie und ethnologischen Theoriebildung.* Wiesbaden.

Murray, O. 1970. Hecataeus of Abdera and Pharaonic Kingship. *Journal of Egyptian Archaeology* 56:141–71.

———. 1972. Herodotus and Hellenistic Culture. *Classical Quarterly,* n.s., 22:200–213.

———. 1980. *Early Greece.* Stanford.

Murray, R. D. 1958. *The Motif of Io in Aeschylus' Suppliants.* Princeton.

Myres, J. L. 1896. An Attempt to Reconstruct the Maps Used by Herodotus. *Geographical Journal* 8, no. 6 (December): 605–31.

Nagy, G. 1996. *Poetry as Performance: Homer and Beyond.* Cambridge, Eng.

Nagy, I. 1973. Remarques sur le souci d'archaisme en Egypte à l'époque Saite. *Acta Antiqua Academiae Scientiarum Hungaricae* 21:53–64.

Nauck, A., ed. 1889. *Tragicorum Graecorum Fragmenta.* 2d ed. Leipzig.

Neel, J. 1988. *Plato, Derrida, and Writing.* Carbondale, Ill.

Nibbi, A. 1975. *The Sea Peoples and Egypt.* Park Ridge, N.J.

Nightingale, A. W. 1993. The Folly of Praise: Plato's Critique of Encomiastic Discourse in the *Lysis* and *Symposium. Classical Quarterly* 43:112–30.

———. 1995. *Genres in Dialogue: Plato and the Construct of Philosophy.* Cambridge, Eng.

———. 1999. Plato's Lawcode in Context: Rule by Written Law in Athens and Magnesia. *Classical Quarterly* 49:100–122.

Nock, A. D., and A.-J. Festugière, eds. 1972–73. *Corpus Hermeticum.* 4 vols. New ed. Paris.

Norden, E. 1924. *Die Geburt des Kindes.* Leipzig.

Nunn, J. 1995. *Ancient Egyptian Medicine.* London.

Oakley, J. H., and R. H. Sinos. 1993. *The Wedding in Ancient Athens.* Madison.

Ober, J. 1998. *Political Dissent in Democratic Athens: Intellectual Critics of Popular Rule.* Princeton.

O'Connor-Visser, E. A. M. E. 1987. *Aspects of Human Sacrifice in the Trage-dies of Euripides*. Amsterdam.

Oertel, F. 1970. *Herodots ägyptischer Logos und die Glaubwürdigkeit Hero-dots*. Bonn.

Olmstead, A. T. 1948. *History of the Persian Empire*. Chicago.

Ormand, K. 1999. *Exchange and the Maiden: Marriage in Sophoclean Trag-edy*. Austin.

Otto, E. 1969. Das "Goldene Zeitalter" in einem ägyptischen Text. In *Religions en Égypte hellénistique et romaine*, 93–108. Paris.

Padel, F. 1995. *The Sacrifice of Human Being: British Rule and the Konds of Orissa*. Delhi.

Padel, R. 1992. *In and Out of the Mind: Greek Images of the Tragic Self*. Princeton.

Parke, H. W. 1933. *Greek Mercenary Soldiers*. Oxford.

———. 1967. *The Oracles of Zeus*. Oxford.

Pasquali, G. 1924. Ammonre nelle *Supplici* di Eschilo. *Rivista di filologia e di istruzione classica* 52:246–48.

Payen, P. 1990. Discours historique et structures narratives chez Hérodote. *Annales ESC* 45:527–50.

Pearson, L. 1939. *Early Ionian Historians*. Oxford.

———. 1960. *The Lost Histories of Alexander the Great*. New York.

Pease, A. S. 1926. Things Without Honor. *Classical Philology* 21:27–42.

Pédech, P. 1984. *Historiens Compagnons d'Alexandre: Callisthène-Onésicrite-Néarque-Ptolémée-Aristobule*. Paris.

Pelling, C., ed. 1997. *Greek Tragedy and the Historian*. Oxford.

Pendlebury, J. D. S. 1930. *Aegyptiaca: A Catalogue of Egyptian Objects in the Aegean Area*. Cambridge, Eng.

Petre, Z. 1986. Le décret des *Suppliants* d'Eschyle. *Studii clasice* 24:25–32.

Pickard-Cambridge, A. W. 1968. *The Dramatic Festivals of Athens*. 2d ed. Revised by J. Gould and D. M. Lewis. Oxford.

Pippin, A. N. 1960. Euripides' *Helen:* A Comedy of Ideas. *Classical Philology* 55:151–63.

Podlecki, A. 1975. Reconstructing an Aeschylean Trilogy. *Bulletin of the Institute of Classical Studies* 22:2–8.

Polignac, F. de. 1995. *Cults, Territory, and the Origins of the Greek City-State*. Translated by J. Lloyd. Chicago.

Porter, J. I. 1993. The Seductions of Gorgias. *Classical Antiquity* 12:267–99.

Posener, G. 1936. *La première domination perse en Égypte*. Cairo.

Pratt, M. L. 1992. *Imperial Eyes: Travel Writing and Transculturation*. New York.

Pritchard, J. B., ed. 1969. *Ancient Near Eastern Texts Relating to the Old Testament*. 3d ed. Princeton.

Pritchett, W. K. 1993. *The Liar School of Herodotus*. Amsterdam.

Pucci, P. 1992. Human Sacrifices in the *Oresteia*. In R. Hexter and D. Selden, eds. 1992, 513–36.

————. 1997. The *Helen* and Euripides' "Comic" Art. *Colby Quarterly* 33: 42–75.

Raaflaub, K. 1987. Herodotus, Political Thought, and the Meaning of History. *Arethusa* 20:221–48.

————. 1989. Contemporary Perceptions of Democracy in Fifth-Century Athens. *Classica et Mediaevalia* 40:33–70.

Radermacher, L. 1951. *Artium Scriptores*. Vienna.

Raeck, W. 1981. *Zum Barbarenbild in der Kunst Athens im 6. und 5. Jahrhundert v. Chr.* Bonn.

Ramage, E. S., ed. 1978. *Atlantis, Fact or Fiction?* Bloomington.

Ray, J. D. 1986. The Emergence of Writing in Egypt. *World Archaeology* 17: 307–16.

————. 1987. Egypt: Dependence and Independence (425–343 B.C.). In *Achaemenid History I: Sources, Structures, and Synthesis*, edited by H. Sancisi-Weerdenburg, 79–85. Leiden.

————. 1988. Egypt 525–404 B.C. In *The Cambridge Ancient History*, 2d ed., vol. 4, edited by J. Boardman, N. G. L. Hammond, D. M. Lewis, and M. Ostwald, 254–86. Cambridge, Eng.

————. 1994. Literacy and Language in Egypt in the Late and Persian Periods. In A. K. Bowman and G. Woolf, eds. 1994, 51–66.

Redfield, J. 1982. Notes on the Greek Wedding. *Arethusa* 15:181–201.

————. 1985. Herodotus the Tourist. *Classical Philology* 80:97–118.

Redford, D. B. 1986. *Pharaonic King-Lists, Annals, and Day-Books: A Contribution to the Study of the Egyptian Sense of History*. Mississauga, Ontario.

Rehm, R. 1994. *Marriage to Death: The Conflation of Wedding and Funeral Rituals in Greek Tragedy*. Princeton.

Reich, N. J. 1933. The Codification of the Egyptian Laws by Darius and the Origin of the "Demotic Chronicle." *Mizraim* 1:178–85.

Reisner, G. A. 1923. *Excavations at Kerma, Parts I-III*. Cambridge, Mass.

Ricoeur, P. 1985. *Temps et recit*, vol. 3, *Le temps raconté*. Paris.

Riginos, A. S. 1976. *Platonica: The Anecdotes Concerning the Life and Writings of Plato*. Leiden.

Rives, J. 1995. Human Sacrifice among Pagans and Christians. *Journal of Roman Studies* 85:65–85.

Roberts, J. T. 1994. *Athens on Trial: The Antidemocratic Tradition in Western Thought*. Princeton.

Robins, G. 1993. *Women in Ancient Egypt*. Cambridge, Mass.

Robinson, D. B. 1979. Helen and Persephone, Sparta and Demeter. In Bowersock, Burkert, and Putnam 1979, 162–72.

Robinson, E. 1999. Thucydidean Sieges, Prosopitis, and the Hellenic Disaster in Egypt. *Classical Antiquity* 18:132–52.

Romm, J. S. 1992. *The Edges of the Earth in Ancient Thought: Geography, Exploration, and Fiction*. Princeton.

Rose, M. A. 1979. *Parody//Metafiction*. London.

————. 1993. *Parody: Ancient, Modern, and Post-Modern*. Cambridge, Eng.

Rosenthal, F. 1975. *The Classical Heritage in Islam*. Translated by E. and J. Marmorstein. London.

Rosivach, V. J. 1999. Enslaving *Barbaroi* and the Athenian Ideology of Slavery. *Historia* 11:129–57.

Rösler, W. 1993. Die Schluss der "Hiketiden" und die Danaiden-Trilogie des Aischylos. *Rheinisches Museum für Philologie* 136:1–22.

Rossellini, M., and S. Saïd. 1978. Usages des femmes et autres *nomoi* chez les "sauvages" d'Hérodote. *Annali della Scuola Normale Superiore di Pisa* 3, no. 8:949–1005.

Rowe, C. J., ed. 1986. *Plato: Phaedrus*. Warminster.

Sachau, E. C., ed. 1992. *Alberuni's India*. 2 vols. 1910. Reprint, New Delhi.

Said, E. W. 1978. *Orientalism*. New York.

———. 1993. *Culture and Imperialism*. New York.

Saïd, S. 1984. Grecs et Barbares dans les tragédies d'Euripide. La fin des différences? *Ktema* 9:27–53.

Sallis, J. 1999. *Chorology: On Beginning in Plato's Timaeus*. Bloomington.

Salmon, P. 1965. *La politique égyptienne d'Athènes (VIe et Ve siècles avant J.-C.)*. Brussels.

Sansone, D. 1985. Theonoe and Theoclymenus. *Symbolae Osloenses* 60:17–36.

Sauneron, S. 1960. *The Priests of Ancient Egypt*. Translated by A. Morrissett. New York.

———. 1982. *L'écriture figurative dans les textes d'Esna*. Esna 8. Cairo.

Sauneron, S., and J. Yoyotte. 1959. La naissance du monde dans l'Égypte ancienne. In *La naissance du monde*, 17–91. Paris.

Saussure, F. de. 1959. *Course in General Linguistics*. Translated by W. Baskin. New York.

Saxonhouse, A. W. 1996. *Athenian Democracy: Modern Mythmakers and Ancient Theorists*. Notre Dame.

Sbordone, F., ed. 1940. *Hori Apollonis Hieroglyphica*. Naples.

Schenkel, W. 1971. Zur Struktur der Hieroglyphenschrift. *Mitteilungen des deutschen archäologischen Instituts, Abteilung Kairo* 27:85–98.

———. 1976. The Structure of Hieroglyphic Script. *Royal Anthropological Institute News* 15:4–7.

———. 1979. Atlantis—die "namenlose" Insel. *Göttinger Miszellen* 36:57–60.

———. 1983. Wozu die Ägypter eine Schrift brauchten. In A. Assmann, J. Assmann, and C. Hardmeier, eds. 1983, 45–63.

Schott, S. 1950. *Hieroglyphen: Untersuchungen zum Ursprung der Schrift*. Wisebaden.

Schürer, E. 1973–87. *The History of the Jewish People in the Age of Jesus Christ (175 B.C.–A.D. 135)*. Revised and edited by G. Vermes, F. Millar, and M. Goodman. 3 vols. Edinburgh.

Schwab, R. 1984. *Oriental Renaissance: Europe's Rediscovery of India and the East, 1680–1880*. Translated by G. Patterson-Black and V. Reinking. New York.

Schwenn, F. 1915. *Die Menschenopfer bei den Griechen und Römern*. Giessen.

Seaford, R. 1980. Black Zeus in Sophocles' *Inachus*. *Classical Quarterly* 30: 23–29.

———. 1987. The Tragic Wedding. *Journal of Hellenic Studies* 107: 106–30.

———. 1990a. The Imprisonment of Women in Greek Tragedy. *Journal of Hellenic Studies* 110:76–90.

———. 1990b. The Structural Problems of Marriage in Euripides. In *Euripides, Women, and Sexuality*, edited by A. Powell, 151–76. London.

Segal, C. P. 1971. The Two Worlds of Euripides' *Helen*. *Transactions of the American Philological Association* 102:553–614.

Selden, D. L. 1998a. *Aithiopika* and Ethiopianism. In *Studies in Heliodorus*, *Proceedings of the Cambridge Philological Society*, suppl. vol. 21, edited by R. Hunter, 182–217. Cambridge, Eng.

———. 1998b. Alibis. *Classical Antiquity* 17:290–412.

Serres, M. 1979. The Algebra of Literature: The Wolf's Game. In *Textual Strategies: Perspectives in Post-Structuralist Criticism*, edited by J. V. Harari, 260–76. Ithaca.

Sethe, K. 1922. Die aegyptischen Ausdrücke für rechts und links und die Hieroglyphenzeichen für Westen und Osten: Ein Beitrag zur Urgeschichte der Aegypter. *Nachrichten von der Gesellschaft der Wissenschaften zu Göttingen. Philologisch-Historische Klasse:* 197–242.

Shore, A. F. 1987. Egyptian Cartography. In *The History of Cartography*, vol. 1: *Cartography in Prehistoric, Ancient, and Medieval Europe and the Mediterranean*, edited by J. B. Harley and D. Woodward, 117–29. Chicago.

Sicherl, M. 1986. Die Tragik der Danaiden. *Museum Helveticum* 43:81–110.

Sickinger, J. P. 1999. *Public Records and Archives in Classical Athens*. Chapel Hill.

Siddhantaratna, N. 1935. *Adhyatmaramayana*. Calcutta.

Silk, M. S., ed. 1996. *Tragedy and the Tragic: Greek Theatre and Beyond*. Oxford.

Silverman, D. P., ed. 1997. *Ancient Egypt*. Oxford.

Simms, R. R. 1989. Isis in Classical Athens. *Classical Journal* 84:216–21.

Sissa, G. 1990. *Greek Virginity*. Translated by A. Goldhammer. Cambridge, Mass.

Skon-Jedele, N. J. 1994. *Aigyptiaka: A Catalogue of Egyptian and Egyptianizing Objects Excavated from Greek Archaeological Sites, ca. 1100– 525 B.C., with Historical Commentary*. 4 pts. Ph.D. dissertation, University of Pennsylvania.

Skutsch, O. 1987. Helen: Her Name and Nature. *Journal of Hellenic Studies* 102:188–93.

Smelik, K. A. D., and E. A. Hemelrijk. 1984. "Who Knows Not What Monsters Demented Egypt Worships?" Opinions on Egyptian Animal Worship in Antiquity as Part of the Ancient Conception of Egypt. *Aufstieg und Niedergang der römischen Welt* 17, no. 4:1852–2000, 2337–57.

Snowden, F. 1970. *Blacks in Antiquity: Ethiopians in the Greco-Roman Experience.* Cambridge, Mass.

———. 1976. Iconographical Evidence on the Black Populations in Greco-Roman Antiquity. In *The Image of the Black in Western Art,* vol. 1: *From the Pharaohs to the Fall of the Roman Empire,* edited by L. Bugner, 133–245. New York.

———. 1983. *Before Color Prejudice.* Cambridge, Mass.

Solmsen, F. 1934. ΟΝΟΜΑ and ΠΡΑΓΜΑ in Euripides' *Helen. Classical Review* 48:119–21.

Sommerstein, A. 1977. Notes on Aeschylus' *Suppliants. Bulletin of the Institute of Classical Studies* 24:67–82.

———. 1997. The Theatre Audience, the *Demos,* and the *Suppliants* of Aeschylus. In *Greek Tragedy and the Historian,* edited by C. Pelling, 63–79. Oxford.

Sommerstein, A. H., S. Halliwell, J. Henderson, and B. Zimmerman, eds. 1993. *Tragedy, Comedy, and the Polis: Papers from the Greek Drama Conference, Nottingham, 18–20 July 1990.* Bari.

Spivak, G. C. 1988. Can the Subaltern Speak? In *Marxism and the Interpretation of Culture,* edited by C. Nelson and L. Grossberg, 271–313. Urbana.

Steiner, D. T. 1994. *The Tyrant's Writ: Myths and Images of Writing in Ancient Greece.* Princeton.

Stephens, S. A. Forthcoming. *Seeing Double: The Politics of Poetry in Ptolemaic Alexandria.* Berkeley.

Stephens, S. A., and J. J. Winkler, eds. 1995. *Ancient Greek Novels: The Fragments: Introduction, Text, Translation, and Commentary.* Princeton.

Stewart, A. 1993. *Faces of Power: Alexander's Image and Hellenistic Politics.* Berkeley.

Stoddart, S., and J. Whitley. 1988. The Social Context of Literacy in Archaic Greece and Etruria. *Antiquity* 62:761–72.

Strasburger, H. 1956. Herodots Zeitrechnung. *Historia* 5:129–61.

Suleri, S. 1992. *The Rhetoric of English India.* Chicago.

Sullivan, S. D. 1997. *Aeschylus' Use of Psychological Terminology: Traditional and New.* Montreal.

Svenbro, J. 1993. *Phrasikleia: An Anthropology of Reading in Ancient Greece.* Translated by J. Lloyd. Ithaca.

Symonds, R. 1991. *Oxford and Empire: The Last Lost Cause?* Corrected ed. Oxford.

Tait, W. J. 1988. Rush and Reed: The Pens of Egyptian and Greek Scribes. In *Proceedings of the XVIIIth International Congress of Papyrology, Athens 25–31 May 1986,* 477–81. Athens.

Taylor, A. E. 1928. *A Commentary on Plato's Timaeus.* Oxford.

Taylor, T. 1820. *The Commentaries of Proclus on the Timaeus of Plato.* Vol. 1. London.

Te Velde, H. 1985–86. Egyptian Hieroglyphs as Signs, Symbols, and Gods. *Visible Religion* 4–5:63–72.

———. 1988. Egyptian Hieroglyphs as Linguistic Signs and Metalinguistic Informants. *Visible Religion* 6:169–79.

Tefnin, R. 1984. Discours et iconicité dans l'art égyptien. *Göttinger Miszellen* 79:55–72.

Teltscher, K. 1995. *India Inscribed: European and British Writing on India 1600–1800.* Delhi.

Thiry, J. 1973. *Napoléon Bonaparte. Bonaparte en Égypte, décembre 1797–24 août 1799.* Paris.

Thomas, R. 1989. *Oral Tradition and Written Record in Classical Athens.* Cambridge Studies in Oral and Literate Culture 18. Cambridge, Eng.

———. 1992. *Literacy and Orality in Ancient Greece.* Cambridge, Eng.

———. 2000. *Herodotus in Context: Ethnography, Science, and the Art of Persuasion.* Cambridge, Eng.

Thompson, D. J. 1988. *Memphis under the Ptolemies.* Princeton.

———. 1994. Literacy and Power in Ptolemaic Egypt. In A. K. Bowman and G. Woolf, eds. 1994, 67–83.

Thompson, L. A. 1989. *Romans and Blacks.* Norman, Okla.

Thomson, G. 1973. *Aeschylus and Athens.* 4th ed. London.

Too, Y. L. 1995. *The Rhetoric of Identity in Isocrates: Text, Power, Pedagogy.* Cambridge, Eng.

Traunecker, C. 1979. Essai sur l'histoire de la XXIXe dynastie. *Bulletin de l'institut français d'archéologie orientale du Caire* 79:395–436.

Trigger, B. G., B. J. Kemp, D. O'Connor, and A. B. Lloyd. 1983. *Ancient Egypt: A Social History.* Cambridge, Eng.

Tuplin, C. 1999. Greek Racism? Observations on the Character and Limits of Greek Ethnic Prejudice. In *Ancient Greeks West and East,* edited by G. R. Tsetskhladze, 47–75. Leiden.

Turner, E. G. 1974. A Commander-in-Chief's Order from Saqqara. *Journal of Egyptian Archaeology* 60:239–42.

Usher, S. 1994. Isocrates: Paideia, Kingship and the Barbarians. In *The Birth of the European Identity; The Europe-Asia Contrast in Greek Thought 490– 322 B.C.,* edited by H. A. Khan, 131–45. Nottingham.

Valbelle, D. 1990. *Les neufs arcs: l'égyptien et les étrangers de la préhistoire à la conquête d'Alexandre.* Paris.

Van der Horst, P. W. 1984. *Chaeremon: Egyptian Priest and Stoic Philosopher.* Leiden.

Vegetti, M. 1992. Dans l'ombre de Thoth. Dynamique de l'écriture chez Platon. In M. Detienne, ed. 1992, 387–419.

Verbrugghe, G. P., and J. M. Wickersham. 1996. *Berossos and Manetho, Introduced and Translated: Native Traditions in Ancient Mesopotamia and Egypt.* Ann Arbor.

Vergote, J. 1939. Clément d'Alexandrie et l'écriture égyptienne. *Le Muséon* 52: 205–7.

Vermeule, E. 1979. *Aspects of Death in Early Greek Art and Poetry.* Berkeley.

Vernant, J.-P. 1982. *The Origins of Greek Thought.* Ithaca.

———. 1983. *Myth and Thought among the Greeks*. London.

———. 1990. *Myth and Society in Ancient Greece*. Rev. ed. Translated by J. Lloyd. New York.

Vernant, J.-P., and P. Vidal-Naquet. 1990. *Myth and Tragedy in Ancient Greece*. Translated by J. Lloyd. Rev. ed. New York.

Vernus, P. 1977. L'écriture de l'Egypte ancienne. *L'espace et la lettre: Cahiers Jussier* 3:60–77.

———. 1982. Espace et idéologie dans l'écriture égyptienne. In *Écritures, systèmes idéographiques et pratiques expressives*, edited by A.-M. Christin, 101–16. Paris.

———. 1985. Des relations entre textes et représentations dans l'Egypte pharaonique. In *Écritures II*, edited by A.-M. Christin, 45–69. Paris.

———. 1991. Les "décrets" royaux *(wd-nsw)*: l'énoncé d'auctoritas comme genre. In *Akten des vierten Internationalen Ägyptologen Kongresses: München 1985*, edited by S. Schoske, 239–46, vol. 4 of *Studien zur altägyptischen Kultur: Beihefte*. Hamburg.

Veyne, P. 1988. *Did the Greeks Believe in Their Myths? An Essay on the Constitutive Imagination*. Translated by P. Wissing. Chicago.

Vidal-Naquet, P. 1986. *The Black Hunter: Forms of Thought and Forms of Society in the Greek World*. Translated by A. Szegedy-Maszak. Baltimore.

———. 1995. Atlantis and the Nations. In *Politics Ancient and Modern*, ch. 2. Translated by J. Lloyd. Cambridge and Oxford. Originally published in *Critical Inquiry* 18 (1992):300–25.

———. 1997. The Place and Status of Foreigners in Athenian Tragedy. In *Greek Tragedy and the Historian*, edited by C. Pelling, 109–19. Oxford.

Vlastos, G. 1983. The Historical Socrates and Athenian Democracy. *Political Theory* 11:495–516.

von Kaenel, F. 1980. Les mésaventures du conjurateur de Serket, Onnophris et de son tombeau. *Bulletin de la societé française d'Egyptologie* 87–88:31–45.

Vürtheim, J. 1928. *Aischylos Schutzflehende*. Amsterdam.

Waddell, W. G., ed. 1940. *Manetho*. Loeb Classical Library. Cambridge, Mass.

Walker, S. 1983. Women and Housing in Classical Greece: The Archaeological Evidence. In *Images of Women in Antiquity*, edited by A. Cameron and A. Kuhrt, 81–91. London.

Weinfeld, M. 1972. The Worship of Molech and of the Queen of Heaven and Its Background. *Ugarit-Forschungen* 4:133–54.

West, M. L. 1985. *The Hesiodic Catalogue of Women: Its Nature, Structure, and Origins*. Oxford.

———. 1997. *The East Face of Helicon: West Asiatic Elements in Greek Poetry and Myth*. Oxford.

West, S. 1984. Io and the Dark Stranger (Sophocles, *Inachus* F 269a). *Classical Quarterly* 34:292–302.

———. 1985. Herodotus' Epigraphical Interests. *Classical Quarterly* 35:278–305.

———. 1991. Herodotus' Portrait of Hecateus. *Journal of Hellenic Studies* 111:144–60.

Whaling, F. 1980. *The Rise of the Religious Significance of Rama*. Delhi.

Whitehouse, H. 1995. Egypt in European Thought. In *Civilizations of the Ancient Near East*, edited by J. M. Sasson, vol. 1, 15–31. New York.

Wilcken, U. 1967. *Alexander the Great*. Translated by G. C. Richards. With a preface by E. N. Borza. New York.

Wilcox, S. 1943. Criticisms of Isocrates and his φιλοσοφία. *Transactions of the American Philological Association* 74:113–33.

Wildung, D. 1977. *Imhotep und Amenhotep: Gottwerdung im alten Ägypten*. Berlin.

Wilkinson, A. 1990. *Gardens in Ancient Egypt: Their Location and Symbolism*. London.

Winkler, J. J. 1992. Lollianos and the Desperadoes. In R. Hexter and D. Selden, eds. 1992, 5–50.

Winnington-Ingram, R. P. 1983. *Studies in Aeschylus*. Cambridge, Eng.

Witt, R. E. 1966. Isis-Hellas. *Proceedings of the Cambridge Philological Society* 192:48–69.

Wolff, C. 1973. On Euripides' *Helen*. *Harvard Studies in Classical Philology* 77:61–84.

Wood, E. M., and N. Wood. 1986. Socrates and Democracy: A Reply to Gregory Vlastos. *Political Theory* 14:55–82.

Woodford, S. 1994. Palamedes Seeks Revenge. *Journal of Hellenic Studies* 114: 164–69.

Woodward, A. M. 1962. Athens and the Oracle of Ammon. *Annual of the British School at Athens* 57:5–13.

Wright, R. 1979. How Credible Are Plato's Myths? In G. Bowersock, W. Burkert, and M. Putnam, eds. 1979, 364–71.

Wunderlich, E. 1925. *Die Bedeutung der roten Farbe im Kultus der Griechen und Römer*. Religionsgeschichtliche Versuche und Vorarbeiten 20. Giessen.

Wüst, E. 1942. Palamedes. *RE* 18:2500–12.

Young, R. 1994. Egypt in America: *Black Athena*, Racism, and Colonial Discourse. In *Racism, Modernity, and Identity: On the Western Front*, edited by A. Rattansi and S. Westwood, 150–69. Cambridge, Eng.

Yoyotte, J. 1980–81. Héra d'Héliopolis et le sacrifice humain. *Annuaire de l'École Pratique des Hautes Études. Résumés des conférences et des travaux* 89:31–102.

Yoyotte, J., P. Charvet, and S. Gompertz. 1997. *Strabon: Le voyage en Égypte: Un regard romain*. Paris.

Zecchini, G. 1989. Linee di egittografia antica. In *Egitto e storia antica dall' Ellenismo all' età araba: bilancio di un confronto*, edited by L. Criscuolo and G. Geraci, 703–13. Bologna.

Zeitlin, F. I. 1981. Travesties of Gender and Genre in Aristophanes' *Thesmophoriazousae*. In *Reflections of Women in Antiquity*, edited by H. P. Foley, 169–217. New York.

————. 1996. The Politics of Eros in the Danaid Trilogy of Aeschylus. In *Playing the Other: Gender and Society in Classical Greek Literature*, 123–71. Chicago.

Zizek, S. 1991. *Looking Awry: An Introduction to Jacques Lacan through Popular Culture*. Cambridge, Mass.

Zuckert, C. 1996. *Postmodern Platos: Nietzsche, Heidegger, Gadamer, Strauss, Derrida*. Chicago.

Zuntz, G. 1960. On Euripides' *Helena*. In *Euripide*, 199–241. Entretiens Fondation Hardt 6. Geneva.

Index

Abram (Abraham), 46–47
Abu Simbel, 26
Abusir, 21, 25
Achaemenes, 26
Achaemenids, 20–23. *See also* Persia;
  Persian Wars
Achilles, 246, 254
Achilles Tatius, 186
Adhyatma-ramayana, 62–64
Aegyptiaca, 116–17, 289–305
Aegyptus, 5, 42; sons of (Aegyptiads),
  5, 33–58, 68–74
Aeschylus, 12, 16, 31; and Alexander,
  253, 287–88; association of blackness and death, 47–53; on Egypt as
  locus for male fertility, 43–47; and
  ethnicity of Danaids and Aegyptiads, 40–43; marriage with Egyptians in, 53–58; on Nile's fertility,
  43–47, 277; status of Egypt in,
  33–40, 69–74; and writing, 138,
  143–46, 176, 179–82; *Agamemnon*, 54; Danaid trilogy, 33–58,
  68–69, 69–74; *Oresteia*, 41; *Persians*, 45; *Prometheus Bound*, 43–
  44, 48, 91n28; *Suppliants*, 12, 33–
  58, 65, 68–74, 143–46, 180, 253
Africa, 19
African Americans, 15–16, 19
Afrocentrism, 15–16
Agamemnon, 255

Agatharchides of Cnidus, 279
Agesilaus of Sparta, 23, 27, 29
Akhenaten, 107, 173
Akhetaten, 107
Akhoris, 22, 244
Alcibiades, 27, 274
Alcidamas, 194
Alexander III ("the Great"), 6–7, 11–
  12, 17, 21, 23, 246–47; and Am-
  mon, 272–75; and Aristotle, 261–
  65; body of, 251; conquest of Egypt
  by, 248–88; dream of, 255, 269;
  founding of Alexandria by, 268–
  72; and Herodotus, 256–61;
  and Homer, 253–55; mausoleum
  (Sema) of, 251–52; and Napoleon,
  282–88; restoration of Egyptian
  sanctuaries by, 267–68; and search
  for Nile's source, 275–82
Alexander-Romance, 273, 268n71,
  279n122
Alexandria, 109, 247, 251, 255, 268–72
Alloula, Malek, 38
Amasis, 25, 26, 80, 83, 86, 117, 274
Amazon, 25
Amenhopis III, 267
Amenhotep, 130
Americas, 15–16, 249
Ammianus Marcellinus, 182
Ammon, 27–28, 272–75, 285; Am-
  monias, 27

Amun, Amun-Re, 27, 72, 154, 173, 268, 272, 274
Amymone, 40n18
Amyntas III, 262
Amyrtaios, 21, 22, 27
analogy, 94. *See also* polarity
Anaxagoras of Clazomenae, 276
Anaxandrides, 98
Anaximander, 37, 88
Anaximenes of Lampsacus, 231
aner theoretikos, 242n55
annals, 128–30
Anticleides of Athens, 58n65, 138n4
Antipater, 262–63
Antiphon, 184
Antonius, Marcus, 284
ants, gold-digging, 260
Apelles, 253
Aphrodite, 24, 43
Apis bull, 21n34, 86, 117, 266–68
Apollo: temple of, 24
Apollodorus, pseudo-, 40n18, 185–86
Apries, 25, 26
Arabia, Arabic, 9, 91, 118, 281
Aramaic, 20, 22n38, 271
Arcesilas IV, 273
"archaeography," 245
archaism: in Greek accounts of Egypt, 110–35, 264
Archedice, 24
Archelaus, 252
Archilochus, 69n95
architecture: Egyptian influence on Greek, 28–29
archive, 146
Argos, Argives, 39, 41–43, 44, 45, 70–71, 144–45. *See also* Pelasgus
Aristagoras of Miletus, 116–17; fragments of, 296–98
Aristobulus of Cassandreia, 261
Aristophanes, 33n1, 59n68, 274. *See also* comedy
Aristotle, 4; and Alexander, 247, 249, 253, 255, 256, 261–65, 271, 275, 277, 279–82; and Atlantis, 232, 234; on Egyptian doctors, 212–13; on encomia, 194; on Herodotus,

95; on language and metaphysics, 151, 158, 174, 181; on Nile/Delta, 45, 86n20, 91n30, 279–82; and polarity, 97; representative in themes, 264; on tyranny, 82, 86n20, 264–65; Aristotelian treatise on the Nile, 281–82; *Generation of Animals*, 95; *The Glories of Riches*, 263; *On Interpretation*, 158n56; *On Kingship*, 263; *Metaphysics*, 97; *Meteorology*, 86n20, 91n30, 277, 281–82; *Physics*, 151; *Politics*, 82, 212–13, 263, 264, 271; *In Praise of Colonies*, 263
Arrian, 187, 258–61, 269, 273
Artaxerxes III Ochus, 21, 23, 266, 267, 281
Aryandes, 21
Ashdod, 23
Asia, Asians, 19, 90–91, 93, 254, 286; Asia Minor, 22; West Asia, 5, 8, 16
Assmann, Jan, 3–5, 160–62, 169, 173, 174–75
Assyria, 4, 9, 23, 24, 118
Asuchis, 143
Aswan, 276
Atalante, island, 234
Athena, 233; temple of, 26
Athenaeus, 45, 194
Athens, 2, 6, 12–13, 15, 22–29, 31, 69–74, 77, 87, 104–6, 112, 133–35, 144, 184, 190, 204, 207–15, 216–47, 271, 274; and Atlantis, 216–47; Egyptian cults in, 27–28; empire of, 133–35; expedition to Egypt of, 26–27, 31, 244; Egyptian origin of classes in, 230; Herodotus' attitude to, 105–6, 109, 112, 135, 145–46. *See also* democracy
Atlantis, 15, 31, 216–47
Atum, 154
Augustus (Octavian), 248, 284
al-Azhar, 285

ba, 172–74
Babylon, Babylonians, 4, 6, 118
Bacchae, 192

Bacchylides, 252
Baines, John, 127, 167, 171
Bakhtin, M. M., 206
barbarian, barbarians, 31–32, 34, 40–
    43, 60, 69, 118–19, 125, 126, 180,
    184n3, 214, 222, 252, 262–63, 288
Bartlett, W. H., 101n46
Bartoli, Giuseppe, 236
"beans," 260, 280
Bentresh Stela, 129
Bernal, Martin, 16–17, 200n37
Bernand, André, 72
Bhabha, Homi, 207
Bible, 3–4, 16, 18, 111, 249; Genesis,
    46–47; Jeremiah, 35n46
al-Biruni, 9, 99–100, 137n2, 248–49
black, blackness, 12, 34–35, 37–38,
    41, 47–53
Blake, William, 11–12
Bonneau, Danielle, 276
Borges, Jorge Luis, 205
Bosworth, A. Brian, 250, 280n128
Bourdieu, Pierre, 170, 235
Bowersock, Glen W., 256
Boylan, P., 152
brands, 79–82
Brauron, 192
Brecht, Bertolt, 206
British Empire, 9, 247, 283
Burckhardt, Jacob, 183
Burkert, Walter, 149
Burstein, Stanley M., 10, 115, 117, 282
Burton, Richard F., 36, 77, 257
Busiris, 3, 14, 33n1, 183–215
Butler, Judith, 205

Callisthenes of Olynthus, 231–32, 234,
    256, 261, 262, 278n121, 281–82
Cambyses, 21, 26, 83–86, 115, 130,
    267
Cameron, Alan, 233
Campaspe, 253
canal, 21, 78, 79, 86, 89, 90, 97
Caria, Carians, 23–26
Casaubon, Isaac, 18
caste system, 227–28, 237, 239, 264
Cephalus, 194

Certeau, Michel de, 100, 140
Chabrias, 22–23, 27, 29
Chaeremon, 10
Champollion, Jean-François, 18, 75,
    286
Champollion-Figeac, Jacques-Joseph,
    286
Charaxus, 83
Charitimides, 26
Cheops, 82–85, 143; daughter of,
    82–85
Chephren, 114
China, Chinese, 217
Chios, 24
Chow, Rey, 241
Cicero, 186
Cimon, 27, 28, 71, 274
citizen, citizenship, 27–28, 38, 69–71,
    72n104, 105, 133, 145, 212, 236,
    271
civic ideology, 69–74, 142–46
Clazomenae, 24
Cleisthenes, 133, 271
Clement of Alexandria, 136n1, 240
Cleomenes of Naukratis, 270, 287
Cleopatra VII, 248
coinage, Greek: in Egypt, 25
Colie, Rosalie L., 195
Columbus, Christopher, 249
comedy: Egypt in, 28, 33n1, 184,
    186n6, 190
Conon, 187
Corinth, 24, 29
Cowper, William, 101n46
Crantor of Soli, 226–36
Crete, 9
crocodiles, 260, 280
Critias, 15, 218–26, 236–38, 241
Csapo, Eric, 112, 133–34
Ctesias, 289n1
cults, Egyptian: in Athens, 27–28
Cyrene, 273
Cyrus ("the Great"), 4, 21, 85

Danaids, 33–58, 68–74, 143–44
Danaus, 33–58, 68–74, 144
dance: Plato on, 213

Darbo-Peschanski, Catherine, 119, 123
Darius I, 21–22, 86, 130
Darius II, 22
Darius III, 265–66
dead: Egypt as land of, 12–13, 33–34, 64
death, 34–35, 47–53, 64–69
Deinocrates of Rhodes, 270
Delos, 28
Delta, Egyptian, 22, 23, 24, 90–91, 259, 269–70, 286–87
Demeter, 36–37. *See also* Thesmophoria
Demetrius, 195
democracy, 103–9, 112, 133–35, 142–46, 224–26
Democritus, 276
Demosthenes, 252
demotic, 20, 136, 271, 272
Derrida, Jacques, 14, 59, 142n6, 155–59, 170–71, 174, 225n16
Description de l'Égypte, 283–85
despot, despotism, 5, 83. *See also* tyrant, tyranny
Detienne, Marcel, 148, 222–23
Diodorus of Sicily, 10, 15, 187–89, 212, 230, 232n28, 273, 283
Dionysius of Halicarnassus, 194–95
Dionysius Thrax: scholia to, 138n4, 149n22
Dionysus, 96, 124, 140
Diop, Cheikh Anta, 16
Dioscuri, 39; temple of, 24
Diphilus, 33n1
Djedi, 191
doctors, Egyptian, 212–13
Doniger, Wendy, 63–64
doubles, 58–64
Drews, Robert, 115
Du Bois, W. E. B., 16
Duff Gordon, Lucie, 110n1

Eagleton, Terry, 157–58
Edfu, 21, 25
Edwards, Amelia, 110
Egypt: Alexander's conquest of, 248–88; concept of matter in, 172–76;
exports of, 24; Greek view of art in, 213; Greek view of customs in, 94–95; Greek view of mice in, 194; human sacrifice in, 190–92; as locus for fertility, 42, 43–47; maps in, 88n23; Napoleon's conquest of, 17–18, 245, 266, 282–88; as place of captivity, 16; as place of wealth, 254–55; priests in, 138–40, 209–10, 219–25, 237–38, 246, 267–68; sense of space in, 106–9; sense of time in, 126–31; tradition of Nile's source in, 275–76; views of foreigners in, 8–9; writing system of, 159–76. *See also* Nile; pharaoh; *names of persons, gods, places, and topics as appropriate. For Greek views of, see also authors' names*
Egyptian bean, 260, 280
Egyptian bondage, 3
Egyptian darkness, 3
Egyptian doctors, 212–13
Egyptian herald, 144–45
Egyptian Theatre: in Los Angeles, 13–14
Egyptian voyage, 29–32
Egyptology, 18n30, 245
Egyptomania, 17–18
Ehrenberg, Victor, 272
Elephantine, 26, 276
Elkab, 21
embalming, 53
encomium, encomia, 183–85, 193–207, 210–11, 215
environmental determinism, 48, 94–95
Epaphus, 16, 41, 44, 48
Ephorus, 276, 282
Epicharmus, 48
epideictic speeches, 183–85, 193–207
Eratosthenes, 187, 279n122
eros, 83
Ethiopia, Ethiopians, 9, 16, 118, 275, 279, 280, 281
ethnic identity, ethnicity, 1–6, 34–40, 40–43, 252
ethnocentrism, 9, 92, 94, 95, 101, 116–17, 181, 206, 215, 246

ethnographic present, 113–14

ethnography, 113–14. *See also authors' names*

Eudoxus of Cnidus, 10, 117, 240,
259n33; fragments of, 298–304

eulogy, 183–85, 193–207, 210–11,
215

Euphrates, 106–7, 261

Euripides, 7, 31; and Alexander, 252–
53, 288; and Ammon, 274; association of Egypt, marriage, and death,
64–69; and Busiris, 186, 190; doubles in, 58–64; journey to Egypt
of, 240; status of Egypt in, 33–40,
69–74; and *Ramayana*, 62–64;
Alcestis, 54, 67; *Helen*, 12, 33–40,
58–74, 253; *Hippolytus*, 54; *Iphigenia among the Taurians*, 67;
Iphigenia in Aulis, 54; *Medea*, 54;
Suppliant Women, 54; *Women
of Troy*, 54

Eurocentrism, 246. *See also* ethnocentrism

Europe, 15, 19, 91, 93, 225–26, 286

Evagoras of Cyprus, 22, 244

eye: hieroglyph of, 166

Eyre, Christopher, 131, 167, 171

Fabian, Johannes, 113, 134

fantasy, 38–39, 72–73

Favard-Meeks, Christine, 152, 154

Ferrari, G. R. F., 151

fertility: Egypt as locus for, 42, 43–47

Ficino, Marsilio, 17

Fischer, Henry G., 163–64

fish, 92–93

Flaubert, Gustave, 35–36, 84–85,
110–11

Foley, H. P., 67

Foucault, Michel, 11, 205

Fourier, Jean-Baptiste-Joseph, 283–86

France, 217; invasion of Egypt by,
282–88

Frankfurter, David, 148–49

Fraser, P. M., 271

Frazer, James George, 186n5

Freemasonry, 18

Freud, Sigmund, 12, 56, 73, 217, 280

Froidefond, Christian, 7, 212, 228,
242–43, 264

gadfly, 43, 46n35

Gautier, Théophile, 287

gaze, 29–30, 101–2

Geertz, Clifford, 127

gender conflict, 33–74

genealogy, 37, 123, 139, 239, 245–46

Genette, Gérard, 201

geometry, 89–90

Ghosh, Amitav, 131–32, 134

Gibbon, Edward, 266

goats: intercourse with, 47n37

gods, 123–24, 140; of writing, 146–55

Goldhill, Simon, 71, 201–3

Gorgias, 184, 193–94

Grafton, Anthony, 249

grammatology, 155–59

graphomania, 138–42

Green, Peter, 265

Greenblatt, Stephen, 13n20

Griffiths, J. G., 233n32

Grosrichard, Alain, 72n104

Guérin Dalle Mese, Jeannine, 99

Gynaikospolis, 117

Hades, 48–53, 64, 68. *See also* dead;
death

Hagar, 46–47

Hall, Edith, 6

Hamilton, Edith, 111n4

Hapy, 72, 276

Hare, Tom, 166n76, 172, 175n95, 182

Hartog, François, 29–32, 79, 81, 83,
96, 142, 214, 245, 246, 287–88

Hatshepsut, 108n59

Hebrew: sources, 25n53; tradition,
46–47. *See also* Bible

Hecateus of Abdera, 10, 230–32, 250,
283

Hecateus of Miletus, 37, 88, 91n29,
116, 137–38, 139, 245–46; fragments of, 289–94

Hegel, G. W. F., 15, 115, 241, 246

Heidegger, Martin, 155

Helen, 5, 7, 33–40, 58–74, 121–26, 188, 238, 255
Helice, 234
Hellanicus of Lesbos, 116–17; fragments of, 294–96
Hellenion: at Naukratis, 24
Hellenocentrism, 9, 92, 94, 95, 101, 116–17, 181, 206, 215. *See also* ethnocentrism
Hellespont, 86–87
Hephaistion, 254, 273
Heptastadion, 269
Hera: temple of, 24
Heracles, 14, 123–24, 185–90, 192, 254
Heraclides of Pontus, 234
Hermes Trismegistus, 10, 152n30, 240; Hermetic Corpus, 10, 17–18
Hermocrates, 225
Herodotus, 4, 10, 13, 15, 20, 26, 184, 242, 289; allochronic discourse of, 117–21; and Alexander, 12, 75, 253, 254, 256–61, 268–69, 270, 274, 280, 286–88; and Ammon, 28, 272; on ants, 260; and Apis bull, 21n34, 86, 267; and Athenian democracy, 105–6, 109, 112, 135, 145–46; on blackness of Egyptians, 47–48; and caste system, 227; on crocodiles, 260, 280; on Egyptian bean, 260, 280; and Egyptian space, 9, 75–109; and Egyptian time, 9, 110–35, 245–46; and Egyptian writing, 136–40, 142–46, 171, 176, 179–82, 180–82; and environmental determinism, 48, 94–95; and Fourier, 284–85; on Helen in Egypt, 121–26, 238; Hellenocentrism of, 94; on human sacrifice and Busiris, 185, 187–88; in-between country, 90–91, 268–71, 284; influence on Hellenistic historians, 250; and Macedon, 252; mapping of Egypt, 87–91; on mice, 194; and names, 36–37, 123; in Naukratis, 24; and Nearchus, 75, 257–61; and Nile's behavior, 90–

91, 257–60, 275–77, 280; panopticism of, 100–103; and royal power, 5, 31, 77–87; on Scythia and Egypt, 96–97; sex and death, 52–53; and static history, 112–17, 214; symmetry and inversion in, 92–100; and Thesmophoria, 36–37, 68. *See also names of relevant individuals, places, and topics*
Hesiod, 37n10, 42n22
Hexter, Ralph, 74
Hibis: temple of, 21
hieratic, 136. *See also* writing
hieroglyphs, 136n1, 151–55, 159–76, 181; mutilation of, 143n11, 165–66. *See also* writing
Hindus, 9, 99–100, 137n2
Hippias, 184
Hippocrates, 252; Hippocratic treatise, 48, 94
historians (fragmentary), 116–17, 289–305
historiography. *See authors' names*
history, 3, 15, 110–35, 222–23, 225–26, 241–42, 245–46; of Egypt in Late Period, 20–29
Homer, 23, 45n31, 67, 122, 124–25, 259n33, 269, 277, 286; and Alexander, 253–55, 256; *Iliad*, 23, 45n31, 253–55, 277, 285; *Odyssey*, 23, 67, 254–55, 259n33, 269
Horapollo, 10, 17, 167n79, 182
Hornung, Erik, 107, 109, 127, 128, 153–54
Horus, 9, 124, 270
House of Life, 21
human sacrifice, 15, 185–93
hunting metaphors, 57, 60
Hutcheon, Linda, 200–203
Hymn to the Nile, 276
Hypermestra, 68, 69n95, 73

Iamblichus, 10, 175n96
Ibn Abi Usaibia, 263nn45, 46; 281n130
identity, 30–32
Imhotep, 130
imperialism, 11–12, 16–19, 245. *See*

also Alexander; Athens, empire of;
   British Empire; Napoleon
Inachus, 41
Inarus, 6, 26
in-between country, 90–91, 268–71,
   284
incest, 41, 50n46, 55
India, Indians, 6, 9, 99–100, 137n2,
   250–51, 256, 258–61, 278–82,
   283
Indus, 258–59, 280–81
inversion, 92–100
Io, 16, 37–38, 41–47, 56, 124
Ionia, Ionians, 91. *See also authors'*
   names
Iphigenia, 192
Isis, 27–28, 36–37, 270
Iskandar Dhu'l-Qarnein, 273
Islamic tradition, 17n27, 265n57,
   268n71, 273, 285
Isocrates, 14, 31, 183–215, 226–29,
   243, 252, 287–88; rivalry with
   Plato, 207–15, 227–29; *Busiris,*
   183–215, 226–29, 287
isonomia, 87, 104–6
Israel, 3–4
Issus, 265–66
Ister, 93, 96–97
Iulius Caesar, Gaius, 284
Iykhernofret Stela, 171

Jacoby, Felix, 10
Jeremiah, 25, 240
Jerusalem, 4
John the Lydian, 278n121
Josephus, 16
Jowett, Benjamin, 246–47
Juvenal, 186

ka, 268
Karnak, 25, 267
Khabash, 266
Kharga, 21
Khnum, 276
Khufu, 191
King, Martin Luther, Jr., 16
Kipling, Rudyard, 12

Kircher, Athanasius, 17
kouroi, 28
Kristeva, Julia, 41, 202
Kuchuk Hanem, 35n6
Kurke, Leslie, 78–79, 84n16, 149n23

labyrinth, 81
Lacan, Jacques, 157
Lactantius Placidus, 185
Lane, Edward William, 94
Lane Fox, Robin, 255
languages: Greek knowledge of, 30,
   167n79, 182. *See also* writing
Lant, Antonia, 14, 19
Late Period, 20–29, 129–30, 233, 239
Lateiner, Donald, 77, 94
Laurens, Annie-France, 190
law, laws: Antiphon on, 184n3; Aris-
   totle on, 264; Egyptian, 21–22,
   41–42; Greek, 41–42, 70, 71, 105,
   106, 109, 133–34, 144, 178, 179,
   180, 211; giver of, 210; of parody,
   202; in Plato's dialogues, 212–14,
   222n8, 237, 244
Lefebvre, Henri, 177
Lefkowitz, Mary R., 5
Lesbos, 24
Lévêque, Pierre, 87, 104, 105, 133
Levinas, Emmanuel, 30
Lévi-Strauss, Claude, 30–31, 52
Libya, Libyans, 8, 9, 37, 47, 90–91,
   93, 118. *See also* Ammon; Cyrene
Lindus Temple: chronicle at, 26
Linus song, 120
literacy. *See* writing
Lloyd, Alan B., 128
Locris, 234
logos, 122
Loraux, Nicole, 40, 49, 52, 65, 179, 223
lotus, 260
Lucan, 279
Luce, John V., 234
lustfulness: of Zeus in tragedy, 43; of
   Egyptians in tragedy, 47, 49–53,
   58, 59, 63, 65
Luxor (al-Uqsur), 25, 28, 267–68
Lycophron, 194

Lycurgus, 27–28
Lydia, 113
Lynceus, 68, 69n95, 73
Lysander, 274
Lysippus, 253

maat, 128, 153
Macedonia, Macedonians, 25, 252–53.
    See also Alexander III; Philip II;
    Ptolemy I
MacKinnon, J. K., 57
Magi, 4
Mahmud of Ghazna, 249
Malcolm X, 16
Malkin, Irad, 248
Manetho, 10, 186, 188, 250
matter: Egyptian concept of,
    172–76
marriage, 33–74; of Heaven and
    Earth, 43; in Aeschylus' *Suppli-
    ants*, 53–58; in Euripides' *Helen*,
    64–69
map, maps, 87–91
Marx, Karl, 217, 228
al-Mas'udi, 268n71
Mazakes, 251, 266
measuring, 87–91
Mecca, 285
Meeks, Dimitri, 152, 154
Megabyzos, 26
Megasthenes, 260nn36, 37
Meier, Christian, 21, 135
memory, 111, 130; of Gérard de
    Nerval, 287; and writing, 139,
    141, 147, 150, 152, 180, 221–24,
    225n16
Memphis, 21–22, 25, 266–67, 277,
    282
Memphite Theology, 129–30, 162
Menelaus, 5, 39, 58–66, 124, 188,
    255
mercenaries, 25–27
Mesopotamia, 146, 177
metics, 105, 135, 271
mice: Aristotle and Herodotus on,
    194
Michelet, Jules, 283n136

Migdol, 25
Miletus, 24, 88. *See also authors'
    names*
Miller, Margaret, 112, 133–34
Minos, 123
Mitchell, Timothy, 13
Momigliano, Arnaldo, 30
Montserrat, Dominic, 79–80
Montu-her-khopeshef, 191
monuments, monumentality, 145–46,
    168–76, 177
Moses, 3–4, 240
Mozart, Wolfgang Amadeus, 18
mummies, mummification, 53n54
Murray, Oswyn, 250
music: Plato on, 213
Myceneans, 9
Mycerinus, 83–85
mystery cults, 36n7
mythos, 122

names, 221–22; of the gods, 36–37,
    123
Napoleon I, 17–18, 245, 266,
    282–88
Naukratis, 7, 24–25, 34, 84, 270
Nearchus, 75, 256, 257–61, 262, 275,
    277, 280–82
Nebuchadnezzar, 25
Necho II, 25
Nectanebo I, 24
Nectanebo II, 23, 266, 274
Neïth, 154, 233
Nekos, 86
Neoplatonism, 10, 175n96, 240n51,
    229–30, 263n46. *See also authors'
    names*
Nepherites I, 22
Nerval, Gérard de, 36, 287
Nicomachus, 262
Nietzsche, Friedrich, 155, 157
nightingale, 51–52, 57, 64
Nightingale, Andrea Wilson, 207–8,
    210–11, 212–13
Nile, 61–62, 72, 90–91, 92, 93, 96–
    97, 257–61, 275–82, 285, 286;
    Egypt as gift of, 90–91, 259; fertil-

ity of, 45–47; search for source of, 275–82
Nine Bows, 9
Nubia, Nubians, 8, 25–26, 108

Ocean (river), 88, 260
Octavian (Augustus), 248
Odysseus, 30, 255
Oenopides of Chios, 276
Olympias, 280
Olympiodorus, 240n51
Onesicritus of Astypalaea, 261
"Orient," 35–36, 82–85
Orientalism, 20, 216, 247
Orpheus, 67, 148–49, 180
Osiris, 189, 191, 270
Ovid, 186

Palamedes, 148–49, 180
palm capital, 28
panopticism: of Herodotus, 101–2
Panyassis, 185
papyrus, 177
paradoxical encomium, 183, 193–207, 210–11
Paris, 39, 60–62, 124–25
parody, 184, 193–99, 199–207, 214–15
Pateneït, 240
Pausanias, general, 83
Pausanias, writer, 274n105
Pausiades of Phaleron, 27
Pearson, Lionel, 258
Pease, Arthur Stanley, 193–94
Pelasgians, 119
Pelasgus, 40–58, 70, 143–44
Peloponnesian War, 71
pens, 153n36
performative speech, 168–72
Pericles, 70, 271
periplous, 87
Persephone, 64, 67–69
Perseus, 254
Persia, Persians, 4, 5, 6, 7, 9, 31, 85–87; and Alexander, 250–51, 256, 265–67, 271–72; in Egypt, 20–23, 239, 244; in Herodotus, 85–87,

112–13, 118–19. *See also Persian kings' names*
Persian Wars, 1–2, 121, 125–26, 254, 256
Phaedrus, 240. *See also* Plato
Phalaris, 191
Phanes of Halicarnassus, 26
Phanodemus, 231
phantom, 39, 58–59, 61–62
pharaoh, 128, 153, 171–72, 190, 191, 274. *See also pharaohs' names*
pharmakon, 156, 213n55
Pharos, 58n65, 116, 269, 271
Pherecydes, 185
Philip II, 252, 262, 273
Philodemus, 193n25
Philomela, 51–52
"philosophy," 207–14
Phoenicia, Phoenicians, 25, 118
phoenix, 260
Photius, 279
Phrygia, Phrygians, 141
Phrynichus, 33n1, 48
physiognomy. *See specific characteristics*
Pindar, 28, 47n37, 252, 273–74
Pippin, Anne, 68
Piraeus, 27–28, 274
plants, 56–57
Plato, 4, 5, 9; and Alexander, 247, 262, 266n63, 287; and Atlantis, 15, 216–47; on Egyptian art, 213; on Egyptian music, 213; on Egyptian dance, 213; on Egyptian doctors, 212–13; and encomia, 194, 198, 210–11; and Eudoxus, 117, 240; and Hegel, 15, 241, 246; and history, 15, 222–23, 225–26, 241–42, 245–46; and language, 14, 31, 138, 140–43, 146–51, 155–59, 159–60, 167–68, 172–73, 174–76, 179–82; rivalry with Isocrates, 207–15, 227–29; *Cratylus*, 159; *Critias*, 15, 140, 180, 216–47; *Laws*, 151, 212–14, 237, 243; *Letters*, 151; *Phaedrus*, 146–51, 154–55, 155–59, 168, 194, 223–24, 240; *Philebus*, 141–

Plato *(continued)*
   42; *Politicus,* 266n63; *Republic,*
   159, 209–10, 217, 218–19, 224,
   228–30, 237, 239, 246; *Sympo-*
   sium, 198; *Timaeus,* 15, 140, 141,
   180, 216–47, 287
Pliny the Elder, 16, 138n4, 263
Plutarch, 10, 179, 188, 231, 234, 240,
   241n53, 261, 263, 271, 285
polarity, 92–100
Polignac, François de, 104–5
Polybius, 249–50, 252
Polycrates, sophist, 194–99, 208–9
Polycrates, tyrant of Samos, 123
polytheism, 4–5
Porphyry, 186
Porter, James I., 199
Posidonius, 232n30
Potasimto, 26
pottery: Greek, in Egypt, 24–25
Pratt, Mary Louise, 13, 101
priests: in Egypt, 138–40, 209–10,
   219–25, 237–38, 246, 267–68
primeval mound, 108–9
Proclus, 229, 231, 240, 241n53
Procne, 51–52, 57
Procopius, 186
Procrustes, 191
Prometheus, 43–44, 148, 180. *See*
   also Aeschylus, *Prometheus*
   Bound
Protesilaos, 254
Proteus, 64–66, 124, 125
prytany, 133–34
Psammetichus I, 7, 23–26, 130, 141
Psammetichus II, 25–26, 130
Psammetichus III, 21
Psenophis, 240
Ptah, 153–54, 162, 267
Ptolemaic Egypt
Ptolemies, 6, 175, 248, 251–52, 269,
   270
Ptolemy I, 248, 251, 256, 273
Pucci, Pietro, 59
pyramids, 81–85, 264, 286; builders
   of, 114–15
Pyramid Texts, 107, 154

Pythagoras, Pythagoreans, 87, 209,
   228, 242

Quran, 273, 285. *See also* Islamic
   tradition

racism, 35. *See also* ethnocentrism
Rama, 62–64
Ramage, E. S., 235
Ramayana, 62–64
Rameses II, 78n6, 129
Rameses III, 130
Rameses V, 130
rape, 33–74
Ravana, 62–64
Ray, J. D., 22
Redfield, James, 96
Redford, Donald B., 130
Red Sea, 21
Renaissance, 17–18, 75
Rhakotis, 269
Rhodes, 24, 29
Rhodopis, 24, 82–85
Ritner, Robert K., 33–34
rivers. *See* Indus; Nile
Rives, James, 192
Rose, Margaret, 201
Rosetta stone, 245, 285–86

Said, Edward W., 11, 12, 33, 35–36,
   242, 282–83
Saïs, 21, 24, 115, 130, 219, 224, 229–
   36, 237, 239, 242, 246
Samos, 24
Sanseverino, Roberto da, 98–99
Santorini, 234–35
Sappho, 83
Saqqara, 152n30, 266–67
Saranyu, 63–64
sati, 65
satrap, satrapy: in Egypt, 21–23. *See*
   also Persia
Sauneron, Serge, 165
Saussure, Ferdinand de, 162, 181
Savary, Claude Étienne, 283
scapegoats, 192
Schenkel, Wolfgang, 233n32

Schlegel, August Wilhelm von, 201
Schwab, Raymond, 20
sculpture, 28–29
Scythia, Scythians, 6, 96–97, 120
Seaford, Richard, 55–56
Segal, Charles P., 59
Sechnuphis of Heliopolis, 240
Selden, Daniel L., 15–16, 74, 107–9, 168, 269, 271
self/other, 1–3, 205; and selfhood, 30–32, 36–40
self-reflexivity, 30–32
Sesostris, 77–79, 89–90, 115, 142–43, 264
Seth, 9
Sethos, 121–22, 143
sex: and "Orient," 35–36
Sextus Empiricus, 186
Shabako, 23
Shelley, P. B., 113
Shrine of the Bark, 267–68
sign, linguistic, 160–68
Sissa, Giulia, 52
Sita, 62–64
Siwah, 251, 272–75, 285
sky: in Egyptian thought, 107; hieroglyph of, 162
slave, slavery, 79–82, 86–87
Socrates, 14–15, 195, 207, 208–9, 252; and Atlantis, 218–26, 237–40; and language, 141–42, 146–47, 149–51, 156–59, 168, 179. *See also* Plato
Solon, 141, 219–26, 231, 237, 242, 245–46, 286
Sommerstein, Alan H., 71
Sonkhis, 240
sophists, 184. *See also individual names*
Sophocles, 37–38, 48, 53n54, 54, 94, 98, 253; *Antigone*, 54; *Inachus*, 37–38, 48; *Oedipus at Colonus*, 98; *Oedipus Tyrannus*, 48, 54; *Phineus*, 53n54; *Women of Trachis*, 54
Sotades, 25
space, 75–109

Sparta, Spartans, 22, 24, 29, 31, 61–62, 179, 212, 274
speech, 156–59, 168–72, 173. *See also* writing
Spivak, Gayatri Chakravorty, 38
splitting: of Danaids, 40–43
Steiner, Deborah T., 14, 82–83, 142, 179
stereotypes, 11, 12–13, 14–15, 206–7, 215
Stesichorus, 39, 121, 149n22
stigmata, 79–82
Strabo, 10, 15, 45, 47n37, 187n91, 232n30, 240, 259–61, 283
Subaltern Studies, 11
Suleri, Sara, 3
supplication, 40–58, 65–66, 69–74
surveying: as narrative technique, 87–91
Svenbro, Jesper, 170
symmetry, 92–100, 106–9
Syria, 118

Takhos, 23
tattoos, 79–82
Tell Defenneh (Daphnae), 25
Teltscher, Kate, 9
temple: in Egypt, 108–9
temporality, 110–35
Teos, 146
Tereus, 51–52
Thales, 242, 276
Thamus, 14, 147–51, 224, 240
Thebes, Egyptian, 89, 91n30, 101, 102, 106, 123, 130, 139, 188, 191, 277
Thebes, Greek, 122, 274
Theoclymenus, 5, 39, 58–66
Theodectes, 33n1, 69n95
Theonoe, 58–66
Theopompus, 257, 262
Theopompus, pseudo-, 231
Theoprastos, 45
Theseus, 192
Thesmophoria, 36–37, 68, 70–71
Theuth, 14, 141–42, 147–51, 180, 224, 240
Thomas, Rosalind, 146, 178

Thonis, 124
Thoth, 147–48, 151–55. *See also* Theuth
Thothmes III, 267
Thrace, Thracians, 25
Thrasyalces, 276
Thucydides, 7, 31, 234, 270
Timaeus, 225
time, 110–35
Timesitheus, 33 n1
tourist, 31–32
tragedy: Egypt and, 33–74
triremes: sacred, 27
Troy, Trojans, 39, 58–64, 71, 254; Trojan War, 121–26
Tuplin, C., 119 n18
Tulsi Das, 63
Typhon, Typhonian men, 188–89
tyrant, tyranny, 70, 77–87, 142–46, 264–65. *See also* despot, despotism

Udjahorresnet, 130
United States of America, 15–16

Valla, Lorenzo, 75
vases, 48, 189–90
Vernant, Jean-Pierre, 70, 104, 145
Veyne, Paul, 286 n148
Vidal-Naquet, Pierre, 58, 69, 87, 104, 105, 133, 218, 236–37

Virgil, 186
Volney, Constantin François de Chasseboeuf, 283
voyage in Egypt, 29–32

Walker, David, 16
water-carriers: Danaids as, 52
West, Stephanie, 142
Wilamowitz-Moellendorf, Ulrich von, 29
writing, 14, 136–82, 212–13, 220–26; writing and control, 176–81

xenophobia: stereotype about Egyptians, 188. *See also* Busiris
Xenophon, 285
Xerxes, 22, 86–87, 130

Yama, 64
Yamani, 23

Zeitlin, Froma I., 43, 55, 68, 71
Zeus, 37–38, 41–50, 62
Zeus Ammon, 27–28, 272–75, 285; Ammonias, 27
Zizek, Slavoj, 72 n104
Zoilus of Amphipolis, 194
Zoroastrianism, 4. *See also* Persia

Text: 10/13 Aldus
Display: Aldus
Composition: G & S Typesetters, Inc.
Printing and binding: Thomson-Shore, Inc.